ARTHUR KOESTLER

Arthur Koestler was born in Budapest in 1905. He attended the University of Vienna before working as a foreign correspondent in the Middle East, Berlin and Paris. For six years (1932–38) he was an active member of the Communist Party, and was captured by Franco's troops in the Spanish Civil War and imprisoned under sentence of death. In 1940 he came to England, adopting the language with his first book in English, *Scum of the Earth*. His publications manifest a wide range of political, scientific and literary interests, and include *Darkness at Noon*, *Arrow in the Blue* and *The Invisible Writing*. He died in 1983 by suicide, having frequently expressed a belief in the right to euthanasia.

ALSO BY ARTHUR KOESTLER

Novels

The Gladiators
Arrival and Departure
Thieves in the Night
The Age of Longing
The Call-Girls

Autobiography

Dialogue with Death
Scum of the Earth
Arrow in the Blue
The God that Failed (with others)

Essays

The Yogi and the Commissar
Insight and Outlook
Promise and Fulfilment
The Trail of the Dinosaur
Reflections on Hanging
The Sleepwalkers
The Lotus and the Robot

The Act of Creation
The Ghost in the Machine
Drinkers of Infinity
The Case of the Midwife Toad
The Roots of Coincidence
The Challenge of Chance
(with Sir Alistair Hardy and
Robert Harvie)
The Heel of Achilles
Suicide of a Nation? (editor)
Beyond Reductionism:
The Alpbach Symposium
(editor with J. R. Smythies)
The Thirteenth Tribe
Life After Death
(with Arnold Toynbee and others)
Janus – A Summing Up

Theatre

Twilight Bar

Reader

Bricks to Babel

ARTHUR KOESTLER

The Invisible Writing

The Second Volume
of an Autobiography: 1932–40

VINTAGE

To Dorothy

16

Vintage
20 Vauxhall Bridge Road,
London SW1V 2SA

Vintage Classics is part of the Penguin Random House
group of companies whose addresses can be found
at global.penguinrandomhouse.com.

Penguin
Random House
UK

This edition reissued by Vintage in 2019
First published in Great Britain by Collins
with Hamish Hamilton in 1954
First Published by Vintage in 2005

www.vintage-books.co.uk

A CIP catalogue record for this book is available
from the British Library

ISBN 9780099490685

Printed and bound in Great Britain by Clays Ltd, Elcograf S.p.A.

Penguin Random House is committed to a sustainable future for
our business, our readers and our planet. This book is made
from Forest Stewardship Council® certified paper.

MIX
Paper from
responsible sources
FSC
www.fsc.org FSC® C018179

TO DOROTHY

Une vie d'analyse pour une heure de synthèse!

FUESTEL DE COULANGES

Everything becomes legend, if the gentlemen will have the goodness to wait.

NORMAN DOUGLAS

Contents

PART IV. THE INVISIBLE WRITING
1936–40

EPILOGUE

Illustrations

Author's Note to First Edition

THE previous volume of this autobiography covered my first twenty-six years, up to my joining the Communist Party in 1931. The present, second volume ends with my escape to England in 1940, and my settling down in that country. An epilogue brings the narrative up to the present date.

To write one's memoirs before one has reached the age of fifty may seem a premature and somewhat presumptuous undertaking. But if one's past is worth recording at all, this should be done before its colour and fragrance have faded. Gains in distance and perspective must be balanced against losses in emotional freshness, for facts are more easily retained than feelings. Facts can be complemented by files and newspaper records, emotions not.

This point will become painfully apparent to the reader through the first five or six chapters of this book, which deal with my early Communist days in Berlin and Russia. I found it impossible to revive the naïve enthusiasm of that period : I could analyse the ashes, but not resurrect the flame. I disliked writing these chapters, but felt the chronicler's compulsion to record material which appears to him trivial and boring, in the hope that at some future date it will appear less so. The reader is advised to get through these opening chapters as best and as quickly as he can.

I am indebted to Laurie Lee for his friendly help with the translations of Attila Jozsef's poems, and to my former secretary, Cynthia Patterson-Jefferies, for her infinite patience with this and several earlier books. The following is a list of the works from which I have quoted with the kind permission of the authors and publishers concerned : *One Sky to Share* by L. Bruckberger (P. J. Kenedy and Sons); *To Dusty Death* by Manes Sperber (Allan Wingate (Publishers) Ltd); *My House in Malaga* by Sir Peter Chalmers Mitchell (Faber & Faber

Ltd); *Handbook For Spies* by Alexander Foote (Museum Press Ltd); *Warrior Without Weapons* by Dr. Marcel Junod (The Macmillan Company); *I Was Stalin's Agent* by W. G. Krivitsky (Hamish Hamilton Ltd); and my own *Darkness at Noon, The Yogi and the Commissar* (Jonathan Cape Ltd), and *The God that Failed* (Hamish Hamilton Ltd.).

A.K.

London, December 31, 1953

Note to the Danube Edition

The Invisible Writing is the continuation of *Arrow in the Blue*.

I have called it 'a typical case-history of a member of the educated middle classes of Central Europe in the first half of our century.'

Two episodes in it—imprisonment during the Spanish Civil War and living through the French apocalypse of 1940 —I have described in greater detail in two companion volumes, *Dialogue with Death* and *Scum of the Earth*.

A.K.

Alpbach, Tyrol, July 1969

Part One

EUPHORIA

1932

When one burns one's boats, what a very nice fire it makes.

DYLAN THOMAS

I. Bridge-Burning

I went to Communism as one goes to a spring of fresh water.

PABLO PICASSO

I WENT to Communism as one goes to a spring of fresh water, and I left Communism as one clambers out of a poisoned river strewn with the wreckage of flooded cities and the corpses of the drowned. This, in sum, is my story from 1931 to 1938, from my twenty-sixth to my thirty-third year. The reeds to which I clung and which saved me from being swallowed up were the outgrowth of a new faith, rooted in mud, slippery, elusive, yet tenacious. The quality of that faith I cannot define beyond saying that in my youth I regarded the universe as an open book, printed in the language of physical equations and social determinants, whereas now it appears to me as a text written in invisible ink, of which, in our rare moments of grace, we are able to decipher a small fragment. This volume, then, is the account of a journey from specious clarity to obscure groping.

I joined the Communist Party on December 31, 1931. Seven months later I emigrated from Germany to Soviet Russia. These seven months of transition are divided into two periods. During the first, I was a secret member of the Party; during the second, an open one.

In *The God That Failed* I have told in some detail the story of my enlistment, and how I was drawn into the Party's Intelligence network. I shall therefore confine myself to a brief outline of these events.

My written application for membership of the K.P.D.—*Kommunistische Partei Deutschlands*—was addressed to the Central Committee of the Party. It was answered a week or more later by a rather mystifying letter, typed on blank paper and bearing an illegible signature, in which I was invited, 'with reference to your esteemed of December 31st' to meet 'a representative of our firm' at the offices of a certain paper-mill in Berlin.

The man whom I met at the appointed place and hour was Herr Ernst Schneller, head of the Department for Agitation and Propaganda (AGITPROP) of the German Communist Party, and at the same time chief of one of the Comintern's secret *apparats* or intelligence networks. In yet another capacity, Schneller was *Reichstagsabgeordneter*, a member of the German Parliament. This double existence as an official dignitary and as an underground conspirator was by no means exceptional. A large proportion of the Communist membership lived, and still lives, to use French Party slang, *à cheval*—a term borrowed from roulette and referring to a player who backs two numbers simultaneously. Nor is such an existence considered dishonourable. To exploit fully the constitutional liberties provided by bourgeois society for the purpose of destroying them is elementary Marxist dialectics.

I had two meetings with Ernst Schneller, and after these I never saw him again. A few years later he died in a Nazi prison where he was serving a six-year sentence of hard labour. He was an insignificant-looking, shy, thin, bony man with a pinched face and an awkward smile. He told me that he was a vegetarian and lived mostly on raw vegetables and fruit; also, that he never read any newspapers except the Party press. At first I took him for a narrow-minded bureaucrat, but my initial feeling of condescension soon changed into respect for his quiet and astute manner of arguing. I told him of my desire to throw up my job and go as a tractor-driver to Russia; but within a few hours Schneller had convinced me that I would be more useful to the Party by keeping my convictions secret, carrying on as a journalist, influencing, within the limits of my possibilities, the policy of my paper, and passing on to the Party any inside information that came my way. The Party, he explained, though still enjoying the privilege of legality, would probably quite soon be outlawed and forced underground. In that event people like myself, who were in respectable positions and untainted by suspicion, would be even more valuable than at present in the struggle against

Fascism and imperialist aggression. Everything he said sounded so plausible that by the end of our first meeting I agreed to his proposal and became, without being fully aware of the fact, a member of the Comintern's intelligence service.

At our second and last meeting, Schneller handed me my Party card, made out under the alias 'Ivan Steinberg'. He had also brought along a dark, blowsy girl named Paula who would serve as a liaison with my future superior in the *apparat*, named Edgar. Thus from the moment of joining the Party I found myself plunged into a strange world of conspiratorial twilight, populated by 'Edgars' and 'Paulas' without a surname or address—fleeting, elusive shapes like the phosphorescent creatures of the deep sea.

Edgar and Paula were my only contacts in the *apparat*. We usually met in my flat, where Paula took down on a typewriter what information I was able to supply, while Edgar would pace up and down the room and put in a question now and then to clarify a point. He was a slim, smooth, smiling young man of thirty, blond, with an open face and frank eyes. His real name I only discovered more than twenty years later, in the following footnote in Alexander Weissberg's book, *Conspiracy of Silence* (London 1952) :

'In *The God that Failed* Koestler mentions a man named Edgar . . . "Edgar" was a revolutionary worker from Hamburg. His real name was Fritz Burde. He was a decent fellow and a good comrade. I met him in 1936 in Moscow when he had a high position in the Red Army Intelligence service. . . . For a long time the G.P.U. and the War Commissariat had been fighting for control of this important secret organisation abroad. Once Tukhachevsky was arrested, the G.P.U. had a free hand. They recalled almost all the military secret agents from abroad and arrested them. Fritz Burde was in charge of the secret service of the Red Army in Scandinavia, and when he was recalled with the others he told friends that he was going to his death, but that he had no alternative.'

Without knowing what fate had befallen him, I used 'Edgar' some ten years later as a part-model for Bernard, the young Nazi agent in *Arrival and Departure*. I was trying to visualise a handsome and winning Nazi who would capture the reader's sympathy—and found myself, quite unintentionally, describing the smiling appearance and manners of Edgar, the Communist. He fitted the part perfectly.

My contact with the *apparat* remained a peripheral one, and after two or three months came to a dismal end. I was at that time foreign editor of the *B.Z. Am Mittag* and science editor of the *Vossische Zeitung*—two daily papers published by the Ullstein Trust, Germany's largest Liberal newspaper concern. In my capacity as foreign editor I had access to virtually all confidential information of a political nature that converged in that important nerve centre of the Weimar Republic. My assistant at that post was a young man of twenty-one, von E., the son of a retired German ambassador. With only five years separating us, we soon became friends; I preached the Marxist doctrine to von E., and became the kind of *guru* to him that Peter and Karl had been to me. After a fortnight or so, he had made sufficient progress to be roped into the service of the Cause. The von E.s entertained at their house members of the German general staff and of the diplomatic corps; my young friend's task was to keep his ears open and report to me anything of interest—in particular information relating to 'the preparations for the war of aggression against the Soviet Union by Germany and the other imperialistic powers'.

For a few weeks all went well. Then young von E. was seized with remorse, and one morning after a sleepless night, he presented me with an ultimatum : he must either reveal our treasonable activities, or shoot himself. He had written a letter of confession, addressed to the managing director of the firm; but he would only hand the letter in if I gave my consent. He placed the long, hand-written letter on my desk.

Logically this demand made no sense. In the terms of the law, we had committed no punishable offence. We had not stolen military secrets or sold political documents. Von E. had merely passed on some parlour gossip to me which I in turn had related to my political friends. But these arguments failed to impress the young man. To be a Marxist, or a Socialist, he said, was one thing; to pass on information to agents of a foreign power, quite another. It was treason; and whether, in the strictly technical sense, we were spies or not had no bearing on this fact. Unless I consented to his making a full confession, it was impossible for him to go on living.

I did not take young von E.'s threat entirely seriously, and was unable to convince myself of the reality of the scene. The boy, standing in front of the desk—he had refused to sit down—looked ghastly, with black stubble on his white face and red, swollen eyes. He was perhaps unconsciously dramatising the situation, and the thrills derived from self-dramatisation were not unknown to me. On the other hand, he seemed quite capable of carrying the act to the point of really shooting himself. His demand that I should expressly consent to his handing in of the letter was quixotic and absurd. Yet I consented without further argument—and without even reading the letter that would inevitably put an end both to my professional career and to my usefulness to the *apparat*.

The only reasonable course would have been to read the letter carefully and discuss its contents in detail; to explain away certain points, ridicule others, and put a harmless interpretation on the rest; to blur and confuse the issue, make young von E. feel a fool, and then to gain time by asking him to think the matter over. With a certain amount of psychology and persuasion, it would perhaps have been possible to make the young man see matters differently, to make the harsh contours of fact dissolve in doubt and dialectical twilight. Even if I could not save my job, I could save my standing with the *apparat* by putting up a fight and denying von E.'s accusations. Yet, strangely enough, I could not get myself to argue, not even to read that letter on which my future depended. The whole scene had a touch of dreamlike unreality; and as I stuffed the letter back into von E.'s pocket and told him to hand it in with my blessings and to go to hell, I was acting with a dreamy inner certitude that made me indifferent to the consequences.

Such was the end of my hard-earned position in the newspaper world, the end of the road to respectability, and the beginning of another seven lean years. I had been prepared to sacrifice my future for the Party, but not to throw it away in such an apparently senseless manner. Now, however, after twenty years, it seems to me that my ready consent to von

E.'s denunciation and to the destruction of my career was senseless only in appearance. In reality it conformed to a recurrent, unconscious urge to burn my bridges, which I have tried to analyse earlier in these memoirs. I have mentioned there that all the crucial decisions which have altered the course of my life had in appearance been contrary to reason and yet in the long run had turned into spiritual blessings. It seems as if on these crucial occasions a type of logic were entering into action entirely different from the reasoning of the 'trivial plane'; as if one's decisions in these rare moments, however paradoxical or apparently suicidal, followed the commandments of the invisible text, revealed for a split second to the inner self.

To vary the metaphor : as I look back on the past, I see myself as a blind man painfully groping with his stick along the crowded pavement, while his absent-minded dog trots along on a loose leash and might as well not exist. Yet at the critical moment when the street has to be crossed and the stick becomes useless, the blind man feels a reassuring tug of the leash and knows that his seeing eye has taken over.

In this particular case the blessings of unreason soon became apparent. My quixotic gesture towards von E. saved me from the imminent danger of becoming a full-fledged *apparatchik* —the Party's homely slang-name for its agents. A short time before the disaster, Edgar had suggested that I go to Japan for the *apparat* under the guise of a news-correspondent. I had agreed at once, and though this scheme did not materialise, some similar assignment was bound to turn up sooner or later. As yet I was still an amateur, drifting on the periphery of the vortex; a few more weeks or months and I would inevitably have been drawn into a zone from which there is no turning back. Thanks to von E.'s confession, however, I not only lost my job with the Ullsteins but also my usefulness for the *apparat*—and this in a manner which to Edgar and Schneller proved my total unfitness for secret work. They dropped me without ceremony.

A few days after the letter was handed in, the Ullsteins gave me notice on the pretext of reductions in the staff, and offered me a lump sum in compensation for the remaining term of my five-year contract. Not a word was said about von E. and the Communist Party; they were anxious to avoid a scandal. So was the Party; Edgar instructed me to accept the settlement and leave it at that.

Except on one occasion, I never saw either him or Paula again. Paula was later killed by the S.S. in Ravensbrück. Edgar's and Schneller's fate I have already described.

II. Portrait of the Author as a Comrade

HAVING lost my job, I was free from the fetters of the bourgeois world; having lost my usefulness for the *apparat*, there was no longer any reason for keeping my Party-membership secret. I gave up my flat in the expensive district of Neu-Westend, and moved into an apartment-house on Bonner Platz known as the Red Block, for most of the tenants were penniless writers and artists of radical views. There I joined the local Communist cell and was at last permitted to lead the full life of a regular Party member.

Our cell was one among several thousand in Berlin, and one among the several hundred thousand basic units of the Communist network in the world. Cells exist in every country where the Party is legally tolerated; in countries where Communism is outlawed, a system of 'groups of five' or 'groups of three' replaces the larger legal units. The term 'cell' is not purely metaphorical; for these are living, pulsating units within a huge, sprawling organism, co-ordinated in their function, governed by a hierarchy of nervous centres, and susceptible to various diseases—to the Titoist virus, to bourgeois infection or Trotskyist cancer. The part of the white phagocytes is played by the various defence mechanisms of the Party, from the Central Control Commission to the G.P.U.

Our cell comprised about twenty members. The consciousness of being one unit among millions in an organised, disciplined whole was always present. We had among us several *litterateurs*, such as Alfred Kantorowicz and Max Schroeder, who are now both back in Communist Eastern Germany; a psychoanalyst—Wilhelm Reich, who broke with the Party in 1933 and is now the director of the Institute for Orgone Research in Rangeley, Maine; several actors from an *avant-garde* theatre called The Mouse Trap; several girls with intellectual ambitions; an insurance agent and a number of working men. In so far as the majority of us were intellectuals, our cell was untypical in its structure, yet entirely typical in its function—that is, in our daily work and routine.

Half of our activities were legal, half illegal. The cell met officially once a week, but the more active members were in daily contact with each other. The official meeting always started with a political lecture by an instructor from District Headquarters (or by the cell leader after he had been briefed at H.Q.), in which the line was laid down concerning the various questions of the day. This was followed by discussion, but a discussion of a peculiar kind. It is a basic rule of Communist discipline that, once the Party has decided to adopt a certain line regarding a given problem, all criticism of that decision becomes deviationist sabotage. In theory, discussion is permissible before a decision has been reached; in practice decisions are always imposed from above, without previous consultation with the rank and file. One of the slogans of the German Party said: 'The front-line is no place for discussions.' Another said: 'Wherever a Communist happens to be, he is always in the front-line.' So our discussions always showed a complete unanimity of opinion.

During that fateful spring and summer of 1932, a series of elections took place which shook the country like a succession of earthquakes—the Presidential elections, two Reichstag elections, and an election for the Prussian Diet; all in all four red-hot election campaigns within eight months in a country on the verge of civil war. We participated in the campaigns by door-to-door canvassing, distributing Party literature and turning out leaflets of our own. The canvassing was the most arduous part of it; it was mostly done on Sunday morning, when people could be expected to be at home. You rang the door bell, wedged your foot between door and post, and offered your pamphlets and leaflets, with a genial invitation to engage in a political discussion on the spot. In short, we sold the World Revolution like vacuum cleaners. Reactions were mostly unfriendly, but rarely aggressive. I often had the door banged in my face, but never had a fight. However, we avoided ringing the bells of known Nazis. And the Nazis in and round our block were all known to us, just as we were all known to the Nazis, through our rival nets of cells and *Block-warts*. The whole of Germany, town and countryside, was covered by those two elaborate and fine-meshed drag-nets.

That last summer of Weimar Germany was for the Party a period of transition; we were preparing to go underground, and accordingly regrouping our cadres. We might be outlawed overnight; everything had to be ready for this emergency. The moment we were forced into illegality, all Party cells would cease to function, and would be superseded by a new, nationwide structure, the 'Groups of Five'. The cells, whose membership ranged from ten to thirty comrades, were too large in size for underground work, and offered easy opportunities for *agents provocateurs* and informers. The breaking up of the cadres into Groups of Five meant a corresponding diminution of risks. Only the leader of the Group was to know the identity and addresses of the other four; and he alone was to have contact with the next higher level of the Party hierarchy. If he was arrested, he could only betray the four individuals in his group, and his contact-man.

So, while the cell still continued to function, each member was secretly allotted to a Group of Five, the idea being that none of the groups should know the composition of any other. In fact, as we were all neighbours in the Block, we each knew which Group was secretly meeting in whose flat; and, on the night of the burning of the Reichstag, when Goering dealt his death-blow to the Communist Party, the Groups scattered and the whole elaborate structure collapsed all over the Reich. We had marvelled at the conspiratorial ingenuity of our leaders; and, though all of us had read works on the technique of insurrection and civil warfare, our critical faculties had become so numbed that none of us realised the catastrophic implications of the scheme. These preparations for a long underground existence in decentralised groups meant that our leaders accepted the victory of the Nazis as inevitable. And the breaking up of the cadres into small units indicated that the Party would offer no open, armed resistance to Hitler's bid for power, and was preparing for sporadic small-scale actions instead.

But we, the rank and file, knew nothing of this. During that long, stifling summer of 1932 we fought our ding-dong battles with the Nazis. Hardly a day passed without one or two being killed in Berlin. The main battlefields were the *Bierstuben*, the smoky little taverns of the working-class districts. Some of these served as meeting-places for the Nazis, some as meeting-places (*Verkehrslokale*) for us. To enter the wrong pub was to venture into the enemy's lines. From time to time the Nazis would shoot up one of our *Verkehrslokale*. It was done in the classic Chicago tradition : a gang of S.A. men would drive slowly past the tavern, firing through the glass panes, then vanish at break-neck speed. We had far fewer motor-cars than the Nazis, and retaliation was mostly carried out in cars either stolen, or borrowed from sympathisers. The men who did these jobs were members of the R.F.B. (*Roter Frontkämpfer Bund*), the League of Communist War Veterans. My car was sometimes borrowed by comrades whom I had never seen before, and returned a few hours later with no questions asked and no explanations offered. It was a tiny, red, open Fiat car, and most unsuitable for such purposes; but nobody else in our cell had one. It was the last relic of my bourgeois past; now it served as a vehicle for the proletarian revolution. I spent half my time driving it round on various errands : transporting pamphlets and leaflets, shadowing certain Nazi cars whose numbers had been signalled to us, and acting as a security escort. Once I had to transport the equipment of a complete hand-printing press from a railway station to a cellar under a greengrocer's shop.

The R.F.B. men who came to fetch the car for their guerrilla expeditions were sometimes rather sinister types from the Berlin underworld. They came, announced by a telephone call or by a verbal message from District H.Q., but the same men rarely turned up twice. Sometimes, on missions of a more harmless nature, I was myself ordered to act as driver. We would drive slowly past a number of Nazi pubs to watch the goings-on, or patrol a pub of our own when one of our informers in the Nazi camp warned us of an impending attack. This latter kind of mission was unpleasant; we would park, with headlights turned off and engine running, in the proximity of the pub; and at the approach of a car I would hear the

click of the safety-catch on my passengers' guns, accompanied
by the gentle advice 'to keep my chump well down'. But I
was never involved in any actual shooting.

Once the R.F.B. men who came to fetch the car disguised
themselves in my flat before starting out. They stuck on
moustaches, put on glasses, dark jackets and bowler hats. I
watched them from the window driving off—four stately,
bowler-hatted gents in the ridiculous little red car, looking
like a party in a funeral procession. They came back four hours
later, changed back to normal, and made off with a silent handshake. My instructions, in case the number of the car was
taken by the police during some action, were to say that it had
been stolen and that I had found it again in a deserted street.

From time to time a rumour got round that the Nazis were
going to attack our Red Block, as they had attacked other
notorious Communist agglomerations before. Then we were
alerted, and some R.F.B. men turned up to mount guard. One
critical night some thirty of us kept vigil in my tiny flat, armed
with guns, lead-pipes and leather batons, like a huddle of
stragglers from a beaten army. A few weeks later, von Papen
staged his *coup d'état* : one lieutenant and eight men chased
the Socialist government of Prussia from office. It was the beginning of the end.

The Socialist Party, with its eight million followers, did
nothing. The Socialist-controlled trade unions did not even
call a protest strike. Only we, the Communists, called for an
immediate general strike. The call fell on deaf ears. Like inflated currency, our verbiage had lost all real meaning for the
masses. We lost the battle against Hitler before it was joined.
After the 20th of July, 1932, it was evident to all but ourselves
that the K.P.D., strongest among the Communist parties in
Europe, was a castrated giant whose brag and bluster only
served to cover its lost virility.

A few months later everything was over. Years of conspiratorial training and preparations for the emergency proved
within a few hours totally useless. Thaelmann, leader of the
Party, and the majority of his lieutenants were found in their
carefully-prepared hide-outs and arrested within the first few
days. The Central Committee emigrated. The long night descended over Germany.

I threw myself into the activities of the cell with the same ardour and complete self-abandonment that I had experienced at seventeen on joining my duelling fraternity in Vienna. I lived in the cell, with the cell, for the cell. I was no longer alone; I had found the warm comradeship that I had been thirsting for; my desire to belong was satisfied.

Only gradually did I become aware of certain undercurrents that existed beneath the free and easy surface. I noticed that individual friendships within the cell were, though not exactly reprehensible, yet regarded as slightly ambiguous and suspect of political 'factionalism'. 'Factionalism' —the formation of groups with a policy of their own—was a capital crime in the Party, and if two or more comrades were known to be often together and to take the same line during discussions, they inevitably became suspect of forming a secret faction.

As in boarding-schools and convents intense personal ties are suspected of having an erotic background, so friendships within the Party automatically aroused political suspicion. This attitude was not unreasonable, for between people whose life was entirely dedicated to and filled by the Party, nonpolitical friendships were hardly possible. The slogans of the Party emphasised the diffuse and impersonal 'solidarity of the working class' instead of individual friendship, and substituted 'loyalty to the Party' for loyalty to friends. Loyalty to the Party meant, of course, unconditional obedience, and meant, furthermore, the repudiation of friends who had deviated from the Party-line, or for some reason had fallen under suspicion. Almost unconsciously I learnt to watch my steps, my words and my thoughts. I learnt that everything that I said in the cell or in private, even to a girl comrade whose pillow I shared, remained on record and could one day be held against me. I learnt that my relations with other members of the cell should not be guided by trust but by 'revolutionary vigilance'; that reporting any heretical remark was a duty, failure to do so a crime against the Party, and that to feel revulsion against this code was a sign of sentimental, *petit-bourgeois* prejudice :

You and I can make a mistake. Not the Party. The Party, comrade, is more than you and I and a thousand others like

*you and I. The Party is the embodiment of the revolutionary
idea in history. History knows no scruples and no hesitation.
Inert and unerring, she flows towards her goal. At every bend
in her course she leaves the mud which she carries and the
corpses of the drowned. History knows her way. She makes no
mistakes. He who has no absolute faith in History does not
belong in the Party's ranks. . . . The Party's course is sharply
defined, like a narrow path in the mountains. The slightest
false step, right or left, takes one down the precipice. The air
is thin; he who becomes dizzy is lost ('Darkness at Noon').*

I learnt that the rules of common decency, of loyalty and
fair play were not absolute rules, but the ephemeral projec-
tions of competitive bourgeois society. Antiquity had one code
of honour; the feudal era another; capitalist society still another, which the ruling class was trying to sell us as eternal
laws. But absolute laws of ethics did not exist. Each class, as it
became dominant in history, had re-shaped these so-called
laws according to its interests. The Revolution could not be
achieved according to the rules of cricket. Its supreme law
was that the end justified the means; its supreme guide the
method of dialectical materialism.

*The true revolutionary is cold and unmerciful to mankind
out of a kind of mathematical mercifulness. . . . A conscience
renders one as unfit for the revolution as a double chin. Conscience eats through the brain like a cancer, until the whole of
the grey matter is devoured ('Darkness at Noon').*

The intense fascination of the dialectical method can only
be understood through a study of its masters—by reading,
say, Engels' *Feuerbach*, Marx's *Eighteenth Brumaire*, or
Lenin's *State and Revolution*. I now lived entirely in a mental
world which earlier I have described as a 'closed system', comparable to the self-contained universe of the medieval School-
men. All my feelings, my attitudes to art, literature and human
relations, became reconditioned and moulded to the pattern.
My vocabulary, grammar, syntax, gradually changed. I learnt
to avoid any original form of expression, any individual turn of
phrase. Euphony, gradations of emphasis, restraint, nuances

of meaning, were suspect. Language, and with it thought, underwent a process of dehydration, and crystallised in the ready-made schemata of Marxist jargon. There were perhaps a dozen or two adjectives whose use was both safe and mandatory, such as : decadent, hypocritical, morbid (for the capitalist bourgeoisie); heroic, disciplined, class-conscious (for the revolutionary proletariat); *petit-bourgeois*, romantic, sentimental (for humanitarian scruples); opportunist and sectarian (for Right and Left deviations respectively); mechanistic, metaphysical, mystical (for the wrong intellectual approach); dialectical, concrete (for the right approach); flaming (protests); fraternal (greetings); unswerving (loyalty to the Party).

However, certain refinements of language were permitted and even encouraged. Thus irony was a desirable method in polemics, but its application was restricted to the use of inverted commas; e.g. : the 'revolutionary' past of Trotsky; the 'progressive' measures of the 'Socialist' government; and so on. Equally popular was the use of what one may call semantic spoonerisms, initiated by Marx's famous pamphlet against Proudhon, *The Philosophy of Poverty and the Poverty of Philosophy*. This delightful game could be varied endlessly : 'the war on profits and the profits of war', 'the psychology of adolescence or the adolescence of psychology', 'the laws of terror and the terror of the law', and so on. There were also certain luxury words whose use was regarded as good form. For instance, in one of his works Lenin has mentioned Herostratus, who burnt down a temple because he could think of no other way of achieving fame. Accordingly, one often heard and read phrases like 'the criminally herostratic madness of the counter-revolutionary wreckers of the heroic efforts of the toiling masses in the Fatherland of the Proletariat to achieve the second Five Year Plan in four years'.

Few among the intellectuals in the Party realised at the time that their mentality was a caricature of the revolutionary spirit; that within the short span of three generations the Communist movement had travelled from the era of the Apostles to that of the Borgias. But the process of degeneration had been gradual and continuous, and the seeds of corruption had already been present in the work of Marx : in the

vitriolic tone of his polemics, the abuse heaped on his opponents, the denunciation of rivals and dissenters as traitors to
the working class and agents of the bourgeoisie. Proudhon,
Dühring, Bakunin, Liebknecht, Lassalle, had been treated by
Marx exactly as Trotsky, Bukharin, Zinoviev, Kameniev *et
alia* were treated by Stalin—except that Marx did not have
the power to shoot his victims. During these three generations,
the uses of the dialectic had also been vastly simplified. It was,
for instance, easy to prove scientifically that everybody who
disagreed with the Party-line was an agent of Fascism because
(*a*) by disagreeing with the line he endangered the unity of
the Party; (*b*) by endangering the unity of the Party he improved the chances of a Fascist victory; hence (*c*) *objectively*
he acted as an agent of Fascism even if *subjectively* he had his
kidneys smashed in a Fascist concentration camp. It was
equally easy to prove that charity, public or private, was
counter-revolutionary because it deceived the masses regarding the true nature of the capitalist system, and thereby contributed to its preservation.

Our literary, artistic and musical tastes were similarly reconditioned. The highest form of music was the choral song
because it represented a collective, as opposed to the individualistic approach. The same argument led to a sudden
and unexpected revival of the Greek chorus in the Communist *avant-garde* plays of the 'twenties. Since individual
characters could not be altogether banished from the stage,
they had to be stylised, typified, depersonalised. The Communist novel was guided by similar principles. The central
character was not an individual, but a group : the members
of a partisan unit during the Civil War; the peasants of a village in the process of being transformed into a collective farm;
the workers of a factory striving to fulfil the Plan. The tendency of the novel had to be 'operative', that is, didactic;
each work of art must convey a social message. And here
again, as individual heroes could not be entirely dispensed
with, they had to be made into typical representatives of a
given social class, party or political attitude.

Stripped of its exaggerations this conception has, of course,
a certain validity in the field of the political and ideological
novel. In later years I have written several essays criticising

the Marxist theory of art, and trying to reconcile the striving for social relevance with the conflicting claims of aesthetics and psychology. But such critical exercises did not prevent me from falling into the very errors that I had pointed out. The effects of years of indoctrination reached deeper than the conscious mind, and are easily traceable in my novels even ten years after the break.

Nevertheless, the Marxist approach has produced valuable results both in literary criticism and in creative writing. At least two among the leading contemporary critics, Edmund Wilson and Lionel Trilling, owe much to it. The orthodox 'proletarian' literature of the 'thirties appears today shallow and dated; but a whole generation of poets and novelists, who took Marx in small and digestible quantities, have added an essential feature to the civilisation of the twentieth century. Among them are Auden, Isherwood, Spender and Day Lewis in England; the early Dos Passos, Steinbeck, Caldwell and Sinclair Lewis in the United States; Barbusse, Rolland, Malraux, Sartre and Sperber in France; Becher, Brecht, Weinert, Renn, Seghers, Regler, Plivier in Germany—to mention only a few.

My own development was different from that of the enthusiastic 'fellow-travellers' of the 'thirties. I began to write my first novel when I was already disillusioned, and on my way out of the Party. The reason is that emotionally and in artistic taste I remained an adolescent to my late twenties. But this retarded development is again partly due to my seven years in the Communist Party. So long as I remained a true believer, my faith had a paralysing effect on my creative faculties, such as they are. The Marxist doctrine is a drug, like arsenic or strychnine, which in small doses have a stimulating, in larger ones a paralysing, effect on the creative system. The large majority of 'socially conscious' writers of the 'thirties were stimulated by it because they did not enter the Party, and remained sympathisers from a safe distance. The few of us who actually took the plunge—such as Victor Serge, Richard Wright, Ignazio Silone—felt frustrated during their active Party career, and only found their true voice after the break. One wonders what would have happened to Catholic novelists like Mauriac, Evelyn Waugh, or the late Bernanos, had they accepted the discipline of monastic life, or at least taken holy orders.

The Russian writers belong to a different category. They could not remain distant sympathisers; from the early 'thirties onward literature in Soviet Russia was regimented, and literary criticism wielded by the Party as a disciplinary weapon, with punishments ranging from the silencing of the discordant voice to the liquidation of its owner. A number of our Russian colleagues—among them the greatest, Alexander Blok—saw long before us where the régime was drifting and committed suicide. The majority, who made Soviet literature great during the first decade of the Revolution, were officially or secretly liquidated during the Purges. Those who survived have either lost their voices, or become Stalin-prize court jesters. The same is true of those non-Russian Communist writers who have remained in the Party—e.g., Johannes R. Becher and Louis Aragon.

My fanatical allegiance to the Party did not cause complete mental blindness to the more absurd phenomena in my new environment. I noticed that the political instructors sent by District Headquarters to the meetings of our cell knew nothing of the world outside the narrow field of working-class politics —that is, strikes, demonstrations and trade union developments. They did not know or believe that the Christian-Democratic Chancellor Bruenning was genuinely opposed to Hitler, or that there was a difference between a British Tory and a German Nazi. For them, democracy was 'a camouflaged form of the dictatorship of the capitalist ruling class' and Fascism 'its overt form', while 'the class-content' of both régimes was the same. The political struggles between the various 'bourgeois' parties were merely a symptom of the 'internal contradictions of the capitalist system'; the real alignment of social forces was along the class frontier. All this to my mind was both true and untrue. It was untrue because it was a crude over-simplification of a complex reality; but in the long view of History nuances did not matter, and my sophistication did not matter, and the dialectical telescope revealed the essential truth.

There were things even more difficult to swallow, particularly in the field of language and literature. After a speech in the cell, in which I had repeatedly used the word 'spontaneous', a well-wishing comrade tipped me off that I had better avoid it in the future, because 'spontaneous manifestations of the revolutionary spirit' were part of Trotsky's theory of the Permanent Revolution. I was at the very beginning of my party career, and though I agreed that such semantic purism was part of the necessary 'revolutionary vigilance', I did so, for the first time, with my tongue in my cheek. This reaction was soon to become more frequent.

A comrade, on his return from the Soviet Union, quoted to me the contents of a lecture he had heard, given by a Party instructor to a literary circle of workmen in a Russian factory. 'To regard poetry as a special talent which some men possess and others don't,' the instructor had explained, 'is bourgeois metaphysics. Poetry, like every other skill, is acquired by learning and practice. We need more class-conscious proletarian poetry; we must increase our poetry output on the literary front. Beginners should start with five or ten lines a day, then set themselves a target of twenty or thirty lines, and gradually increase the quantity and quality of their production.'

Later on I myself heard a Russian lecturer explain that the vogue of excessively long poems in Germany during the 'twenties was the ideological reflection of the currency inflation with its floods of printed paper. I constantly came across nonsense of this kind in Russia, but told myself that it didn't matter; it was merely a touching symptom of the exuberance and enthusiasm of a backward people awakening from centuries of apathy and oppression. The 'backward masses' could not be expected to develop overnight the sophistication of an ex-editor of Ullstein's.

After a few months in the Party my faith began to assume a more supple and lasting form. Everything that I disliked I explained to myself as 'the heritage of the Capitalist past', or as 'the inevitable measles of the Revolution', or finally as 'temporary expedients'. The higher interests of revolutionary strategy often necessitated tactical measures which seemed cruel, absurd or downright despotic. But Marxists must not judge 'mechanistically' by appearances, as the bourgeois Press did; their duty was to discern the hidden dialectical meaning; and their public utterances must be kept on the level of the backward masses.

Thus my originally naïve faith gradually changed into a private, esoteric creed which was more malleable, and shock-proof against reality. If the outsider asks how intelligent people could stand the wild zigzags of the Party line, the answer is that every single educated Communist, from the members of the Russian Politbureau down to the French literary côteries, has his own private and secret philosophy whose purpose is not to explain the facts, but to explain them away. It does not matter by what name one calls this mental process—double-think, controlled schizophrenia, myth addiction, or semantic perversion; what matters is the psychological pattern. Without it the portrait of the author as a comrade would not be comprehensible.

There existed, however, a barrier beyond which I was unable to carry self-deception. My language and reasoning became reconditioned to the Party's jargon; but this mimicry remained confined to the spoken word. When it came to writing, I encountered an unconscious resistance. Though a seasoned journalist, I was unable, during my whole Communist career, to write a single article for the Party Press—even when I found myself on the verge of starvation. At the beginning I composed broadsheets and leaflets for our cell, but though correct regarding the line, they were too unorthodox in style, and the District Committee stopped them. Much later, during the Saar campaign of 1934, I edited a comic Party paper, but this too was stopped after the first issue. I was capable of making speeches in the orthodox Party manner and of keeping them strictly on the level of the 'backward masses', while my esoteric truth and private opinion remained locked away in an air-tight compartment of the mind. But when I tried to apply the same process to writing, I became paralysed : I got involved with the syntax, made inkblots on the paper, was unable to concentrate, and caught myself drawing arabesques or a naked goddess holding up a hammer and sickle to the sun.[1]

Thus there were limits to my capacity for double-think. I

[1] I have tried to describe this mental torment in the chapter 'Fatigue of the Synapses' in *The Age of Longing*.

had been unable to argue with von E. though my job was at stake; I was unable to write in the Party's style; later on, as will be seen, I failed at other tasks. Perhaps, despite my ardour, I was only a mediocre Marxist. The fact that in spite of my growing misgivings I stuck to the Party through seven years, seems to indicate that my limitations as a Communist were of an unconscious rather than of a rational order. I was still chasing after the arrow in the blue, the absolute cause, the magic formula which would produce the Golden Age. Arrows may drift with the wind, and apparently change their direction relative to the rotating earth; but, unlike guided missiles, they cannot be forced into a zigzag course.

A special feature of Party life that had a profound and lasting influence on me was worship of the proletariat and contempt for the intelligentsia. Intellectuals of middle-class origin were in the Party on sufferance, not by right; this was constantly rubbed into us. We had to be tolerated, because during the transition period the Party needed the engineers, doctors, scientists and literati of the pre-revolutionary intelligentsia. But we were no more trusted or respected than the so-called 'useful Jews' in Hitler's Germany, who were given a distinctive armlet and allowed a short respite before their usefulness expired and they went the way of their kin. The social origin of parents and grandparents is as decisive under a Communist régime as racial origin was under the Nazi régime. Accordingly, Communist intellectuals of middle-class origin tried by various means to give themselves proletarian airs. They wore coarse polo-sweaters, displayed black finger-nails, talked working-class slang. It was one of our undisputed articles of faith that members of the working-class, regardless of their level of intelligence and education, would always have a more 'correct' approach to any political problem than the learned intellectual. This was supposed to be due to a kind of instinct rooted in class-consciousness. There is again a distinct parallel here with the Nazis' contempt for 'destructive Jewish cleverness' as opposed to the 'healthy and natural instinct of the race'.

This atmosphere provided wonderful nourishment for my chronic inferiority complex. In the chapters dealing with my childhood I have explained the depths and tenacity of this affliction, and its ties with anxiety and guilt. In later years I gradually managed to build up a brash façade, but this still further deepened the conviction that I was a sham who deserved his failures and humiliations, and obtained his successes by fraud. I felt a constant longing to be 'myself and nothing else beside'; yet for a person suffering from this type of affliction it is easier to climb Mount Everest than to be his own self. We know that Demosthenes, the stammerer, practised speech with his mouth full of pebbles until he became the foremost public orator of Greece; but we are not told whether he ever learnt to speak with a natural voice to his friends.

Now the working-men with whom Party-life threw me into contact did speak in their slow natural voice, and did more or less behave as their natural selves. That a truck-driver or a dynamo-fitter can be just as neurotic as a literary critic, and that he merely lacks the articulateness to express it, was a much later discovery. At the time it seemed to me that the proletarian members of our cell were all strong, silent, hard and kindly men, not only appointed by History to inherit the earth from the decadent bourgeoisie, but also mentally more hale and sane than the clever phoneys of my type. In short, the class-conscious proletarian was the Marxist equivalent of Rousseau's Noble Savage, of Nietzsche's Superman, of Hitler's *Blut und Bodenmensch*, and became a kind of collective super-ego for the Communist intelligentsia. For reasons that I have just explained, my own responses in this respect were particularly deep and lasting.

It is relatively easy to explain how a person with my story and background came to become a Communist, but more difficult to convey a state of mind that led a young man of twenty-six to be ashamed of having been to a university, to curse the agility of his brain, the articulatenesss of his language, to regard such civilised tastes and habits as he had acquired as a constant source of self-reproach, and intellectual self-mutilation as a desirable aim. If it had been possible to lance those tastes and habits like a boil, I would gladly have submitted to the operation.

A recent American study, embracing people from all social classes and races including Negroes, has shown that the majority of young Americans who joined the Communist

Party were prompted not by economic distress, but by some conflict within the family. I have said before that such psychological facts neither prove nor disprove the validity of Marxist theory. But *vice versa*, it is not Marxist theory in itself which turns people into rebels, but a psychological disposition which makes them susceptible to revolutionary theories. The latter then serve as rationalisations of their personal conflict—which does not exclude the possibility that the rationalisation may be a correct one.

To sum up this aspect of the story. As a child I had been taught that whatever I did was wrong, a pain to others and a disgrace to myself. At the age of five, the permanent awareness of guilt and impending punishmnet resulted in a mild attack of persecution mania, described in an earlier chapter. A few years later, the feeling of inferiority manifested itself in paralysing shyness, then focused on my slow growth and juvenile appearance. Now, at twenty-six, this floating mass of anxiety and guilt, always ready to fasten on the first peg in sight, turned against my bourgeois background, my powers of reasoning and capacity for enjoyment. To bask in the sun, to read a novel, to dine in a good restaurant, to go to a picture gallery, became guilty exercises of a privilege that others could not share, frivolous diversions from the class struggle. True Communists, like Catholics, live in a constant awareness of original sin.

I deplore the logical error that led me into the Communist Party; but I do not regret the spiritual discipline that it imposed. Purgatory is a painful experience; but no one who went through it is likely to wish that it should be erased from his past.

The one 'diversion from the class struggle' that did not make me feel guilty was love. In an earlier chapter I have described the phantom-chase after Helen's image that obsessed me during some twenty years. With most men, at least in the Anglo-Saxon countries, sex is the main source of guilt and anxiety. In my case it was the only pursuit exempt from guilt —perhaps because my attitude to women remained basically naïve and romantic, imparting to each liaison a flavour of uniqueness; and the feeling of uniqueness seems to me the only criterion of purity in matters of sex. The squalor of promiscuity prompted by mere pleasure-seeking lies in the drawing of comparisons. To be compared in one's most intimate behaviour to others is a degrading and wounding thought, and probably the main reason why we set so much store on exclusive possession. The phantom-chaser, however, who discovers Helen's image in each beloved face, feels each time that 'this is the real thing', set apart from all other experiences, past and future, and hence not comparable with them. It is a feeling that automatically conveys itself to the other person, and creates an oasis of innocence round both, leaving regret but no resentment when the illusion dissolves.

Some of the women with whom my life interlinked during my two years in Berlin have remained permanent friends; two were killed in air bombardments; two died in concentration camps; one of tuberculosis, and one achieved the rare distinction of marrying a dentist in Persia.

I wish one could write about one's sentimental curriculum in the same manner as one writes about one's political or literary evolution. The trouble is not that it would shock the reader, but that it would bore him. The experience of uniqueness is always confined to the protagonists. The oasis, however strange and fascinating, has only room for two. And yet—as some French writer is sure to have said somewhere—one learns to think through books; one learns to live through women.

Two episodes concerning women with whom I was not personally involved deserve to be related here because they are characteristic of the atmosphere of Berlin during the feverish months of *Götterdämmerung* that preceded the Nazis' seizure of power. The first is pretty ghastly, and hard to believe for anyone who has not experienced the mass-hysteria that conquered the German people during the last days of Weimar. It happened to a colleague of mine at Ullstein's, whose name has slipped my memory—it sounded something like von Ehrendorf, so I shall call him that.

During the carnival season of 1932, Ehrendorf went to a dance and picked up a tall, pretty blonde. She wore a large swastika brooch on her breast, was about nineteen or twenty, gay, uninhibited and brimful of healthy animal spirits—in short, the ideal *Hitler-Mädchen* of the Brave New World. After the dance, Ehrendorf persuaded her to go back with him to his flat, where she met his advances more than half-way. Then, at the climactic moment, the girl raised herself on one elbow, stretched out the other arm in the Roman salute, and breathed in a dying voice a fervent 'Heil Hitler'. Poor Ehrendorf nearly had a stroke. When he had recovered, the blonde sweetie explained to him that she and a bunch of her girl friends had taken a solemn vow, pledging themselves 'to remember the Fuehrer every time at the most scared moment in a woman's life'.

The *tricoteuses* of the French Terror had found their successors in the Valkyries of the Hitler era. I use this opportunity to confess that I have always held a reactionary view of the part played by women in politics. Taking history as a whole, female interference in matters of State seems to add up to a rather nefarious balance. The male tyrants of history are on the whole cancelled out by an equal number of reformers; but where are the female humanists to compensate for the long series of monsters, from Messalina to Catherine the Great, to Irma Griese of Buchenwald? There are countless books for boys about great men, and no books for girls about great women; yet an anthology about the harpies who left their imprint on history would be an international best-seller. I am talking of women who took a direct hand in politics; their indirect influence *via* husbands and lovers is a different problem altogether—though even here it seems that they have acted on the whole more as catalysts of ambition than as neutralisers of aggression.

The second story is the counterpart of the first. Alfred Kantorowicz, our cell leader, had asked a girl comrade to tea in his flat. There were only the three of us present. The girl, whom I had not met before, was dark and slim and would have been moderately attractive but for her slovenly manner of dressing, and a curiously distraught look. She took no part in the conversation, and did not even pretend to listen. Suddenly she said to Kantorowicz : 'Do look out of the window now, and see whether he is there; but be careful.'

Kantorowicz peered into the street from behind the curtain.

'There is nobody,' he said reassuringly.

'When I came in, he was hiding behind a lamp-post,' said the girl.

She spoke in a quiet, resigned voice, without any emotion. Kantorowicz now explained to me that comrade Hilda was in trouble : a man had been shadowing her for days, but he had been unable to gather from her story whether she suspected the Police or somebody else.

'It is not the Police,' the girl said, in the same resigned voice. We pressed her to explain, and after a long pause she said :

'It is a chap from the *Bezirksleitung*' (the District Committee of the Party).

With great effort and with lenghtening intervals, during which the girl relapsed into silence and became *incommunicado* behind a fixed stare, we extracted from her a confused story to the effect that a man from the District Committee (our immediate superiors in the Party hierarchy) had wanted to sleep with her; that she had refused; that subsequently he had been accusing her of some unnamed crime against the Party, and was now following her round, hiding behind doorways and lamp-posts after dark.

Kantorowicz and I discussed this for a while, trying to think of a way of helping her. But the girl no longer took an interest in us. She had now completely withdrawn into herself; her stare had become fixed and glassy. She sat upright and immobile at the table, as if petrified. Gradually her upper lip began to lift, baring her teeth and her gums, and remained fixed in a snarl. A few tears detached themselves from the corners of her eyes and slid slowly down her face; but she neither sobbed nor gave any other sign of emotion; and that snarl, like a dead rabbit's, had become a permanent feature. It was obvious that a case of latent paranoia had suddenly entered its acute phase; the girl had gone insane before our eyes. We somehow got her into a taxi, and Kantorowicz drove her to a hospital.

I once took a rabbit, caught by a spaniel, from the dog's fangs. The rabbit was apparently unhurt but died a few moments later, probably from fright or shock. Comrade Hilda's face, with the bared gums and glassy stare, had worn the same expression. It was a pitiful and horrifying experience, that in moments of anxiety haunted me for a long time. The transformation of a face into a mask, of a human being into an automaton, bore the familiar sign of Ahor—the archaic horror of my childhood. That unfortunate girl would probably have gone insane in any case, Communist or not. But the particular form which her insanity took was characteristic of the atmosphere in which we lived. No doubt there was a grain of truth in the story around which her fantasies had crystallised. In former days, persecution manias focused on devils and incubi; for poor Comrade Hilda the fiend was 'a chap from the District Committee' denouncing her crimes against the Party.

The hysterical Valkyrie and Comrade Hilda certainly do not represent German womanhood; but they do represent, as extreme cases, the 'politically awakened' part of it, anno domini 1932.

III. 'Sink into the Mud'

A SHORT time before I lost my job, I had organised a caucus of Communist sympathisers among the Ullstein staff. The group met once a week in my flat, and comprised about a dozen columnists, sub-editors, magazine artists, theatre and film critics. Its purpose was to exchange information, and to counteract the pro-Nazi tendencies within the trust. Only two of us were members of the C.P.—Kantorowicz, who was a free-lance contributor to several Ullstein papers, and myself; and we were the only ones who punctually attended the meetings of the caucus, who took the matter seriously and knew what we were about. We were disciplined members of a civilian army acting under instructions; the others were free agents, divided and confused, as intellectuals always are in matters of practical action, anxious 'to do something', frightened of the consequences, and given to long, rambling, pointless arguments.

I reported every week on the antics of the group through Edgar to the *apparat*, including brief reports on the background and character of each of the members. My instructions were to let them all talk to their hearts' content and just to keep the thing going, while watching the individual evolution of each member with a view to his possible future usefulness. By this slow, patient, apparently aimless method did the *apparat* cast its nets into thousands of similar 'study groups' and 'discussion circles' in universities, editorial offices, government agencies, industrial enterprises all over the world. It was all perfectly harmless and high-minded; and it produced an astonishing harvest of Alger Hisses, Nunn Mays and Donald MacLeans. Yet such big and dramatic catches were rare; of equal importance were the more intangible results of ideological infiltration, the creation of a mental climate in progressive-liberal circles which ranged from benevolent neutrality to active support of the Great Social Experiment, and the equation of all criticism of Russia with a reactionary, Fascist attitude.

Our particular little group was not a successful one, and it petered out after a few months. With the constant dismissals at Ullstein's, and the shadow of Hitler lying across the country like a monster-shaped cloud, our motley little crowd of intellectuals was too scared to be capable of any clear thought. It was easy to win their sympathy for Russia, but almost impossible to make them take a determined stand for their own interests in Germany. The liberals in Germany—and elsewhere—have rarely understood that there are situations in which caution amounts to suicide.

When Franz Höllering, editor of the Ullstein's mid-day paper *B.Z. Am Mittag* was sacked for his leftist views, I tried to organise a collective action of protest. In spite of Höllering's great popularity amongst his colleagues, not one of them was prepared to sign the quite moderate letter that I had drafted. Some shrugged and muttered : 'You are a young man, but I have my family to consider'; others talked of 'Communist methods'. This last remark reveals the ambiguity of the whole problem. Whenever Communists took the lead in actions of social protest—in defence of anti-Fascists, Negroes, and natives, or in the war-time resistance movements in any part of the world—they certainly acted for devious motives of their own. But at the same time they behaved with courage, discipline and determination, which won them grudging admiration and gave them a considerable moral advantage over their soft and undecided progressive allies. It was this fearless, active, knight-errant aspect of Communism which attracted me and millions of others to the movement, and which compensated us for our disappointments.

Another episode, that I still remember with considerable satisfaction, concerns the threatened eviction of a destitute woman and her child from a flat in our vicinity. When we heard of this, some thirty of us marched in a body to the landlord and told him that if he insisted on carrying out the eviction, the police would first have to knock every one of us cold before they could get the woman out, and that we would take good care that the story got into the press. The landlord desisted, and we subsequently called a public meeting that resolved : 'no more evictions around the Red Block.' These were actions spontaneously undertaken by our cell without any order from District H.Q. Sooner or later we would have got into trouble for 'Trotskyism' or 'Leftist deviation'; but Hitler came in first.

The Ullstein-caucus of sympathisers disintegrated soon after my dismissal. Having lost my position in the Trust, I also lost my authority in the group, for, as one of them coldly put it : 'You no longer have anything to lose—we still have.' That was, of course, true, but not for long. The jobs to which they clung so fearfully, without regard to principles and without understanding that only concerted and courageous action could save them, they all lost a few months later. Their fate was symbolic of the undignified end of the Weimar Republic. Their cowardice and helplessness filled me with contempt, and made me glad and proud to be a Communist.

Outside the cell which had become my universe I now had few friends and social contacts. Even these were either Communists or sympathisers. With others I no longer had a common language. We were moving into the totalitarian era; all relations became polarised and tense. It was a process like the requisitioning of private telephones near the front-line. The possibilities of human communication were rapidly narrowing.

Among the Communist intellectuals who were prominent in pre-Nazi Berlin, my favourite was Hans Eisler, the composer. His family belonged to the high Comintern aristocracy and deserves a brief description.

The three Eislers—Hans, Gerhart and Ruth—came from Vienna; their father was the respected author of several works of sociology. Ruth (alias Ruth Fischer) is probably the most brilliant woman in Communist history. In 1918 she founded the Austrian Communist Party and became its charter member No. 1; later she was elected chairman of the Berlin C.P., a Deputy of the Reichstag, and a member of the Praesidium of the Comintern. She was excommunicated for 'Left deviationism' in 1926. Now she is the most ardent and temperamental among the ex- and anti-Communists, but also the author of the most scholarly work on Comintern history.[1]

The third of the Eisler siblings, Gerhart (alias Hans Burger), started his Party career on the wrong foot as a 'Right deviationist'. He managed, however, to work himself back into Stalin's personal favour and in 1929 was sent—disguised as a salt merchant—to China, to liquidate the Party's revolt against Stalin's pact with Chiang Kai Shek (the Stalin-Chiang pact of 1927 was a forerunner of the Stalin-Hitler pact of 1939). Gerhart's experiences as a Comintern agent in China inspired his brother Hans' opera *The Punitive Measure*, book by Bert Brecht, which has since become a Communist classic. Later on Gerhart was a Comintern official in Moscow (where I met him in 1933), a Comintern agent in France (where we were interned together in the concentration camp of Le Vernet), and in the United States (where he was arrested in 1950 and, after jumping bail, was smuggled out of the country on board a Polish liner). At the time of writing he is head of the propaganda department of the Soviet Zone of Germany.[2]

Though all three Eislers were Communists, the characters of Hans, Gerhart and Ruth were entirely unlike each other. Ruth Fischer—a short, stout woman with an explosive temperament—revolted against the strait-jacket which Stalin put on the revolutionary movement. Gerhart, a smooth-faced, smooth-mannered careerist, succeeded in maintaining his place in the Comintern hierarchy by intrigue and self-abasement. Hans was neither an enthusiast like Ruth, nor an opportunist like Gerhart. He was a musician, who also happened to be a member of the Communist Party. He did not care a fig about political intrigues, and managed to remain almost miraculously detached amidst the earthquakes and tempests of Party life. As music is further removed from politics than literature or painting, composers were at that time still left relatively alone; the Politbureau's thunderbolts against Shostakovich and the Formalists only came twenty years later. Amiable Hans was a bald, moon-faced little man with a wealth of humour and self-mockery. To listen to him

---

[1] *Stalin and German Communism*, Cambridge, U.S.A., 1948.
[2] At the time of going to Press, he no longer is.

hacking out on the piano his revolutionary songs and singing
the words in his cracked, croaking voice was pure joy. These
songs—'The March of the Unemployed', 'Hymn of the
Comintern', etc., with words by Becher or Erich Weinert—
were at the same time sentimental, stirring and didactic. They
were the only successful works of popular art that the European Communist movement has created, the beginnings of a
revolutionary folklore.

The most fashionable poet among the snobs and parlour-
Communists of the period was Bertold Brecht. I have never
met Brecht in person, but it is impossible to evoke the last
years of the Weimar period without mentioning him. His plays
had a success far surpassing the Auden-Spender-Isherwood
productions in England. Some of them were set to music by
Hans Eisler, others by Kurt Weill. They were full of catchy
melodies, easy to hum, sentimental in the tradition of the German ballad, but with a dissonant, modern orchestration which
gave them a ring of sophisticated mockery. You were moved,
but at the same time remained ironically superior, as when
listening to a tear-jerking Victorian ballad. Against this ambiguous musical background was set a text of great brilliance
and intellectual dishonesty.

Brecht's greatest success, *Die Dreigroschenoper*, was a
modernisation of Gay's *Beggar's Opera*. It was a highbrow
épatez le bourgeois-prank in praise of thieves and whores. One
of its refrains, which compressed Brecht's message into a single
formula, became a catchphrase in pre-Hitlerite Germany :
'First comes my belly, then your morality'. (*Denn erst kommt
das Fressen, und dann kommit die Moral.*)

The theme of another Brecht success, the didactic play *A
Man is a Man (Mann ist Mann)*, can also be reduced to a formula : 'To hell with the individual.' A soldier disappears from
his regiment; he is replaced by a man caught at random in
the street and pressed into service. It makes no difference
whatever, for all men are interchangeable regarding their
function within the collectivity : 'The sun doesn't care on
whom it shines.'

The dreary message of these plays was made attractive by
Brecht's considerable lyrical talent, by the catchy tunes of the
songs, and above all by their stylised and exotic settings : Ala-

bama, China, India, the slaughterhouses in Chicago, the Kingdom of the Dead. Some of the songs were lifted, without acknowledgment, from Kipling, others from Villon. When a leading German critic exposed the plagiarism, Brecht coolly answered that he did not recognise individual property in literature any more than in economics. This statement was acclaimed by the progressive intelligentsia as highly original and daring.

The climax of Brecht's literary career, and at the same time most revealing work of art in the entire Communist literature, is the play *Die Massnahme* (*The Punitive Measure*). It will, I believe, be quoted by historians in coming centuries as the perfect apotheosis of inhumanity. As it has not been translated into English, I feel justified in describing its contents in some detail.

The play takes the form of a trial. Three Comintern agents return from a secret mission in China, and explain before a Party tribunal, in the form of flashbacks, why they had been obliged to kill their fourth, young comrade and to throw his body into a lime pit. The tribunal is represented by an anonymous, Greek 'Controlchorus'. The three agents are equally anonymous—they wear masks on their mission, having effaced their personality, their will and feeling, by order of the Party :

'You are no longer yourselves. No longer are you Karl Schmitt of Berlin. You are no longer Anna Kyersk of Kazan, and you are no longer Peter Savich of Moscow. You are without a name, without a mother, blank sheets on which the Revolution will write its orders.

'He who fights for Communism must be able to fight and to renounce fighting, to say the truth and not to say the truth, to be helpful and unhelpful, to keep a promise and to break a promise, to go into danger and to avoid danger, to be known and to be unknown. He who fights for Communism has of all the virtues only one : that he fights for Communism.'

The 'young comrade' however, was unable to live up to this ethical code. He was guilty of four crimes, having successively fallen into the traps of pity, of loyalty, of dignity and righteous indignation. In the first episode he is described as one of a gang of coolies pulling a boat up the river. He tries to help some exhausted comrades, thereby attracts attention, and the agents have to decamp. In the second episode he comes to the defence of a workman beaten up by the police, with the same result.

In the third, he is sent to negotiate with a representative of the Chinese bourgeoisie, who is willing to arm the revolutionary coolies to get rid of his British competitors. All goes well until the fat bourgeois sings a song in praise of business profits; the young comrade is so disgusted that he refuses to accept food from the bourgeois, and the deal falls through. The moral is driven home by the Controlchorus, who asks the rhetorical question :

Controlchorus : But is it not right to place honour above all ?
The three agents : No.
Controlchorus : What vileness would you not commit to exterminate vileness? . . . Sink into the mud, embrace the butcher, but change the world : it needs it.

The climax of the play is the fourth episode, in which the young comrade deviates from the Party line. The line, it should be remembered, was the Stalin-Chiang pact of 1927, one of the most terrible episodes of Comintern history, which led to the wholesale massacre of Chinese Communists by Chiang, and with Stalin's passive complicity. It should also be remembered that Gerhart Eisler had played a decisive part in implementing this policy, and that Hans Eisler wrote the music for the play. We may, therefore, assume that Brecht knew exactly what the consequences of the 'line of 1927' had been. The young comrade in the play refuses to implement that line. He tears up 'the scriptures of the Party classics', and cries out :

'All this no longer has any bearing. At the moment when the fight is on, I reject all that was valid yesterday and do my human duty. My heart beats for the Revolution.'

He tears his mask off and shouts to the coolies :

'We have come to help you. We come from Moscow.'

So the agents, who 'in the dusk saw his naked face, human, open, guileless', have to shoot him. But before they do that, they ask the young comrade whether he agrees to be shot. He answers :

'Yes. I see that I have always acted incorrectly. Now it would be better if I were not.'

The three agents : 'Then we shot him and threw him into the lime pit and when the lime had absorbed him we returned to our work.'

Controlchorus : 'Your work has been blest. You have propagated the Principles of the Classics, the ABC of Communism. And the Revolution is on the march here too, and here too the ranks of the fighters have been formed. We are in agreement.'

The play reads like a glorification of the anti-Christ. Perhaps the most uncanny scene in it is the young comrade's confession, and his acquiescence in his own liquidation. Written in 1931, it seems to be a prophetic forecast of the Moscow show trials that were to start five years later. The young comrade stands in reality for the old bolshevik guard, the generation of the civil war, who had to be thrown into the lime pit because they had retained some vestiges of humanity; and above all, because they were old-fashioned revolutionaries 'whose heart beat for the revolution', and who put the interest of the coolies before those of the 'controlchorus'.

Certain scenes in the play have the rugged and hostile greatness of a moon-landscape; others read like a vitriolic parody of the Communist creed. Yet the idea that it may be viewed as a parody never occurred to author, actors, and audience. The play had the inhuman consistency of a schizophrenic vision; and once you accept its two basic tenets, that the Party can never do wrong, and that the End justifies the Means, its apparently prophetic foresight becomes merely logical extrapolation.

In his excellent analysis of Brecht, Herbert Lüthy has shown how the ex-anarchist, ex-libertarian poet became attracted 'not by the workers' movement—which he had never known—but by a deep urge for a total authority, a total

submission to a total power, the new Byzantine State Church
—immutable, hierarchic, founded on the infallibility of the
leader'.[1]

The immense success of his plays was a symptom of the
morbid death-wish of German democracy. The leading part in
the play which made Brecht's reputation, *The Beggar's Opera*,
was played by a remarkable actress, Carola Neher, Brecht's
mistress, muse, and closest friend. A few years later she went
on a tour to Russia and shared the fate of the 'young comrade'.
Brecht did not protest; he has remained faithful to this day
to his party and his creed : 'sink into the mud and embrace
the butcher.'

I was waiting for my visa to Russia. When I lost my job
I had asked the Party for permission to emigrate. This was
regarded as a rare privilege, for the duty of every Communist
was to work for the Revolution in his own country. However,
I still enjoyed a certain reputation as a liberal journalist (the
reasons why I had to leave the Ullsteins were not known in
public), and the Party was willing to exploit this advantage.
It was agreed that I should go to Russia and write a series of
articles on the first Five Year Plan, maintaining the fiction
that I was still a bourgeois reporter. I accordingly entered into an agreement with a literary agency, the Karl Duncker Ver-
lag,[2] who undertook to syndicate the series on some twenty
newspapers in various European countries. But the months
passed by, and my visa did not arrive.

Meanwhile I had to live. The sum which the Ullsteins had
paid me as a final settlement I sent to my parents; it would
keep them going for two or three years—that is, until after the
victorious Revolution. I had only kept the amount required
to pay my fare to Moscow, as I had optimistically assumed
that once the Party had agreed to my going to Russia, my visa
would be granted at once. Fortunately I managed to sell a
detective serial to the *Münchner Illustrierte Zeitung* for a
fairly large sum; besides, I also worked as a free-lance journalist for my former paper, the *Vossische Zeitung*. To be fired by
one's employers as a Communist agent, but permitted to go on

---

[1] H. Lüthy : *Du Pauvre Bert Brecht, Preuves*, March, 1953.
[2] Not to be confused with the Communist editor, Herman Dunker.

working for them informally, was one of the amiable para-
doxes of bourgeois liberalism which I held in such contempt.

I would probably still be waiting for my visa if Johannes
R. Becher had not arrived in Berlin from Moscow.

Becher, the Communist poet laureate, was President of the
'League of Proletarian Revolutionary Writers of Germany'.
He was a tall, sturdy Bavarian with a fleshy, nondescript face,
made even more inscrutable by thick-lensed, steel-rimmed
spectacles. One could take him for a teacher of mathematics
or the director of an insurance company—for anything but a
poet. But behind this calm poise and neutral façade was a
complex and fascinating personality.

Becher became known in Germany in the mad years after
the first World War, partly as a young expressionist poet,
partly as the lucky survivor of a suicide pact. He had shot the
girl with whom he was determined to die, neatly through the
head, but had himself survived through some accident. Subsequently he was acquitted by a German court on the grounds
of having been mentally irresponsible at the time when the
act was committed.

Becher's outstanding quality was a cynical humour, very
unusual in Party circles. Together with this went an astute
judgment of men, remarkable cunning in handling situations,
and a ruthless capacity for manœuvring in troubled waters.
It is probably this combination of abilities, so rare in a poet,
that has enabled him to survive the Purges and the traps which
threaten the Communist writer at every step. In the inner
circles of the Party he was sometimes called 'the tightrope
walker'—a name which, in view of his heavy build, sounded
both ludicrous and slightly sinister.

Becher took a liking to me which I reciprocated and in a
manner still do, regardless of the fact that he has since publicly denounced me as a war criminal, a gangster and a spy,
and has variously demanded that I should be exterminated
or put into a mental asylum. But to issue statements of this
kind is no more than an inescapable formality for Party members; the Soviet citizen who, as a matter of routine, signs a
resolution asking that this or that fallen leader should be 'shot
as a mad dog' has no ill feeling against the victim and would
be surprised if told that the latter resented his performing such

a simple act of duty. When one knows the rules of the game one does not take these matters seriously, and when one's former friends and comrades keep calling one every name out of the Zoo there is no need even for forgiveness; one knows that they cannot act otherwise.

So Becher and I got on well, and he procured me an official invitation from MORP,[1] the 'International Organisation of Revolutionary Writers', to write a book on the Soviet Union : *Russia through Bourgeois Eyes.* The idea of it was similar to that of the articles for which I had signed up with Dunker : Mr. K., a liberal news-correspondent, starts his journey with an anti-Communist bias, is gradually converted by the results of the Five Year Plan, and ends up as a friend and admirer of the Soviet Union. As MORP was *de facto* a branch of the Comintern, and Becher himself occupied a high position in it, my visa was now at last granted.

I had few possessions, having always lived in hotel rooms or furnished flats; the books about which I cared filled no more than a large crate. But I still had my car, the little red Fiat that had rendered such faithful services to the cell. It was known in the Party under the petname 'Gretchen'. One day Becher happened to ask me whether I intended to sell Gretchen before I left. I told him that I intended to leave her to the Party.

'The Party,' said Becher, 'is a large body. The German branch of MORP is affiliated to it. It would be logical to leave Gretchen to us.' I agreed that it would be logical. As Becher happened to be chairman of the German branch of MORP, it was also logical that he took personal possession of Gretchen, and a few days after I had left for Russia, he went off in her to find inspiration in the Black Forest. As a sign of his appreciation, he procured me a contract for my book with the Russian State Publishing Trust against a cash advance of three thousand roubles. This amiable deal gave me the first intimation that a writer's existence in the Soviet Union depended entirely on his standing with the Party.

By the end of July 1932, I was at last ready to turn my back on the bourgeois world and head for the Promised Land. It

[1] *Meshdunarodnoe Obyedinenie Revolusionnykh Pisateley.*

was six months before the Germany of Weimar became Nazi-land. It was also six years and six months after I had emigrated to the first Land of Promise, Palestine. I felt the same exhilaration at having burnt my bridges, the same hectic expectation of a journey into Utopia. It took me many years to discover that the restless traveller has only one goal: to escape from himself.

This time there was no crowd of friends on the platform to sing anthems and wave me good-bye. The members of the cell were political allies, not personal friends; I had not asked any of them to come to the station. One girl alone stood outside the window of my third-class compartment: Lotte, the last and most faithful among the Helenas of vanished Weimar. As the train moved out of the Bahnhof am Zoo, she made a mocking curtsey; I never saw her again. When I turned away from the window, I felt, for a moment, a very lonely voyager. Then I became immersed in a pamphlet on the increase of steel production under the second Five Year Plan.

Part Two

UTOPIA

1932–33

*They believe everything they can prove,
and they can prove everything they believe.*

'The Age of Longing.'

IV. The Sorting Machine

THE chapters which follow describe my travels in Russia in 1932-33. Conditions have, of course, considerably changed since that time; yet I believe that certain basic values and characteristic features of the Soviet Régime have remained substantially the same.

My first destination was not Moscow but Kharkov, then capital of the Soviet Ukraine. I had friends living in that town, who had invited me to stay with them until I found my feet in the new world. They were Alex Weissberg and his wife; and they are going to play an important part in my life.

Eva, a dark, strikingly beautiful girl, was a painter and designer of ceramics. I had known her since my childhood; she appears in *The God that Failed* as Eva, and elsewhere under a different pseudonym. Alex was a physicist, and a member of the Austrian Communist Party. I had first met him in Eva's studio in Berlin, before they married and left for the Soviet Union, where an important research job was waiting for him. I had no inkling at that time that they were heading for years of prison and torment in Russia; nor that Eva was to supply, from her own tragic experience, the background material of a future novel, *Darkness at Noon*. In my Preface to Alex's autobiographical book, *Conspiracy of Silence*,[1] I have described our first meeting :

My first impression of Alex was that of a prosperous and jovial business man with a round face, rounded gestures, a great gusto for telling funny stories and a curious liking for

[1] London and New York, 1952.

sweets—there were little trays with chocolates about, which he kept gobbling up absentmindedly by handfuls. I failed to see what Eva found so remarkable about this character until the other guests were gone and we became involved in an argument on some of the finer points of Marxist theory. Then Alex's eyes became narrow and piercing, every trace of humour left him, and he made dialectical mincemeat of me. He had a lucid, trenchant and relentless way of arguing, and, not content with knocking his opponent down, he continued to hammer away at him. After a while he became jolly and jovial again.

What enabled him to hold out [under G.P.U. interrogation] was his great physical and mental resilience—that jack-in-the-box quality which allows quick recuperation and apparently endless comebacks, both physical and mental; a certain thickskinnedness and good-natured insensitivity: an irrepressible optimism and smug complacency in hair-raising situations.

Practically all of my Central-European friends have had experiences of varying severity in prisons and concentration camps. I don't know a single one who, after three years in the hands of the G.P.U. and five years hunted by the Gestapo, has emerged physically and mentally so unscathed and pleased with this best of all possible worlds as Alexander Cybulski Weissberg. He looked like a prosperous business man when I first met him twenty years ago, before the roof collapsed over our heads; and he still looks like a prosperous business man, with rounded gestures, a fondness for Viennese coffee-house stories, munching pralinés or his favourite Turkish delight.

My idea of Russia had been formed entirely by Soviet propaganda. It was the image of a super-America, engaged in the most gigantic enterprise in history, buzzing with activity, efficiency, enthusiasm. The motto of the first Five Year Plan had been to 'reach and surpass' the Occident; this task had been completed in four years instead of five. At the frontier I would 'change trains for the twenty-first century', as another slogan had promised.

A few trivial episodes of the journey are sharply outlined in my memory even after twenty years. First, the Customs examination at Shepetovka, the frontier station. As a travelling reporter, I had gone through frontier controls in nearly all European and several Oriental countries; but the Customs examination at Shepetovka was different from any previous experience. The Soviet Customs officials did not follow the usual routine of plunging their hands into a suitcase, feeling their way along its sides and bottom, or pulling out a few objects for closer examination. They completely unpacked the contents of every suitcase in every traveller's possession and spread them out on the customs counters and on the grimy floor. They unwrapped every object packed in paper, opened every box of chocolates or collar studs, examined every book and printed sheet. Then they re-packed everything again. It took half a day. Meanwhile the train in the station could not be boarded by the travellers : the empty compartments were being subjected to the same minute search.

Most of the travellers in the train were Russians, and most of the contents of their baggage was food. Hundreds of pounds of sugar, tea, butter, sausages, lard, biscuits, and conserves of every variety were piled on the counters and grimy floor of the Customs shed. I was startled by the look on the Customs officials' faces while they were handling these foodstuffs. It was a look of greed and resignation. I had suffered hunger myself; the way a hungry man takes a piece of salami into his hands—the deference of his touch, and the pathetic gleam in his eyes—cannot be mistaken.

The train puffed slowly across the Ukrainian steppe. It stopped frequently. At every station there was a crowd of peasants in rags, offering ikons and linen in exchange against a loaf of bread. The women were lifting up their infants to the compartment 'windows—infants pitiful and terrifying with limbs like sticks, puffed bellies, big cadaverous heads lolling on thin necks. I had arrived, unsuspecting, at the peak of the faminine of 1932–33 which had depopulated entire districts and claimed several million victims. Its ravages are now officially admitted, but at the time they were kept secret from the world. The scenes at the railway-stations all along our journey gave me an inkling of the disaster, but no understanding of its causes and extent. My Russian travelling companions took pains to explain to me that these wretched crowds were *kulaks*, rich peasants who had resisted the collectivisation of the land and whom it had therefore been necessary to evict from their farms.

Another incident was so slight that I only registered it half-consciously. As our train was approaching a river across which a bridge was being built, the conductor came walking down the corridor with an armful of square pieces of cardboard and blocked up all the windows. When I asked why this was done, my travelling companions explained with smiles that bridges were military objectives, and that this precaution was necessary to prevent anybody from photographing them. It was the first of a series of equally grotesque experiences which I put down as examples of revolutionary vigilance.

The next surprise came in Kharkov when I found that my friends had not turned up at the station. When I tried to telephone them, I discovered that the only public telephone at the central railway station of Kharkov was out of order. Instead of taxis, there were only horse-drawn droshkys which seemed to come straight out of Chekov. I did finally find the Weissbergs' flat; the telegram which I had sent before leaving Berlin arrived eighteen hours after myself. In 1932, letters in Russia often took several weeks to arrive; inland telegrams took several days, while long-distance calls could only be made by Government and Party officials.

I reacted to the brutal impact of reality on illusion in a manner typical of the true believer. I was surprised and bewildered —but the elastic shock-absorbers of my Party training began to operate at once. I had eyes to see, and a mind conditioned to explain away what they saw. This 'inner censor' is more reliable and effective than any official censorship.

To illustrate this point, I shall quote a passage from the travel-book that I started to write a few weeks after my arrival. Working on the book was a means to work all doubts and misgivings out of my system by ridiculing my own bewilderment. It was a strenuous effort, as the style of the excerpt reveals; it is a description of the author's first impressions on Russian soil :

. . . Let us not deceive ourselves: this writer did not stand up very well to the test of the first few days. He splashed about

*rather helplessly in the bottomless porridge of impressions
which he had found instead of the neat and tidy contours of
socialist life anticipated in his imagination. He had visualised
the Soviet Union as a kind of gigantic Manhattan with enormous buildings sprouting from the earth like mushrooms after
rain, with rivers queuing up before power stations, mountains
being tossed into the air by faith, and people breathlessly
racing, as in an accelerated film, to fulfil the Plan. Yet the
first Soviet town in which he set foot gave the impression of a
huge village of seven hundred thousand sleeping souls, lazy as
the Orient, timeless as the steppes. From the railway station a
heavy peasant crowd was clumping through the dusty streets
as if heading for a fair; and this was not a backward village,
but the capital of the second largest Republic in the Union.
In the antique tram-car the conductress sits ensconced among
the passengers, chewing sunflower seeds, and if you ask her for
a street she looks at you reproachfully from under her peasant
kerchief and shrugs. The droshkys look like relics in a
museum: high up on his lofty seat the isvoschik wields his
whip, cursing the mother and grandmother of his skinny
mare; an occasional motorist clatters, wildly hooting, with
creaking axles along the unpaved road; stalls with gory posters depicting the tortures of the Inquisition lure the mushiks
inside to enjoy modern art—which is further represented by
the street photographers' backdrops, showing palaces with
marble columns and lotus-covered ponds. Foreign newspapers
are unobtainable, telegrams travel slower than the trains, a
telephone call takes longer than a journey in the tram.*

*Yet in the centre of this sleepy village with its dusty streets,
milling crowds, and overcrowded tram-cars, there is a square
with two modern skyscrapers; and next to it the new telephone
exchange all in steel and glass; and there is a new model hospital, and the new tractor factory—the second largest in
Europe; and the sports stadium, the amusement park, the
workers' club, and so on and so on. . . .*

*It looks like a film which, through a mistake, has been twice
exposed by the photographer: once in the past and once in
the future. The two pictures overlap and interlace; the result is chaos. Only slowly does the newcomer learn to sort
things out, to distinguish between the two layers, to discover*

in the confusing maze the dominent pattern. It will take him even longer to understand the people of this country, these men and women who are again a mixture of two different epochs: of the race that plods barefoot through the mud, and another that carries briefcases and wears horn-rimmed lenses. Their heredity is the shapeless vagueness of the steppes; their environment the hard precision of the Plan.

Only slowly does the newcomer learn to think in contradictions; to distinguish, underneath a chaotic surface, the shape of things to come; to realise that in Sovietland the present is a fiction, a quivering membrane stretched between the past and the future....

The chapter from which I have quoted was suppressed by the censor. The book appeared two years later in a mutilated version, with half of its contents cut out, under the title *Red Days and White Nights* (the 'White Nights' referred to the Arctic regions). But writing it was occupational therapy : it helped me to overcome my doubts and to re-arrange my impressions in the desired form. I learnt to classify automatically everything that shocked me as the 'heritage of the past' and everything I liked as the 'seeds of the future'. By setting up this automatic sorting machine in his mind, it was still possible in 1932 for a European to live in Russia and yet to remain a Communist.

All foreign comrades I knew, and also the more mentally alert among the Russians, had that automatic sorting machine in their heads. They knew that official propaganda was a pack of lies, but justified this by referring to the 'backward masses'. They knew that the standard of living in the capitalist world was much higher than in Russia, but justified this by saying that the Russians had been even worse off under the Czar. They were nauseated by the adulation of Stalin, but justified it by explaining that the *mushik* needed a new idol to replace the ikon on the wall.

When conditions became insupportable, men react according to their temperament in roughly three ways : by rebellion, apathy or self-deception. The Soviet citizen knows that rebellion against the largest and most perfect police machinery in history amounts to suicide. So the majority lives in a state of outward apathy and inner cynicism; while the minority lives by self-deception.

I belonged to this minority. The Communist mind has perfected the techniques of self-deception in the same manner as its techniques of mass propaganda. The 'inner censor' in the mind of the true believer completes the work of the public censor; his self-discipline is as tyrannical as the obedience imposed by the régime; he terrorises his own conscience into submission.

The Weissbergs occupied a small but, by Russian standards, luxurious flat attached to the Institute where Alex worked. It was the Ukrainian Institute for Physics and Technology (UFTI)—one of the largest experimental laboratories in Europe. The new factories, universities and research centres all had their own housing developments, and many also their own farms or vegetable plots; their personnel thus became even more directly dependent on their jobs. The flat consisted of three rooms, shared by Alex, Eva and Eva's mother; frequently they also had visiting physicists from abroad billeted on them.

I stayed with the Weissbergs for about a fortnight. Then I set out on my travels, but later on returned on several occasions to that haven of friendship and comfort. The appalling fate that was in store for them we did not guess. I also met a number of Alex's colleagues, among them some of the leading physicists of the Soviet Union. Again, had a prophet whispered to us that the same men would denounce Alex as a Gestapo agent and a terrorist, we would have thought him crazy.

During that first fortnight I visited Kharkov's factories and workers' clubs. My Russian was ungrammatical, but fairly fluent. I had acquired it during my last four months in Berlin by the same pressure-cooker method by which I had learnt modern Hebrew before setting out for Palestine. My vocabulary consisted of about a thousand words which I juggled around in the manner of hotel porters and tourist guides, without paying attention to grammar and syntax. Thus I was able to get around alone, to travel by tram instead of in official cars, to do my own shopping and talk with everybody with whom I came into contact.

The only public conveyances in Kharkov were old-fashioned electric tram-cars which ran at intervals of twenty to thirty minutes. Inside, they were crammed to three times their normal capacity, and on the outside they were covered with grapes of people clinging in acrobatic postures to bumpers, fenders, running boards, windows and roof. On my first journey on a tram not only my wallet was stolen from my hip pocket, but also my fountain pen from my breast pocket and my cigarettes from my trouser pockets; the squeeze and pressure in the tram was such that they could have cut off my trouserlegs without my feeling it. The chronic overcrowding of public conveyances, offices and places of entertainment made Russia into a paradise of pickpockets who displayed a virtuosity as nowhere else. They were mostly *bespirisornys*, the notorious waifs and strays who had been roaming about the country like a plague of locusts ever since the Civil War.

The only goods easily obtainable in Kharkov in 1932 were fly-paper, contraceptives and postage stamps. The co-operative stores, which were supposed to supply the population with the necessities of life, were empty. Misled by the relatively lavish supplies in my own privileged foreigners' co-operative, I did not realise the extent of the Ukrainian famine until much later; but the lack of consumer goods struck me from the first day. There were no boots and no clothes to be bought anywhere; no typewriting paper, or carbon paper, or combs, hairpins, nails, or pots or pans, or even primus-needles—those indispensable instruments for cleaning the nozzle of the primus cooker, operated by paraffin, that all Russian households use. Later on, when the Kharkov Power Station broke down and the town remained without electricity for several winter months, the supply of paraffin ran out too.

If it became known that any kind of goods had turned up in a store, the news spread immediately and everybody rushed to buy—whether the goods in question were toothbrushes, acid drops, soap, cigarettes, oil wicks, or frying pans. Wherever the people in the street saw a queue, they hurried to join it. Often, when the queue formed an angle round a street corner, the people in the rear had no idea 'what they were selling', and amused themselves by passing on rumours and guesses. I soon became addicted to this sport, and, on my second day in the Soviet Union, brought home as trophies a mouth organ and a bottle of stain-removing liquid which burnt a hole in Alex's best suit.

Less amusing, because difficult to contemplate without a feeling of constriction in the throat, was the bazaar. This was a permanent market held in a huge, empty square. Those who had something to sell squatted in the dust with their goods spread out before them on a handkerchief or scarf. The goods ranged from a handful of rusty nails to a tattered quilt, or a pot of sour milk sold by the spoon, flies included. You could see an old woman sitting for hours with one painted Easter egg or one small piece of dried-up goat's cheese before her. Or an old man, his bare feet covered with sores, trying to barter his torn boots for a kilo of black bread and a packet of mahorka tobacco. Hemp slippers, and even soles and heels torn off from boots and replaced by a bandage of rags, were frequent items for barter. Some old men had nothing to sell; they sang Ukrainian ballads and were rewarded by an occasional kopeck. Some of the women had babies lying beside them on the pavement or in their laps, feeding; the fly-ridden infant's lips were fastened to the leathery udder from which it seemed to suck bile instead of milk. A surprising number of men had something wrong with their eyes : a squint, or one pupil gone opaque and milky, or one entire eyeball missing. Most of them had swollen hands and feet; their faces, too, were puffed rather than emaciated, and of that peculiar colour which Tolstoy, talking of a prisoner, describes as 'the hue of shoots sprouting from potatoes in a cellar'.

The bazaar of Kharkov was one of those scenes one imagines one could paint from memory, even after twenty years. Officially, these men and women were all *kulaks* who had been expropriated as a punitive measure. In reality, as I was gradually to find out, they were ordinary peasants who had been forced to abandon their villages in the famine-stricken regions. In last year's harvest-collecting campaign the local Party officials, anxious to deliver their quota, had confiscated not only the harvest but also the seed reserves, and the newly established collective farms had nothing to sow with. Their cattle and poultry they had killed rather than surrender it to the *kolkhoz*; so when the last grain of the secret hoard was eaten, they left the land which no longer was theirs. Entire villages had been abandoned, whole districts depopulated; in addition to the five million *kulaks* officially deported to Siberia, several million more were on the move. They choked the railway stations, crammed the freight trains, squatted in the markets and public squares, and died in the streets; I have never seen so many and such hurried funerals as during that winter in Kharkov. The exact number of these 'nomadised' people was never disclosed and probably never counted; in order of magnitude it must have exceeded the modest numbers involved in the Migrations after the fall of the Roman Empire.

Officially the famine did not exist. It was only mentioned in the terms of veiled allusions to 'difficulties on the collectivisation front'. *Trudnesty*—difficulties—is one of the most frequent words in Soviet parlance; it serves to minimise disasters in the same proportion as achievements are magnified. The Soviet citizen automatically understands that a 'gigantic victory of the revolutionary forces in Britain' means that the Communist Party has increased its vote by one half per cent, whereas 'certain difficulties in the health situation in Birobidjan' means that the cholera is raging in that province.

After a week, I had incorporated into my vocabulary some of the essential household words of Soviet life such as *pyatiletka* (the five year plan), *komandirovka* (official journey), *propusk* (permit), *nachalnik* (chief), *remont* ('in repair'). I learnt that *valuta* (foreign currency) could buy one any otherwise unobtainable goods; that *si-chass* meant literally 'at once' but was in fact the equivalent of the Spanish *mañana*; that a *kulturny choloveik*, a 'cultured person' was one who did not spit and swear, who used a handkerchief, and could do sums without an abacus. I learnt that Soviet watches, gadgets and machines had to 'go to remont' every three months; I learnt to write on the coarse, grey sheets which served as writing paper, and to wash under a kind of samovar with a drip-tap, fixed to the wall. I learnt that no map or policeman could help you to find an address because all streets had new names but were called by their old ones; and that officials and employees were permanently being moved about the country as in a game of musical chairs. All this I learnt eagerly and with a great sense of exhilaration, for I knew that everything that annoyed me was the heritage of the past and everything that I liked a token of the future. Besides, I have always had a deep longing for the primeval chaos, a nostalgia for the apocalypse; and here I found myself in the middle of both.

One of my favourite pastimes was to walk through the streets trying to guess the meaning of the mysterious abbreviations by which every institution, office or shop, was called. Thus my co-operative store was called INSNAB; the organisation that looked after me, MORP; the Institute for which Alex worked, UFTI, which was a branch of NARKOM-TASHPROM (People's Commissariat for Heavy Industries), which depended on SOVNARKOM (the Government), and was controlled by GOSPLAN (the Government Planning Committee) jointly with the CKSP(B)CS (Central Committee of the Social Democratic Party, Bolshevist Fraction, of the Soviet Union). Most difficult to remember were the initials of my publishers in Kharkov because they were not in Russian but in Ukrainian. The abbreviation ran : URKDERSHNAZ-MENWYDAW, and meant : Ukrainian State Publishing Trust for National Minorities. The reason for this epidemic of initials was that enterprises could no longer be called after their proprietor or trade-name; it was a symptom of the de-personalisation so typical of Soviet life.

In trying to understand everyday life in a totalitarian state, one should beware of over-simplification. In the period preceding the murder of Kirov in 1934, which started the Terror, people in Russia did not live in permanent fear, but rather in a world of diffuse insecurity, of floating apprehension. An incautious remark did not, as a rule, entail immediate retribution. The citizen merely knew that his remark would remain on the record, and that the day might come, perhaps in a year, perhaps in ten years, when he would slip up on his job or get involved with a jealous woman or a neighbour coveting his flat, and on that day the G.P.U. would hold against him every dubious conversation and encounter of his past. In other words, the Soviet citizen was no more acutely frightened than a Catholic is of the Last Judgment—except that the G.P.U.

operate this side of death, and that he had nowhere to turn for confession and absolution.

In 1932, it was still possible among intimate friends to pass on a joke that was politically off-colour. To understand the sample that follows, one must know that before he was exiled, Trotsky had advocated a harsh policy towards the peasants for the benefit of the industrial workers, whereas Bukharin had advocated concessions to the peasants at the expense of the workers. The story purports to list questions put to candidates for Party membership, and the correct answers thereto :

Question: What does it mean when there is food in the town but no food in the country?
Answer: A Left, Trotskyite deviation.
Question: What does it mean when there is food in the country but no food in the town?
Answer: A Right, Bukharinite deviation.
Question: What does it mean when there is no food in the country and no food in the town?
Answer: The correct application of the general line.
Question: And what does it mean when there is food both in the country and in the town?
Answer: The horrors of Capitalism.

One of the Soviet citizen's permanent apprehensions was that he might be sent on a *komandirovka* to some remote part of the country—the Urals, or Eastern Siberia, or Kazakstan. This was not necessarily a punitive measure; it could happen to practically anybody, in any job, any day. A *komandirovka* is an official mission, and in a State-owned economy everybody is a State official.

A *komandirovka* may be a permanent or a temporary one. A considerable proportion of the higher officials in any branch of activity—administration, industry, education, publishing, etc.—seemed to be constantly travelling about on urgent *komandirovkas*. One of the reasons for this was the slowness and unreliability of communications by mail, telegram or telephone. Important or complicated matters could only be settled by personal contact. In a completely centralised State no local executive could make any important decision without consulting his superiors in the heirarchy. As a result, if you tried to see a person of consequence outside Moscow, the answer would be as often as not that he was away on a *komandirovka*, and would be back maybe next week, maybe the week after.

All this may give the impression that travelling in Russia was an easy matter. It was not. In theory, at that time the Soviet citizen still had the right to travel anywhere he liked inside the country. But in practice the unbelievable over-crowding of all means of transport made travelling only possible for those in possession of an official priority order called a *broni*. People without *bronis* had to queue up at the ticket counter for several hours or several days, according to circumstances; and, when in possession of a ticket, they had to camp at the station, again for hours, and sometimes for days, until their turn came to be crammed into a freight train or a local train that took them to the next junction. There were millions of campers, choking all the railway stations in Russia, squatting amongst their bundles of bedding and other baggage, on the grimy floors of platforms and waiting-rooms, patient and resigned to their fate. It was the period of the great upheaval officially referred to as 'nomadism in agriculture and industry'. The famine had turned a considerable percentage of the population into railway-nomads who were travelling thousands of miles, attracted by vague rumours of better conditions in some other region.

Among citizens of the privileged categories who travelled armed with *bronis*, the speed with which they obtained a train reservation depended on the 'strength' of their *organizacia* —meaning the administrative department, trust, factory, state-farm or other body for which they worked. The G.P.U. had absolute priority; next to it came the Party, then the government administration, army, heavy industry, light metal industry, consumer industries, trade unions, research centres, etc., approximately in that order. The same system of hier-archic priorities was applied to the allocation of flats, rooms, or a share in a room, through the City Soviet's Housing Department, and to the allocation of a bed in a hotel room, for travellers arriving in a town, by the Central Hotel Management Trust. The same system of priorities determined to which food co-operative you belonged; the same system decided whether you gained access to an official parade or theatre performance. The first question one was asked when applying for any commodity or facility, from railway tickets to ration cards, was always 'What is your *organizacia*?' The rights and privileges of the individual were entirely dependent on the rank which his 'organisation' occupied in the social pyramid, and on the rank which he occupied inside that organisation. There has never perhaps been a society in which a rigid hierarchical order so completely determined every citizen's station in life and governed all his activities.

We all remember from pre-revolutionary Russian novels descriptions of the kind : 'Ivan Ivanovich Golupchine, an official of the 13th Grade'. This traditional hierarchic system, formerly confined to the civil service, now embraces the entire nation. Though he has no official number to grade him, every citizen knows his exact place on the pyramid.

The standing of a political leader, for instance, which in other countries is dependent on achievements, election results and popular favour, is in the Soviet Union defined by (*a*) the place allotted to him on the official platform at the annual parades on May Day and at the October Celebration; and (*b*) the place which his name occupies on the official list of those present at a meeting or ceremony. Foreign diplomats and journalists have learnt to take their cues from this Byzantine ritual.

Another peculiarity of the hierarchic system is that every demotion, each step down the slopes of the pyramid, is final and irrevocable. In other countries, governments and individuals have their ups and downs. In the Soviet Union there are few examples of a come-back for a politician, bureaucrat, technocrat, scientist, writer or artist, once he had started moving down the slope.

V. Journey's Start

A FREE-LANCE writer ranked somewhere near the bottom of the hierarchy. However, I was not a simple free-lance; I had an 'organisation'—the MORP—which, being affiliated to the Comintern, was situated somewhere in the middle range of the pyramid. Moreover, I was a Party member, which improved my grading; but only a member of the German, not the Russian Party, which lowered it. I also carried on me a letter from AGITPROP EKKI (Department of Agitation and Propaganda of the Executive Committee of the Communist International) which again considerably improved my grading.

Such 'to whom it may concern' letters serve as a kind of passport in the Soviet Union. It is on their strength that the citizen obtains his permits, his accommodation, ration card, and so on. Accordingly, these letters are very carefully worded and graded, to convey the exact degree of priority to which the bearer is entitled. Mine was a 'strong' letter, signed by the head of AGITPROP EKKI, Comrade Gopner, in person. It said that I was a delegate of the Revolutionary Writers' League of Germany, and that I was travelling under the sponsorship of the Comintern.

On the other hand, I was also a bourgeois foreign correspondent, working for several important newspapers, and duly accredited as such with the Press department of NARKO-MINDYEL, the Ministry of Foreign Affairs. This placed me in one of the top grades on another side of the pyramid, as it were. It entitled me to accommodation in INTOURIST Hotels where such existed; to travel in the 'soft class' on trains; and to buy my food at INSNAB, the co-operative stores re-

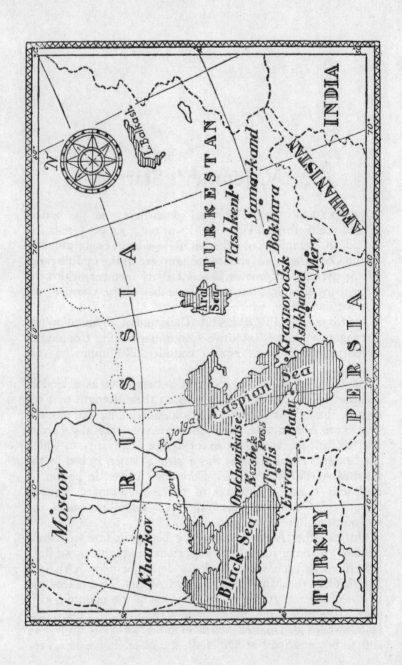

served for the diplomatic corps, the foreign Press and foreign technical advisers. I disliked availing myself of these bourgeois privileges, but as I was travelling alone through remote and famine-stricken regions of the country, it was often the only way of obtaining food and shelter.

I was careful never to show my bourgeois, NARKOMIN-DYEL documentation at the Party offices and factories that I visited, nor to travelling companions, for the immediate result would have been to arouse distrust and suspicion. On the other hand, I never showed my Comintern letter to hotel managers, railway officials and co-operative store managers— it would have deprived me of the preferential treatment for bourgeois tourists who have to be humoured for reasons of propaganda. Such a double existence was not regarded as dishonourable. On the contrary, it reflected the basic dualism of 'NARKOMINDYEL line' and 'Comintern line'—the two aspects of the Soviet Union as a respectable international power, and as a clandestine centre of the world revolution. To bear this duality constantly in mind was one of the first lessons taught to every Party member.

Thus I travelled symbolically in two different guises, and literally with one set of documents in my right-hand pocket, another in my left-hand pocket. I never mixed them up, thanks to the simple memorising device that the Comintern was 'on the left'.

Even so, it would have been impossible for me to travel alone without falling back on the help of the only organisation that functioned efficiently everywhere throughout the country : the G.P.U. In every railway station in the Soviet Union there was a G.P.U. Commissariat which maintained a minimum of order in the chaos. The function of the 'Station G.P.U.' was not political surveillance, but to act as railway officials, travel agents and information centres for official travellers. When I got out of the train in a new town, I went straight to the Station G.P.U., presented my papers, and was provided, as a matter of routine, with those basic necessities which no individual traveller can obtain without the 'organisation' behind him : a room or bed, ration-card, means of transportation. My sponsors were the Comintern and the Foreign Ministry, neither of which had branch offices in small places; so the Station G.P.U. took me under its wing until it was able to hand me over to the care of the slow-moving local Party Committee or Government Guest House. In short, the Station G.P.U. had none of the sinister associations of that notorious body, of which it formed a kind of administrative public-service branch. It was, as I have said, the only efficient institution throughout the country, the steel framework which held the pyramid together. Yet it was characteristic that this frame should have been subordinated not to the general machinery of governmental or municipal administration, but to the Political Security Department. It is not the Terror, but the existence of this ubiquitous organisation without which nothing can be done, and which alone is capable of getting things done, that defines the structure of the totalitarian police state.

My idea for the book, and for the series of articles which would constitute its backbone, was to describe a journey across the Soviet Empire from its most northerly to its most southerly point, from the Arctic regions to the frontier of Afghanistan. My superiors in the Party had approved the project. The Arctic I had visited the year before, as a member of the 'Graf Zeppelin' Polar expedition;[1] this was to provide the contents of the first part of the book. Part two was to be devoted to the achievements of the Five Year Plan in Russia proper and in the industrial Ukraine; part three to the development of the backward regions of Central Asia. The latter part of the journey took me across the Caucasus into the three Autonomous Soviet Republics of Georgia, Armenia and Azerbeijan; then across the Caspian and through Turkestan from Krasnovodsk to Ashkhabad and the oasis of Merv in the Karakum desert; then down to the Afghan frontier and up again to Bokhara, Samarkand and Tashkent, capital of Uzbekistan and administrative centre of Soviet Central Asia; then via Kazakstan back to Moscow. Altogether I spent five months on this journey, travelling by railway, steamship, paddle-steamer, motor-car and on horseback. This last means of locomotion was by far the most comfortable; you can't overcrowd a horse. Some of these Central Asian regions had not before been visited by

[1] See *Arrow in the Blue.*

Europeans, except by Russian Government officials.

Yet all this was less exciting than it may sound. It was a unique opportunity to explore a little-known, exotic part of the world; my itinerary led through some of its most striking landscapes and towns—the Caucasus, Mount Ararat, the Karakum desert, Tiflis, Baku, Samarkand. In a foolish and unpardonable way I spoiled it all, for, encased as I was in my closed universe, my eyes and mind were focused on statistics, factories, tractor stations and power plants; to landscape and architecture, to flower and bird, I paid little attention.

It had also been hammered into my head, and into the heads of two hundred million Russians, that to pay undue attention to relics and monuments of the past was a sign of a morbid, sentimental, romantic and escapist attitude. The old folk songs were forbidden all over Russia; they would have evoked an unhealthy yearning for bygone days. Some classics which expressed a 'socially progressive attitude'—for instance, *War and Peace, Oblomov* and *Dead Souls*—were read in school and reprinted in cheap editions by the State Publishing Trust; the rest, including most of Dostoievsky, were, if not exactly banned, condemned to oblivion by the simple means of not reprinting them. (The State monopoly in publishing is in the long run a more decisive feature of the Communist régime than the concentration camps and even the one-Party system). The Communist's duty was not to observe the world but to change it; his eyes were to focus on the present and the future, not on the past. The history of mankind would start with the World Revolution; all that went before was merely a chaotic, barbaric overture.

The same was true of philosophy, architecture and the fine arts; and this attitude was by no means confined to fanatical Party bureaucrats. Professor Landau, the outstanding genius among Russian physicists, once tried to convince me during half-an-hour that to read any philosopher earlier than Marx was a simple waste of time. Auden's call 'to clear from the head of the masses the impressive rubbish' expressed a similar attitude. It was less absurd than it appears today; born out of the despair of world war and civil war, of social unrest and economic chaos, the desire for a complete break with the past, for starting human history from scratch, was deep and genuine. In this apocalyptic climate dadaism, futurism, surrealism, and Five-Year-plan-mystique came together in a curious amalgam. Moved by a perhaps similar mood of despair, John Donne had begged : 'Moist with a drop of Thy blood my dry soule'. The mystic of the nineteen-thirties yearned, as a sign of Grace, for a look at the Dneiper Dam and a three per cent. increase in the Soviet pig-iron production.

So I set out for Mount Ararat and the city of Bokhara, not to feast my eyes and delve into the past, but to see how they were doing on the Central Asiatic cotton production front. There were of course occasional lapses of discipline, a peep now and then round my self-imposed blinkers; even a travelling salesman may notice that a sunset lends colour to the sky. But on the whole I stuck with a deplorable purposefulness to my programme and spent most of my time visiting factories, *kolkhozi*, workers' clubs, kindergartens and Party offices. The people who took charge of me when I arrived in a new place, knew little or nothing of the history, architecture and pre-revolutionary folklore of their town. They were all members of the Party, schooled by the Party, conditioned by the Party. A seventeenth-century church or a fifteenth century mosque was for them 'just an old building', dismissed with a shrug. If the visitor betrayed interest in a Byzantine mosaic or a carved column, this romantic, bourgeois attitude was passed over with a lenient smile; foreign comrades were expected to be backward in their ideological training.

Another factor which helped me to stick to my programme is the uniform dreariness of the average Russian town and its lack of architectural character. New Bokhara, though located in the heart of Asia, is a typical Russian garrison town, hardly distinguishable from Kharkov or from a suburb of Moscow. This uniformity reminds one of the middle-towns of America —but of an America made up entirely of the slummy parts 'on the wrong side of the tracks'. It was a lucky circumstance that had made me start my travels in Kharkov and not in Moscow. Thus from the beginning I became acquainted with everyday life in the provincial towns of the Soviet Union, as little known abroad as the dark side of the moon. The face that is turned towards Europe is Moscow—the only town where foreign diplomats and journalists are permitted to congregate. But Moscow is less typical of the rest of the Soviet Union than any other capital in relation to its country. It is the centre of a centralised empire, the seat not only of the Government and Party, but of the managing personnel of all branches of industry and agriculture, of production, distribution and every other national activity. Hence Moscow has absolute priority in supplies, from food and fuel to tooth brushes, lip-sticks and other luxuries unknown to the rest of the country. The living standard of Moscow in 1932 was about that of a Welsh mining town during the slump; but even so it was exceptional and enviable compared with any other place in the Soviet Union that I visited in the course of a journey covering several thousand miles.

The Revolution had brought little change to the townscape in the peripheral regions. There may be a new factory in the suburbs; privileged citizens may possess a radio and even a telephone; but the overcrowding and neglect of the buildings and the emptiness of the shops, the disappearance of all little marks of opulence, of all colour and *joie de vivre*, have made the Soviet middle-town even sadder and drearier.

A Communist writer—a woman whom I greatly admired— once made an unguarded remark that has stuck in my memory. She was telling us, a small circle of Party members, about a clandestine meeting of hers with a comrade in a forest in Austria. It had been spring, and despite the circumstances she greatly enjoyed her walk in the woods. When she met the other person, a Party official, he had launched at once into an 'analysis of the difficulties confronting the movement and the means of overcoming them'. From that moment it had seemed to her that the birds had become silent, and the air had lost its fragrance. She was and is a devoted Communist, and this experience greatly disturbed her. 'Why,' she asked pathetically, 'why is it that the leaves die wherever we go?'

In retrospect my overall impression of life in Russia has become tinged with the sadness and desolation of this remark.

The first part of my travels was intended to be a broad survey of the achievements of the Five Year Plan in the industrial

D

regions of the Russian and Ukrainian Republics. I started with 'S.K.1', the newly founded synthetic rubber factory in Yaroslavl. From there a paddle steamer took me down the Volga to Russia's Detroit, the automobile works of Gorki (which is the new name of the fabulous Nishni Novgorod). In the chapter that I wrote about Nishny, two pages were devoted to the factory, and half a page to this most fascinating of all ancient Russian towns.

From Nishny I returned to Moscow, then undertook my pilgrimage to the holy of holies : the Dnieper dam. It inspired the following rhapsody :

In the shrill light of the August morning the white semi-circular dam offers a supernatural sight. The savage river rears and foams in the throttling grip of this lassoo of cement, but in vain: it is overwhelmed, deflected, forced to race through the pressure chambers where nine flaying turbines drain its accumulated fury and transform it into electric power. If these turbines were tilted up, each would be higher than a four-storey house, and each of them is a match for ninety thousand horses—the next largest turbines, at the Niagara Falls, have only seventy-five thousand H.P. Vibrating high-tension wires of altogether six hundred miles' length convey the stream of electrones, fed with energy from the stream of water drops, to the new giants of industry which will transform the rural Ukraine into an industrial base of the Red Continent, second only in importance to the Urals.

After the Dnieper dam, I intended to visit the coal mines of the Donetz basin but failed to obtain the necessary permit. Next I was to make a tour of the German *kolkhozi* in the Ukraine, but my permit was cancelled at the last minute. These collective farms with a population of half a million Germans, the descendants of colonists who had come to Russia under Catherine, were among those worst struck by the famine. A few years later the survivors were deported to Siberia, simultaneously with the liquidation of the Volga-German Republic. Both populations have since vanished as if the earth had swallowed them.

The famine was at its peak and AGITPROP became

anxious to pack me off to regions where language barriers would cut me off from contact with the natives; but this of course I only understood later. At any rate, I had seen enough factories in European Russia, and my impressions were beginning to fall into shape. When the Party had agreed to the outline of the book that I submitted, they had not realised that, as a one-time student of engineering and a former science editor, I possessed a more specialised knowledge of technology and industrial efficiency than the average newspaper reporter. The picture of Soviet industry at the end of the first Five Year Plan that I had gained was that of a young giant who was in turns afflicted with paralysis of the limbs and by epileptic fits. The cause of the crisis was not sabotage and not bureaucratic incompetence as such, but the rigid, hierarchic centralisation. It 'instilled a grotesque fear of initiative and responsibility in all branches of the administration. It reduced every official to a cog; it often brought the whole machine to a standstill—or worse, it made the machine turn in the wrong direction by sheer force of inertia whenever the man at the top failed to press a button in time.'[1]

It so happened that the year I spent in the Soviet Union—1932–33—was perhaps the most crucial year in its history. The régime was at a crossroads. Forced collectivisation and rigid centralisation of industry had led to the famine and to the near-collapse of production. The common cause of both disasters was the general breakdown of incentives to work.

I have tried to analyse this astonishing new social phenomenon in *The Yogi and the Commissar*. In an equally disastrous situation in 1923, Lenin had introduced the New Economic Policy : a compromise between collectivistic and liberal economy. Nine years later Stalin was faced with the choice between two possible methods of overcoming a similar crisis : either to make the régime more elastic or to make it more rigid. The first method—Lenin's choice in 1923—would have implied concessions to the peasants amounting to a New Economic Policy in agriculture; a certain amount of decentralisation in industry, the restoration of the Trade Unions' independence of the State, the raising of the workers' living standards through the free interplay of collective bargaining, and so on.

[1] I. Deutscher, *Stalin,* Oxford, 1949.

But this would have meant softening up the whole hierarchic structure of the régime; and this risk Stalin could not afford. He chose the opposite way : the pyramid was made even more rigid, fortified with steel and concrete. At the top of the pyramid, exorbitant discriminatory rewards were created for the benefit of 'shock-brigaders', 'Stakhanovites' and the new 'proletarian millionaires'. At the bottom of the pyramid, incentives were replaced by 'educational coercion' (even the forced labour camps are officially called 'Re-education Camps'), which led, step by step, to more generalised forms of terror.

Before I left European Russia, I finished a first series of six articles on the achievements of the Five Year Plan, and took them to the Moscow headquarters of MORP. It had been agreed that MORP would exercise a kind of preliminary censorship under the guise of 'comradely advice', before the articles were delivered by me to the official censor at the Press department of the Foreign Office.

At this point my first difficulties in Russia began. MORP did not like my pieces. They were partly over-critical in a mechanistic way, and partly they expressed a romantic attitude. This verdict was communicated to me by Sergei Tretyakov, who was then, I believe, chairman of the Russian section of MORP, in the presence of Paul Dietrich, representing the German section of the Comintern.

Tretyakov, author of several successful novels, was then at the height of fame and official favour. His manners were so distant and reserved that I can hardly remember what he looked like, except for the vague impression of a tall, gaunt man with cautious gestures and a Mongoloid face. He was shot as a spy in 1938.

Paul Dietrich, on the other hand, my official liaison with the German section of the Comintern, was a jovial and rotund native of the Saar. He was of working-class origin, an easygoing and amiable character and a henpecked husband, married to a hysterical female called Lilly, who repeatedly tried to commit suicide in the Comintern's famed Hotel Lux. Paul and I were on friendly terms; three years later we again worked together during the campaign which preceded the Saar referendum; he was called back to Moscow in 1936 and shot as a spy in 1938.

Our meeting with Tretyakov was short and stiff. I dutifully accepted his verdict, promised to exercise more Bolshevik self-criticism in the future, and to rewrite the articles. On our way back to the Comintern building in the Maneshynaya, Paul comforted me with the reflection that, as Tretyakov and Becher were rivals, and as I had arrived with a letter from Becher, I could not reasonably hope for a better reception.

I touched up my articles and sent them again to MORP. They were returned without a word of comment. This I interpreted as a tacit approval, and now took the batch to be officially censored at the Press Department of NARKOMIN-DYEL, the People's Commissariat for Foreign Affairs.

Head of the Press Department at that time was Constantin ('Kostya') Umansky, a short, elegant and handsome young man in his thirties. Thanks to his personal charm, cynical wit and apparent frankness he was on excellent terms with the foreign correspondents in Moscow; the fact that he got away with these dangerous qualities was ascribed to the personal favour of Stalin. Umansky was later appointed Consul in New York, then Ambassador in Mexico; he was killed during the war in a mysterious aeroplane accident.

He received me most affably, and we often met later on. He read my articles on the spot and approved them after a few insignificant cuts. When I told him about my experiences with Tretyakov, he laughed, patted me on the shoulder, and advised me to steer clear of MORP :

'You are officially a bourgeois correspondent, so you had better stick to us here in the NARKOMINDYEL and keep away from those Comintern zealots. We'll look after you—but keep your mouth shut about your Party membership and Comintern connexions. Officially, I know nothing about them.'

Working on the 'NARKOMINDYEL line', Umansky was full of departmental animosity against the 'comrades on the Comintern line'. I have spoken before of this dualism between the two aspects of Soviet power. In their mentality and style of living, Comintern and NARKOMINDYEL are two worlds apart. The people in the diplomatic service are supposed to be men of the world, to mingle with bourgeois society and lead a respectable existence. The Comintern people, quite to the contrary, are supposed to live up to a puritan and ascetic ideal. Hence their hearty dislike for each other.

Umansky was not only contemptuous of the zealots of the Comintern; he was also a clever propagandist who knew that effective propaganda in the capitalist Press must be camou-flaged by an attitude of critical objectivity. Fellow-travellers and Communist writers whose Party membership was not generally known to the public (as was my case), were the more useful the better they succeeded in convincing their readers of their ·detached neutrality. Criticism of minor blemishes of the régime was from the Foreign Ministry's point of view not objectionable so long as it served as a bait to put some key-motive of Soviet propaganda across.

Having obtained Umansky's clearance for my articles on European Russia, I set out, some time in the autumn of 1932, for the Caucasus and Central Asia.

VI. Onions and Odkolon

THE train from Moscow to Orchonikidse in the Caucasus took, in 1932, four days and three nights; I doubt whether it takes much less nowadays. These four days and three nights I spent in a sleeping-car compartment with citizen Vera Maximovna who occupied the berth above mine.

I never spent a more chaste eighty hours alone with a woman. The Russians think nothing of throwing men and women together in sleeping cars; it is an old Russian tradition like swaddling their babies and whipping each other with birch-rods in the steam-bath. It is also one of the reasons why *komandirovkas* are so popular among the higher ranks of the hierarchy who are entitled to sleeping compartments. Every long train journey becomes a kind of lottery game where the prizes are unknown beforehand. A bribe to the conductor, however, often improves the chances.

I did not bribe the conductor to pair me off with citizen Vera Maximovna. She was well over forty and dressed in the fashion of the 'twenties : in a short, green skirt with a wasp-waist, a pink blouse with a lace décolletage over her flat chest, and a pink ribbon over her forehead. Her hair was dyed with the intention of making it appear blonde, but Soviet dye is apt to play unpredictable tricks, doubtless owing to sabotage on the cosmetics front. From under the pink head-ribbon, some frivolous curls were peeping out. During the day, Citizen Vera mostly lay on her upper berth, doing her nails and chewing sunflower seeds. At night, she exchanged the ribbon for a white nightcap with lace embroidery. Otherwise she did not undress, except for taking off her blouse while I waited in the corridor; Russian sleeping-cars provided no sheets. In the morning, she rubbed her neck with *odkolon,* the Russian version of *eau de cologne*; the water supply of the sleeping car was *in remont.* Our compartment reeked of a mixture of sweet *odkolon* and raw onions, of which I had brought a liberal supply from Moscow, to keep up the vitamin balance.

I was hammering away on my typewriter, or reading, during most of the journey, and on the first and second days successfully avoided getting involved in conversation. On the third day I got out as usual at a station to queue up for hot water to make tea with. When I got back to the compartment with the pot of hot water I found a note on my bed, typed on my typewriter. It said, in pidgin German :

> '*Now you have worked enoff and myust pay a little courtship to Mademoiselle Vera Maximovna.*'

The courtship consisted mostly in Vera Maximovna talking about herself. She talked without restraint, for she took me for a bourgeois newspaperman, and as she regarded me, despite the onions, as a *kulturny choloveik* from abroad, she took it for granted that I must loathe the Bolshevik régime as much as she did. Her hatred for it was nearly hysterical, for she was full of the snobbery of the *déclassée* petite-bourgeoise 'who has seen better days'. I became suddenly fascinated in talking to her, for I had never met a real counter-revolutionary in the flesh—little though there was of it on poor Vera Maximovna. If she had found the courage and the opportunity, she would certainly have become a saboteur. She also inspired in me the heretical idea that, contrary to all that Marx said, the only truly class-conscious social stratum was the lower middle class with their ambiguous situation between middle- and working-class, and the half-caste's obsessional yearning for respectability. They, and not the revolutionary workers, were carrying the day in Germany, and Vera Maximovna would have made an excellent little Fascist. She actually was an assistant book-keeper in a Trust in Leningrad, a position that entitled her to one hot meal a day in the Trust's canteen, less than a pound of black bread, an occasional salted herring, a few tea-leaves from the co-operative, and little else. She only had the scantiest provisions for the long journey; I suspected that she kept nibbling her sunflower seeds to stay her hunger. Yet, in contrast to the hearty Russian habit of sharing all provisions on a journey, she would only accept the daintiest morsels from mine, 'to try the taste of it'. It was so pathetic to watch her watch me eating that I, too, ate very little by day and stuffed myself secretly at night under my blanket; but I feared that she might hear me chewing. She was one of those persons who, when you sleep in the same room with them, always make you feel that they are awake and holding their breath.

Vera Maximovna was of a romantic disposition. She made frequent references to her soul, and occasional ones to mine. She also got into the habit of letting at night one thin arm dangle down from her berth, slowly moving her manicured fingers in the void, as if in her sleep. She probably expected me to blow a kiss at the moving fingertips, accompanied by a groan of passionate torment. She got so much on my nerves that I was tempted to climb into her berth and pummel her black and blue under the pretext of passion, but she would probably have screamed and brought the train to a halt— provided the emergency chain was not *in remont*.

Her destination was Yessentucki, a Caucasian spa where she was going to spend her annual leave. A holiday in Yessentucki was a coveted privilege, quite out of keeping with Vera Maximovna's inferior position in the hierarchy; but she had made one or two allusions to a friend 'high up in the Trust' whom she was to meet there. Evidently she was the mistress of this important member of the bureaucracy, who either had an eccentric taste, or a fixation on a deceased maiden aunt. It is also possible that I underestimated the attractions of Vera Maximovna, for I had noticed glances from other male passengers in the corridor who clearly envied me for the privilege of our cosy den, with its enticing odour of onion-cum-*odkolon*.

Among the stories Vera Maximovna told me, I remember one, about the famine of 1920, which sounded gruesome and incredible. At that time she lived in the province of Samara which, emerging from the Civil War, was in a state of chaos. The peasants had reverted to a kind of semi-savagery, and cases of cannibalism were not infrequently reported. One wintry evening, walking through a dimly lit street, a lassoo was thrown over her head from a ground-floor window. She screamed, and some passers-by saved her while she was being dragged towards the window. Just in time—otherwise poor Vera Maximovna would have been roasted and eaten.

Strange as it may seem, I believed her story to be quite possibly true. There was something in the way she told it that had the ring of an actually lived experience. Sporadic outbreaks of cannibalism during the famine of 1920 are admitted by Soviet historians. That first famine was a direct consequence of the counter-revolution and foreign intervention, so a full disclosure of its horrors served the interests of Soviet propaganda. Regarding the famine of 1933, the situation was, of course, reversed.

Did similar horrors take place in 1932-33, while I was actually touring the country? The answer is, probably yes. When the gates of the German extermination camps were opened after the second World War, it became known that the eating of human flesh, dead or not-quite-dead, had been a repeated occurrence in the camps and was officially listed by the Germans as a capital crime. The history of polar explorations and of shipwrecked men adrift abounds with similar examples. In short, cannibalism is not quite so remote from civilisation as we commonly believe; but one rarely meets people who have come into direct contact with it, or can plausibly pretend to have done so. This was one of the reasons why meeting Vera Maximovna made such an impression on me.

The other reason is the profession she had practised before the Revolution. I had asked her once or twice what she had been doing in those bygone days, but her only answer had been a coy smile and the promise that she would tell at the moment when we were 'to part for ever'. She kept the promise on the platform in Orchonikidse, where I left the train. By then I had grown quite fond of her. She took my arm—which caused me a curious sensation, mixed of affection and goose-flesh, as it were.

'I promised to tell you what I was before,' she said. 'Can you guess?'

I couldn't.

'Up to my twenty-fifth year,' said Vera Maximovna, 'when

the Bolsheviks closed down all convents and monasteries in Russia, I was a nun in the Convent at Yaromir.'

I had never seen her say her prayers. Perhaps, underneath her hysterical hatred for the Bolshevika, she regarded them as her liberators.

VII. A Dream in the Caucasus

CROSSING the Caucasus has retained a curious significance in my life. The name itself has a magic ring in my
memory, as if a bell were tolling with heavy reverberations.
On the farther side of the white mountain range which divides
Europe from Asia I was to run into my first emotional conflict
with the Party and to meet some exceptional human beings
who, many years later, appeared as characters in *Darkness at
Noon*. It was, of all places, between Tiflis and Baku that I lost
my political innocence.

The railway line from Moscow to Tiflis does not cross the
Caucasus; it throws a huge loop around the forbidding mountains, by-passing them along the Caspian Sea. But in summer,
when the passes are open, one can take a short-cut by car
over the famous Georgian Military Highway. It starts at Orchonikidse (formerly Vladikavkas), and leads across the
nearly 7,500 feet high Kasbeck Pass straight down into the
vineyards north of Tiflis. Thus the Georgian Military Highway served the strategic purpose of saving me a further eight
hundred miles in the company of Vera Maximovna.

It was early in the afternoon when I left the train at Orchonikidse. By the time the Station G.P.U. got me a bed, a
dinner voucher and a reservation for a seat in a car travelling
to Tiflis on the next day, it was evening. There was not much
point in visiting Party headquarters, so I went for a stroll
through the darkening streets. Orchonikidse is a small town in
the foothills of the Caucasus, built on a plateau some 2,500
feet high on both banks of a wild mountain river, the Terek.
Its background is a jagged skyline of glaciers and peaks,
brought close by the deceptive transparence of the air. In the

distance, a second line of white cones, even higher, hang motionless, suspended from the sky. I had now been travelling by myself for several weeks, but for the first time I felt alone in a strange land. After three days in that airless den in the train, the mountain air had a toxic effect which, however, was depressing rather than exhilarating. I took refuge in the international sanctuary for the lonely, the cinema. They played an old silent film with Harold Lloyd, *Safety Last*—that delightful seasick-making picture in which the comedian keeps hanging on by one hand to the roof of a skyscraper, or balancing at impossible angles along its edge. The suspense was increased by the film breaking every five minutes, and leaving the howling audience in darkness. That night I had a significant dream. I was climbing up a bare rockface, when I suddenly felt a slackening of the rope to which I was attached, and giddiness overcome me. I woke up trembling, still waiting for the headlong fall to begin.

The dream had apparently two levels of meaning, but the second only unfolded itself twenty years later, when I was beginning to write the present chapter and, aided by the pages of *Red Days*, memories came surging back. At the age of fifteen and sixteen, I had been an ardent Alpinist. This passion came virtually to an end one Sunday in 1925 on the *Schneeberg*, a popular and treacherous mountain near Vienna. Secured to a rope, I was climbing down a rather difficult rockface (a so-called 'chimney') when I saw on a ledge, a hundred feet beneath me, the immobile figure of a man sprawling on his stomach. It was the first corpse I had ever seen. The man must have broken his neck during his fall, for his head was grotesquely tucked under his body. There was no blood, except a few drops at the back of his shirt where he had scraped against the rock in falling. My comrade and I managed somehow to complete the descent, but this meeting with Ahor—the archaic horror which had haunted my childhood—deprived me of the one indispensable quality of the Alpinist, *Schwindelfreiheit*—freedom from giddiness. I had lost my innocence in dealing with mountains. I went on climbing in the Alps for a while, but soon gave it up, for I now had to avoid exposed rock faces, no longer trusting myself not to get giddy.

Obviously the Caucasian peaks, combined with the film, had revived that *Schneeberg* memory. But as I am a chronic nightmare-dreamer, there must be a special reason for my remembering this particular anxiety-dream after twenty years (there is no mention of it in the pages of *Red Days*). This reason, or level of meaning, is not easy to formulate. The key-word is 'loss of innocence'—towards the mountain, and towards the Party. The sudden slackening of the rope with the resulting giddiness and its terrifying implications, stand for the unconscious fear of losing faith in Russia and the Communist ideal. At that date, this would indeed have meant for me a headlong fall into the physical and spiritual void.

The next morning and during the following happy fortnight, all forebodings were forgotten. The car journey of a hundred and thirty miles across the Caucasus Mountains lasted nearly eight hours and was the most exciting landscape experience since the glaciers of Francis Joseph Land through the 'Graf Zeppelin's' window :

This gigantic ice-hewn doorstep of Asia has a number of peaks several heads taller than Mont Blanc. They make you dizzy by their sight, and drunk with their breath of snow. In the white silence of the highland valleys stand isolated peaks of bare rock like lonely bachelors on Christmas Eve. We started at eighty-five degrees in the shade. Two hours later our noses were red with frost, but the water in the radiator was boiling. We crept through rocky gorges, barren like dead craters on the moon, crawled round hairpin bends, passed castles in ruins, and the crumbling citadel of the loveliest man-devouring amazon of all times, the Georgian reine soleil, Tamara. Every half-hour we were traversing the territories of another tribe or nation of which the Caucasus counts more than forty-five, each stranger than the next: one of the tribes still wore a few years ago steel-plated shirts and mail; a second inhabits an inaccessible valley which the Revolution has not yet reached . . .

The road leads over a pass 7,500 feet high. But before that point is reached there is a mountain village called Kasbek, suspended between heaven and earth like Mohammed's tomb.

Our eyes still dazzled by the crystalline glare of the glaciers, we crowded into the semi-obscure taproom of an inn where men in tall fur-caps and with silver cartridge-belts were moving through a mist of charcoal smoke and mutton smell, engaged in a competition of smashing mutton bones with their bare fists, or throwing the bones into the air and cutting them into two in their flight with a stroke of their daggers. We had mutton stew, and tankards of hot tea that tasted of mutton, and cigarettes that tasted of mutton, and some of the men sat with us smelling of ram. My experienced traveller's eye informed me at once that they were either Georgians or Armenians, provided they were not Ossiets, Abchasi, Lesgins, Tchechins, Mountain-Jews, Tats or Assyrians (who also call themselves Aissors); not excluding the possibility that they were Gessids, Gypsies, Kurds or Talichi. Later on, we were joined by the Commander of the Kasbek militia and all his forces, numbering three. The Commander asked for news of Lady Astor and George Bernard Shaw, who, it seems, had jointly passed through Kasbek back in the early 'twenties. He also treated us to several bottles of Kachetinian Burgundy, whose fulminating effect on us he explained by the rarefied air which accelerates the diffusion of the alcohol molecules in the veins. We then climbed a peak to inspect the ruins of an altar of fire-worshippers, and so back into the car which had meanwhile cooled its temper.

The southern slopes of the range are gentler. The setting sun seemed to conduct a symphony: the green staccato of the vineyards was followed by the adagio of golden foliage; then came a presto furioso: the foaming gorges of the Kura racing towards the Asiatic lowlands: and finally the andante majestuoso of the great power dam, Zages. On both sides, the white dam is flanked by the spires of two crumbling, abandoned monasteries; in between, in line with the centre of the gorge, on a huge column of concrete stands a giant in bronze. His left hand tucked nonchalantly in his trouser pocket, an intelligent sharp smile on his lips, Vladimir Ilyich Lenin stands on the doorstep of Asia and points with his right arm into the valley...

(From *Red Days*.)

I loved Tiflis more than any other town in the Soviet Union.
Perhaps because it was still so untouched by the drabness and
monotony of Soviet life. The town has an irresistible charm of
its own, neither European nor Asiatic, but a happy blend of
the two. It has a carefree and leisurely rhythm of life which is
bohemian rather than Oriental; but its fastidious architecture
and the courteous poise of its citizens, make one constantly
aware that it is the product of one of the oldest Christian
civilisations. In the distance the Caucasus provides the town
with a background of austere grandeur; but its immediate
surroundings are gently undulating hills with the amiable profile of the vineyards of Tuscany; and the Kura River, daughter
of glaciers, displays a Danubian mellowness under the handsome old bridges.

(Having been brought up on the shores of the Danube, I
have always felt sorry for towns without a river and conse-
quently without bridges. A city without bridges is like a
woman without necklace and adornments; and the citizens of
riverless towns—Moscow and Berlin, for instance—seem to be
tenser and harsher than those of typical river towns like Paris
or Vienna.)

The fortnight that I spent in Tiflis was a happy interlude
during which I acquired a great fondness and admiration for
the Georgian people. A small ethnic enclave, surrounded by
far more powerful neighbours, their history is one of almost
continuous wars against Assyria, Armenia, Persia, Byzantium,
Tartars, Turks and Russians; yet in spite of countless in-
vasions and occupations, they succeeded in preserving their
national culture and traditions. In this respect they were not
unlike the Hungarians, also a small ethnic minority, wedged
in between Slavs and Germans and constantly menaced by
them—a parallel that might partly explain my sudden affection for the Georgians. They are a stubborn but lovable people,
with an innate genius for music, architecture, the gold- and
silversmith's craft, and for standing up to phenomenal quantities of wine.

The Georgians have never become reconciled to Russian
rule (which dates from 1783), and have always maintained
the silent hope that one day it would come to an end as the
Armenian, Persian and Turkish occupations had come to an

end. They were the only national minority in the Soviet Union
which rose in open revolt after the consolidation of the Soviet
régime. In none of the National Republics through which I
travelled have I sensed such an intense and generalised anti-
Russian feeling. If you asked anybody in a street or tramcar a
question in Russian he would invariably answer in Georgian
—though they all speak Russian, which is compulsory in the
schools. After the 1924 insurrection, Stalin exclaimed that 'all
of Georgia must be ploughed under'. It was done, brutally and
repeatedly—the last time during the 1935-38 Purge, when
virtually the entire Party leadership of Georgia was exterminated.[1] There is little hope that the friends whom I made in
the Georgian capital are still alive.

A few days after my arrival in Tiflis I was asked to address
a mass meeting held in the National Opera House in com-
memoration of some revolutionary event. The other four or
five speakers spoke, of course, in Georgian, while I had no
choice but to speak in Russian. My neighbour on the platform
was an elderly Georgian poet, one of the Bolshevik Old
Guard and a member of the Central Committee of the Party.
Before my turn to speak came, I asked him half-jokingly in
a whisper whether my addressing the meeting in Russian
would make a bad impression. He whispered back with an
amiable grimace : 'Your Russian is so awful that they'll like
it.' Addressed to a stranger, this was a politically risky remark,
and typical of the devil-may-care atmosphere in Tiflis. As for
my speech, the audience listened to it in polite boredom, until
the last phrase. This—the obligatory slogan 'Long live the
World Revolution'—I pronounced in Georgian. I had learnt
the words by heart so carefully that I still remember them :
'*Gawmargios mossoplios revolutias!!!*' The audience roared
with delight.

With that meeting my Party activities in Tiflis were concluded. To my lasting shame I did not visit a single factory
in Georgia, and did not even study the Plan-fulfilment figures.
A curious holiday spirit had come over me. After a couple
of days at the Intourist Hotel I had moved to the house of a
newly-acquired friend, the Minister of Education, Oragvilidze. He was an extremely well read, thoughtful and quiet

[1] Another purge has started in Georgia while this was being written.

young man in his early thirties, who shared a tiny house of
three rooms with his mother—an old, big-boned, straight-
backed Georgian peasant woman. She cooked, washed and
cleaned the house for her son, a member of the Government,
and at night would sit and sip her wine with the two of us and
other guests, matron and servant at the same time. Oragvilidze had studied in Berlin and Moscow, and was Euro-
peanised in his habits and way of thinking; yet he had remained true to Asiatic tradition in one respect, by accepting his
mother's menial services as a matter of course, and treating
her with the courtesy and respect due to an old family retainer.

When I had paid my first visit to this house, I had found to
my utter astonishment German editions of Trotsky's *My Life*
and of his *History of the Russian Revolution* openly displayed
on the bookshelf, next to the works of Lenin and Stalin. I
asked naïvely : 'But can you permit yourself to do that?'
Oragvilidze answered non-committally : 'Censorship does not
apply to members of the Central Committee.' It is true that
this was Tiflis, and that the year was 1932, long before the
murder of Kirov; nevertheless, it was an attitude that betrayed
great daring and independence. I was impressed, and became
very attached to my host. He was a stout, slow-moving young
man, with the face and comportment of a somewhat shy
undergraduate. His colleagues and friends—mostly members
of the Government and of the top strata of the Party hierarchy
—treated him with respect and affection. He usually left the
talking to others, but was an attentive listener, and all his remarks went straight to the point. His thinking was entirely
imbued with the Marxist method, but instead of the arid dialectics of the German C.P., he displayed the shrewd realism
of Lenin. For all that he had an undergraduate's sense of
humour with a native Georgian twist, and like all the men
whom I met in Tiflis, he was a heavy and expert wine drinker.

One evening he took me for dinner to a garden restaurant in
the hilly outskirts of Tiflis. There were candles on the tables,
a gypsy orchestra, and the sweet smell of dying autumn leaves
in the air. I had not known that such places still existed in the
Soviet Union. The dinner, with *zakushka, shashlik, shushke-
bab, lulakebab*, and the rest, was monumental. Halfway
through it, we were joined by two of Oragvilidze's friends :

the local head of the G.P.U., and the director of the National
Picture Gallery, Professor Migrelidze. We talked Georgian art,
the prospects of Hitler, the curriculum in bourgeois universities, and all the time the number of empty bottles on the table
increased at a speed such as I had never seen before, not even
at the famed *Kneipe* orgies of 'Unitas' in Vienna. By midnight I counted fourteen of them—and there were only the
four of us. It is true that we kept on eating dish after greasy
dish. The wine was the famous Kachetian—a light but full-
bodied Beaujolais type of wine, which elsewhere one can only
get in a doctored state, for it does not travel well. I had been
unwise enough to boast about the drinking prowess of my odd
duelling fraternity, and now I was challenged to live up to its
reputation. Counting the fourteen bottles whilst sitting still
reasonably upright in the chair, I was silently congratulating
myself, when to my horror I saw four bottles of *white* wine
arriving, one for each of us. It was of the sweet Sauterne type,
and I knew that drinking it would be disastrous; yet neither
my Marxist nor my psychiatric training, nor the presence of
the G.P.U. chief, nor the fact that I represented the 'Proletarian Revolutionary Writers of Germany' could overcome my
cowardly fear of being laughed at if I stopped. We drank not
only our bottle a head, but shared another two between the
four of us. I was sick all night and the next day, but managed
to hold out until we got home.

The way we got home was memorable. The Professor and
the G.P.U. chief had somehow vanished, and Oragvilidze and
I walked with arms round each other's shoulder for mutual
support. We swayed and lurched in semicircles, in a manner
that I had only seen before in cheap farces on the stage. Yet,
though thick-tongued, we talked earnestly and coherently. We
had little control over our bodies, but full control over our
minds—a state of Dionysian bliss only known to wine drinkers
with a solid stomach who abstain from hard liquor. It was a
memorable evening, followed by a bad physical, but no moral,
hangover.

'What did your mother say,' I asked on the next day, 'about
the state we were in when we got home?' He shrugged : 'She
knows that every man must get drunk now and then, or he is
no man.' It was part of the Georgian philosophy of life. To be

able to get occasionally drunk without a feeling of guilt has always seemed to me the state of innocence before the Fall.

Of all this there is no mention in *Red Days*. I was afraid of compromising Oragvilidze. Today, unhappily, this fear is no longer justified. The chances that he may have survived the purges are practically nil. Even if by some miracle he had been spared, my stay with him, and the volumes of Trotsky on his bookshelf, are anyway on the G.P.U.'s record.[1]

The chapter on Tiflis in *Red Days* thus became a piece of camouflage rather than an account of my experiences—a technique which I began to use more and more extensively. The chapter is called 'Caucasian Mosaic' and consists entirely of the short biographical sketches of three local celebrities: Delavassera, Piroshmanoshvili, and Kamo. The first one was an adventurer of the picturesquely boring kind whose only claim to celebrity was his hobby of collecting foreign newspapers. He had assembled specimens in a hundred and four different languages, among them a copy of the *Neue Rheinische Zeitung* of May 19, 1849, containing the text of the expulsion order issued against the paper's editor-in-chief, and angrily annotated with pencilled exclamation marks by that editor, Karl Marx.

The second local celebrity was a primitive painter, Niko Piroshmanoshvili, Georgia's Le Douanier Rousseau. He was an illiterate and a *kinto*. The *kintos* in old Tiflis had been a guild of Villonesque vagabonds, costermongers, ballad-singers, thieves, cut-throats and pimps. According to Trotsky, the Georgian members of the Politbureau used to call Stalin among themselves contemptuously the *kinto*. Piroshmanoshvili was a permanently drunk member of the guild who passed his life in taverns, and painted signs for the tavern-keepers in exchange for food and drink. After his death, his paintings were collected from all over Georgia by Professor Migrelidze —our drinking companion on that memorable evening. They filled two rooms in the Tiflis National Museum—scenes from Georgian rustic life, peasants, ox-carts, village fairs, tavern brawls. All were painted on black cardboard or black canvas,

[1] I have only altered the names of such chance acquaintances in Russia who occupied no public position, and whose contact with me may have escaped the attention of the authorities.

with oil-paint of the illiterate artist's own making. They were very impressive indeed, in a style somewhere between Rousseau and Chagall. I bought several photographic reproductions which, to my great regret, I have since lost. I also had several of the *kinto* songs translated for me into the Russian by a collector of Georgian folklore. One is called : 'Song of the Young Bride' :

> My heart is of glass, fragile glass, fragile glass.
> Beware my beloved, beware, beware,
> For if it breaks—plim, plim—
> Not even the fire of love can weld it again.

Others are satirical :

> I wanted to make my little son—into a vendor of fruit,
> To buy him a little donkey—and send him on the road.
> But the Devil was riding me—I sent him to school,
> And now he's in the Komsomol—the Devil take the fool;
> Plim—plim.

The third biography was that of Simon Ivanovich Petrossian, alias Kamo, the famous Armenian terrorist, perpetrator of some of the most daring and successful bomb outrages of all times. He had been condemned to death four times in four different countries, and escaped on each occasion (the last time from a lunatic asylum after having simulated madness for eighteen months). He died, after the victorious Revolution which had no use for him, in a manner strangely reminiscent of the death of T. E. Lawrence. While riding on a bicycle through one of the main streets of Tiflis, he was run over by a lorry and killed on the spot.

Kamo-Petrossian had been an intimate friend of Stalin's before the Revolution. They were born in the same village, and it was Stalin, then nicknamed Koba, who gave his companion the nickname Kamo. Not only the history of Kamo, but all Tiflis is, of course, full of memories and stories associated with Stalin. Yet, on re-reading after twenty years the chapter on Tiflis in *Red Days*, I was surprised to find only one single tortuous reference to him, and even in this case I had managed to avoid mentioning him by name. It reads :

The birth of Simon Ivanovich Petrossian, alias Kamo, took place in 1882 in the same village of Gori where the son of the cobbler Vissarion Dugashwili, who was later to be called 'The Man of Steel', had also been born into this world . . .

I had written *Red Days* in 1932, as a Communist living in Soviet Russia; and a description of Georgia by a Communist writer ought to be saturated with references to Stalin. Puzzled by this strange omission, I now re-read the entire book looking for references to the Father of the People, the Leader of the Blind, the Sun of the Revolution, etc., etc. In the 480 pages of the book I found nearly a hundred references to Lenin, and not a single mention of Stalin.

Luckily, there was no index to the book, or I would have been lost. And yet this fantastic omission was entirely unconscious. I would never have dared to write a book with the deliberate intention of passing The Name in silence. Obviously, the political libido is also subject to inhibitions and repressions, which came from the same source as the dream of the slackening of the Alpinist's cord.

VIII. Mount Ararat

SOVIET Caucasia was at that time divided into three 'Trans-Caucasian Autonomous Socialist Soviet Republics': Georgia, capital Tiflis; Armenia, capital Erivan; and Azerbaijan, capital Baku. Armenia was the second Republic that I visited.

The distance between Tiflis and Erivan is approximately 240 miles, but the journey takes sixteen hours as the train has to climb over six thousand feet high to wind its way across the Little Caucasus. Only two trains of five or six coaches joined the two capital cities, one a day in each direction. My train was to leave at 9 p.m., but when I arrived at the appointed time at the station, I was told that it had got stuck somewhere in the mountains on the return journey from Erivan and would be several hours late.

The waiting-room of the station in Tiflis had the same look as stations everywhere else in the Soviet Union—the look of a battlefield strewn with corpses. Resigned, I settled down amidst my baggage on the grimy stone floor, surrounded by bundles, baskets, and sleeping human shapes. Only one girl, in an embroidered Ukrainian blouse, was sitting up erect, watching my cumbersome, luggage-laden progress with a mocking smile. I chose my camping-place as near as I could get to her. She was a strapping girl with a typically Ukrainian, broad peasant face, her blonde hair tucked away under a coloured kerchief, with round arms made to pitch hay with effortless ease.

We soon got talking. She talked readily about the sights of Tiflis and Kharkov—she had been born in a village a few miles from the Ukrainian capital—but her answers to ques-

tions regarding herself were rather laconic. She had been doing farm work in her village until the year before; then she
had left to look for work as a domestic servant in Kharkov.
Why had she left? She shrugged : 'Oh, everybody left the village.' But why? She shrugged again : '*Nichevo*—we all just
left.' She had worked for a while in Kharkov—as a cleaning
woman, and later as an unskilled hand in the tractor factory.
Then she had managed to get on a train to Dnieprostroy, and
had worked for a year building the famous dam. I remarked
how beautiful the dam was. She laughed out aloud : 'Beautiful? A dam? It is all cement.'

She obviously found me, with my foreign accent and out-
landish dress, very stupid and funny. I asked her whether she
was a member of the Party or the Komsomol. She laughed
again : 'Me? A Komsomolka? Do I look like one? No more
than you!' The idea that a foreigner with, by Soviet standards, luxurious suitcases and clothes, should be a Communist
was to her so obviously absurd that I left it at that. I had a
bottle of wine and lots of food in my luggage, and as there was
no sign of the train, we spread out a newspaper on the floor
and settled down to an enjoyable meal. I found out that she
was going to Leninakhan, the second town in Armenia, because her sister's husband was working there as a mechanic;
her sister had written to tell her that the food situation in
Armenia was better than elsewhere, and that her husband
would find her work. The wine and the food had made her
more confiding, and when I asked her again why she and her
people had abandoned their village, she said impatiently :
'But don't you know about these things?' I asked : 'Because
you had to join a *kolkhos*?' She said, in a voice of boredom
and contempt : '*Kolkhos!* We were all dying. What do you
foreigners know?' I remembered the scene in the bazaar of
Kharkov and did not press her further.

Some time around midnight the train arrived, and the
waiting-room became a battlefield. Two officers of the Station
G.P.U., who had been advised of the presence of a 'Comintern
Delegate', came to rescue me and escort me to the sleeping car
reserved for the privileged. They asked me with broad smile
whether I would like the girl (to whom they referred as 'your
Comrade') also accommodated in the sleeper; the other berth

in my compartment, they said, happened to be free. The girl blushed, but came along happily. It obviously never occurred to her to refuse the undreamt-of luxury of a sleeping car.

That night on the train is agony to remember to this day. The girl took it for granted that she was expected to pay in the approved manner for the favour bestowed upon her. She was a peasant girl whose grandparents had probably been serfs; I was a member of the new privileged class which had replaced the feudal landlords. The only difference between then and now was that in Czarist days these privileges were exercised a little less crudely, or, at least, with a certain seigneurial style.

She was pretty, tipsy, and desirable. Her surprise at the wonders of a sleeping compartment was pathetic and embarrassing. When I tried to explain that I had been merely acting in a 'comradely' way and that she ought not to feel under an obligation, she obviously regarded me as an even greater fool than before. To end the absurd situation, I tried to overcome the inhibiting feeling of guilt, which by now had become physical, and made an even greater fool of myself. Such incidents are merely grotesque in retrospect, but very disturbing to a vain and complex-ridden young man. The girl's undisguised derision was an echo of the healthy proletarian's contempt for the bourgeois intellectual, under which I had suffered in my early Party days. At the same time my humiliation was also a symbolic punishment, the revenge of the starving peasants on the hated bureaucracy with which I had become identified. I thought that I had become impotent for life, and the dream of falling off the mountain assumed yet another sinister meaning.

At the first light of dawn, we reached Leninakhan, and struggling with her bundles and without saying good-bye, the girl got out. I remembered her saying, earlier on, something like 'you are, of course, accustomed to finer ladies'—and only now did it occur to me that, to complete the disaster, I had also hurt her feminine vanity. I watched through the window the white peak of Mount Ararat coming into sight, and for the first time realised how total and deadly my involvement with the Party had become if it could take control to this extent of the involuntary reactions of my nervous system.

The first, unearthly sight of Mount Ararat in the rising day-light makes one understand why legend has chosen it as the site where the Ark came to rest. Owing to some optical delu-sion, the middle regions of the mountain up to some twelve thousand feet seemed non-existent—they had dissolved and become one with the misty sky; only the white peak, nearly twenty thousand feet high, was visible, suddenly emerging at the top of the window, hovering over the earth without sup-port, like a space-rocket on its way to the moon. The people in Erivan told me that Ararat often appeared to them in this hallucinatory aspect. It seemed only too possible that it had hovered in the same aloof manner over the receding flood.

Yet Ararat is not popular among Armenians. They call it a bad mountain, for a strangely ironic reason. Armenia is a dry land, poor in water, and Ararat contributes none of it. Its rival, Mount Alagoez, is a good mountain : it gives rise to the River Arax. Ararat is bad because its hygroscopic rock swal-lows all the water from heaven and does not yield a single drop to the thirsty valley. The water that it swallows often makes its belly rumble, and when that happens there is an earth-quake. Earthquakes are frequent in Armenia, and they all are Ararat's fault.

The mountain is not located on Soviet territory, but just across the frontier, in Turkey. From time to time some opti-mistic Americans equip an expedition to climb Ararat and look for the Ark. They usually find some weathered object which they identify as Noah's tiller or oar, and they usually get arrested as spies by the Turks if they have started out from Soviet territory, or by the Soviets if they have started from the other side. In the guest-book of the only hotel in Erivan I found traces of the last such expedition. It was called the 'Ararat Expedition of the Chicago Geographical Society' and consisted of a Mr. H. Wells, his wife and a photographer. The guest-book entry also showed a little elephant, drawn by Mr. Wells, and the prophecy that Erivan would soon become a new Mecca for tourists from all over the world. The Wellses must have been particularly efficient, for I was told that they found the Ark on the first day of their search, in the foothills on the Soviet side of the mountain; which was all the more lucky as they had no Turkish visas. I would have loved to go Ark-hunting myself, but in Communist circles this is strictly not done.

The few days that I spent in Erivan lifted my flagging morale a little. Erivan was then a kind of Tel Aviv, where the survivors of another martyred nation gathered to construct a new home. They were full of hope, and as grateful to the Soviet régime which had provided them with an Autonomous Republic as the Jews had been to England in the days when Balfour promised them a National Home. The new capital looked like a huge building site. At the end of the first World War it had been a dirty Asiatic village, crammed with refugees who has escaped massacre by the Turks; by now it was well on its way to becoming a modern capital. 'It is almost incredible how much has been achieved here within a few years with very modest means,' Fridtjoff Nansen, the High Commissioner for Refugees, had reported in 1926 to the League of Nations, and the evidence before our eyes confirmed what he had said.

The massacre of two million Armenians in World War I was probably the greatest organised crime in history before the Nazis beat that record by killing six million Jews. Like most other people, I had vaguely heard about the 'Armenian massacres', but not until I read, in Tiflis, the books by Nansen and Pastor Lepsius, did I realise the enormity of the facts. There was, for instance, the famous cable, addressed by the Turkish Minister of the Interior, Talaal, to the provincial governors on September 15, 1915 :

'As already communicated to you, the Government by order of the Committee has decided to exterminate all Armenians on Turkish territory. Whosoever opposes this order cannot be regarded as loyal to the Government. However regrettable it may be to resort to the means of extermination, it is nevertheless necessary to put an end to their existence without regard for women, children or sick people, without listening to the voice of sentiment of conscience. Signed—Talaal.'[1]

It sounded incredible, a pernicious propaganda fake, yet it

[1] Quoted from Nansen, *Betrogenes Volk, Eine Studienreise durch Georgien und Armenien als Oberkommissar des Völkerbundes*, Brockhaus, 1928.

was true. And this was merely the last chapter of a story which in cynicism and horror has few parallels, and in which each of the great European powers had played a shameful and treacherous part. Since I had become a Communist, I had so often heard and repeated the cliché about 'the crimes of Imperialism' that it had gone stale on me. Now it again assumed a fresh and terrible meaning through the indictments of the Norwegian explorer and the German clergyman, neither of whom could be suspected of a Marxist bias.

As I have said before, I have always suffered from an emotive condition that I have called 'chronic indignation'. Since I was living in Russia where, according to my credo, the Revolution had abolished all injustice, I had found no legitimate cause to wax indignant. The iniquities of Soviet life had to be dialectically explained, and indignation in such cases was entirely illegitimate. This unconscious but constant effort to repress all angry reactions may explain why the story of the Armenian persecutions had such a sudden impact on me. It was so strong that echoes of it can be found in a novel written twenty years later (*The Age of Longing*), whose hero is a descendant of Armenian martyrs.

I am dwelling at some length on this experience because it provides a sidelight on the Communist psyche. Communists are not as singleminded as outsiders believe. Their progress does not follow a straight, but a wavy line; they are exposed to recurrent crises comparable to the periods of temptation and doubt in the case of religious believers. I have said earlier on that the two poles of the Communist's faith are longing for Utopia and rejection of the existing social order. The first exerts a pull of attraction, the second a repellent push. In moments of disgust with Russia or the Party, when the fraudulent character of Utopia becomes temporarily evident, every Communist is tempted—in varying forms and degrees—to turn back. I know of one or more such crises in the life of nearly every comrade who has been near to me. And on every occasion it was some repellent aspect of capitalist society which put him back again on the road. I would probably have left the Communist Party after my return from Russia in 1933, had not Germany meanwhile gone Nazi. The show-trials of 1936–38 disgusted many European Communists, but the Fascist menace, symbolised by the Spanish Civil War, disgusted them even more. Just as, at the time of writing, the decay of French Parliamentary democracy and the imbecilities of the American visa departments provide a good deal of the repellent force which puts doubt-stricken Party members and fellow-travellers back on the road to Moscow.

Thus my visit to Erivan staved off the first approaching crisis. I watched the great and hopeful effort that went into the reconstruction of the Armenian national home, and approved of it. I read the Czarist ambassador's classic advice to Abdul Hamid : '*Massacrer, Majesté, Massacrer,*' and said to myself, 'back to that past? Never.' Party jargon calls attacks of doubt 'belly-aches'. In the ghastly documents of pre-1914 European diplomacy I had found the emetic for them. Of course, Stalin's régime was not perfect either. But it had to be understood as a transitory phenomenon, and Stalin's person was purely accidental. So accidental that I never even mentioned his name in my book.

The more I saw of Erivan, the more it reminded me of Tel Aviv. The enthusiasm, the muddle, the errors and bad taste which accompanied the fever of construction were all touching and familiar reminders. Here, too, drab, cheap, ugly utilitarian buildings were superseding the charming, colourful and filthy Orient. Erivan, too, was an informal and chaotic pioneer-town, the unfinished streets, between half-finished buildings, a labyrinth of pipes and cables. There were as yet so few telephones that calls were made by asking the exchange for the name, and not the number, of the subscriber. Familiar, above all, was the Babel of languages, for a sizeable part of the population were refugees and immigrants from Turkey, Armenia, Europe and America. It often happened that, when I asked my way from a passer-by in halting Russian, the answer was given in fluent German or French. The town had a lively and well-informed intelligentsia whose political orientation, in contrast to Tiflis, was very friendly towards Russia and the Soviet régime.

I returned to Tiflis greatly comforted. I could not foresee how shortlived the reprieve of the Armenians would be. The Great Purge swept through the neighbourhood of Ararat like a new Flood. Its destructions in Armenia were, perhaps, even worse than in the other minority republics, for the proximity of the Turkish and Persian frontiers made the whole border-district an unreliable and suspect area. As for the Armenians scattered over other parts of the Soviet Union, they were, as usual in the history of that unhappy nation, among the first to be singled out for special persecution. In Kharkov, for instance, there existed a small colony of about six hundred Armenians, most of them illiterate boot-blacks and cobblers. In the autumn of 1937 they were arrested and imprisoned to the last man.[1]

---

[1] See, i.a. Weissberg, op. cit.

IX. Nadeshda

AFTER another few days in Tiflis I continued my journey to Baku, capital of Azerbaijan and centre of Russia's oil resources. As I still had an itinerary of several thousand miles through Soviet Central Asia before me, I only intended to stay a week. I stayed nearly three, partly because the town fascinated me (see the passages about Baku in *The Age of Longing*), and partly because I had fallen in love and became involved in a harrowing personal conflict.

It again started on a train. This is not surprising, for the long train journeys in Russia are the social equivalent of transatlantic boat crossings, and for the foreigner one of the main opportunities for making acquaintances outside his official contacts.

While the train was still standing at the station in Tiflis, there was one of the usual short-circuits, and the light went out in the sleeping car. I was sitting alone in the darkness of my compartment when a girl came in, followed by a tall officer of the Red Army. The officer had somehow got hold of a candle, and it was by its flickering light that I had my first startling glimpse of Nadeshda Smirnova. I saw a slim girl of about twenty-five, as tall as her escort, her slimness emphasised by a black tailored suit. She had soft brown hair which shimmered in the light of the candle, and a profile of classic, haughty purity. It was in profile that I saw her first, and I still think that it was the most beautiful that I have ever seen, with an almost abnormally tall, vaulted forehead and the chiselled lips of an adolescent Greek youth. Then she turned her head and I saw that hers was one of the faces which offer a disturbing contrast between profile and frontal view. Her profile had been forbidding in its beauty; *en face*, she looked charming, but different. Her very large dark eyes, with pupils dilated in the candlelight, gave the impression of faint short-sightedness, as if wanting her face to be brought closer to yours but being restrained in that impulse, and this gave the in-human perfection of her features a touching, wistful quality. In profile, Nadeshda looked like an unapproachable great lady; *en face*, sometimes, like a very young girl. Her move-ments, too, were swift and impulsive; the whole slim appari-tion brought to mind the legendary ballerinas of the St. Peters-burg Opera which I had never seen.

It was an apparition that only lasted a few seconds. They had obviously entered the wrong compartment; the officer apologised in a soft, polite voice, and Nadeshda with a silent and charming bow of her head. Then they moved on to the next compartment. There was an air of graceful courtesy and breeding about both of them which made them appear com-pletely out of place in this drab proletarian world. Soon the train departed and I went to sleep with an aching and guilty nostalgia for the world of the decaying bourgeoisie where women had Nadeshda's grace and poise, smelt of scent and spent hours in their bathtubs.

Early in the morning I went out into the corridor for fresh air, and the first person I saw was Nadeshda. She was stand-ing at the window facing her compartment, which was next to mine, looking at the landscape.

I planted myself at my own window, but felt so awestruck by her beauty that I could not find a word to say. The agonis-ing timidity of my schooldays had returned, and I knew that if I were to speak to her it would sound false and gauche. I comforted myself in cowardly fashion with the existence of the tall Red Army officer as an excuse. We both stood there in silence for perhaps five minutes, then Nadeshda went back to her compartment. Later on she was to ask me why I had looked so sullen and arrogant instead of talking to her, and when I told her that I had been too shy, she wouldn't believe me.

I went to the dining-car for breakfast, and a minute later Nadeshda appeared at the door. The waiter directed her to the empty seat opposite mine, and she sat down, repeating the silent, charming little bow of the previous evening. After a moment of wild panic, I at last found a sufficiently original opening, by asking the apparition whether she was going to Baku. (Baku was the only place where the train was going.) 'Yes,' said Nadeshda, 'and you too?' Thus started the saddest affair of my life, whose memory was to haunt me for years.

I had fallen immediately and desperately in love with Nadeshda Smirnova. To watch her hands move, or her head bend over the tea-glass, filled me with boundless joy. I knew that I was in love, for the boldest of my desires was to be permitted to hold her hand in mine, short of dying for her on the spot. I was twenty-seven and had again fallen victim to the eternal romantic deviation.

The dining-car was exceptionally well stocked. One could get black bread, cucumber, salted herrings, vodka, tea and red caviar. I ordered everything. In the Caucasus it is not unusual to start a day with a hearty *zakushka* of this kind, but as far as I was concerned it was the first time that I drank vodka at eight o'clock in the morning. Its effect was wonderful. I had learnt the classic way of drinking vodka in the Ukraine : you down a small tumblerful of the pure, transparent, fiery liquid; (*vodka* or *vodichka* are tender diminutives of *voda*= water); then you hold a chuck of the black rye-bread to your face and inhale its potent, sour smell to clear your head; then you take a bite of the huge cucumber pickled in salt-water and dill. Nadeshda looked at first faintly shocked, then smiled, watching me with puzzled, amused eyes over her glass of tea. Then she suddenly tossed her hair back, pushed the insipid tea aside, and held out the empty tumbler, which the waiter had put next to her plate, across the table. I felt jubilant with delight; that gesture of her arm holding out the glass was like the signing of a covenant.

We stayed in the dining-car until midday, talking and eating red caviar, but only drank one small bottle of vodka. I learnt the blissful news that the tall officer had remained in Tiflis—he was, she said, a casual friend who had only accompanied her to the train. I also learnt with some incredulity of Nadeshda Smirnova's occupation. She worked as a clerk on the Water Supply Board of the Baku Town Soviet, and was on her way back from her annual fortnightly leave, which she had spent in Kislavodsk, a Caucasian spa. She spoke fluent French with that melodious Russian drawl that has always seemed to me the only legitimate maltreatment of the French language. She also spoke a few words of German, and when she became animated, she recited passages from Pushkin and Mayakovsky. Her manner was one of restrained gayness, amused rather than amusing, but behind it I felt the impenetrable reserve of the *jeune fille de bonne famille* with a papa who is a staff officer of medium rank and who has just managed to offer his daughter an education at the *Sacré Coeur*. That, and the Water Board of the Baku Town Soviet just didn't make sense. I told her so. She opened her large eyes even wider, to indicate surprise. She had a way of doing that, without asking a question, and of bringing her shining eyes to within a few inches of one's own, which almost drove me out of my mind. I repeated that the Water Board just didn't seem to make sense. 'Why?' she asked. 'What else would you do in my place, *skazitye pazalsta*—tell me, please?' I told her truthfully that I had thought she was an actress at the Bolshoi Theatre or a prima ballerina, or at least the wife of a People's Commissar. She smiled and said with faint irony, but in a tone which closed the subject : 'The Water Board assures one a quieter life.'

She was an amused listener and I did most of the talking. In fact, during three or four hours I talked my head off—about Paris and Vienna and Egypt and the North Pole. Nadeshda was egging me on, casually at first, but gradually her questions about life in Europe betrayed a pathetic eagerness, a nostalgic thirst. I was familiar with that hopeless longing of educated Russians for a glimpse of a world which they know they will never be permitted to see. My heart was aching for her and I became dimly aware—for the first time, I believe—of the monstrousness of a régime that cuts its two hundred million citizens off from the rest of the planet. As Nadeshda pursued her questions, some intelligent, some disarmingly ignorant and naïve, I saw the slim, haughty girl transformed into a sick child, tied to its bed by some paralysing disease, hungrily asking questions about the children's party to which she could not go. The discrepancy between the unapproachable classic profile and that faintly pathetic quality in her face became more pronounced, but also less puzzling.

When we had to leave the dining-car, she invited me to her compartment. We stayed there until the train arrived in Baku, looking at snapshots Nadeshda had taken during her holidays and at the books I had brought from Europe. Then, on a sudden impulse, she showed me two treasures that she had somehow got hold of through a friend of a friend in Kislavodsk : a woollen jumper and a pair of suède shoes of foreign make, both quite plain and ordinary, but of a quality unobtainable in the whole of Russia. When she noticed my slightly puzzled reaction, Nadeshda became confused. She had been unable to resist the temptation of showing off her hoard, and now her pleasure was spoilt. I told her that the next time I came from Europe I would lay all the treasures of the world before her, from Lyons silks to Persian nard, and I said this actually on my knees on the floor of the compartment. (I wore high Russian boots and knee-breeches on all my travels in Russia, as these were the most practical.) Nadeshda rewarded me with a regally serene touch of her lips on my forehead, Russian fashion.

The train arrived in Baku about dinner time, and I proposed to Nadeshda that we spend the evening together. She explained that she lived with an aunt. So we took a horse-carriage and drove to the Intourist Hotel where we left my luggage, and then drove on to the aunt's flat. It was a small, two-roomed flat; a bedroom and a drawing-room, where Nadeshda slept on a sofa. The furniture was antique, battered and shabby. The aunt was a wizened little woman, colourless and reserved, meticulously dressed in an old-fashioned manner, with lace round her neck. She spoke excellent French. I feared that she might be upset by Nadeshda's arriving with a stranger in tow, but if she was she did not show it. She was devoid of curiosity. She made tea while Nadeshda was freshening up, and after a quarter of an hour's dragging and desultory conversation, we went off. Nadeshda wore her new jumper and the new suède shoes, and catching my eye, smiled in touching self-mockery, but made no comment. The aunt, however, had noticed the jumper and the shoes and exclaimed :

'*C'est joli.*' She had said no more, and it had been her only remark made with some animation.

In the street Nadeshda clutched my arm and chattered like a bird escaped from its cage. I asked her what her aunt was doing. 'Nothing,' she said. 'She is a widow.' I asked her what her uncle had been, and learnt that he had been the consul of a European power in Czarist days. As for her own parents, Nadeshda merely said : 'They are dead.'

A few days later I mentioned to a friend in the G.P.U.—about whom I shall presently say more—Nadeshda's aunt. The day after, this friend told me in a voice which still rings in my ears :

'I have asked my *nachalnik* (boss) about your girl's aunt. The *nachalnik* had laughed and said : "*Staraya, sta-raya spionka*—an old, old spy." ' As for Nadeshda, she was merely 'under observation'.

I had become involved with the G.P.U. in Baku in two independent ways. To understand what follows it must again be remembered that these events took place in the pre-Terror days of 1932, and secondly, that in spite of my occasional 'bellyaches', I was still a true believer. As such, I looked upon the 'Comrades of the G.P.U.' much as a loyal Englishman looks at Scotland Yard. It was the most, and in fact the only, efficient organisation in the Soviet Union. To work for the G.P.U. was the highest distinction for a Party member, a sign of his absolute loyalty. 'Every Bolshevik must be a *Chekist*,'[1] Lenin had said—and for every Bolshevik, Russian or foreign, this was a self-evident truth. After my break with the Party, when I lived for a while in fear of assassination, the fateful initials became for me a symbol of terror, more menacing than the swastika. But in 1932 they represented a paternal authority, ubiquitous and omnipotent. In short, the 'Comrades of the G.P.U.' had come to replace the knowing *shamans* of my early years, and I regarded them with a child-like trust. In this respect I was probably more naïve than the majority of

[1] The *Cheka* ('Extraordinary Commission for Combating Counter-Revolutionary Activities') was the forerunner of the G.P.U. in the heroic days of the Revolution.

my Party comrades—a consequence of the infantile streak of
which I have made repeated mention before.

On my second or third day in Baku, I went to buy food at
INSNAB, the foreign specialists' co-operative store. There was
red caviar, which had become my staple diet, and little else
to buy. Next to me in the queue stood a slight youth with a
deformed shoulder, who talked, like myself, with a pronounced
foreign accent. While our rations of caviar were being
wrapped in copies of last week's *Pravda*, I got into conversation with the person who, seven years later, appeared as Little
Loewy in *Darkness at Noon*. We left the shop together.

The name of my new acquaintance was Paul Werner. He
was small and nimble like a weasel and looked both frail and
tough, with the pale, pinched face of a child of the slums.
His right shoulder was higher than the left; it looked as if it
were permanently raised to protect his face against a threatening blow. One could imagine him as a newsboy, racing down
the Friedrichstrasse and crying out the evening paper, or selling fruit from a barrow in a London street—except for his
soft, brown eyes. They were the eyes of a sad, ageing hunch-
back. Their quiet, contemplative gaze was a strange contrast
to his nimble gestures and sharp features. They seemed to
say : 'Forget how I look and behave; I am really a quite different person.'

I took to Werner at once. It was very exciting to meet, in
this remote part of the world, a comrade of the German C.P.
who spoke the same language, and the same jargon within that
language; with whom one could talk shorthand instead of
stammered Russian, and crack private jokes. I had not known
how much I had felt the need of it. Werner had felt it even
more. He had been working in Baku for over a year, and as
we tramped through the drizzle of the depressing streets with
their all-pervading odour of petrol, there was an aura of
pathetic loneliness around him. He explained to me that he
worked in PROFSAYUS, the Trade Unions. I found this
rather strange, and asked him what earthly use the Azerbai-
jani Trade Unions had for a German youngster from Leipzig? He shrugged with the shoulder that was higher, and said
that as a political refugee he had been directed by the Party

from one job to another, and that at present he was serving as a kind of instructor or lecturer on European Trade Union movements. It did not sound convincing. I was naïve, but not quite as naïve as that, and the thrilling thought occurred to me that my new friend was a 'Comrade from the G.P.U.' who had been assigned a fictitious cover-job with PROFSAYUS. This hypothesis was based partly on certain discrepancies in his story, and partly on a kind of instinct that had developed in me through my contact with Schneller's *apparat* and with other comrades who had some hush-hush assignment. But naturally I could not be sure.

I invited him to a glass of vodka in my hotel, and we talked for several hours, until I had to meet Nadeshda. At some point during our talk I asked Werner whether he knew how I could get hold of material on foreign espionage in Baku for my book. He looked rather shocked, and said that I had better lay off that subject. I told him that I thought the matter was politically important. The capitalist Press was constantly be-rating the Soviet Union for its distrust of foreigners, its strin-gent visa and security regulations. I needed material to prove that these measures were justified, that espionage and sabotage did in fact exist. And Baku, Russia's oil centre, close to the Turkish and Persian frontiers, was the obvious locale for cloak-and-dagger intrigues. I wanted one or two striking cases to illustrate my point.

Werner remained uneasy and sceptical. Then I had an idea. '*Weisst du was?*' I told him. 'I shall go straight to the horse's mouth. I shall go to the G.P.U. and ask them for material. Naturally, the names, details and so on, will have to be camouflaged.'

Werner burst out laughing. 'How long have you been in the U.S.S.R.? Six months? You are crazy. One does not go to the G.P.U. to ask questions. One goes to the G.P.U. to answer questions. *Du bist verrückt!* They will throw you out head first, and you will get into serious trouble with the Party.'

I remained, however, adamant. We made an appointment for lunch for the next day. For an employee of the hard-working PROFSAYUS, Werner had a remarkable amount of free time on his hands.

The next morning I betook myself to the Baku headquarters

of the G.P.U. It was housed in an imposing building in Byeligorod, the modern European quarter. The atmosphere inside the building did not impress me in any particular way. The people in the entrance hall who were queuing up at the porter's cubicle looked shabby and morose, as people did in any other queue in Russia. If they were frightened or distressed, I did not notice it. The porter or concierge, called *Kommandant* as in every official building, was a scruffy, grubby little man with a distinctly unpleasant face; this I remember because it surprised me. I also remember that all the people in the queue, except myself, had typewritten summonses which the *Kommandant* stamped, marking the hour and minute when they had entered the building. This too is a matter of routine in official Soviet bureaux. As I had no summons, the *Kommandant* asked me gruffly what I wanted. I showed him my Comintern letter—not, of course, my bourgeois Press accreditation—and asked to see a 'responsible comrade in the department dealing with espionage'. He asked me what for. I said I could not tell him, and repeated my request. He said : 'It is called the Economic Department.' This detail, too, has remained in my memory, because I cannot understand to this day why even the G.P.U., whose official business it is to deal with espionage, has to use a cover-name for it. But euphemisms and camouflage are part of the ever-present conspiratorial ritual of the Communist world.

The *Kommandant* went to another sound-proof cubicle where he telephoned upstairs. Then he told me to wait. I waited for about half an hour. Then a uniformed guard took me up in a lift to a higher floor, led me along some corridors, and showed me into an office. It was a small room, furnished with a large desk and three chairs. Behind the desk sat a tall officer with a shaven skull. He asked me, unsmiling, to sit down and tell him what I wanted. His manner was coldly polite and stiff. I showed him my papers and briefly told him the purpose of my visit. He studied all my papers with extreme care for several minutes, re-examining some of them two or three times as if he were learning them by heart. Then he said, looking at me with an expressionless stare : 'We do not give information of the kind you require, citizen.' I resented that he had called me citizen, not comrade. I repeated the arguments I had used with Werner. While I talked, there was a knock at the door and another officer came in. He saluted my interviewer in military fashion and laid a bundle of letters before him on the desk. While the latter was signing these, the other officer remained standing and studied me with what seemed to me an amused smile. He was tall and slim, with a dark, handsome face and easy manners. In contrast to him, the officer behind the desk, with his shaven skull, the flat eyes, and the stiff, creaking uniform, seemed to belong to a primitive race, a kind of Neanderthal bureaucrat. I registered in a half-conscious way that while he had scrutinised my papers with such pedantic care, he put his signature on the letters before him after only a cursory, absent-minded glance. As the dark officer left, he again saluted gracefully, while the man behind the desk acknowledged the salute with a curt, stiff nod. Then he turned to me, and, cutting me short, said : 'I shall discuss your request with my colleagues. You will probably hear from us.' I asked whether I should call again after a few days. He said : 'That is not necessary. Please wait until you hear from us.' With that I was dismissed. I never heard from them. It had obviously been intended to teach the foolish little foreigner a chilling lesson. I never again set foot in a G.P.U. building, in Baku or anywhere else.

But that short, silent scene between the two officers had made a curiously vivid impression on me. It had seemed unreal in an undefinable way. A few days later I found out why —from Werner. By that time he no longer pretended to work for the PROFSAYUS. When I described to him my visit to headquarters, he laughed his head off—he had a pleasant, boyish way of laughing. Then he said : 'They played a routine trick on you. The dark, elegant one was the *nachalnik*. The one behind the desk is his subordinate. The *nachalnik* came in under a pretext because he was curious about you.' I asked what purpose was served by this reversal of parts, and he explained : 'Don't you know that the *kibitz* is always in a better position to observe?' (A *kibitz* is the silent onlooker in a game of cards or chess.)

This, and my emotional involvement with Nadeshda, reinforced even more the vividness of my image of that strange scene, so that even after years I could evoke it unimpaired be-

fore my mind's eye. Six years later, when I was searching my
memory for visual models for two characters in a novel, the
image flashed up almost like a hallucination, and the two
officers became Ivanov and Gletkin in *Darkness at Noon*.

The exact sequence of events during my stay in Baku is
blurred in my memory. At my second or third meeting with
Werner, over a copious meal with some vodka, I told him
straight to his face that I was sure he was working with 'the
Comrades of the G.P.U.'; and he saw that it was no use trying
to deny it. He then told me that he had been detailed to ac-
cost me and make friends with me, but that after a couple of
days he was told to drop the matter because information
about me had arrived from Moscow and the *nachalnik* had
simply said : 'Your friend is okay. No need to bother about
him.'

I was, of course, greatly pleased by this honourable exemp-
tion. Werner was perhaps even more pleased. He felt very
lonely indeed—only after we had parted did I fully realise the
depth of his loneliness—and he had an almost physical need
to talk to somebody in whom he could confide without reserve. On two consecutive days he told me the story of his life.
It is the story of Little Loewy in *Darkness at Noon*, except for
its ending.

He had grown up in Leipzig, Saxony, as a working-class
child—a cross between the street-urchin that he still looked,
and the bookworm and dreamer who was reflected in his
gentle eyes. He had joined the Young Communist League, and
in due time had graduated into the Party. The Party needed
weapons for its guerilla warfare against the Nazis, and Werner
participated in a daring *coup* to procure some arms, as a result of which he was forced to flee abroad. For about a year
he tramped through Belgium and France. There were times
when he lived on stolen food, and times when he killed stray
cats and sold their furs for half a loaf of bread and a packet
of pipe tobacco. At last he found contact with one of the
Party-*apparats*, which took him over. He carried out various
clandestine duties; the last of these was the liquidation of an
apparat-man turned traitor. Werner talked about the murder he had committed without visible emotion, but with the
air of acute embarrassment of one who confesses to a foolish

act which makes him appear ridiculous, and about which he nevertheless feels an irresistible urge to speak. At moments his embarrassment became so acute that he avoided my eyes; at others he looked full into my face with a soft, questioning look, as if probing my reaction. When he had finished, I asked him whether he had occasional dreams about it. He said no— the only nightmares he had were about killing cats, and the eyes of dead cats, and their smell.

After that episode, he was whisked off to Russia where he was given asylum as a political refugee, and finally his present job. That job was, as I knew, somehow related to G.P.U. work; its precise nature he did not tell me and I did not ask.

Werner's disclosures about Nadeshda and her aunt came a few days after he had told me his story. From this point onward my memory becomes confused, with only a few scenes standing out vividly, like islands in a fog. I seem to have been wandering through a murky emotional labyrinth which I find difficult to map out without simplifying or dramatising.

Topmost in my reaction was shocked incredulity. That two women living alone, one the widow of a foreign consul, the other a striking beauty, should attract suspicion was almost inevitable. The Party taught that social origin was a decisive test of political reliability, and the social origin of the two women was unmistakably the Russian aristocracy or upper middle class. I could not believe that the aunt was really a spy—it sounded rather too crude and obvious. Perhaps in bygone days the consul, and even she herself, had done some routine intelligence work, and the expression 'staraya spionka' referred to that; but precisely that conspicuous past seemed to make her unfit for carrying on any such activity. As for Nadeshda, the idea of her being a foreign agent was simply preposterous. She was under observation—all right. If Werner wanted to meet her, he was welcome; it would only help to convince him of the absurdity of the whole thing.

That was, of course, precisely what Werner wanted. Whether it was originally he who made the suggestion or I, I cannot remember, and it makes no difference. I believe that Werner suggested I should pretend to her that we had known each other in Germany, so as not to arouse her suspicion. If he did make the suggestion, I turned it down, probably on the grounds that I am a bad liar. There was, of course, no question of telling her what Werner was doing. That would have been a breach of Party discipline amounting to treason, and entirely inconceivable to me at that time.

We met for lunch in one of the two 'free-market restaurants' in Baku. 'Free-market restaurants', as distinct from professional canteens, were at the time tolerated but considered disreputable places which only foreigners, black marketeers, and other 'parasitic survivors of the N.E.P.' would frequent. Every town had one or two such restaurants—most famous among them the Café Metropole in Moscow—and it was common knowledge that every word spoken at such a place could an hour later be found on the desks of the G.P.U. But they were the only places where you could get abundant food and drink (at exorbitant prices) in an almost pre-Revolutionary atmosphere, with smiling waiters and a gypsy orchestra. And the attraction of this was so strong that although it meant a black mark against one's name to be seen in one of these places, they were always crammed full.

In spite of the *shashlik* and the drinks and the gypsies, it was an unhappy lunch. Nadeshda had not wanted to come. She had, in fact, at first proudly refused to come, but her eyes, shimmering with curiosity and desire, had betrayed her. I felt a wrench each time I saw the wistful little girl appear behind the classic profile; it made my heart choke with misery, and I would almost have preferred her to remain haughty and unapproachable. To hold a young Greek goddess in your arms, as I now was occasionally privileged to do, is blasphemy and sacrilege. During the whole phantom-chase for Helena, the need to worship had always accompanied desire; now I discovered, with awe and joy, that the need to worship may be stronger than desire.

It was an unhappy meal. Nadeshda had come after all, but not in her new jumper and suède shoes. She was wearing her black tailored suit. There was almost a hush in the restaurant as she wended her way among the tables with her floating, weightless walk, to the corner where Werner and I were waiting for her. Werner's eyes for a moment became round and goggling. She greeted us with the graceful little bow of her head that I knew so well. But I felt that she disliked Werner at first sight.

I cannot remember whether I ever told Nadeshda that I was a member of the Party. But if I didn't, she had guessed it. About Werner I had only told her that he was a young German whom I had met by chance in the co-operative store, and that he was working at the PROFSAYUS. Now I realised that bringing them together had been a mistake. Werner and I obviously lived in two different words, and yet there was an equally obvious intimacy between us, a common tie which, given the circumstances, could only be the Party. At first, I thought that Nadeshda was jealous of this intimacy from which she was excluded; then I realised that she was not only jealous but frightened, and that her distrust of Werner automatically included me. I felt that a disaster was happening, that irreparable damage was being done, and that I could do nothing to prevent it.

I had seen Nadeshda frightened before, on a single occasion, when for the first time we were alone in my room and some unhappy experience of the past made her expect that something inconsiderate or even brutal would be done to her. So I knew what she looked like when she was frightened, and that now she was frightened of Werner. She was frightened in the manner of the brave. She held her head a little higher than natural, and a great stillness came over her; her body seemed becalmed, waiting without motion for the axe to strike. I had told her, only half mockingly, that on that earlier occasion she had made me think of Marie Antoinette under the guillotine. Now, as I watched her sitting at our little table, I again saw her hold her head slightly higher than natural, and the revealing stillness of her poise. In Russia it is not considered a sign of cowardice to behave in an affable manner towards people of whom one is afraid, and personal pride is not considered a virtue. But Nadeshda did not smile at Werner a single time. She was polite, cool, wrapped in her stillness and miles removed from us, though I could inhale her scent.

In cold despair, I drank glass after glass of wine. With the second bottle the tension somewhat eased, but only on the surface. Then, on top of all this, I discovered that Werner's unusual timidity was not merely a homage to Nadeshda's beauty, that he was also labouring under a social inferiority complex. When we were alone, there had been no sign of it; in the Party, relations between working-class and middle-class were reversed. But at that restaurant table he was a minority of one against two, with a different technique of manipulating knives and forks—and against that perennial nightmare not even Marxism is a remedy. To complete the nightmare, there was my own deep-rooted feeling of guilt towards the proletariat of which Werner was the perfect symbol—the deformed street-urchin, the cat-killer, the hunted and persecuted, who had already made a hundred times greater sacrifices for the Party than I, the middle-class intellectual, ever would. I could do nothing to comfort Nadeshda and allay her apprehensions; she had become incommunicado. But at least I could put Werner at his ease by stressing the intimacy and solidarity between us. Nadeshda's behaviour must seem to him simply upper-class arrogance. Her manner turned Werner and me into allies. In every triangle there are two corners on the base, and the third one is the lonely apex. As the meal progressed, Nadeshda became the lonely apex.

I was not conscious of a choice. I was pushed into it. I made it unthinkingly and automatically. But that excuse applies to most betrayals. One does not decide at a given moment : 'I am going to be a traitor.' One slides into treason by degrees.

After that meal there was a period of a week or ten days out of my three weeks in Baku, when Nadeshda avoided me. On the telephone she pretended to be busy. There had been no quarrel, not even an unfriendly word. Then we met by chance in the street, and from that moment until my departure all was again as it had been before—on the surface. Below the surface nothing is ever 'as it had been before'. She gave no explanation why she had avoided me, and I did not press for one.

One day I had to go to the post office. I received my mail *poste restante*. Nadeshda accompanied me. There was a cable for me from Berlin which said something like this : 'Stockholm and Madrid settled. Zürich and Warsaw doubtful. Cable itinerary and rush material.' It was from my agent, Karl Duncker, and referred to the serialisation of my articles in the foreign press. But to anybody who did not know that, it must have sounded puzzling and suspicious.

I stuffed the cable into my overcoat pocket. On the way back Nadeshda, according to her habit, walked at my side with her hand in the pocket of my overcoat, her fingers locked in mine. We parted at her office. When I got home, the cable was no longer in my pocket.

It may have fallen out by chance. For a variety of technical reasons this was unlikely.

I had no explanation for this episode at the time. Today I have. If I had had it at the time, I would have carried a considerably smaller load of guilt during the past twenty years.

There seemed to be only two explanations. Firstly, that Nadeshda herself worked for the G.P.U., and that her whole behaviour, including her apparent distrust of Werner, had been an elaborate comedy. I would not have resented that beyond a slight hurt to my vanity. I was on the side of the G.P.U., and the G.P.U. was on my side. It would have been a wonderful relief to know that I had merely been made a fool of by the *shamans*. But this hypothesis was untenable for a simple reason. The G.P.U. read all my cables anyhow, quite officially, in the censor's office; they had no need to steal them.

If, on the other hand, Nadeshda was a foreign agent, an assumption which every fibre in my body rejected, I still could not see what foreign power could be interested in a cable addressed to a Mr. Arthur Koestler, journalist. The whole thing was absurd. But then I remembered how, in my *apparat* days, I had eagerly collected every scrap of information, relevant or irrelevant, to fill my reports to Edgar. This made the assumption a little less absurd.

In the end, I reported the incident of the cable to Werner.

There is one aspect of time-travel in which science-fiction writers have never been interested, and which for a while interested me to the point of obsession. If a time-machine could be made, it would be possible to undo what one has done in the past.

Denunciation is an elementary duty of every Party member, and a test of his loyalty. During the Purges, women denounced their husbands, and boys were made to sign public statements demanding that their fathers be hanged. Denunciation is a scientifically fostered epidemic, the Party's principal method of waging germ-warfare against the human spirit.

During my seven years in the Communist Party, the only person whom I denounced or betrayed was Nadeshda, and she was the person dearer to me than anybody during those seven years. It is no exaggeration when I say that I would have died for her readily and with a glow of joy. The Party to which I betrayed her I did not love; I had qualms and doubts about it, and moments of exasperation. But I was part of it, as my hands and my guts were part of myself. It was not a relationship; it was an identity.

The mitigating circumstances, which I kept and keep repeating to myself, are that I rather over-emphasised to Werner the possibility that the cable had simply fallen out of my pocket; that he did not seem to take the matter seriously at all; that I was quite sure that the all-knowing *shamans* would find out the exact truth of the matter, and that it would turn out to be a harmless solution which had escaped me. Lastly, I could not know at the time that a denunciation of this kind would be regarded, when the Terror started three years later, as sufficient grounds to condemn any person, and to turn Nadeshda's fate into Marie Antoinette's.

The explanation which came to me too late, and which I feel to be true, is the most unbearable part of this story. Nadeshda had never asked me any personal question beyond what I told her about myself. She was curious about Paris and Berlin, and the Jordan and the Nile; she seemed to have no curiosity regarding my personal circumstances. In my blindness I did not realise that there is no woman without a devouring curiosity about her lover. Nadeshda, the haughty ballerina's profile, had been too proud to betray her curiosity. Nadeshda, the wistful captive child, had pinched the cable to know whether it came from a mistress or a wife in far, far-away glittering Paris or Berlin. It was the child whom I had denounced.

There is only one comforting aspect to all this.

One day Werner asked me with apparent casualness why I did not take Nadeshda with me on my journey through Central Asia. A leave from the Town Soviet could be arranged, she would officially act as my interpreter, and I would have a wonderful time.

The suggestion obviously originated from Werner's superiors. It could again be interpreted in two different ways. The first was that the G.P.U. wanted to use Nadeshda to keep me under observation. But I had already asked her, more than once, to come with me, and she had refused. If she were working for them she would have accepted, according to their instructions.

The remaining possibility was the reverse one. They wanted to use me to keep *her* under observation. I told Werner frankly that I thought this was the purpose of his suggestion. He said with an unusual undertone of seriousness : 'If she is all right, as you believe that she is, this is the best way to help her.' Logically, he was right.

I again begged Nadeshda to come with me. She refused : she could not leave her aunt, nor her job. I said that I could probably arrange for her to get leave for a *kommandirovka* as my interpreter. She asked with a little smile, bringing her eyes close to mine so that they shimmered in a faint squint : 'Arranged—through whom?' I said : 'Through Intourist.' It must have sounded quite natural, for she watched me with a puzzled look. The guides and interpreters of Intourist were, of course, all working for the G.P.U., but I did not necessarily have to know that. For a moment she seemed to hesitate, and everything was in the balance. Then she tossed her head back with a single, final 'No.' It sounded almost fierce, but a moment later she proposed gaily that we have dinner at the 'free-market restaurant' to hear the gypsies. I said I had thought that she did not like to be seen there. She answered again with a single word, a smiling *nichevo*.

I reported my failure to Werner. He said with his little grimace and his soft, steady gaze : *'Du wurdest gewogen und zu leicht befunden'*—'Thou hast been weighed and found wanting.' This talk took place one or two days before my departure from Baku. From my hotel window I could sometimes hear the wail of the little steam-boat on the Caspian Sea which would take me away to its Eastern shore. There was a pause, then Werner said very deliberately : 'Why don't you tell her to get herself a job in some other town?' He then explained, more by hints than by direct statements, a curious fact of which I was unaware at the time, but which I have since found confirmed in the reports of a number of refugees from Russia. If a not very important person attracted the suspicions of the local G.P.U., he or she could usually escape the consequences by taking up residence in another part of the country. The overworked G.P.U. rarely bothered to follow up the cases of such insignificant people, once they were removed from its local sphere and responsibility. It would have been quite impossible to keep track of the millions who had fallen under suspicion in a country where millions were on the move. If Nadeshda could be persuaded to leave her ominous aunt and go to live somewhere else—in Leningrad, for instance, where she had friends—the chances were that she would be safe. If, on the other hand, she stayed in Baku, sooner or later she was bound to get into trouble.

By passing me this tip, Werner had given me proof that he believed in Nadeshda's innocence, and that he wanted to help her. This was the one comforting aspect to which I have referred. There was even a faint possibility that he had not considered the story of the cable worth reporting. Whether he had done so or not, I shall never know. Sometimes I believe in one possibility, sometimes in the other.

My boat was to have left shortly before midnight. There had been the usual delay. By four o'clock in the morning Nadeshda and I were still tramping up and down the deserted docks of Baku. There is a fine black snow falling day and night on Baku from the oil-towers and the huge chimneys of the refineries. About one o'clock in the morning a drizzling rain had started. Nadeshda's hair was soaked; she never wore a hat or scarf. She did not mind it getting wet; she only minded the smell of petrol which got into her hair with the rain. Shampoo was unobtainable in Baku. The image of Nadeshda washing her lovely hair with kitchen soap made me ache.

I has said good-bye to Werner at the hotel so that Nadeshda would see me off alone. We were engaged in a monotonous argument that had gone on for hours. I had told Nadeshda that it would be better for her to take a job in Leningrad. She had asked why. I had said: 'Just because.' She had asked again. I had given the same answer. It was impossible for me to say more. My Russian vocabulary was limited. So was Nadeshda's French. What remained unsaid could fill a volume.

It was understood that there would be letters, and that after completing my journey I would come back to Baku. Neither of us believed in it. There was nobody around in the docks, except an occasional Red Army patrol. The other passengers were already on the boat, asleep. We tramped up and down through the drizzle and the smell. I clutched her cold fingers in my overcoat pocket, and every minute was added torture. Then it started again : 'Why did you tell me to go to Leningrad?' She had never before been so insistent. Yet it was impossible for me to say more.

In the darkness, Nadeshda's face looked the same as it had appeared to me for the first time in the door of the sleeping-car compartment, an eternity of three weeks ago. It had reverted to its haughty, forbidding purity. There was nothing else to say. Her hand in my pocket had become a lifeless object, a polite loan.

I waited for the redeeming whistle of the boat, as a man about to be hanged must wait impatiently for the trap to open under his feet, to get it over. At last the whistle sounded. We walked slowly to the gangway, then stopped. I wanted to kiss her, and could not. She made no move. She bent her head, her hair dripping, and looked at her shoes. They were the new suèdes. She said : 'Now they are ruined.' Those were the last words that I heard from her.

I walked up the planks and was shown into the stuffy dormitory full of snoring corpses. For some security reason nobody was allowed up on deck. So I could not even wave Nadeshda good-bye.

The crossing of the Caspian, from Baku to Krasnovodsk, takes about twenty-four hours. During that time I did not move from my bunk. I was in a state of apathy which, during the day, turned into acute physical discomfort. Then I discovered that I was ill. Or rather, I found a previous notion confirmed that Nadeshda was ill and that now I was to share her illness.

The illness was gonorrhœa. I accepted it without shock or surprise, with only an aching tenderness for the slim, lonely figure left behind on the quay in Baku. I felt so dead and alone in the middle of the Caspian Sea that I cherished my affliction because it was part of her. That type of affliction has become practically extinct since the mass production of antibiotics began. But at the time, in Russia, with its primitive standards of hygiene, it was epidemic. In men, if treated in time, it was usually cured within a fortnight or three weeks. In women, it was more stubborn and serious. That Nadeshda had had another lover before me, I knew. That this humiliation should have befallen her, just her, the pure and lovely apparition from a banished world, seems to me the perfect symbol and fulfilment of her destiny.

I have hesitated for a long time whether to mention in these pages our illness, or whether to suppress it. I feared, not so much to arouse indignation, but to provoke a snigger. I believe that to omit certain facts is legitimate so long as the omissions are not relevant to the essence of the narrative. But I feel that this sickness is relevant because it sums up the degradation of human substance, the annihilation of human dignity, the poisoning of human relations which was inherent in the time and place. And also, because it proves that the gods delight in reserving their worst tortures for their darlings, the innocents.

My letters to Nadeshda Smirnova remained unanswered. Whether they arrived, I do not know. The G.P.U., like the gods, are capricious. I never heard from her again. Nor from Werner.

During the Great Purge, all German Communists in Russia with a handful of exceptions, were arrested, deported, or handed over to the Gestapo. During the war, the entire native Volga-German Republic, and the German minorities in the Ukraine shared the same fate. The chances that Werner survived the Black Death of the Purge are small. If he did survive, then, as in the case of Oragvilidze, what I have written here can do him no harm. Twenty years have passed, and the facts are in any case on record.

As for Nadeshda, if she remained in Baku, she was lost. If she left in time she may have survived. Sometimes I make my-

self believe that this is the case, and I try to visualise her leading a normal life in Moscow or Leningrad. It does not work,
because another image keeps intruding—the scene in the
restaurant where she refused to lie even to the extent of a
single smile for Werner, and where she had held her head so
unnaturally high and still. She was one of those who, in the
words of the Koran, carry their destinies fastened round their
necks.

I have mentioned before that having denounced Nadeshda,
I never denounced anybody again, neither as a Communist
nor later as an anti-Communist. What happened to me in
Baku made me into a bad Communist, and a bad anti-
Communist, and thereby a little more human. I had my first
glimpse of the invisible writing. If I were a Catholic I would
detect in my betrayal of Nadeshda the dialectics of Provi-
dence, and derive comfort from it. But I am not.

X. Storm Over Turkestan

THE prevailing mood of my first fortnight in Turkestan was a sullen, brooding dejection in a sullen and dejected part of the earth. The deserts of Turkestan and the deserts of Arabia were once the most explosive trouble-centres of this planet; their energies exhausted, they have both reverted to semi-barbarism and decay. The nomads from the Arabian desert were the scourge of the ancient Middle Eastern Empires whose last sally carried the banner of Islam to India and Spain; the desert of West Turkestan, between the Caspian Sea and the Pamir plateau, was the main area of high pressure that precipitated the great migrations.

It is the part of our planet where the influence of cosmic changes on human destiny became manifest in the most palpable way. For the cause of the pressure which initiated the fateful moves of the people of Central and Western Asia was simply desiccation, and this process can be observed to this day. The Oxus and Jaxartes, now called Amu Darya and Syr Darya, have drastically changed their courses in historical times, and the level of the Aral Sea is still falling with astonishing rapidity. Countries which were once rich and fertile, and have changed into deserts through desiccation and erosion, become imbued with a haunting sadness, and the same mood characterises the wandering nomads who people them. During three years of travel in Syria, Palestine and Iraq, I had become familiar with this atmosphere of decline and desolation, so that the deserts of Turkestan gave me a feeling of *déjà-vu*. It accompanied me all through the endless, slow train journey through the Kara Kum, the Desert of Black Sands. I recognised the familiar landscape of barrenness and desolation, of hostile drifting sands sparsely dotted with black tents, tufts of mean thistles, and phlegmatic camels—the bulgy-eyed, melancholy maiden aunts of the animal kingdom. I also became conscious of being back in a Moslem country. The various tribes of Turkestan are certainly very different from the Arabs of the Middle East, but towards Europeans they seemed to share the same characteristic attitude, based on their common religion. Hidden under a jovial, or polite, or non-committal surface, one felt the surly fanaticism of Islam —that harsh faith, born in the desert, which has never been reformed and liberalised, which became petrified at the stage of development that Christianity had left behind in the days of the Inquisition.

But the country was familiar to me for yet another curious reason. West Turkestan, between the Caspian and the Pamir, is also known as the 'Turanian Basin', and is supposedly the place of origin of the Hungarian people. As a child I had learnt to regard the expression 'Turanian' as synonymous with 'Hungarian'; so in a sense I had come home.

Echoes of this far-fetched relationship accompanied me all through Central Asia. Whenever I mentioned to any literate person that I was a Hungarian, the name of my illustrious compatriot, Armin Vámbéry, was flung at me with broad smiles. Vámbéry was the first European who, in 1863, pene-trated into the forbidden Khanats of Khiva and Bokhara and into the city of Samarkand, by disguising himself as a Turkish Dervish and joining a band of pilgrims on their return jour-ney from Mecca. His fantastic feats of endurance were made even more fantastic by the fact that he was congenitally lame and walked on two crutches. His *Travels in Central Asia* were classics of travel literature; as a schoolboy I had de-voured them, together with the works of Sven Hedin. Now I found them everywhere in the libraries of Soviet Central Asia, and also found that his name was as well known and popular in Bokhara as it had been in Budapest. Everybody told me that I was but the second Hungarian who had visited the cradle of his nation—and for all I know this may be true, for the Emirates of Central Asia remained forbidden countries to Europeans even after the Emirs became vassals of the Czar, and under Stalin they became forbidden countries again. Today they are more jealously guarded than ever, for this is the remote part of the Soviet Empire where the first Russian atomic bomb was exploded in September 1949.

Thus this inaccessible area seems to assume for a second time a curious significance for human destiny. The first time, the drying up of its rivers and lakes precipitated the great migration; this time, an explosion of a different type threatens another Asiatic invasion of the West. It is a region of the earth where short-circuits are frequent between Nature and History.

Soviet Central Asia was divided at that time into three Autonomous Republics: Turkmenistan, Uzbekistan and Tadzhikistan. Among these Turkmenistan is the most desolate. Its borders are the Caspian in the West, Persia and Afghanisstan in the South, the Amu Darya in the East and the Autonomous Kazakh Republic in the North. It is approximately the size of Germany, but its population in 1932 was less than a million. Its surface is almost entirely desert, only habitable on its fringes, where sparse water-courses make irrigation possible. The chief product of the irrigated areas is cotton.

There are few towns. One cluster of oases lies in the North, round the mouth of the Amu Darya, where it flows into the Aral Sea. This is the former Khanat of Khiva, which in 1932 was still something of a Shangri-la, inaccessible from the South except by camel-caravans. The remaining towns are strung in a single line along the Central Asiatic Railway which skirts the Kapet Dagh hills along the Persian frontier. In spite of their picturesque names, these towns—Kizyl Arvat, Bakharden, Geok Tepe, Ashkhabad, Merv—are not oriental in character but typical Russian garrison-towns. In fact, the main feature of the towns of Turkmenistan was that they were not inhabited by Turkomans but by Russians—government officials, railway workers, soldiers, merchants, artisans and colonials; the natives were left to their semi-nomadic existence. The change only started with the industrial revolution under the Five-Year Plan. The new factories drew native labour into the towns, and the creation of a 'class-conscious native industrial proletariat' became a declared aim of Soviet policy in all national republics. Even so, in 1932 the Turkomans were still a minority in the towns of Turkmenistan, including Ashkhabad, the capital.

The result was a complete absence of local colour and local architecture in these Czarist garrison-towns which cover like pockmarks the noble face of Asia. The Bolsheviks completed the process which Russian Imperalism had begun. The aim of Czarist colonisation had been to keep the natives in their state of semi-barbarism and ignorance—at the time of the Revolution there were less than one per cent literates in Turkmenistan. The Communist régime took an apparently opposite line which in fact, however, completed the tragedy. The natives were drawn into the towns, educated, Russified and Stalinised by the pressure-cooker method. The children of the nomads were brought to school, processed, indoctrinated, and stripped of their national identity. All national tradition, folklore, arts and crafts, were eradicated by force and by propaganda. Everywhere in Asia primitive tribes and nations were transformed into a nondescript, colourless and amorphous mass of robots in the totalitarian State.

With two exceptions—old Bokhara and Samarkand—I have almost no visual memory of the places I visited in Central Asia. In retrospect, Krasnovodsk, Ashkhabad, Merv, Tashkent, all dissolve in the same uniform dreariness of the Russian provincial small-town, except that they were even poorer and drearier. On the screen of memory they appear as vague grey blurs, as if their image had been absorbed by blotting paper.

Up till now I had been travelling alone. In Ashkhabad I found unexpected and pleasant company for the remainder of my journeys in Central Asia.

The capital of Turkmenistan had no hotel. The Station G.P.U. of Ashkhabad billeted me on the *dom sovietov*—the so-called Soviet House, which serves as a hostel for visiting officials. I was given a room which had an iron bed and no other furniture, and was rather like a prison cell. It smelt of the latrine across the corridor, which was blocked and permanently overflowing. I was, since Baku, in a state of acute depression. I lay down on the iron bed and felt forsaken by God in a godforsaken country. On the journey from the station to the hotel in the G.P.U. car I had seen all there was to be seen in the Turkmen capital, and it had been exactly like a suburb of Kharkhov. What on earth was I doing in Ash-khabad?

As I lay on the sheetless bed, enveloped by gloom and stench, counting the familiar stains on the wall which crushed bed-bugs leave behind, I heard the sound of a gramophone in the next room. The record was cracked, and it played the then popular tear-jerker sung by Sophie Tucker, 'My Yiddishe Momma'. It sounded eerie in the *dom soveitov* of Ashkhabad, and I got up to find out who my neighbour was. I knocked at his door and found a young American Negro squatting in front of a portable gramophone in a bare room similar to mine, and in a state of gloom similar to mine. He turned out to be the poet Langston Hughes, whose 'Shoeshine Boy' I had read in Berlin and greatly admired. It was difficult not to say 'Dr. Livingstone, I presume'

Hughes was then around thirty. He was slim, of medium height, and moved with the graceful ease of his race; but behind the warm smile of his dark eyes there was a grave dignity, and a polite reserve which communicated itself at once. He was very likeable and easy to get on with, but at the same time one felt an impenetrable, elusive remoteness which warded off all undue familiarity.

He offered me some vodka and camel sausage (which, together with sweet Turkestan melon, was to replace in Asia my former staple diet of red caviar), and over these delicatessen he told me the tragi-comic story of how he had come to be stranded in Ashkhabad. He had arrived in the Soviet Union several months before, together with a troupe of some forty American Negro actors and singers. They had been invited by MESHRABPOM, the leading Soviet film trust, to make a film on the persecution of the Negroes. Hughes was to write the script. But by the time they arrived in Moscow a political *rapprochement* had begun between the U.S.S.R. and the U.S.A. which was eventually to lead to the official recognition of the Soviet régime by America in 1933.[1] One of the American conditions for resuming normal diplomatic relations was that Russia should renounce its propaganda campaign among

[1] The United States was the last among the greatest powers to give official recognition to the Soviet régime.

the American Negroes. Accordingly, MESHRABPOM overnight dropped the project of the film.

For several weeks Hughes and the troupe were left to kick
their heels in Moscow. Then the troupe was taken by Intourist
on a pleasure-trip to the Crimea, and sent home with polite
smiles and expressions of regret. As for Hughes, who, because
of his great reputation in America, could not be got rid of in
such a summary manner, they proposed that he should write a
book comparing conditions in the cotton-growing regions of
Central Asia with those on the plantations of the American
South. Hughes at that time was deeply sympathetic towards
the Soviet régime, but as far as I remember not a Party member. He was a poet with a purely humanitarian approach to
politics—in fact, an innocent abroad. He had no clear idea of
the connexion between the Russo-American negotiations and
the dropping of his film, nor had I. We probably both dimly
guessed what had happened, but, according to etiquette, did
not talk about it.

So, accepting the proposal, Langston Hughes had duly
travelled down to Ashkhabad. Here he had run out of money.
MESHRABPOM had advanced him a certain sum for the
voyage and promised to wire the remainder. This, however,
was a period when the Soviet Government pursued a policy
of ruthless monetary deflation, in consequence of which all
branches of administration and production were desperately
short of cash and for weeks on end unable to meet their com-
mitments, including salaries and workers' wages. Stranded in
Ashkhabad, Hughes had kept sending wires to MESHRAB-
POM which were never answered. For the last three weeks he
had lived as a kind of pensionnaire of the Ashkhabad G.P.U.
in the *dom sovietov*, getting what food was available in the
G.P.U.'s canteen and co-operative stores on tick. He told me
all this as a kind of shaggy-dog story—one of those funny
things that inevitably happen in a country which has embarked on a great revolution.

Later in the evening, more people arrived in Hughes's room,
and I discovered that we were not the only intellectuals in Ashkhabad. First to arrive was a timid little mouse of a man with
a wizened Tartar face, who hardly ever spoke but listened to
everything that was said with an immutably admiring smile.

He was Shaarieh Kikiloff, the President of the Turkoman Writers' Federation. What he wrote, neither Hughes not I were ever able to find out, though we travelled together for about a fortnight. Nor did we ever discover whether he was married, where he lived and how he lived.

Next came a large, hulking and vague youth who was to become our second travelling companion. He had a ship's anchor tattooed on his chest and a mobile nude on his biceps; he was a Ukrainian, and an ex-sailor of the Pacific Merchant Navy, called Kolya Shagurin. Kolya, too, was a writer, engaged in writing a pamphlet for the Ukrainian State Publishing Trust on the over-fulfilment of the Five Year Plan in Central Asia. We never saw him taking notes, or asking any pertinent questions on our journey; one day in Merv he picked up a native *komsomolka* who was said to write Uzbek songs, and vanished from our lives as abruptly and mysteriously as he had appeared.

It became quite a party. Kolya sang Ukrainian songs and Hughes Negro spirituals. Later on three more guests drifted in. One was Mark May, a film director from the Baltic provinces, who had come with a travelling documentary unit to make a film about the construction of a sulphur factory in the heart of the Kara Kum desert, where rich mineral deposits had recently been discovered. He was an imperturbably matter-of-fact, impeccably dressed young man, who squatted on the floor of Hughes's room amidst this Asiatic crowd with the same efficient, self-confident, no-nonsense air which movie producers display in Hollywood, Ealing or Berlin-Spandau. Finally, there was a tall and pleasant Red Army officer of Udgurian nationality, by the name of Anvar Umorzakov. He was the colonel of a frontier unit in the Pamir Mountains, had been sent on a *kommandirovka* to Ashkhabad, and on the way had married a charming little Uzbeg girl, with dark plaits falling to her shoulders, who sat smiling next to her martial husband on the floor and never said a word during the whole evening. The next day I wrote down Colonel Umorzakov's story. It is a typical sample of countless biographical sketches that I collected in Central Asia. I am quoting from the text in *Red Days* :

Anvar Umorzakov was born in Kashgar, Chinese East Turkestan. One night in 1915, when he was seven, his family fled across the frontier into Russian Turkestan to escape imprisonment for failing to pay taxes after a bad harvest. They settled somewhere in the territory which is now the Tadzhik Autonomous Soviet Republic, north of the Himalayas. After a while they became indebted to the local Bey and father Umorzakov had to sell his small farm. When the news of the Russian Revolution had percolated down to Central Asia, he joined a Red partisan band, and later the Red Army. In 1923 he and his wife were murdered by the Basmachi—*the counterrevolutionary guerilla bands in Central Asia. Anvar, then fifteen, was made to watch while the* Basmachi *tied his father and mother to the bedpost and cut their heads off. The boy was allowed to escape, became a vagabond like millions of other waifs and strays, found work in the German travelling circus Yupatov first as a handyman, later as a trapeze artist, then joined the Komsomol, and finally the Red Army. At eighteen, he was sent to the University for Asian Minorities in Tashkent, and from here was comissioned as an officer in the Red Army. He had distinguished himself in fighting the* Basmachi *in the Alai region near the Chinese frontier, and at twenty-four had attained the rank of colonel. . . .*

I have no recollection of his features except that he was tall, friendly, restrained, with an open face and smile. He was typical of many young Red Army officers. They seemed to belong to a race different from the Party bureaucrats, and that distinction held good from Leningrad down to the Afghan frontier.

Indignant at the treatment of Hughes, I sent, unknown to him, a long telegram to the Comintern, explaining his predicament and the repercussions to be expected in America if it were to leak out that its leading Negro poet had been lured under false pretences to Central Asia and simply forgotten there. It had an unexpected effect : Hughes's money arrived a few days later. The explanation is, I believe, that I was dealing with the German section of the Comintern, Hughes with the American; and that, according to the traditions of inter-

departmental rivalry, the German section was probably delighted at this opportunity to annoy their American colleagues
by reporting the matter straight to the Praesidium.

In the meantime, Hughes, Kikiloff, Kolya and myself had
become organised into an 'International Proletarian Writers'
Brigade', and it was decided that we should continue our journey into Uzbekistan together. I don't remember on whose initiative this was done, but it was not difficult to understand
that the powers-that-be had become uneasy about us motley
characters knocking around in Turkestan. It was also fairly
obvious that Shaarieh Kikiloff, the silent, smiling, wizened
Turkoman bard, was meant to act as our shepherd. At any
rate, he was the only one who knew the native language, and
we needed an interpreter. Hughes's Russian was even sketchier
than mine; Kikiloff would translate from the Turkoman into
the Russian and I from Russian into English. In Merv, both
Kolya and Kikiloff faded out of the picture, and the latter's
place was taken by a Russian schoolmaster who had appeared
somehow out of the blue. I have forgotten his name, which is
not mentioned in *Red Days*, probably because both Hughes
and I disliked him at first sight. He tried to boss us around as
if we were a couple of schoolboys, and as we could not get rid
of him by polite hints, we at last told him to go to hell. But
by that time we had arrived in Tashkent, our Asiatic
terminal.

Before leaving Ashkhabad with the 'Writers' Brigade', I
dutifully visited all its sights, which consisted of a silk factory,
Mark May's mobile film studio, and the People's Court where
a purge trial was being held.

The silk factory in Ashkhabad is the oldest in Turkmenistan; it was founded in 1928. Before that, the word 'factory'
did not exist in the Turkoman vocabulary. It was the most
picturesque factory that I had ever seen, except perhaps for
the great pottery in Seville's Triana :

*In the little garden which serves as a factory yard, some
twenty native factory girls are squatting on the ground, smoking over their bowls of* khok-chai, *the green Persian tea. They
all still wear their colourful national costumes, complete with*
boerk. *The* boerks *are tall cylindrical hats, wrapped in multi-*

*coloured silks, and adorned with coins and amulets; each must
weigh several pounds. They smoke black mahorka, which
looks like flaky pipe tobacco and is loosely filled into five-inch-
long cornets rolled out of newspaper. Apart from the slow
movements required to sip their* khok-chai *and lift the paper
cornets to their lips, they are entirely immobile. The sky is
blue, the sun stabs down in pitiless rays, a camel ambles past;
little white mahorka clouds float out of the immobile girls'
nostrils. It looks as if they hadn't moved a limb for the last
three hundred years. Then the factory whistle sounds, the girls
carry the* chai *bowls unhurriedly to a corner, smooth their
medals and amulets and, holding the smoking paper-cones
between their teeth, vanish one by one through the concrete
vault of the factory gate, tripping along like painted figures
on a medieval clock-tower. The step across the factory gate
takes them in one move from the seventeenth century straight
into the twentieth....*

*Thou and I, we shall die and never learn what news the
first spaceship will bring home from another planet. We shall
not learn what ideas, machines and courting habits the citizens of the future will employ. Our curiosity will never be
assuaged. But look at these girls. The fetters which had tied
them to medieval Islam have suddenly snapped; they rubbed
their eyes, sat down in Wells' time machine, and alighted three
centuries later. Their curiosity is satisfied. I envy them.*

Re-reading, after twenty years, passages like the above from
Red Days, I am constantly amazed by their crude naïveté.
They express, however, what I believed at the time—or rather
one set of beliefs to which I clung with desperate tenacity. I
did not see, because I did not want to see, that for the
tradition-bound people of Asia the enforced voyage in the
time-machine amounted to their deportation into a discon-
solate and incomprehensible world. I saw one half of the truth,
indicated by dozens of stories like Anvar Umorzakov's—that
a storm was brewing over Asia, and that the Revolution of
1917 had merely been the first blast. I did not see the barren
desolation which the storm would leave in its wake everywhere, from China to Georgia. Nor that it would merely mean
a change from partial enslavement by landlords, tax-collectors

and money-lenders, to total enslavement by the State, which is landlord, tax-collector and money-lender all in one.

By a strange hazard I stumbled on the first great show trial in Central Asia—a foretaste of things to come.

The only sizeable building in Ashkhabad was the City Soviet, the equivalent of a Town Hall. I had walked past it several times with Kikiloff and wanted to have a look inside, but the smiling little man had each time side-tracked me with a vague 'They are very busy there' or 'It is not a good time'. Puzzled by his manner, I at last insisted and simply walked into the building with the anxious Kikiloff in tow. Inside, there was a courtyard from which a staircase led to the offices; and opposite the gate there was a large door, with red draperies over it, leading into the City Hall. People were drifting in and out of that hall; it looked as if a meeting were in progress there. I walked in and sat down in the last row, Kikiloff unhappily huddled beside me.

The hall was rectangular, with a raised platform which on other occasions served as a stage for the performances of the Turkoman National Theatre. On that platform now sat the People's Court, consisting of the Judge who, Kikiloff said, was a workman from a cotton-mill, his two Assessors, the State Prosecutor, the Lawyer for the Defence, a translator and a stenographer. Facing them sat the audience on rows of chairs and benches. The first three rows were occupied by the defendants; there were twenty-nine of them. Behind them in the otherwise empty fourth row, sat three militiamen with bayonets fixed on their rifles. Behind these the public : men, women, and a class of school-children between the age of ten and fifteen. Only about half of the seats for the public were occupied. One of the accused was testifying in a droning, monotonous voice. Everybody seemed half asleep—the Court, the accused and the audience : Turkomans in tall sheepskin hats, Uzbeks with coloured skull-caps. Russians in cloth-caps, women with tall *boerks* or coloured scarves on their heads.

The accused was talking in Turkoman; after each couple of sentences his statement was translated into Russian. We had come in near the beginning of his testimony. According to my notes, this is what he said :

His name was Changildi. At the age of seven he had become an orphan, and was employed as a shepherd by the local Bey. One day he had stepped on a thistle, and his foot started festering and had to be amputated. Then he had sold milk, and later had become an opium-smuggler on the Persian frontier. Then he had been arrested, fined four hundred roubles, and put into prison.

Then Citizen Attakurdov had got him out of prison and made him an official of the District *kolkhoz* Centre. (Attakurdov, as I gradually gathered, was the principal accused : he was the former Chairman of the Town Soviet and a member of the Central Executive Committee of the Party.) In 1931, Changildi was dismissed from the District *kolkhoz* Centre, but Attakurdov's brother-in-law got him a new job in the R.D.I.[1]

As a member of the R.D.I., Changildi had dissolved a certain *kolkhoz* whose members had embezzled melons to the value of fifteen hundred roubles belonging to the State (in other words, they had eaten the melons instead of surrendering them). However, the members of Attakurdov's clan within the guilty *kolkhoz* got away without punishment because he, Changildi, felt himself indebted to Attakurdov. Moreover, after the *kolkhoz* had been dissolved, and individual property had been restored to its members, he, Changildi, had seen to it that the *kulaks* (rich peasants) got the best irrigated plots, whereas the *bedniaks* (poor peasants) only received dry plots. This also was done on Attakurdov's orders. . . .

Gradually, through Changildi's testimony, and through the reports in the local newspaper during the following days, I got the hang of the affair. The trial had been on for several weeks. It was expected that it would last for another number of weeks. The City Hall was the only large public meeting place in Ashkhabad; whenever it was needed for a meeting or a theatre performance, the trial was adjourned. The twenty-nine defendants were accused of Sabotage and Counter-revolutionary Conspiracy.

Attakurdov had been the leading personality in the young Turkmen Soviet Republic. He had been chairman of the Ash-

[1] 'Workers and Peasants Inspectorate'—a permanent control commission of the State administration.

khabad Soviet; his brother-in-law, Ovez Kouliev, chairman of
the District R.D.I.; another of his in-laws had been editor of
the official Party paper. They were now all in the dock. It
looked as if Attakurdov and his clan had been running the
Republic, and were responsible for all the troubles that had
befallen it.

Changildi's testimony provided a revealing glimpse into the
nature of these troubles. An entire *kolkhoz* had been disbanded
because of a hundred and fifty melons. Moreover, private
property of the collectivised land had been restored to its former owners, against the policy and law of the Government.
Neither the Judge nor the Public Prosecutor had commented
on this unheard-of event. When I asked Kikiloff about it, he
shrugged and smiled : 'There are difficulties.' But if such an
event was possible, and accepted as a matter of course, the
collectivisation-programme in Turkmenistan must be in a
state of chaos. I did not draw these conclusions; but I vaguely
guessed them. I did not doubt that Attakurdov and his people
were bad, guilty men; but the eerie unreality pervading the
courtroom made me at the same time feel that they were being used as scapegoats.

There was another, more familiar aspect to it all. I knew,
from my past sojourns in Syria and Palestine, how tenaciously
the ancient clan-divisions survived in the politics of modern
Moslem countries. In Palestine, for instance, Arab public life
had been dominated by two powerful clans, the Husseinis and
the Nashashibis. Before the Revolution, Turkmenistan had
been an even more primitive country than Palestine, divided
into tribes, and within the tribes into clans. Attakurdov and
his numerous in-laws had evidently been running the country,
as the Grand Mufti's clan had been running Palestine. Historically this was only natural, for in a country with less than
one per cent literates, educated people with administrative
ability could only be found in the upper crust of the wealthier
clans. On the other hand, for the socialist State it was a vital
necessity to destroy the coherence of the traditional clan-
structure in the backward areas. This was another implication
of the trial with its constant emphasis on 'in-laws' and
'cousins' in the administration; it was intended to demonstrate

that such relationship in itself was a counter-revolutionary tie.

I stayed at the trial for several hours, but did not return the next day or after. It had been too depressing, and I was avoiding, by instinct, more depressing experiences. There had been a strange unreality about the proceedings. The defendants, for instance, were allowed to smoke in the courtroom. Everybody else, too, of course. Changildi, the one-legged former opium smuggler, had testified with a dead cigarette stump stuck in his dead, ashen face. The Judge and his Assessors hardly seemed to listen. Now and then, when Changildi broke off, the Judge or the Prosecutor (both of whom were Russians) would prompt him, or ask him a question in an indifferent, remote murmur. Counsel for the Defence (one Counsel for the twenty-nine accused) never opened his mouth. He was the youngest person on the platform, a shy native youth, looking like a bewildered student at an examination who does not quite know what is expected of him next. There was no sign of any interest or tension in the room. The spectators seemed to doze, except when they shook Mahorka into a new paper-cone with slow, lazy movements. The school-children, who sat directly behind the bayonets of the guards, did not giggle, nor crane their necks. Several of them were asleep. There was an atmosphere of informality and amateurishness about the whole thing which made it quite impossible to believe that twenty-nine men, among them the leading figures of the Republic, were on trial for their lives.

After Changildi's testimony there was a pause. The Judge and the Public Prosecutor exchanged a few casual, whispered words. Then they all sat for several minutes, and nothing happened at all. No word was spoken. Time seemed to have come to a standstill. Some of the defendants now and then shuffled their feet. Then the Judge seemed to come regretfully back to life. He said something to one of the accused in the second row. The man got up obediently like a schoolboy, and said that Attakurdov had told him that the Russian people wanted to oppress the people of Turkmenistan. As he went on denouncing Attakurdov in a flat, impersonal voice, he seemed to vanish as an individual; all that remained of him was a limp puppet without a will of its own, manœuvred by the

arch-fiend, Attakurdov. The latter was apparently the Trotsky, or perhaps the Tito, of Turkmenistan.

From my place all I could see of Attakurdov was an occasional view of the back of his head. It was a round head,
with close-cropped dark hair, set on a powerful neck and
powerful shoulders. The head never turned or moved.

After some time a little man, who seemed to be something
like an usher or clerk, came up to us in the last row and said
something to Kikiloff. Kikiloff said to me smilingly that the
Court was inviting me as a 'distinguished visitor' to sit on the
platform. I had noticed him earlier whispering to the little
man; then the latter had walked up the dais and had whispered to the Judge. So now we had to follow him to the platform. Two chairs were brought, and we had to sit down on
them, on the edge of the platform, facing the audience.

As a 'foreign delegate' in Russia, I had been in the habit of
sitting on platforms at all sorts of meetings and celebrations.
But this time I felt a painful embarrassment. As we walked
up to our two conspicuous chairs, the Judge seemed to take no
notice of us, and neither the accused nor the audience gave
any sign of curiosity. The Judge was probably thinking that
once this foreigner had managed to butt in, one might as well
humour him with a place on the grand-stand; and the others
were probably thinking that we were Party officials somehow
connected with the case.

I could now see the accused. Attakurdov is described in my
notes as having the 'round, bloated, greyish-yellow face of a
Turkish tax-collector'. I do not remember his features. I remember that he gave me one single glance of his flat eyes,
penetratingly incurious like a dead man's, which made me
avert mine.

I also remember that he wore a high-necked, embroidered
Russian shirt, because most of the other accused wore dirty,
European shirts with the collars missing. They were a miser-
able lot—yellow-faced, unshaven, creased and crumpled, like
vagabonds on police photographs. Yet these were the men
who had, a short while ago, held the highest offices in the
Party and State. And, unlike the faces on police photographs
which stare with an angry or sullen or frightened look into the
camera, the men sitting in front of the guards' bayonets all

wore expressions of complete indifference and apathy. So did the spectators behind the guards. In fact, the expressions of the spectators were the same as those of the accused. I must have vaguely felt, even then, that they were all one—the defeated victims, the people down there before us; and that we who faced them from the raised platform were their conquerors and rulers. Not the representatives of the Workers' State and the People's Court; but simply the rulers. They did not hate us. They were too apathetic and resigned even for that. How much of this did I consciously understand at the time? I am unable to decide; but I do vividly remember feeling, while I sat exposed on that raised platform, that not the accused but I was being pilloried.

The German Communist Party had a motto which used to appear every day on the top right corner of the official Party paper: *'Wo es Stärkere gibt, immer auf der Seite der Schwächeren'*—'Where there is Power we are on the side of the Powerless'. On that platform I was obviously on the wrong side. It gave me the same guilty feeling that I had experienced towards the Ukrainian peasant girl in the sleeping-car to Erivan. And again, on a different level, towards Nadeshda. And again in my daily contacts with the common people who had no access to privileged co-operative stores, no priorities for food, housing, clothing and living. They were the powerless and I was on the side of the Power, and so it went on wherever I turned in Russia. A revolutionary can identify himself with Power, a rebel cannot; but I was a rebel, not a revolutionary.

The trial of Attakurdov and accomplices was an exotic and amateurish forerunner of the great show-trials in Moscow. It was still on when I left Ashkhabad, and I never knew its outcome. Back in European Russia I found that nobody had ever heard about it. It had only been reported in the local papers of Turkmenistan, and passed over in silence everywhere else. I had walked into it by pure chance. I wonder how many similar trials had been conducted in the same silence in various parts of the vast Soviet Empire, long before the Moscow purges revealed that weird, Kafka-esque pattern to the incredulous world.

XI. To the Afghan Frontier

FOR a week or ten days our 'Writers' Brigade' explored the cotton plantations surrounding the oasis Merv.

Merv occupies a strategic position at the point where the Murghab River, which originates in the mountains of Afghanistan, loses itself in the sands of the Kara Kum. Before it is absorbed by the desert, the river divides into several branches, and each branch again into a number of capillaries : the artificial irrigation channels which make this oasis the central cotton-growing region of Turkmenistan.

At the same time, Merv controls the strategic approaches to Afghanistan and Persia from the North-East. It is one of the oldest towns in the world, mentioned in the *Zend-Avesta* and in the Hindu scriptures, and is regarded by Hindu and Arab tradition as the site of the Paradise and the cradle of mankind. It was also referred to variously as 'the Town of Plenty' and 'the Queen of the World'. But nothing of its past splendour remains, except crumbling ruins not worth the time to visit them—or so we were told, for the Brigade was never allowed to see Old Merv. When we alighted from our train one morning at four o'clock, we were taken to New Merv, which is another dreary Russian garrison town on the railway, at a few miles distance from the ancient city. Whenever I asked to see the old city, I was put off with smiles to the next day. It is unlikely that there were any secret military installations there. More probably, the District Party Committee, which only possessed one old Ford car, really thought that it was a waste of time and petrol to indulge in the bourgeois-romantic whim to look at ruins of the bygone past.

Extracts from my travel notebook

Collective Cotton Plantation Farm Aitakov.

A huge, dry, dusty field, stretched to the dust-coloured horizon, covered with mean-looking shrubs. A line of women slowly advanced on a broad front spread out across the field, their bodies in shapeless black garments, bent forward at ninety degrees so that their backs are parallel to the earth; from the distance they look like ravens on a stubblefield. They pick the white tufts from the knee-high shrubs with rapid automatic movements, with unseeing eyes, unerring fingers. In their wake, all the cotton has vanished from the shrubs into their bodices and aprons, and as the line approaches, their breasts and bellies swell into monstrous bulges. At the near side of the field they stop and empty the contents of these bulges on to heaps of white cotton. Amidst the heaps stands the foreman, an old, gaunt and gnarled Turkoman in a sheepskin cap, making marks in his tattered notebook with a stub of pencil. He is the only male in sight on the field, except for the Writers' Brigade. He is called Medshur Baba, and he is not a 'foreman' but a 'brigadier', and the thirty black-clad women are his 'brigade'. *Kolkhoz* Aitakov, like all other *kolkhozi* from the Afghan frontier to the Arctic circle, is subdivided into 'brigades', which vie with each other in Socialist Competition to fulfil the Plan and win the battle on the Agricultural Front. The same military terminology is used on the Industrial Front and on the Cultural Front.

The meeting between the Writers' Brigade and the Cotton Brigade was not a success. The women did not talk to us and did not glance at us—not even at Hughes, though he was certainly the first Negro they had seen, and a handsome one, too. The women of Turkestan have shed their black veils, but only physically. One feels that, when looked at by a stranger, they still feel naked without the veil that used to hide a woman's most intimate features : her eyes and lips. On the other hand, two of them plop out their breasts from under the black sackcloth without a trace of embarrassment and feed their infants in front of us. These infants they were carrying on their backs, in another fold of their garments. There were five or six of them carrying their babies in this fashion, on backs bent nearly horizontal to the ground, for seven hours a day. Moslem women are used to hard work, but not to regular, organised work. They are also used to carrying their babies on their backs, but not while on a back-breaking job in the fields. When the Cotton Brigade had emptied the contents of their bodices and aprons, and had gone on to the next trip, we tackled Medshur Baba on these subjects.

Medshur Baba speaks no Russian, so Kikiloff had to translate. Medshur Baba is tall, morose and monosyllabic; Kikiloff short, wizened and all creased smiles. Of each word that Medshur Baba mumbled between two spittings of mahorka juice, Kikiloff made a well-rounded phrase. He explained the system. *Kolkhoz* Aitakov had around two hundred and fifty members, half of them were women. The latter were divided into four brigades of thirty to forty, who were now engaged in harvesting the cotton.—And why no men?—Because the men were engaged on the more exacting work of digging irrigation canals. (Something in the manner of Kikiloff told us that he had doctored Medshur Baba's answer. Nowhere in *Kolkhoz* Aitakov did we see men digging at irrigation canals, though we asked to see them. But we saw plenty of men talking and smoking in the *chai-khana*—the tea house.) The *kolkhoz* has its Production Plan, and each brigade has its Production Plan. The brigade that we were watching had surpassed its Plan figures by sixty-five per cent, whereas the whole *kolkhoz* had only surpassed it by twenty-nine per cent. The earnings of the *kolkhoz* are distributed among its members according to the work done by each member. The work is measured by 'work-day units'. The work-days, however, are not measured in actual time. They are measured on a piece-rate scale. A work-day is the equivalent of thirty-two kilogrammes of harvested cotton. If a woman picks forty kilogrammes of cotton then she is credited with one and a quarter work-days. One of the *udarnitsas* ('shock-brigadier', forerunner of the 'Stakhanovite') was alleged to be able to pick sixty-five kilogrammes of cotton a day.—Which one was it? —Medshur Baba pointed vaguely at one of the black, doubled-up figures with an infant straggled on her back.—And why was she carrying the child instead of leaving it in the nursery? —Medshur Baba shrugged.—Did *Kolkhoz* Aitakov have no nursery?—It did have one. But it was too far from the field for nursing mothers.—Then why were nursing mothers not employed on work closer to it?—Medshur Baba shrugged. Kikiloff explained that it was important to fulfil the Plan and that the women were used to it, anyway.

Midday break. We are all squatting on the edge of an irrigation canal which is now dry, sharing the women's midday meal. It consists of melons, soup and tea. The soup is being prepared in an iron pot over a fire of dry thistles and twigs. During the three or four days that we spent on the cotton plantations, all meals consisted of the same fare. We never had any solid food, not even bread, except on one occasion. This occasion was an official reception for the Writers' Brigade late one night, at which only the dignitaries of the District were present. We saw no sign that the workers of the *kolkhoz* ate anything but the liquid fare of melon, soup and tea.

During the midday break, a pretty, adolescent native girl had joined the cotton pickers. She was carrying a book, and squatted down for a few minutes next to each woman in turn, whispering to her. Kikiloff explained that she was the teacher, and that she was going over their lessons in reading and writing with the women. In the evening, after work, they were too tired to learn. . . . They seemed even more tired now, and paid little attention to the little teacher, except for an occasional giggle and a covert glance at us. It was impossible to say whether the midday lesson was daily routine, or put on for our benefit. Kikiloff explained that before the Revolution there were only twenty-four women in the whole of Turkmenistan who could read or write. Somebody must have counted them. Now there are just over forty per cent literates among the adults of both sexes. But 1934, according to Plan, illiteracy will be liquidated everywhere in Soviet Asia.

(*End of extract*)

In the early years of the Revolution, the Soviet Government had replaced the Arab and Persian scripts all over Soviet Central Asia by the Latin alphabet. But a few years after my visit, in 1934 or '35, the Latin was replaced by the Russian alphabet. By the middle 'thirties, the revolutionary policy of encouraging the development of national cultures had been replaced by the unitarian concept of 'a single culture with a single common language'—Russian. So the women in the cotton brigade of *Kolkhoz* Aitakov were supposed to learn first the Latin, and then the Cyrillic alphabet; and all that during a half-hour's midday break, in between feeding their babies and drinking their soup.

Only one of them asked us, messengers from a distant world, a question. She was a youngish woman with an alert expression. Lowering her eyes, she asked Medshur Baba to ask us whether the country of America was ruled by Negroes.

When the women returned to their work, the four of us, led by Medshur Baba, wandered off to the *chai-khana* for some more tea. We wandered for a mile or two along one dry irrigation canal and then another. Now and then we saw a black tent or a clay hut, planted somewhere among the cotton fields without apparent plan or reason. The Turkomans are a nomadic race, and tradition proved stronger than regulations. The entire life of the *kolkhoz* is planned, counterplanned, regimented and directed—in theory; but the members of the *kolkhoz* still build their *kibitkas* (tents) and mud houses wherever they fancy putting them. Aitakov is not a proper village; nomads hate crowding together. The *kibitkas* and clay huts are dispersed over an area of something like a square mile.

The *chai-khana* was a kind of clay-cube bigger than the other clay-cubes. It consisted of a large room, whose only furniture was a rug on the stamped mud floor, and a smaller one which contained a table and several chairs. The smaller room served also as an office where most of the official business of the *kolkhoz* was transacted. On the rugs of the large room squatted several men, silent and motionless like Indian fakirs. They were drinking green *khok-chai* out of tiny cups. The atmosphere was so much like that of an opium den that I wondered whether it was not really an opium den. But I had long ago given up the hope of getting to the bottom of any problem in Turkestan.

In the smaller room, the one with a table and chairs, sat an Uzbek militiaman, a Russian agronomist and a third, nondescript person without definable occupation, such as can be found in any Levantine café or Asiatic *chai-khana*. They asked us for tobacco, and I tried to pump the militiaman, who spoke Russian, regarding the pre-revolutionary habits and folklore of Turkestan. I tried that more or less with every Turkoman, and never got anywhere. The answer to all questions starting with 'How was this or that before the Revolution?' was invariably a monosyllabic: 'Bad, very bad.' One rarely got beyond that. An impenetrable wall seemed to stand between the present and the past—one of those walls of baked mud of which everything here was built. Beyond the wall lay the land of memories which were taboo. Sometimes that laconic 'Bad, very bad' would be accompanied by a wistful, faraway smile—the smile of adults whom children ask naïve questions about forbidden subjects. The land of memories had become transformed into a land of mysteries, where the Muezzins called from the minarets, and women's eyes flashed secretly behind black veils, and the smell of spices hung over the bazaars, and where there was sometimes hunger and sometimes a slaughtered sheep. It was a land where the sky was blue and the air full of colour, and where men argued and fought, and women gossiped and laughed—in the days before the great silence descended.

'How were the women before the Revolution?' we asked the militiaman. 'Bad, very bad.' 'How did a young man get himself a wife?' 'He could not because he had no money to buy her.' 'So the poor all died out?' 'All the money and all the women belonged to the Beys. It was bad, very bad.'

We sat in that *chai-khana* all afternoon. Something seemed to have gone wrong. Since we were going to stay in the village, the Ford of the District Committee had gone back to Merv. Only gradually did it dawn on us that there was no village, or rather that the *chai-khana was* the village, and that we had arrived at our destination, so to speak. Kolya, the Ukrainian sailor-writer, had at the last minute decided to go back with the Ford, and we never saw him again. We were sorry to lose him for he had been a gay and resourceful companion with a gift for ferreting out food and lodgings in the middle of the desert. We needed that badly. On our arrival in Merv, the four of us had been billeted in one room containing two beds, one of which was already occupied. We had tossed for the other, and Kikiloff had got it. Perhaps Kolya had gone back to take possession of the bed. On the cotton-field he had tried to show off the tattooings on his arm to the women, but it had not been a success. Now that he had vanished, I wondered again why he had never taken notes or asked a question, and it occurred to me that I had never seen him use a pen or read a newspaper. I cannot swear to it, but I have a suspicion that one of the members of our Writers' Brigade was illiterate.

Darkness descended abruptly on the steppe, and we were still marooned in the *chai-khana*: Hughes, Kikiloff, myself and Medshur Baba, who seemed to have become permanently attached to us. Several hours earlier we had been told that our sleeping-quarters were being prepared, and that they would be ready presently. Then we had given up inquiring, and had sipped cup after cup of green tea which had a calming effect on our hunger. Since we had left Ashkhabad, the Brigade had been living on tea, melons, an occasional chunk of camel sausage, and *lepioshkas*—flat unleavened bread. We were also unable to get cigarettes, and had taken to smoking mahorka from paper-cones. As the melons gave all of us more or less chronic diarrhoea, we did not suffer too much from hunger. Yet the Brigade had been photographed in Ashkhabad, photographed in Merv, interviewed by the local Press and fêted everywhere it went. If, in spite of this, we were not better nourished, it was because we happened to be travelling through a country stricken by famine, without an efficient propaganda department to hide the truth from the visitors. Kikiloff knew about the famine; Hughes and I saw it every day more clearly, but did not talk about it.

When it became completely dark, Kikiloff and Medshur Baba held a conference, and decided that it was time to go. It was a moonless, starry night, and suddenly very cold. Shivering, we stumbled through the darkness in single file, led by Medshur Baba, for perhaps a mile. The night is nowhere as immense as in the starlit steppe, and we no longer regretted our visit to Aitakov. At the junction of two canals, a very old man attached himself to us. He walked beside Kikiloff, who engaged him in conversation and later on, when we had arrived, translated the dialogue for Hughes and me :

'How old are you, comrade uncle?'

'Sixty, perhaps seventy, who knows?'

'And still working?'

'I have worked all my life.'

'Can you read and write, comrade uncle?'

'Yok!' (No.)

'Why don't you learn it?'

'I am too old.'

'You should try, nevertheless.'

'What for? What I see I see, and what I know I know. I shall not be able to read my tombstone, anyway.'

'Have you ever travelled on a train?'

'Yok!'

'But you have seen the train with your eyes?'

'Yes, in Merv. I have once been to Merv.'

'But you have seen aeroplanes?'

'Yes, we saw them all the time. But I did not know that there were people sitting in them. They told me, but I would not believe it. Until my son wrote a letter and it said that he had flown in an aeroplane himself.'

'Where did he fly, comrade uncle?'

'He works in Tashkent in the Cotton Trust. Then they sent him to Samarkand, and so he flew to Samarkand. By Allah, he flew to Samarkand.'

Kikiloff was in an unusual mellow and unbuttoned mood. He was a native of the region of Merv, born somewhere around here, and for the first time since we had known him he struck a personal note in conversation. As we stumbled along through the darkness, he told us about the annual bloody feuds over water in the village where he had lived before the Revolution. The various strips of land were to be irrigated in an agreed order, but there was never enough water, and somebody always stole up at night to a sluice-gate to get more for his plot. In one of the brawls that grew out of such incidents Kikiloff's brother was killed—a neighbour bashed in his skull with a wooden plough. That was perhaps the incident which had turned him into a revolutionary.

Later on, commenting on what the old man had said about aeroplanes, Kikiloff told us another story. He had travelled among the Tadzhiks in the Pamirs—a people even more primitive than the Turkomans. One day a Red Army patrol on bicycles had arrived in a Tadzhik village. The villagers fled in panic. They had seen plenty of aeroplanes, but never a bicycle. They took aeroplanes for granted—why, they were just machines. But a human being riding on a thing which had only two wheels and no support—surely that must be a miracle worked by the Devil.

Our billet, we found, was the communal day nursery. It was a large and fairly clean room, containing several rugs and no other furniture—except for the propaganda posters on the walls which preached hygiene and displayed enlargements of fearful infectious germs.

Later in the night, there was a party attended by the natives of the district. Two *bakhshi*—bards—sang ballads, accompanying themselves on two-stringed *taras*. It was, as far as Hughes and I could make out, quarter-tone music of Chinese origin. It meant little to our Western ears, but much to our hosts, who listened avidly and gradually fell into a trance-like stupor. The room was filled with twenty or thirty men, squatting on the floor, and the air soon became unbreathable with mahorka smoke. The bards were a teacher and an official of the District Committee, and the ballads, Kikiloff explained, were about 'heroism', about 'tragic love', and again 'heroism'.

After each strophe the *bakhshis* threw their heads back and uttered a kind of guttural scream, which sounded to us like ee-ee-ee-ee . . ., sustained for a whole minute or more, until the bards' eyes were bulging out and their faces began to get blue. These screams were apparently much appreciated, and the more so the longer they lasted; sometimes one of the listeners joined in with a high-pitched ee-ee of his own. No women were present except the doctor, a determined female comrade from European Russia, who soon vanished into the night without being bidden a single good-bye.

The singing went on for several hours with nothing but tea

to sustain us; yet there had been promising winks and whispered rumours about a sheep being slaughtered in our honour. Then, just after daybreak, unexpectedly and miraculously, the sheep arrived. It arrived in an enormous wooden bowl. The first rays of the rising sun glittered on the gravy. Globules of fat floated like water-lilies on the surface, and in between them were compact islands of meat. Next, a pile of steaming *lepioshkas* appeared, two for every man, and lastly a wooden spoon.

The ritual of the feast was much the same as in Arab countries. The spoon, filled with gravy, made three times the round from mouth to mouth, under the ironic stare of the germs on the posters. Then the spoon was put aside, sleeves were turned up, and the great dunking of *lepioshkas* in the bowl took its ritual course. Finally came the turn of the meat, picked delicately, unhurriedly, courteously, with outstretched fingers. Every man present would rather have died than betrayed haste or greed.

When the sheep was finished there was more tea; and then the majority of the men wandered off into the warming daylight, whilst the remainder of us lay down where they happened to be sitting, and after a few contented belches rolled over into sleep.

One day Kikiloff took Hughes and me to visit a school in Merv. Over the entrance-gate a streamer greeted us: 'WELCOME OUR PROLETARIAN REVOLUTIONARY WRITER COMRADES FROM AMERICA AND EUROPE'. We were first taken to the advanced class who were having a lesson in German. At a sign from the teacher, the class rose and chanted in a chorus:

'*A giten Tog.*'

They should have said: '*Einen guten Tag*'. I glanced at the teacher, and had to take a hard bite at my tongue. He was a gentle, young Byelo-Russian Jew from Minsk. The future intelligentsia of the oasis Merv, near the cradle of the Aryan race, thought that they were learning German—but they were in fact learning Yiddish.

Next, we assisted at the History lesson of a lower form, and witnessed the following dialogue (in Russian) between teacher and pupil, which I quote from *Red Days*:

The teacher is a girl of about fifteen, who comes from the cotton district and who, five years ago, was herself still illiterate. The child is a little girl from the same region. It has huge doll's eyes in its little Tartar face, and a dripping nose, in spite of it being constantly rubbed with its shirt.

Teacher (*adjusting her scarf in honour of the Heroic Brigade*) : *Well, children, what occasion are we soon going to celebrate?*

Child (*pulls tip of index finger out of nose, holds it up in the air*).

Teacher : *Well, Ashar, you know what it is?*

Ashar : *We are going to celebrate the fifteenth anniversary of the Fifth Year Plan.*

Teacher (*mortified*) : *No, Ashar, you mean the fifteenth anniversary of the Revolution.*

Ashar : *Yes, the Revolution.*

Teacher : *So—when did the Revolution happen?*

Ashar : *A long, long time ago.*

Teacher : *Well, fifteen years ago. Because we are celebrating its fifteenth anniversary.*

Ashar : *The Revolution was fifteen years ago.*

Teacher : *So—who is older? You or the Revolution?*

Ashar (*thinks hard*) : *The Revolution.*

Teacher (*beaming*) : *And what was before the Revolution?*

Ashar (*promptly*) : *The burchuys.*

Teacher : *So—the bourgeois lorded over us, and the workers and the peasants and the shepherds were very poor—yes?*

Ashar (*nods*).

Visitor (*butting in*) : *What is a burchuy?*

Ashar : *You are a burchuy.*

Visitor (*nettled*) : *Why am I a burchuy?*

Ashar (*picks her nose, laughs*).

Teacher (*goes red as a sunset over the steppes*).

Voice from the rear : *I know what a burchuy is.*

Teacher (*doubtfully*) : *Well?*

Voice : *A burchuy is a Kaiptalist.*

Visitor (*stubbornly*) : *And what is a Capitalist?*

Ashar : *A Kaiptalist was a Bey . . .*

Voice (*with gathering speed*) : *The Kaiptalist Beys had swollen bellies because they were eating everything and the workers were all hungry. Then there were* Mullahs. *The* Mullahs *invented Allah. In the Kaiptalist countries which have no Revolution there still are Kaiptalist Beys and* Mullahs.

Teacher (*recovering*) : *So—who owned the factories before the Revolution?*

Chorus : *The bur-chuys.*

Teacher : *And who owned the land?*

Chorus : *The bur-chuys.*

Teacher : *And who owned the canals and the herds?*

Chorus : *The bur-chuys.*

Teacher : *And to whom does everything belong now?*

Chorus : *To the Soy-salist Fa-therland.*

The most out-of-the-world place to which I have ever been is a village near the Soviet-Afghan frontier, called Permetyab. It is inhabited by Afghani and Baluchi tribesmen, compared to whom the Turkomans are a nation of sophisticated intellectuals. I have never seen Permetyab mentioned on any map. It lies some fifty miles south-east of Merv, across the desert.

We went there in the old Ford, equipped with three spare tyres, spades, and a goodly provision of melons and *lepioshkas*. There was no recognisable road or track; the driver had to navigate by doubtful landmarks, guided by the District-Kultprop (Party official responsible for disseminating culture and propaganda). The Kultprop was an energetic Russian Orientalist who spoke fluent Turkoman and knew every *kibitka* of his district. We got repeatedly stuck in axle-deep sand, and had one tyre after another punctured by the thorny thistles in which camels delight. (Camel tongue is considered a local *delicatesse*, but it requires strong teeth to bite through the varicose veins between the furuncular taste-buds.)

Then we came to a canal, some six or seven feet wide, with no bridge anywhere in sight. But at a distance of about half a mile we saw a *kibitka*. An old Turkoman sat in it, smoking. Next to it stood a second, half-finished *kibitka*. Directed by the Kultprop, we all fell to dismantling it. We pulled out the tent-poles, carried them to the canal, threw them across the watercourse and dug the ends into the two banks. Then we took the mats of artfully-woven reeds, which decorated the inner walls and floor of the *kibitka*, and laid them over the poles. Then we solidified the structure with clay, put some more reeds on top, tested the resistance of our bridge, and it fell into the canal. We started again, and at the second attempt, got across. The old Turkoman had watched the destruction of the *kibitka*, which was perhaps his son's, without a word or a gesture.

We came to a second, narrower canal which we filled up with sand, and when we got across, we dug it open again. We passed an old caravanserai half in ruins, which now served as a cotton storage depot. Camels were unloading huge bales of raw cotton in the courtyard. The walls of the building were covered with the familiar posters : portraits of the leaders, slogans against religion, against illiteracy, against imperialist wars, and drawings illustrating how to fight malaria, trachoma and syphilis. The Russian director at the depot confided to us that it had surpassed its Plan by ten per cent.

In the end, we reached Permetyab. It was a scattered village of black tents interspersed with clay huts. At first view there seemed to be no life in it, except for a few slinking pariah dogs who circled the car from a distance, like hyenas. Nobody came to greet us as we scrambled out of the car. Led by the Kultprop, we all flocked to one of the tents. At the entrance of it squatted a huge, savage-looking, bearded figure in a striped caftan, with a large dirty turban on his head. He was smoking a hookah made out of a hollowed marrow. In the dim interior of the tent we could see the shape of a woman clad in rags, her face averted, arms and ankles hung with brass bangles. On the floor crawled two dirty children with open sores on their faces. Another hollow marrow served as a water jug, and a mat as furniture. The other tents were exactly alike. At each tent the head of the family greeted us with a few murmured words, then went on smoking. The children stared at us in fear, and the women turned their heads away.

At last the Kultprop found the man he was looking for : a youngish man, without beard, who looked a little less fierce than the rest. He was the translator, the only man in the village who spoke some Turkoman (nobody knew any Russian). With his help, a kind of conversation got under way : he translated into Turkoman, then Kikiloff or the Kultprop translated into Russian and I translated into English for Hughes.

When the villagers saw that a palaver was on, they came
sauntering over one by one, until we were surrounded by a
dense ring of staring men. To break the ice, the Kultprop told
Hughes and me to show them our watches and fountain pens.
These objects wandered from hand to hand, and were duly
admired. Then Hughes's cigarette case, Kikiloff's Trade
Union badge, and even my leather belt made the rounds. Not
even among the Arab Bedouins had I seen such ignorance, dirt
and primitiveness. Most of the men had sores and eye diseases; it seemed as if nearly half of them were one-eyed. The
children were little wild animals. Some were sitting in the
dust, de-lousing each other like monkeys.

Owing to the hazards of chain-translation, and the oriental
habit of answering leading questions with enthusiastic affir-
mations, it was practically impossible to extract any concrete
information from them. As far as we could make out, the villagers all came from Afghanistan, Baluchistan and Persia.
Some of the families seemed to have immigrated as long as
two or three generations ago. But 'immigrated' is a misleading
expression : they were wandering nomads who had simply
drifted with their cattle and tents across the invisible frontier-
line somewhere between the Caspian and the Amu Darya,
without realising that they had passed from the sovereign rule
of some Habibullah to that of some Nicholas or Alexander.
Then, at some undefinable date, they had all been rounded up
and concentrated in this village, a kind of desert ghetto. Did
they like it here? They liked it very much, thank God. Did
the Soviet Government treat them well? It treated them very
well, thank God. It built them beautiful houses, thank God,
and it sent all the children to school, thank God, and it provided modern hygiene. At which stage of the translation-
process all these blessings had slipped in, we could not tell.
The words had no relation whatever to the visible facts before us, but this disturbed nobody. This was not a Potemkin
village. It was something more curious. Hughes and Kikiloff
and the Kultprop and I were the victims of a kind of verbal
self-hypnosis. It was a triumph of words over reality. Had they
fulfilled their Plan? Thanks to their unceasing labours and
the heroic efforts of their Shock-Brigaders, and the wise guidance of the Soviet Government, they had over-fulfilled their

Production Plan by twenty-two and a half per cent. What exactly were they producing? Oh, this and that. Cotton? Yes, much cotton was grown in the neighbourhood. Where? Some miles away, here and there. But what did the village itself produce? Many things, for the benefit of the villagers and of the Government. And so on.

We learnt that there were really two Permetyabs: a village and a *kolkhoz*. This was the village, not yet collectivised. The *kolkhoz* was a mile or so further on. We got back into the car and drove on to the *kolkhoz*. Some of the savage turbaned figures waved us goodbye; then they were swallowed up by the dust. The Kultprop asked us how we had liked the village. We said we had liked it very much, thank God.

At first sight, the *kolkhoz* looked only slightly different from the village. There were a few more mud houses than tents (the house, however primitive, is the symbol of progress from the nomadic to a settled agricultural existence; hence Soviet propaganda in Asia leads an intensive campaign in favour of houses and against tents). Some of the younger women did not run away at the sight of strangers. Some of the men had exchanged the turban for the cloth-cap, and some of them no longer wore beards. There was a field with a few people actually working in it, and there was even a tractor to be seen, though in a broken-down state. Compared to the dreamlike stupor of the village, the *kolkhoz* gave the impression of a certain will to activity. We learnt that all the inhabitants of the *kolkhoz* were new immigrants from the neighbouring countries who, unlike the villagers, had come after the Revolution.

We gathered in the only brick building of the *kolkhoz*, which served as a school, medical centre and administrative office for the community of a hundred and fifty souls. There was a Russian doctor—again a woman, as in Aitakov, and of the same admirably tough, determined type. She told us matter-of-factly about her 'difficulties'. Syphilis was endemic among the tribesmen. Very little could be done about it. She concentrated as far as possible on the eye diseases. When she had arrived two years ago, nine out of ten children had suffered from trachoma or conjunctivitis. Now it was a little better; though infant mortality was still around fifty per cent.

The usual practice was for the mother to bite off the newborn's umbilical cord with her teeth. Only a few of the 'politically conscious elements' were beginning to call her in as a midwife. . . . The dead were washed in hot water (the one and only hot bath a person ever had) and buried upright, without coffin, in an earth-shaft. Were the men embarrassed to come to a woman for treatment? No. That kind of shame was unknown to them.

There were some twenty of us squatting on the rugs. We distributed the melons and *lepioshkas* we had brought, and also some tobacco. There was an atmosphere of genuine friendliness. Again our watches and fountain pens were admired and passed around. The members of the *kolkhoz* were as primitive as the inhabitants of the village; they came from the same tribes. But there was an unmistakable difference in the selection of the human material. The villagers were the driftwood of the deserts of Asia, who had at one time drifted across the frontier and did not care where they were or what befell them. These men in the *kolkhoz* had come recently, of their own choice. Through this conscious act of will they had shaken off the fetters of oriental fatalism. They were true revolutionaries, in the original Promethean sense of the word.

After a while, a tall old man was led into the room. Everybody seemed to have been waiting for him. He looked part savage, part Biblical patriarch. He was led to a place of honour and squatted down, and only then did we realise that he was blind. He was, apparently the bard, storyteller and philosopher of the community. Even the Kultprop seemed to be impressed by him. He prodded him at first with a few questions asked in a respectfully hushed manner; then the old man went on talking on his own, in a hoarse, guttural voice, while the translator from the village repeated every phrase in whispered Turkoman and Kikiloff followed in whispered Russian. My notes, of which an extract follows, were based on this third-hand information. The old man's words had no doubt been embellished—or banalised—in the process; but I nevertheless had the feeling that I got the gist of what he said.

. . . *What I think of the tractor? I was blind many suns*

before it arrived. But I have seen it with my hands. It is a beautiful and wise machine of the size of a young camel.

. . . Yes: I know of other machines. Sometimes a carriage comes here. It collects the bones of sheep and camel from the carcass heap. The carriage takes the bones to the Government. They put the bones into a machine. The machine makes paper out of them for printing the Koran. That machine must be even wiser and larger than a full-grown camel.

. . . When we came here? That is several suns back. Ali could walk but he had not yet learnt to run. We came at the time when the Emir Amanullah, the son of Emir Habibullah, fled the country and there was war among the Pashtu. After that came the famine, and at that time we were told that in Russia Lenin was chasing away the Beys, and giving the herds to the shepherds to own, and the lands to the poor; and that the land ploughed itself with machines.

At first we would not believe this. But each time the smugglers came, or merchants, or a caravan, they told this same story. They also told us that there were many Pashtu and Farsi and Baluchi living here in a village called Permetyab, and that they were in good health and had plenty of land and water and cattle. But we were suffering from the famine and the children died of hunger in their mothers' wombs and were dead before they were born.

Then many spoke up and said: we must go over there into the country with this new religion. And others spoke and said: Allah will punish you in his anger as he punishes all who go after new things. And many spoke and answered: Allah is already angry enough as the famine shows, and he can't get more angry anyway—so let us go over into the land where the herds belong to the shepherds and the earth is for the poor. There were many who talked this way, but few did come in the end. For great is the laziness of men, comrades, until they have learnt the ways of Socialism.

. . . Do we all come from the same place? No, we do not all come from the same place. We come from many places and many tribes, and one did not know of the other who was coming. Some are from the Chilchigi and some from the Afridi and some others from other tribes. We did not know of each other, but of the new religion and of the chasing away of the

Beys and the Mullahs everybody knew in Afghanistan. Some say it is a good thing, some say it is a bad thing, but they all speak about it although it is forbidden.

. . . No, I could not read, even when I had my eyes. But I took much thought when I heard about this new religion— for I had much time to think during the famine, although it is forbidden to think about these sacred matters. And now I will tell you the result of my thinking:

A fertile womb is better than the loveliest lips.

A well in the desert is better than a cloud over the desert.

A religion that helps is better than a religion that promises.

And this secret which I found will spread over there where we come from, and more and more will understand it and follow our way. But others will stay where they are and embrace the new religion and preach it to the ignorant . . .

We were driving back towards Merv. The sun was setting, and as it touched the rim of the desert, it set it aflame. It started in the West, but soon the South in the direction of the Persian and Afghan frontiers was on fire, too. It was a wonderful feeling to drive head-on into this great conflagration.

XII. Bokhara and Samarkand

THESE two towns were the hidden jewels of Central Asia during the Middle Ages. Samarkand was the residence of Tamerlane and his successors; Bokhara, Islam's most famous centre of learning. Since my schoolboy days, when I had devoured Vámbéry, the two names had retained a magic ring in my ears. I had never hoped that I would have the lucky chance to visit them during the one short period in their history when they were accessible with relative ease to Europeans. Yet all that remains in my memory are some fragments of beauty inextricably mixed with squalor and decay, and a mood of infinite sadness. The Russians have trampled over these two fabulous towns as mercilessly as the Golden Horde of Jenghiz Khan.

I remember wandering over the desolate Registan of Samarkand, accompanied by an Uzbek officer of the Red Army. He reminded me of Anvar Umorzakov, for he was equally reserved, gentle and polite. But he happened to be a native of Samarkand and, in spite of his thorough indoctrination, he loved his city and its past as an Athenean or Roman loves his own. The Registan of Samarkand must once have been the most imposing, and at the same time the loveliest monument of Islam. It is a large symmetrical square, laid out like a piazza, walled in by the three famous *medresseh*, the medieval universities of Tillikari, Shirdar and Ullug-beg. Its impact is still both graceful and awe-inspiring. The façades are broken up by the infinitely complicated filigree work of carved and laced and enamelled columns and arches. The enamel tiling is a mosaic of turquoise-blue, gold, pink and green—a firework frozen into eternity. I knew the blue-and-golden mosques of Jerusalem, Bagdad and Damascus, and was later to know Granada and Seville; but here the genius of the lame warrior and his successors had achieved a synthesis of Arab, Persian and Far Eastern architecture so unique and moving that one wanted just to sit down in the shade of the decaying turquoise columns and cry. For the arches were crumbling, the tiles peeling off, and broken fragments were strewn among the rubble smelling of dogs' urine.

We wandered on to Tamerlane's Summer Palace. I remembered a Persian verse I had seen quoted : *Samarkand seikeli rui zemin est*—Samarkand is the centre of the world. That centre of power has been drifting in the course of the centuries across the globe like a wandering magnetic pole, and no historian has discovered its law of movement. But there seems to exist a negative rule that the pole never comes to rest at the same place a second time. Attempts to bring it back to a previous location have always ended in failure—Napoleon III, Mussolini, Hitler. Instead of a romantic revival, they produce a parody of the original drama. Will Stalin compare to Timur as Mussolini compares to Caesar?

Of the great conquerors of history, Timur the Lame seems to me the most fascinating personality—more human and palpable than, say, the shadowy Alexander or the ambiguous Caesar. The sources are wildly contradictory about his character—but that could not be otherwise in the case of a limping warrior-scholar, who must have appeared to his contemporaries as mysterious and unpredictable as intellectuals always do. That he was a true intellectual becomes evident at once on entering the *Turbeti Timur*, his burial chapel. In the centre of it there are two marble tombstones side by side, one darkgreen, the other black. Under the green stone lies Timur the Lame. Under the black stone, which is slightly larger, lies his teacher and spiritual guide, Mir Said Berki. To choose one's teacher as one's sole companion for eternity is a gesture unparalleled by any great conqueror of mankind.

The interior of the chapel is both graceful and austere. It is octagonal in shape, and less than twenty feet in diameter. The walls are of alabaster, with golden arabesques on a turquoise-blue ground; underneath it is a room of the same shape which contains the actual graves. The inscription on

Tamerlane's green tombstone consists simply of his name, including his surname (Koeregen), without any title or embellishment.

Vámbéry, in his description of the sepulchre, mentions a copy of the Koran, written on the skin of a gazelle, allegedly by Osman, the second Caliph. That relic is no longer there. On the other hand, I saw fixed to the wall in the lower chamber the white tail of a horse—allegedly the tail of Timur's favourite horse; this Vámbéry does not mention. I wonder whether he overlooked it, or whether the tail is of more recent origin.

Every monument in Samarkand built by Tamerlane himself bears the imprint of self-restraint and of beauty-in-austerity. The pomp and circumstance only came in with his successors, the Mogul rulers of India. Timur's Summer Palace is of modest dimensions, almost unassuming from outside. But inside, the mosaic floors and faïenced walls convey even today an image of perfection. It stands on a garden terrace reached by a flight of forty marble steps, and is again named after one of Timur's spiritual guides and companions—Shah Zindeh, alias Kazim Ibn Abas, one of the pioneers of Islam in Central Asia. Timur had Shah Zindeh's tomb placed in the centre of the garden, under the windows of his main reception room.

His preoccupation with matters spiritual seems to have spread to his household and his immediate successors. One of his wives, a Turkish princess named Bibi Khanüm, built the largest *medresseh* in Samarkand, a seminary able to house a thousand students. She built it after his death, and out of her own pocket. Such enterprise and independence by a woman in Moslem Asia is characteristic of the peculiar atmosphere around Timur. His grandson built the only observatory in Central Asia, which was famous throughout the world.[1]

We returned once more to the Registan. The Uzbek officer looked up and down the decaying glories of the ancient Centre of the World with a wretched expression. A taciturn man, all he said was: 'The Government has granted a hundred and fifty thousand roubles for restoration work.'

[1] To be pedantic, there are reports of an earlier Observatory built under Hellagu in Maraga, but there is no trace of it left.

During a year's puritan living in Russia, I spent nearly ten per cent of that sum.

'Get up, get up, empty your bowels, do your exercises, do your exercises, ten minutes of physical culture, eat your breakfast, eat your breakfast, and now it is time to go to work.'

On my first morning in Bokhara I was woken up by a loudspeaker installed in the public square, blaring out these commands. The public loudspeakers have replaced the Muezzin's call. Their mechanised, hypnotising commands sounded like a scene out of Huxley's *Brave New World*.

Bokhara the Noble was being sovietised more ruthlessly than any other Asiatic town. The entire Old City was being razed to the ground. The bazaars—once the most famous trading centre of Central Asia—are dead. No more stalls offering carpets, silk, textiles, goldsmiths' and coppersmiths' work, Kara-Kul lambskins, rare manuscripts, books and exotic spices. The three hundred and sixty mosques, and the hundred and forty *medresseh* are also dead. A few were converted into schools. The others were torn down. The famous books and manuscripts, which made Bokhara the centre of Moslem learning, have vanished—burnt, pilfered, dispersed. The Minaret of Kokhumbez, from whose two hundred-foot turret offenders against religion were thrown down, has been demolished. The Citadel has been transformed into a college; its large reception hall into a students' dormitory; the Emir's harem into a lunatic asylum. 'Within four years,' the chairman of the Town Planning Committee told us proudly, 'Bokhara will have become a European town.'

The desolation of Samarkand had been heartbreaking. The destruction of Bokhara was not. For the past three centuries Bokhara had been a nightmare town where the fanatic side of Islam had degenerated into a kind of collective insanity. The cruelty of the last Emirs surpassed even that of the half-crazed Khans of Khiva. In Khiva, Vámbéry had witnessed the public gouging out of the eyes of some thirty aged prisoners of war. In Bokhara, offenders were thrown into dried-up wells on the Registan, or hurled down from the top of a mosque, or executed by having their throats cut with a knife in the public square. Every deviation from religious orthodoxy, sexual misdemeanour, or criticism of the absolute ruler was punished by summary execution. Vámbéry describes how the *Raiz* (Guardian of Religion) 'with a cat-o-nine-tails in his hand, traverses the streets and public places, examines each passer-by in the principles of Islamism and sends the ignorant, even if they be grey-bearded men of three-score years, to the boys' school...'[1]

While imposing, by a reign of terror, a rigid puritanism on the populace, the Emir and his court led a fabulous life of debauchery. The only building which, as far as I can remember, the Soviet authorities have kept in relatively good repair, and open to visitors, was the last Emir's palace; it was meant to serve as a reminder of the past. It was built about the turn of the century, and decorated in ludicrously bad taste. The last Emir must have had an obsession about mirrors, for they could be found everywhere, as in certain Paris brothels—on the ceiling over his bed, on portable *paravants*, on walls and doors, and even in the one small lavatory of the palace (the harem was only equipped with a communal latrine). The reception chamber was a grotesque imitation of the Versailles Gallery of Mirrors, containing a portable throne covered with red plush. In a walled-in part of the garden adjoining the harem, there was a small artificial lake where the women of the harem bathed in the nude while the Emir watched them from a small balcony specially built for that purpose. The whole thing looked exactly like the description of an Oriental despot's pleasure haunt in a cheap novel.

The last Emir, Olim Khan, had four official wives, eleven favourites, and altogether some hundred and twenty women and forty boys in his harem—or so I was told. When he fled to Afghanistan in 1920, he only took with him the four official wives and several boys. As over a hundred of the harem-women must have been left behind, I resolved to get hold of one. I went to the City Soviet, which had numerous departments, but none for former harem-women. I went to the Women's Education Department. They sent me to the Press Department. I went to the Press Department. They sent me to Mass Agitation. I went to Mass Agitation. They sent me to Kultprop. Then I got fed up and went to the G.P.U. Twenty-

[1] Vámbéry, *Travels in Central Asia*, London (1868).

four hours later the G.P.U. produced Rakhat Razikhova.

Present at the interview were the head of the Kultprop Department, the head of the Women's Education Department, and a translator. Rakhat Razikhova, former member of the Emir's harem, was now a Trade Union official in the City Soviet. She was a fairly good-looking woman of just over thirty, with a slightly wilted Mongolian face, and neatly parted dark hair with a bun at the back. She was shy, and obviously intimidated by the presence of so many dignitaries. A direct dialogue was impossible; she hardly ever looked at me, and addressed her answers to the woman from the Education Department. So all I got out of her was a rather bloodless synopsis of her life-story. I quote from *Red Days*:

Rakhat Razikhova was born in 1900. She was twelve years old when one night she was woken up in her mother's house —her father was dead. Somebody wrapped her into a large overcoat. She cried until a pillow was stuffed into her mouth. Then she was taken away into the harem adjoining the palace. The next night she slept with the Emir—and then never saw him again.

Only a few among the inmates of the harem were called to the Emir a second time. Except for the wives and favourites, the girls in the harem changed constantly, for after a while the Emir would give them away as a present to one of his courtiers, while his agents were always on the lookout for fresh supplies. The agents were old women, known and dreaded by the whole town. They went from house to house, looking for possible candidates, and when they found a suitable girl or boy, they reported to the Emir. Then, a few nights later, somebody came and took the girl or boy away. The parents were given money.

Rakhat had no sharp memories of life in the harem. It was a gloomy building with small windows and bare rooms with whitewashed walls. I had seen it, and it had reminded me of a Y.M.C.A. hostel. Twice a day the girls were given bowls of pilaw. The meals and the regular hours of prayer were the main events of the day. It sounded more like a convent than a harem. No visitors were permitted; only when a girl became pregnant was her mother allowed to come and see her. The *pregnant women were taken to a special room, and their children brought up at court.*

There was only one hope of escaping from this life of boredom and monotony: to be given away to one of the courtiers. In some cases this happened after a few days, in others it took months or years. Rakhat had to wait five years. When she was married to the former Kushbegi (Chief Officer of the Court), she was seventeen; he was seventy-five. Rakhat became his fourth wife, and bore him a son. Her husband, whose name she has forgotten—she only remembers his first name: Astan-aqull—had for some reason been banished by the Emir to the town of Katerzhi. Her married life was as austere, and she was just as much shut off from the outside world, as in the Emir's harem.

In 1922 her husband died, and the world stood suddenly open for Razikhova—a new world, for the old one had perished two years earlier amidst lightning and thunder. The doors of the harems were thrown wide open; the sack-like paranjahs and black veils fell. Asiatic woman was promoted from the rank of a domestic animal to that of a human being.

Rakhat learnt to read and write. She became a factory worker, then a teacher, finally a Trade Union representative in the Town Soviet. She married a young peasant. She bore him a child—her second—and lived with him for one year. But the marriage did not work, for the peasant was reluctant to learn and laughed at her efforts. So Rakhat Razikhova—one-time member of the Emir of Bokhara's harem, created by God as a slave of men, who could be bought and sold like chattel and was supposed to have no mind and will of her own—Rakhat went to the Registrar's office and obtained a divorce.

'It is time for bed, earth your aerial, make sure that your aerial is earthed. Air your room, air your room. Good night.'

The loudspeakers were silent. The red sickle of the moon hovered over the broken minarets of Bokhara the Noble, which four years later was to cease to exist.

XIII. Hadji Mir Baba

BOKHARA, like every other larger town in the Soviet Union, has its Revolutionary Museum where documents, photographs, models of hide-outs, underground printing presses, and other relics are exhibited. One of the exhibits was a pair of photographs which, in the manner of police photographs, portrayed a person from two different angles. One showed him in profile—the profile of a man in his forties with a bony face, prominent nose and dark hawk's eyes. The second photograph showed him not, as usual, from the front but from the back, with a bared torso. It was, however, not so much a torso as a kind of anatomical study of torn flesh, with strips of skin hanging loosely down, showing the bared sinews. The inscription said that these were photographs of Hadji Mir Baba, one of the leaders of the Bokharian Revolution, taken in 1920 by one of the Emir's officers, after Hadji Mir Baba's arrest and torture.

As I was looking at the photograph, a tall old man with a stoop walked up to me and said in Russian : 'That is I'. And so he was. The old man was the custodian of the museum. In spite of his stoop, his bony frame and hawk's face still gave an impression of unbreakable physical strength and will-power. Twenty years later the memory of Hadji Mir Baba served me as a model for old Arin, the Armenian revolutionary, grandfather of the Soviet bureaucrat Fedya, in *The Age of Longing*.

We became friends, and during four or five evenings Hadji Mir Baba told me his life story over cups of green tea in my hotel room. This time no translator was needed as he spoke fluent Russian; I took down his narrative word by word. It was a long, sprawling story, full of digressions and stories-within-the-story, in the manner and tradition of the Arabian Nights. The following is a textual compression in which the oriental flourishes are left in, and only the stories-within-the-story are left out.

'The Emir Olim Khan was preceded on the throne by his father, Abdull'ahat Khan, and he was preceded by his father, Mozaffer Khan. A very cruel ruler was Mozaffer Khan, he offended the people, levied high taxes, and waged great campaigns for plunder, such as the raid on Dekhan where he had two thousand people slaughtered. Out of their heads he built a pyramid on the Registan, and all Bokhara was drowned in stench. But at that time the Russians came from Samarkand and vanquished the Emir's armies and made him their vassel. A few years later the Emir Mozaffer Khan died. He was followed by the Emir Ahat Khan, and he was even worse than his father.

'The taxes which he levied were beyond counting, and so was the number of boys and girls whom he had carried off to his harem; and what he did not steal himself his officials stole, and the women whom he did not take himself were taken by his officers. He who read a book other than the Koran had his head cut off; and he who spoke a word that the *Mullahs* did not like also had his head cut off. The *Mullahs* pretended that all these barbarities were good for the people and pleasing to God; only we, the revolutionary *Djadidi*, fought for the rights of the people. I, Hadji Mir Baba, was a *Djadid* even in my youth, for as a merchant in Kara-Kul furs I had travelled in many foreign lands and had seen that the people were better off there.

'The Emir Ahat Khan reigned for twenty-seven years, and he was followed by the Emir Olim Khan, and he was even worse than his father.

'The people had a very poor time under Olim Khan for he was a very bad ruler. But one day it happened that the people of Russia deposed their Czar and sent him to the devil, and shortly afterwards our Emir Olim Khan received a telegram from Petersburg from the new Government which said :

' "Liberate the brave Bokharian people stop Kerensky."

'So the Emir invited the representatives of the people to his Palace. And when we arrived at the Palace, twelve of us representing the people of Bokhara, we saw Olim Khan sitting on his red throne, and his golden sword dangled across his belly, for he was as fat as he was lazy. And at his right side sat the *Kazi Kalan*, who is the supreme judge over the believers, and at his left the Representative of the Russian Government, and all around sat the *Bashis* [Pashas] and *Mullahs*, and they looked very angry. The Emir said not a word, but merely pulled a roll of parchment out of his green velvet sachet, and he handed the scroll over to the *Kazi Kalan* to be read aloud. That was the Manifesto.'

[It was a manifesto in which, for the first time in the history of Bokhara, constitutional government was granted to the people. This was in April, 1917. It was soon withdrawn, however, and until the consolidation of Soviet power in Turkestan in 1920, which led to the deposition and flight of the last Emir, the history of Bokhara is a tangle of revolutions, counter-revolutions and civil wars. The *Djadidi* were a radical group of the new, educated middle-class which had come into being after the Russian conquest in 1868. Hadji Mir Baba, who had travelled far and wide, was one of their leaders.—I asked him what the Emir had looked like, and got this description of a previous meeting : 'He was a fat man, sitting on a fat white horse. He wore a silken turban and a golden sword and he had a little pointed beard and small pig's eyes. He pretended to be a descendent of the great Timur, but he looked like a devil greased with codliver oil.' And now let Hadji Mir Baba continue his story] :

'Hardly had the *Kazi Kalan* finished the reading of the manifesto, when the *Mullahs* and the *Bashis* gave out a loud cry. The *Mullahs* yelled : "This is bad. It is against the Koran." And the *Bashis* said : "The manifesto has not been written by our mighty Emir but by others, and it only pleases the enemies of our mighty Emir, this one and that one."

'And the representatives of the people became frightened, and they only said : "Hm, Hm."

'When the Emir saw that there was such a controversy about the authorship of the manifesto, he said nothing but got up and left the room. For he was as cunning as he was cruel.

'We, however, took the manifesto, and had it printed in many copies and distributed among the people; and the next day several thousand people gathered in the street. We marched with our flags through the bazaar, and then we held a big meeting. At the meeting three delegates were elected to go to the Emir and to ask him to accept public responsibility for the manifesto, and to liberate the prisoners as it was promised in it. And the three delegates chosen by the people were: Attakhodja Polat Khodjayev, Abdulrakhim Khan Yussouf Zade, and I, Hadji Mir Baba.

'But meanwhile, the *Mullahs* had not been idle. They had gathered together all the seminarists from the *medresseh* and incited the ignorant people against us. They ran through the streets shouting: "The *Djadidi* are depraved people who spit on the Koran and sleep with their mothers."

'When we climbed into a *droshky* and rode past the crowd on our way to the Citadel, many cried: "Such noble men we shall not let go, for the Emir is going to slaughter them." We, however, said: "Be quiet, good friends, we shall come back with trumpets."

'When we reached the Citadel, the *Tubshi Bashi* asked us what we wanted, and opened the gate. The courtyard was crowded with officers in full battle costume. This was unusual. It was a bad sign and we became frightened.

'At once we were surrounded by soldiers and taken to the *Kushbegi*. The *Kushbegi* was sitting in a large room, and next to him the *Kazi Kalan*. As we entered the room, the *Kazi Kalan* shouted at us angrily:

' "What have you done? What have you done?"

'But we answered just as angrily:

' "What have *you* done? What have *you* done?"

'Outside the windows the mob screamed and yelled because the priests had incited them and they asked for our heads. Then a horde of *Mullahs* came running across the courtyard with wild shouts. The *Kushbegi* had us locked in a room nearby, and two sentries were guarding the door. We were hardly in that room when the *Mullahs* stormed into the big room where the *Kushbegi* was sitting; they bared their heads and shouted:

G

' "The day of God has come, the tempter is amongst us, we shall defend Islam by the sword." And they asked the *Kushbegi* were we were hiding. I saw and heard it all through a crack in the door. The soldier who guarded the door whispered to me : "It looks bad for you, very bad, very bad."

'Yussouf Zade lay down on the floor and stuffed his ears with his thumbs. Polat Khodjayev whispered to me : "Hadji, Hadji, tell us what's happening outside?" But I said : "It doesn't help now to stuff one's ears. When they come we shall shoot and kill ourselves with the last bullet." Meanwhile more and more people had gathered in the *Kushbegi*'s room.

'Then the guard who had spoken to me through the crack in the door, said to one of the *Mullahs* :

' "We are guarding three great criminals in that room, three of the leaders." Thus the *Mullahs* found out where we were hidden, and they all ran to the door and roared :

' "Deliver us those three. We shall eat their flesh and drink their blood."

'And they fought with the guards who defended the door. And my two comrades were lying on the floor, and they cried : "Hadji, Hadji, we shall die by the knives of our enemies." For they had gone quite crazy with fear.

'Then it became calm outside and I heard the *Kushbegi* say :

' "Be patient, please. The mighty Emir will presently give orders that the three be slaughtered on the Registan."

'Finally, the door was opened and several high officers of the Emir's guard came into our room. They stared at us like mad wolves and asked each one of us : "Who art thou and what is thy name and what didst thou come for?"

' "My name is Yussouf Zade, my father came from Ush, my mother from Ferganah. I am a Russian citizen."

'The second said : "My name is Polat Khodjayev, my mother came from Ush, my father from Ferganah. I am a Russian citizen."

'Then my turn came : "My name is Hadji Mir Baba Mukhsin Zade. I am a merchant in Kara-Kul furs, and a citizen of Bokhara."

'Then they drew up a statement, and after a while the *Kushbegi* came in and said :

' "The mighty Emir has just issued the order that Hadji Mir Baba be slaughtered on the Registan." '

[Hadji Mir Baba never said 'executed'; he always used the expression 'slaughtered'. The most common form of execution in Bokhara was indeed to slaughter the delinquent like a chicken by pushing the knife sideways into his neck and cutting his throat by a horizontal twist.]

'. . . My comrades cried : "Hadji, Hadji, why did you not say that you were a Russian citizen?" I, however, shouted "Long live freedom !" Then they led me out.

'In the courtyard a great crowd was assembled, and they shouted :

' "This is Hadji Mir Baba, the enemy of religion, the author of bad books, let us kill him !" And all across the courtyard they hit and kicked me. And I spat out many of my teeth and much blood.

'At the gate the guard took off my *khalat* and my clothes— they only left me my shirt. Now at that time it was law in Bokhara that the executioner should tie your hands before he slaughtered you. Therefore, I searched with my eyes for a man with a cord in his hands, for that one would be the executioner. But I saw nobody with a cord.

'Then I told myself : "Very well, the man with the cord is to the second gate and there they will surely tie your hands." But I got to the second gate and my hands were still free.

'Then I told myself : "Very well, the man with the cord is certainly waiting on the Registan." They led me to the Registan and there was a great crowd, but there was no man with a cord. Instead, they brought a bucket filled with water in which several heavy sticks were soaking.

'A great joy scorched my heart and I thought :

' "Very well, very well, if it is only the sticks, you may perhaps survive them."

'They lifted my shirt and twisted the ends of it round my neck and tied them in a knot. Two men were holding me by my feet and two by my hands. For at that time I was as tall and strong as a camel. And two others each took a stick out of the bucket and began to beat me.

'But I tensed the muscles of my back and held my breath before each stroke, for I had learnt that only in this way could you protect your spinal column from breaking. The strokes were like thunder, and I would have liked to shout because it helps if you shout down the pain, but because I had to watch my breathing I could only moan. I was just on the point of giving up by relaxing the muscles of my back because the strokes were breaking my will, when I saw one of the officers of the Emir who stood in front of the soldiers and winked at me with his eyes. And I recognised him as a member of our secret organisation. And when it was all over, and I collapsed, and the *Mullahs* came running to tear me to pieces, the soldiers of that officer lifted me up and carried me back into the citadel. They threw me into a room which was in darkness; I only noticed by the smell that there were many other prisoners in the room. But they were all common criminals, robbers and murderers, or people accused of such crimes.

'As I lay in the darkness on the floor of that room and gradually resumed my normal way of breathing—for one ought not to do that suddenly—they all crowded round me and asked : "What have you done?" But I was afraid to tell them the truth for they were ignorant and fanatical people, so I answered : "Give me time to recover, then we shall talk." But they were too impatient to wait. And so I asked them :

' "Have you heard that the mighty Emir has promised to set you all free?" [The manifesto of April 1917 had promised a general amnesty.]

' "Yes, yes," they cried.

' "Well, you are ignorant people who cannot read, so the Emir has written his answer to you on my back. There will be no freedom, and you will all die in this prison."

'When I had spoken these words, many began to weep and they told each other : "False is our Emir and false our religion."

'And they said : "He has done this to save us. We know him, he is Hadji Mir Baba, a good man, a rich merchant. Not for his sake but for ours did he receive the sticks."

'And they prepared green *chai*, and they said : "Djafur, give him of your medicine."

'And one who was called Djafur the Smuggler, took from a tin-box a piece of opium as large as my little finger. I said : "If

I eat this piece I shall die of it." But they shouted : "No, no, go on, eat it."

'When I had eaten it and had drunk some hot water, I was overcome by the sweetest feeling that I had ever known. I stretched out on the floor and fell asleep. Each man gave me a piece of his dirty clothes and covered me with it.

'When I woke up it was as dark as when I had fallen asleep. Two men were massaging the palms of my hands and the soles of my feet to draw the blood away from my back. Then these men whom I had thought to be robbers each told his story in turn. They were very interesting stories and I shall now tell them to you. . . .'

It was at this point that Hadji Mir Baba's story branched out. Some of the prisoners' tales sounded indeed like something straight out of the Arabian Nights. I listened to them entranced, while we were both squatting face to face on the mat of my bare room under the light of one naked, fly-soiled electric bulb hanging from the ceiling. But as these memoirs deal with *Red Days* and not with *Arabian Nights*, I must call a halt, and bring Hadji Mir Baba's story summarily to its happy end. After several months in prison he was released as a result of representations from the Russian Provisional Government, spent some time in hospital, and then travelled to Moscow, where he arrived just in time for the October Revolution which brought the Bolsheviks into power. He joined the Party and visited Lenin in Petersburg. Admitted to Lenin's presence, Hadji Mir Baba bared his back and said: 'This is my letter of recommendation.' He returned to Bokhara after the flight of the Emir in 1920, fought with the Red Army against the *Basmachi*, and was elected to the Central Committee. At the time of my visit to Bokhara, he drew a Party pension and no longer exercised any political function —allegedly because he was too old, though he was only in his sixties. Still, as a curator of the little museum he could spend his time browsing through the surviving documents from the archives of the Emirate. I don't know what has happened to Hadji Mir Baba since, and I prefer not to know.

XIV. Instruments of Fate

AFTER a few days in Tashkent, the colourless administrative capital of the Central Asiatic republics, and a week on a State Farm in Kazakystan, my itinerary was completed, and I returned to Moscow. But the pull of my organisation, or my standing with it, was not sufficiently strong to procure me a room by myself where I could write my book; so I went back to Kharkov and the hospitable Weissbergs. I stayed for a fortnight with Alex and Eva, then managed to get a room in Kharkov's Intourist Hotel, where I spent the late winter and spring of 1933, writing *Red Days*.

In the meantime, Hitler was appointed Prime Minister, and a month later the Nazis staged their Saint Bartholomew's Night against our comrades in Germany. I learnt of that event one evening at the Weissbergs' flat—Alex has described the scene in his *Conspiracy of Silence*. We were playing a peaceful poker game for kopeks—Alex, myself, and Professor Shubnikov, head of the Institute's laboratory for low-temperature research. Shubnikov was an endearing elderly Professor, very absent-minded and something of an eccentric. While one of us was dealing, he remarked dreamily, apropos of nothing :

'. . . And so they have burnt down the Reichstag. I wonder now what Hitler did that for?'

'*What?*' we shouted.

'Don't you know? The Nazis have burnt down your Parliament. It was on the wireless.'

Alex and I understood at once what this signified. During the first month of Hitler's premiership in a coalition government, the Nazis had still maintained the appearances of legality and democratic procedure. Now the moment had come for them to drop all pretence : the terror had started, and Germany had become a totalitarian state. It was a development that we had foreseen for a long time; but as always in such cases, the fulfilment of our own gloomy prophecies came as a shocking surprise. I don't remember what I did or said; Alex says in his book that I walked out of the room to pack my bag and go straight back to Berlin, and that he persuaded me to wait for more detailed news. Apparently I still believed that the Party would fight back on the famous barricades which had loomed so large in our orations and revolutionary songs. The news later on that evening destroyed what illusions we still had left. There were no barricades. The Party, which at the last elections had still polled five million votes, surrendered without fighting. Hitler's victory was complete and final.

During that poker game, the pattern of my life had been changed without my being aware of it. I had ceased to be a traveller and had become a political refugee—which I would remain for the next thirteen years.

It is a curious fact that the really important events which alter the whole course of one's destiny usually appear in an insidiously trivial guise. The first symptoms of cancer are much less dramatic than a bruised knee; every psychiatrist knows that the real conflicts of the patient are hidden behind those ideas and dreams which he dismisses as unimportant. If you keep a diary and re-read the entries of several years ago, you will always be surprised to find that the events that mattered most at the time are strangely underemphasised and only mentioned casually. Real tragedy rarely makes good drama. The language of destiny is smooth and full of trivial understatements—like dear old Shubnikov's : 'I wonder now what Hitler did that for?'

For a long time I was not conscious of having lost my privileged status as a leisurely traveller, and having become one of the grey horde of Europe's political exiles. It was a transformation under anaesthesia, so to speak. For the moment it made no apparent difference to my life; I continued to write *Red Days*, and my main worry was neither the future of Europe nor my own, but the problem how to go on working in an unheated room in the grim Ukrainian winter. For, as one of the minor disasters in that disastrous year of famine and general dislocation, the electricity supply of the Ukrainian capital had broken down—and the central heating in the Hotel Regina was operated by electric pumps. In the streets, the temperature often sank to fifty and sixty degrees below freezing point. When one tried to smoke in the open air the moisture froze in the cigarette which became hard as a stick and gave one the sensation of chewing nicotined ice-cream. Inside my room, the water was permanently frozen in the tap, and the temperature rarely rose over freezing point. At first I tried to work in bed, but found this too uncomfortable; so I hammered away at the typewriter, wearing mittens, and a kind of quilt-jacket padded with cotton-wool, called a *vatinka*.

The electricity breakdown lasted all through the winter. The Ukrainian capital lived in a permanent blackout, paralysed by hunger, darkness and frost. The only public conveyances, the electric tram-cars—dreadfully overcrowded even in normal times—now only ran during two hours a day, to get the workers to the factories and back. The people in the offices worked by the light of paraffin lamps, or oil wicks when the paraffin ran out, huddled in their quilts, surrounded by little clouds of condensed breath, like saints in heaven. After eight o'clock in the evening the streets lay deserted like an arctic settlement in the polar night.

One day the chambermaid in our privileged Intourist hotel fainted from hunger, and afterwards confessed that she had eaten nothing for three days because, as she had only just arrived from the country, the Co-operative had withheld her three-day ration of 1,800 grammes (four pounds) of black bread. The bread ration was at the time 800 grammes per day for industrial workers, 600 grammes for other manual workers, 400 grammes for office employees (one pound=450 grammes); and bread, plus a few tea-leaves and an occasional cabbage or salted herring, was the only food to be had on the ration. In the country the people were dying of hunger; in the towns, they vegetated on the minimum survival level. Life seemed to have come to a standstill, the while machinery on the verge of collapse.

Today, the catastrophe of 1932–33 is more or less officially admitted by the Soviet Government, but at the time no allusion to the real condition of the country was permitted to appear in the Soviet Press. The Government was determined to keep the people in the dark regarding its own situation. This apparently impossible task could only be undertaken in a country where all information was centralised at the top of the pyramid, and all communications were a Government monopoly. The Soviet Press is, in fact, controlled to a degree which the Nazis were never able to achieve. Every town in the Union, Moscow included, has two morning papers : a Government organ and a Party organ. All Government papers throughout the country print every morning one uniform leader : the leader of the Moscow *Isvestia*, distributed to them by telegraph and radio. Similarly, all Party papers throughout the country appear with the *Pravda* editorial. All foreign news and home news are distributed by one single agency, TASS. Local events are covered entirely by official hand-outs. The effect of this total news-centralisation in a country with vast distances is that the people are kept in ignorance not only of foreign events, but also of everything outside the range of their immediate neighbourhood.

Thus every morning I learned from my Kharkov paper about plan figures that had been reached and surpassed, about competitions between enthusiastic factory shock-brigades, about awards of the Red Banner, new giant factories in the Urals, and so on; the photographs were either of young people, always laughing and always carrying a banner in their hands, or of some picturesque elder in Uzbekistan, always smiling and always occupied with learning the alphabet. Not one word about the local famine, the typhus epidemic, the dying out of entire villages; even the fact that there was no electricity in Kharkov was never mentioned in the Kharkov newspaper. It gave one a feeling of dreamlike unreality; the paper seemed to talk about some different country which had no point of contact with the daily life that we led. The same was true of the radio. The consequence of all this was that people in Moscow had no idea of what went on in Kharkov, and even less of what went on in Tashkent, or Archangel, or Vladivostok—twelve days' train journey away in a country where travelling accommodation was reserved for government officials; and these travellers were not of a talkative nature.

The enormous land was covered by a blanket of silence, and nobody outside the small circle of initiates was in a position to form a comprehensive picture of the situation.

In other words, news in Russia could only travel up and down the sides of the pyramid, along the lines converging in the top, but could not be exchanged horizontally, as it were. This twin policy of centralisation—plus-atomisation is a basic feature of the Soviet régime. To understand its full significance, one would have to imagine a world in which travelling is only possible by air, and only due North or due South. Thus to get from London to Paris, one would have to fly to the North Pole along the meridian of London, and then descend due South along the meridian of Paris. Precisely this was happening in the Soviet Union when, say, a metal works in Baku wanted to buy machine oil from a local refinery. The transaction could not be concluded locally; the request had to travel up to the Commissariat of Heavy Industries in Moscow, and then come down again. Similarly, a Ukrainian newspaper could not keep a local reporter in its local area. All news had to be reported to the top—to *Pravda, Isvestia* or TASS—and, in duly processed form, sent down again to the regional centre.

I finished *Red Days* some time in April. I had it typed out, top and five copies, and sent the various copies to the various State publishing firms in Moscow, Kharkov, Tiflis and Erivan, who had signed agreements for the Russian, German, Ukrainian, Georgian and Armenian editions of the book. I have explained in *The God that Failed* that these agreements, and the considerable advance payments that went with them, were not the result of my literary reputation—which was nonexistent since I had published no books at that time—but a direct effect of the strong Comintern letter that I carried. When I produced it, in Kharkov or in Erivan, the Director of the State Publishing Trust in question could not refuse signing a contract for the contemplated book, which was described as an important contribution to our fight on the Propaganda Front, without risking to be accused of sabotage. It was in this indirect manner that the Comintern financed my sojourn and travels in Soviet Russia, and similar methods were employed to oblige visiting authors from abroad who were not members of the Party. They were, of course, delighted at the news that the Uzbeks, Tadziks and Eskimos were all eager to read their books, and they would have been very indignant at the suggestion that the advance payments from the various State publishing firms amounted to bribes. This is another miracle which State control over publishing can achieve.

In spite of my numerous contracts, however, only one edition of *Red Days* did, in fact, appear. This was the Kharkov edition in German, intended for the German-speaking national minorities in the Ukraine. It is a thin, paper-bound volume, so thoroughly expurgated that less than half of the original manuscript was allowed to stand. It was published in 1934, after I had left the Soviet Union. I was never sent a presentation copy, and did not know for certain whether the book had been published or not until some thirteen years later —when an unknown American reader sent me a copy that he had picked up by chance on a tourist trip to the Soviet Union.

The Russian edition of the book which, from the point of view of a writer's prestige was the only one that really counted, never saw the daylight. Three months after I had delivered the manuscript I was informed by one of the higher bureaucrats in the Moscow Trust that it had been rejected because it was written in 'a too frivolous and lighthearted style'. This was, of course, a bitter disappointment; but at least I had not been accused of any political deviation, and my Party record remained untarnished.

At about the time when this decision was communicated to me, Paul Dietrich, my friend and immediate superior in the German section of the Comintern, informed me that the Party had decided against my staying in Russia. The leaders and intellectuals of the German C.P. who had managed to escape from the Nazi terror were all gathering in Paris which was becoming the centre of the anti-Fascist propaganda campaign, and I was instructed to join them.

Though in Russia it would have been easy to find a job, whereas in Paris I would have to start from scratch, I received the news with immense relief. I was a Communist, but I found life in Russia terribly depressing. Only now, with the prospect of departure before me, did I admit to myself how depressing it had been. The drab streets, the unrelieved shabbiness and poverty, the grim pomposity of everything said and written, the all-pervading atmosphere of a reformatory school. The feeling of being cut off from the rest of the world. The boredom of newspapers which contained nothing critical or controversial, no crime, no sensation, no gossip, sex, scandal, human interest. The constant exhortations, the stereotyped uniformity of all and everything, the eternal portrait of Big Brother following you everywhere with his eyes. The overwhelming bleakness of an industrialised Neanderthal.

. . . And yet I remained a convinced Communist. I had learned that facts had to be appreciated not on their face value, but in a dynamic way. Living standards were low, but under the Czarist régime they had been even lower. The working classes in the capitalist countries were better off than in the Soviet Union, but that was a static comparison, for here the level was steadily rising, there steadily falling. At the end of the second Five Year Plan the two levels would be equalised; until that time all comparisons were misleading, and bad for the Soviet People's morale. Accordingly, I not only accepted the famine as inevitable, but also the necessity of the ban on foreign travel, foreign newspapers and books, and the dissemination of a grotesquely distorted picture of life in the capitalist world. At first I was shocked when after a lecture I was asked questions like these: 'When you left the bourgeois Press was your ration card withdrawn and were you kicked out at once from your room?' 'What is the average number per day of French working-class families starving to death (a) in rural areas, (b) in the towns?' 'By what means have our comrades in the West succeeded in temporarily staving off the war of intervention which the Monopoly-Capitalists are preparing with the aid of the Social-Fascist traitors to the working class?' The questions were always painstakingly formulated in neo-Russian Djugashwilese. After a while I found them quite natural. There was always a small element of truth in them—this had, of course, been exaggerated and simplified according to the accepted techniques of propaganda; but propaganda was indispensable for the survival of the Soviet Union, surrounded by a hostile world.

The necessary propaganda-lie; the necessary intimidation of the masses to preserve them from error; the necessary liquidation of opposition groups and hostile social classes; the necessary sacrifice of a whole generation in the interest of the next—it may all sound revolting, and yet it was quite easy to accept while one was rolling along the single track of faith. It had all happened before, in the history of the medieval churches, in Byzantium, in the hothouses of mystic sects; but the mental universe of the addict is difficult to understand for the outsider ...' (The God that Failed.)

There was another consideration that helped me, and every other Communist who visited Russia, to get over the shock. It was our conviction that conditions in Russia were what they were not because of any fault in our system, but because of the backwardness of the Russian people. In Germany, in Austria or France, the Revolution would take an entirely different form. There was a saying among German Communists in Russia that could only be pronounced in a whisper : *'Wir werden es besser machen'*—'we shall know better'. In other words, every Communist who had lived in the Soviet Union for some length of time, returned to his country as a Titoist at heart.

It was this conviction that 'we shall know better' that kept my faith alive. It was no longer the naïve faith of a year before, when I had got into the train in Berlin expecting that it would take me straight to Utopia. It had become a rather wistful, rather esoteric faith, but all the more elastic. I no longer believed in Communism because of the Russian example, but in spite of it. And a faith that is held 'in spite of' is always more resilient and less open to disillusion than one that is based on a 'because'.

My last few weeks in Russia I spent in Moscow. I met a number of men in the higher Comintern and Soviet hierarchy, among them Mikhael Kolzov, Karl Radek and Nicolai Bukharin, all of whom have since met with their fate. Bukharin and Radek both made a deep impression on me, but I only met each of them once and in rather formal circumstances, so that I cannot trust my memory to describe them. Besides, I have incorporated certain characteristic features of both Radek and Bukharin into the 'Rubashov' of *Darkness at*

Noon, and after all these years I am quite incapable of disentangling the features of the original models from the composite imaginary figure.

They were all tired men. The higher you got in the hierarchy, the more tired they were. I have nowhere seen such exhausted men as among the higher strata of Soviet politicians, among the Old Bolshevik guard. It was not only the effect of overwork, nervous strain and apprehension. It was the past that was telling on them, the years of conspiracy, prison and exile; the years of the famine and the Civil War; and sticking to the rules of a game that demanded that at every moment a man's whole life should be at stake. They were indeed 'dead men on furlough', as Lenin had called them. Nothing could frighten them any more, nothing surprise them. They had given all they had. History had squeezed them out to the last drop, had burnt them out to the last spiritual calorie; yet they were still glowing in cold devotion, like phosphorescent corpses.

In the generation that followed them, the generation of the Gletkins, a different type prevailed. Its mentality is wonderfully summed up in a statement by a young Soviet official, quoted by J. L. Bruckberger :[1]

'We are believers. Not as you are. We do not believe either in God or in men. We manufacture gods and we transform men. We believe in Order. We will create a universe in our image, without weaknesses, a universe in which man, rid of the old rags of Christianity, will attain his cosmic grandeur, in the supreme culmination of the species. We are not fighting for a régime, or for power, or for riches. We are the instruments of Fate.'

Yet it was neither the 'dead men on furlough' of the Old Guard, nor the Gletkins of the next generation, who made the most lasting impression on me. At the time of my visit, the Soviet Empire occupied one-sixth of the inhabited earth; at present it occupies, directly or indirectly, one-third. It would have been impossible to hold such an immense realm together by terror alone. The apathy and passive acquiescence of the ruled, their self-deceiving hopes and propaganda-fed illusions,

[1] *One Sky to Share*, New York, 1952.

facilitated the task of the rulers, but could never have given sufficient coherence to that vast structure. The bureaucracy of Party and State, which represented roughly one-third of the total population, had, of course, a vested interested in defending the system; but the majority of this bureaucracy, on the lower grades of the pyramid, lived just as wretchedly and insecurely as those whom they ruled. There existed another human element which prevented the colossal machinery from breaking down into its component parts, which kept the creaking transmissions and the dry bearings somehow going. It was a certain category of men that I find difficult to define though I have a vivid impression of the various individuals who belonged to it. I can perhaps best describe them by quoting a Talmudic legend which I recently read in a novel (Manes Sperber's *To Dusty Death*). It is called 'the legend of the thirty-six just men' :

'When I was a child, our Rabbis taught me that if the thirty-six men did not exist, mankind couldn't last a day, it would drown in its own wrongs. The thirty-six are not marked out by any rank or office. They cannot be recognised, they never yield their secret, perhaps they are not even aware of it themselves; and yet it is they who, in every successive generation justify our existence and who every day save the world anew.'

I have met them on my travels in every part of the Soviet Union. Hadji Mir Baba was one of them. Colonel Anvar Umorzakov was another. Oragvilidze in Tiflis; the Kultprop of the District of Merv; little Werner in Baku; the Secretary of the Party Committee in the Kharkov Institute for Physics; a young Komsomol girl in Moscow; an engineer in the Gorky Motor Car Factory; the woman doctor in Permetyab; a G.P.U. guard in a village in Kazakystan; and so on. I could continue my list up to an approximate number of one hundred individuals whom I met in the course of one year of travels. So there must exist thousands, or even tens of thousands of them.

What did these individuals have in common? They were 'not marked out by rank or office'. They had the most varied occupations. They were not fanatical supporters of the régime. They were the people who, when I was lost and despairing, restored my faith in the Soviet Union. They created around themselves little islands of order and dignity in an ocean of chaos and absurdity. In whatever field they worked, their influence communicated itself to their surroundings. It is the ensemble of these human islands, dŏtted over the Soviet realm, which maintains its coherent structure and prevents it from disintegrating.

These men, whether Communists or not, are 'Soviet Patriots' in the sense in which that word was first used in the French Revolution. They are neither heroes nor saints, and their civic virtues all go against the grain of the régime they serve. They are motivated by a grave sense of responsibility in a country where everybody fears and evades responsibility; they exercise initiative and independent judgment where blind obedience is the norm; they are loyal and devoted to their fellow-beings in a world where loyalty is only expected towards one's superiors and devotion only towards the State. They have personal honour and an unconscious dignity of comportment, where these words are objects of ridicule.

Though there are thousands of them, they are a small minority, and always the first victims of every new purge. Yet they do not die out. Those whom I met in Russia were mostly in their early thirties, and belonged to the post-revolutionary generation. Nowadays I again meet with the same type among the post-war Russian emigrés, who belong to an even later generation. These upright, devoted, energetic and fearless men were and are the backbone of a régime that denies all the values for which they stand. As a Communist, I took their existence for granted, for I believed that they were the product of revolutionary education, that 'new type of man' whose coming Marx had predicted. Today I realise that their existence is very nearly a miracle, that they became what they are not because, but in spite of that education—a triumph of the indestructible human substance over a de-humanising environment.

For the pressure of that environment seems almost irresistible—slow and steady like soil erosion, or the action of the tides. It results in that gradual thwarting of the mind which I have tried to describe, and is accompanied by an even more fatal corrosion of the spirit. It cuts man off from his meta-physical roots, from religious experience, from the 'oceanic feeling' in all its forms. Cosmic awareness is replaced by social vigilance, perception of the absolute by brain-acrobatics. The result is a gradual dehydration of the soul, a spiritual dearth more frightening than the famine. In the United States where, for different reasons, a similar flight from the metaphysical, from the tragic facts of existence is taking place, the morti-cians endeavour to transform the dead, with lipstick and rouge, into horizontal members of a perennial cocktail party. In Soviet Russia the method is simpler : there are no funeral rites, death is stripped of its tragic grandeur and mystic im-plications, reduced to a mere statistical event. At a Writers' Congress in Moscow, after listening to countless speeches promising universal happiness in a brave new world, André Malraux asked suddenly : 'And what about the child run over by a tram-car?' There was a pained silence; then somebody said, amidst general approbation :

'In a perfect, planned socialist transport system there will be no accidents.'

I left Russia in the late summer 1933.

A few weeks before my departure, I was sitting on the ter-race of the Café Metropole in Moscow, in a mood of suicidal depression. Inside the café the orchestra was playing a popu-lar song of the period; its refrain, in German, ran something like this :

> ... If you love me, you must steal for me,
> And tell me fairy tales of a happy land. ...

I had had three vodkas, and the last words of the song, to-gether with the sentimental tune and my feeling of misery, had a hypnotic effect. They made me escape into a long day-dream, a 'fairy tale of a happy land' as the sloppy refrain had it, and the day-dream led me to an idea for a play. The idea was that a pair of scouts from an alien planet land on earth in search of colonising space for their overcrowded world. They explain that only happy planets have a cosmic right to exist, and give mankind a last chance to organise its happiness within three days—or else it will gently be put out of its miseries, and the earth turned to better use. Faced with this ultimatum, the government resigns, the opposition washes its hands of the issue, and the dilettants take at last over, appointing a crazy poet called Glowworm to be Dictator of Happiness. And lo, it works, to everybody's surprise : money is abolished, authority if abolished, all taboos are smashed, all curtains raised. Alas, at the end of the three days it transpires that the scouts are imposters; and as there is no longer any need to be happy, the old order is restored and everybody goes back to his former miseries.

I began to write the play then and there, on the paper-napkins of the Café Metropole. It was, of course, an unforgivable heresy : 'escapsim' is almost the deadliest sin for a Communist, and I felt rather like a schoolboy drawing obscene pictures on the blackboard all set for a solemn lesson in History. I finished the play in three weeks, the last act on the train that took me out of Russia. I called it *Bar du Soleil*. It was a play without literary pretensions, a flight from the pressure of reality, and I described it accordingly as 'An Escapade in Four Acts'. It was to have a long and undistinguished stage career.

My last halt in the Soviet Union was, as the first had been, the Weissbergs' flat in Kharkov, where I again stayed for a week or two. We continued to play poker with dear old Professor Shubnikov. Five years later Professor Shubnikov was to testify before the G.P.U. as follows :

'Weissberg came to the Institute from Germany in 1931, where he had been recruited by the Gestapo. His task was to organise sabotage and espionage. He tried to recruit me for his organisation, but as I had already been in the service of a German espionage organisation since 1924, I refused. From that time on we worked parallel but without contact with each other.'[1]

I met most of the leading members of the Institute in Alex's flat : the Head of the Institute, Professor Leipunsky, in charge

[1] A. Weissberg, *Conspiracy of Silence*, London and New York, 1952.

of the Department for Nuclear Fission; Lev Davidovich Landau, the infant prodigy of Russian physics who, together with Leipunsky, played an important part in the development of the Russian atomic bomb; the head of the laboratory for Crystallography, old Professor Obremov; and a British physicist, Martin Ruhemann, whom Alex had brought to Kharkov. Every member of that illustrious crowd of scientists, who used to come to the flat after dinner to play cards or relax over a cup of tea, was to testify five years later that Alex was a Gestapo spy who tried to induce them to sabotage and assassination. They were neither cowards nor evil men; they had to testify as they were ordered. At a later stage of the Purge, they were all arrested in their turn and signed confessions accusing each other and themselves of the same fantastic crimes. At the end of the Purge in 1939, some of them, including Landau, Leipunsky and Shubnikov, were released and allowed to return to their work. Ruhemann was deported to England, and is still a member of the Communist Party. The end of Alex' and Eva's story I shall tell later.

To obtain my exit permit proved almost as difficult as it had been to obtain my visa. When it arrived, the relief was even greater. Alex saw me to the train, chatty, round-faced and jovial as always. His parting words were, as the train started moving:

'Whatever happens, Arthur, hold the banner of the Soviet Union high.'

Part Three

EXILE

1933–36

> I apologise
> For boasting, but once you know my
>   qualities
> I can drop back into a quite brilliant
> Humility. . . .

CHRISTOPHER FRY

XV. Poetic Interlude

THE first lap of my journey into exile took me in a third-class compartment through Poland and Czechoslovakia to Vienna. It lasted nearly three days, most of which I spent in typing out *Bar du Soleil*, blissfully happy to be back in Europe. The moment we passed the frontier a magic change of atmosphere had taken place. The station buffets were piled with foodstuffs I had not seen for a year—sandwiches with cheese, eggs, sausages and ham; coffee and buns and pastry. There were foreign newspapers, books and magazines on the stalls; the platforms and ticket-windows were no longer battlefields; and, what struck me most, the people in the train all had different personalities instead of being molecules in a grey, amorphous mass. They were mysteriously alive, they were individuals, and some of them, oh wonder, even had dogs. Nobody in Russia kept a dog—but I only noticed that now.

I felt excited like a schoolboy who has escaped from an austere college to a matinée in a circus, and this mood was to prevail for several weeks. It was indeed a childish mood, for from a more adult point of view my prospects were grim. My flat in Berlin and all my possessions had, of course, been confiscated by the National-Socialist régime. My career was finished, too : I was a German journalist proscribed in Germany. The savings from my years of prosperity I had given to my parents before I had left for Russia. The roubles that I had earned there could not be converted into foreign currency. I was now nearly twenty-seven, without a job, without a country, and completely destitute for the second time in my life. The first time this had happened to me was at twenty, when I had run away from home and had nearly starved in Palestine. That had been seven years earlier. Strangely enough, exactly seven years later I was to find myself ship-wrecked for yet a third time—in 1940, when Europe foundered and all I could save was a toothbrush and a diary.

To lose one's home, one's hopes and possessions every seven years seems a rather repetitive and humourless type of be-haviour. Insurance companies call a person with that kind of pattern 'accident prone' and regard him, with perfect justi-fication, as a bore and a nuisance. The mitigating factors in my case are that when Hitler took power in 1933, and when he conquered Europe seven years later, the majority of Euro-peans became accident prone. Anglo-Saxon readers (and critics) often miss this obvious point and, rather flatteringly, regard the misadventures of the chronicler as of his own mak-ing, an emanation of his perverse mind. In fact, I was luckier than any of the people who have played a part in this book so far, or who will in pages to come; with few exceptions, they are either dead or have vanished in the dense fogs of the East.

Though I had known penury before, I started on my new career as a political refugee in a kind of holiday mood and without feeling sorry for myself. I do not mean that I am a stranger to the comforts of self-pity. Minor upsets and tribu-lations will release floods of it; but in the so-called major crises of life I have always found a redeeming element of the gro-tesque. There is terror and tragedy, but also an absurd incongruity in the ravages of a flood, when saucepans float down the stream next to a hairbrush and a dead hen, and children have the time of their lives being rescued in rowing boats. Though subject to frequent fits of depression, real dis-asters usually fill me with a wild elation. And though I have always jealously clung to my possessions, and their partial damage or loss (a stolen shirt or a stain on the furniture) make me angry and sad, the total loss of all I had, on each of the three occasions when it occurred, aroused a feeling of liberation, the excitement of a fresh start. It is, I suppose, part of the apocalyptic temperament, of the all-or-nothing type of mentality—a temperament that lacks fortitude in minor crises but thrives on catastrophes.

When I arrived in Vienna, I had not even enough money

left to take a taxi. I left my luggage at the station and proceeded by train to the flat of Dr. Hahn, my old friend of the duelling fraternity 'Unitas'. I had wired him from Moscow, but the wire had never arrived. It was a lovely Viennese late-summer day, but I was still wearing my knee-boots and breeches—my only good suit, was in my suitcase, as I had not wanted to sleep in it for three nights in a railway carriage. I ran into Hahn as I was getting off the Number Eleven tram a few yards from the house where he lived. He found my unexpected arrival in such a costume a capital joke, and asked me whether I had come straight from the icy steppes of the Polar Circle. 'No, from Samarkand,' I said earnestly. 'What a liar you are,' said Hahn. 'The Eleven doesn't go to Samarkand. It's the Seventeen.'

I spent three or four days in Hahn's flat, celebrating a series of sentimental reunions with old friends and girl-friends. It was now quite inconceivable to me that I had ever planned to abandon Europe. But though I had only been away for a year, it was also painfully evident that I was returning to a changed continent. The malignant tumour that Germany had become, was eating into Europe's living tissue, destroying its human substance. The fall of Austria lay still five years ahead in the future, and was accordingly unimaginable; but parliamentary rule and the freedom of the Press had already been strangled by Dollfuss, the bigoted dwarf-dictator. The Social Democratic Party, which in Austria had been more powerful, enlightened, and successful in creative achievement than anywhere else in Europe, was now pursuing the same policy of retreat and piecemeal capitulation which in Germany had led to its ruin. A few months later, in February 1934, the rank and file of the Austrian *Schutzbund* (the Socialists' paramilitary organisation) was to rise, leaderless, in revolt. Their bloody defeat marked the end of a century of socialist progress in Central Europe.

Everywhere in Vienna I felt the same uncertainty and nervous tension, the same foreboding of doom that had haunted me during the last pre-Hitler summer in Berlin. I had become as sensitive to this kind of atmosphere as a rheumatic to approaching changes of the weather. In later years I was to have ample opportunities to exercise this Cassandra-gift, first in

Spain, then in France. It rests mostly on semi-conscious impressions and observations of insignificant detail. The old waiters in the cafés still addressed their old clients as 'Herr Doktor', but the warm familiarity had gone; there was an undefinable estrangement and aloofness, as if everybody were holding something back. The air was full of afterthoughts, of interrogation marks suspended in the cigarette smoke. In the trams, the passengers seemed to be aware of the brand of newspaper their neighbour was reading, of the badge he was wearing. My discomfort became more acute as I strolled into the *aula*, the great entrance hall of the University. Each pillar in the colonnade held its memory; yet in this place, for me the most familiar in Vienna, I also felt the most acutely the change to hostility and estrangement. The dominant types in the *aula* were now burly louts in leather shorts and white knitted knee-stockings. With stupid and provocative stares, they trampled over the mosaic pavement of the *alma mater* in their ridiculous mountaineering attire, displaying hairy legs. White stockings and leather shorts were the unofficial uniform of the Austrian Nazis. They were symbolical of the Austrian brand of Fascism : a fanatical, folksy provincialism. Desolately I searched for the girls—the lovely, lively, sophisticated, flirtatious girl-students of Vienna. They, too, had been either ousted by, or transformed into, a new type—the dowdy, blowsy, sweaty, pigtailed Gretchen. Pigtails, *pigtails* at Siegmund Freud's University! They were intended as a political badge, the counterpart of the bare knees of the young men.

I was told that the traditional Saturday brawls, the spice of my University days, had ceased. Under the colonnades, Nazis, Socialists, Liberals and Zionists exchanged glances of hatred, but no blows. Perhaps because each party felt that this time a fight would not end with black eyes and bloody noses, but with corpses in the *aula*. It did, a few years later.

I felt that Vienna was doomed. But at that time I still believed that the Communist revolution would eventually resurrect it.

A trivial little incident has remained in my memory through all these years. I was sitting with my old friend Bruno Heilig in the Café Herrenhof, the old and famous haunt of Vienna's *littérateurs*. Heilig had been on the Berlin staff of the Ullsteins together with me, and had escaped from the Nazis in the nick of time. Now he was editor of the Austrian Zionist paper *Die Stimme*. He was a man in his thirties, with greying hair and an open, energetic face. We were discussing some harmless non-political subject, when Heilig interrupted me with an amused smile : 'Why do you talk in a whisper?' he asked. 'Do I?' I said, 'I thought I was talking normally.' 'In Berlin you used to yell, and now you whisper,' he said. 'That is all I want to know about Russia.'

Five years later the Nazis caught up with Heilig in Vienna, and sent him to Dachau. He survived and wrote a moving book about his imprisonment (*Men Crucified*, London, 1941).

Before continuing my journey to Paris, I wanted to visit my parents in Budapest. With my remaining roubles I had bought in Moscow a ring with a diminutive diamond stone, which was now my only capital. I sold it in Vienna for a sum which just paid for my return ticket to Budapest, and a few days' living. That was all I needed for the moment, as my railway ticket from Moscow to Paris via Vienna was still valid.

Just before leaving Vienna, however, I learnt that my mother was not in Budapest; she was staying for the summer holidays with my cousin Margit in a village in Slovakia called Kàlna, where Margit's husband, Dr. Miklós, was the village doctor. It was only a short detour on the way to Budapest, so I went to join my cousins in Kàlna. I was received with traditional Hungarian hospitality, stayed for a fortnight, and regained some ten pounds of weight lost in Russia. It was to be the last family reunion. During the next war, Margit, her two adolescent children and her aged mother (my mother's sister) ended their lives in the gas chamber of Auschwitz.[1] Margit's husband was luckier; he died of a tumour before they were all arrested. They were completely unpolitical, harmless provincials—a peaceful village doctor and his family. Their accident-proneness was entirely due to the hazard of a Jewish origin.

I have only a vague memory of their home—a one-storeyed, long and narrow white-washed house, such as the richer Hun-

[1] See *Arrow in the Blue*. My mother's brother, Otto, who lived near Berlin, escaped a similar fate by drowning himself in Lake Koepenick.

garian and Slovakian peasants used to build them. There was a small rose-garden, and a tiny strawberry patch whose scant fruit only the children were allowed to pick. Newspapers were only read on Sundays. Berlin and Moscow were distant abstractions, and their two dictators shadowy, legendary figures like Nero and Caligula.

The outstanding event of my visit was a soccer game, one Sunday afternoon, between the local eleven and a visiting team. As a traveller from distant lands, I was given the honour of acting as referee. The referee in the last game had been beaten up by the sturdy Slovaks of the local team for awarding a penalty against them, but I was assured that, as the Doctor's guest, I would be treated with consideration. All went well except that during half-time, when I walked up to my family seated on the bench of honour, my mother, in full view of both teams and spectators, began wiping my sweaty face and fussing with the scarf round my neck, admonishing me not to run about so much or I would contract pneumonia. A veteran newspaperman and member of the Communist world conspiracy, to her I was still a little boy who would 'catch his death' by getting too hot.

To this day the periods of my life which I spent in jail are passed over in silence by my mother, and the word 'prison' is never mentioned by her. She has never asked me what it was like to be in a concentration camp or under sentence of death, nor how or why I had been reprieved. Such things simply do not happen to 'a young man of good family', which I am still supposed to be, and to remain to my death. The silent assumption is that I made it all up in my books, to make them more interesting. The Victorian generation to which she belongs had the miraculous capacity of wading through the Flood while barely wetting their feet; perhaps because it would have been unthinkable for them to lift their skirts higher than their ankles.

Well rested and fattened up on the ducks, geese, and spring-chickens-with-creamed-cucumber from Margit's backyard—('you didn't have roast goose in Russia for a whole year? Poor boy, how *schrecklich* it must have been')—I proceeded, in a slight haze, and somewhat in doubt about the nature of reality, to my native town, Budapest. I found my father broke as usual, and full of 'colossal' projects. Having just failed to capitalise the invention of salting pigs alive (see *Arrow in the Blue*), he was now negotiating the sale of the entire Hungarian red-pepper harvest to England. Hungarian red pepper, known as *paprika*, is a celebrated spice, much sweeter and milder than chili.

'Have you got a buyer?' I asked cautiously. 'Everybody in England will buy,' he said enthusiastically. 'Who doesn't like paprika?'

I had intended to stay only for a few days. Apart from visiting my parents, my purpose in coming to Budapest had been to sell a few non-political newspaper articles on Central Asia, the cradle of the Hungarian race, so as not to arrive completely penniless in Paris. Instead of a few days, I stayed for nearly three months. The reason was an unexpected stroke of good luck. On the day of my arrival I had given the typescript of *Bar du Soleil* to my old friend, Andor Németh. Two days later he arrived with the startling news that Budapest's leading modern repertory theatre, the *Belvárosi Szinház*, had bought the play for a considerable cash advance.

I have briefly mentioned Németh before; I must now speak of him at some length, for during the next ten years we were to be linked in an intimate and bizarre friendship which included literary partnership, a shared taste for the absurd sides of existence, and shared misery. During my stay in Budapest, and on later occasions in Switzerland and in Paris, we were inseparable, and were known by our mutual friends as 'the firm'. Our association was to end in a ghastly scene which still haunts my dreams.

Andor Németh was the most baroque personality that I have known. In his youth he was regarded as one of the subtlest writers of Hungarian prose of his generation. His tragedy was that owing to incurable laziness, the impossibly high standards that he set himself, and his indifference to popular recognition, he never finished a novel.

He was about ten years my senior. In 1914, at the outbreak of the first world war, he had just received his diploma as a teacher of Hungarian and French litereature, and had been sent on a scholarship to the Sorbonne. The day when France declared war on the Austro-Hungary monarchy, all Hungarians in Paris were ordered to leave the country within twenty-four hours. Németh, typically, overslept the departure of the last train. He was interned, together with all other Hungarian civilians caught in France, in a former monastery on the island of Noirmoutier, and spent the four years of his captivity writing a book about it. There was another Hungarian writer interned in the same place, Aladár Kuncz, similarly occupied. Németh's book was planned as a long psychological novel, Kuncz's book as a straightforward reportage. Németh's book was never finished; Kuncz's book became a best-seller.

When the war was over, Németh took train for Budapest. He only got as far as Vienna, for meanwhile the Communists under Béla Kun had staged their revolution in Hungary and communications were temporarily interrupted. He went to the Hungarian Legation, and found the building deserted except for the newly-appointed Chargé d'Affaires, who happened to be a school friend of Németh's. He asked Németh what his plans were. Németh said that he had no plans, no money, and nowhere to sleep. 'You know what,' said the Chargé d'Affaires, 'so far I have got no staff. Why don't you join me and become First Secretary?' 'Why not, indeed?' said Németh. Three months later, the Communist régime in Hungary was overthrown and Németh, as a member of its diplomatic staff, automatically found himself in the rôle of a political emigré. He had never joined the Party, though. The Chargé d'Affaires had given him an application card, but Németh had forgotten to fill it in.

Admiral Horthy's counter-revolutionary terror led to a mass emigration of Hungarians, including the whole progressive intelligentsia, to Vienna. The emigrés published a daily paper, and Németh joined its staff. While still at school, I had read in that paper—the Bécsi Magyar Ujság—several of his short stories and essays. They seemed to me the strangest and subtlest pieces of Hungarian prose that I had ever seen. Németh was something like a Hungarian Kafka, though at that time—in 1921—Kafka was still practically unknown, and neither Németh nor I had read him. I particularly remember one short story, written in the first person singular. The narrator described how he intended to go out for a walk; how his mother, a wizened little woman, begged him to take her too; how on his refusal she started to cry, then changed into a little grey mouse and crept into his pocket; how in the crowded tramway he had to keep his hands in his pocket to protect her from being squashed; and how his lady friend deserted him because of the mouse in his pocket. On getting home, the mother changes back into her natural shape and resumes the darning of his socks under the oil lamp, while the narrator reflects a trifle sadly that his outing had been rather spoilt. The story did not have the nightmarish quality of Kafka's *Metamorphosis*; it was written in a minor key of melancholy irony. Unlike Kafka's terrible indictment of the tyrannical father, the clinging, clasping mother is accepted with a resigned shrug. Németh was singularly free from resentment, envy and ambition. He was politely bored by people, but I know of not a single example of his showing active dislike for a person. He took it for granted that the world was a hopelessly absurd place, and accepted it with a shrug of his shoulders, speckled with dandruff.

Having read that story, I wrote, after weeks of hesitation, a fan-letter to its author. I have only written two fan-letters in my life, one to Németh, one to Thomas Mann. He answered at once, asking me to come and see him at his office. At sixteen, I still wore short trousers; I was suffering from pathological timidity; Németh was the first writer whom I met in the flesh, and it was the first time that I set foot in that awe-inspiring locale, an editorial office. In spite of all this, and though I was literally covered with cold sweat, I felt instantly and miraculously at ease when I set eyes on the untidy, bulgy-eyed young man behind his desk. It was either the dandruff on his collar and his neglected appearance which gave me back my self-confidence (it was said that Németh's girl-friends occasionally banded together and threw him into a bath-tub) or the mild, goggling stare of his eyes which always seemed surprised at the things they saw, and at the same time took them for granted. It was the kind of stare one meets in the profiled figures on Egyptian murals. The goggling effect was emphasised by a bony, prominent nose, but softened by the ripple in his brown mane. Slightly under medium height, he carried himself with the willowy stoop of a tall scholar. Though certainly not a seducer in appearance, women ran after him like mad—it must have been that bewildered and yet understanding stare which penetrated straight to the core of their elastic defences. It seemed to say : 'My dear lady, why all this fuss? There is nothing new under the sun, and you know very well that you enormously enjoy going to bed. Unless, of course, you would rather prefer a cup of tea.' His voice, soft and elaborately polite, had the same quality of taking everything for granted. It always sounded as if he were saying : 'You like boiled eggs with brilliantine for breakfast? But we all do, of course.' It was the voice of a psychiatrist—friendly, soothing, never shocked. His most endearing quality, however, was his fabulous absent-mindedness, about which countless stories circulated in Budapest. The following is typical and authentic :

One day Németh, completely lost in his thoughts, climbed into a tramcar. The tram was crowded, and Németh was pushed and buffeted about, but took no notice, staring vacantly in front of him. After a while the ticket-collector took him gently by the arm, steered him to a seat occupied by a young woman and whispered into her ear. The woman blushed and yielded her seat to Németh. Németh mumbled absently, 'Thank you, dear lady,' and sat down. A few minutes later, emerging from his reverie, he noticed that everybody was staring at him with looks of commiseration. He found this uncomfortable, took a newspaper from his pocket and began to read. He was promptly thrown out of the tram amidst general indignation.

At our first meeting in that editorial office some time in 1921, I had shown Németh my adolescent efforts at poetry; he read them with benevolent scepticism. During my university years we had met more often, and gradually the ten years difference in age began to lose its significance. In 1926, I had left Vienna for Palestine, and as the Horthy régime was becoming more liberal, Németh had returned to Budapest. Whenever I visited Budapest on leave from the Middle East, and later from Paris, we spent most of our time in each other's company. During one of those visits Németh had given me an idea for a detective story. In the boredom of my last year in Palestine I wrote the story but it became too melodramatic and was no good. Three years later Németh, who was in need of money, rewrote the same story and sent it to me, but this time it had become too highbrow. I rewrote it again, and sold it under our joint signatures to the second largest German magazine, the *Münchner Illustrierte*. That was how 'the firm' had started. I was then living in Berlin and had just been sacked by the Ullsteins. Németh used his half of the fee for a visit to Berlin, where he stayed with me for two or three months. We wrote the synopsis for a second detective story, and also a movie script. We could not sell either, but to discuss some idiotic plot over a bottle of wine amused us vastly.

At that time, the petty guerilla war between Nazis and Communists had been in full swing, and my flat in the 'Red Block' served as a local headquarters for all kinds of illegal activities. One night, some thirty of us were keeping vigil in the flat as we were expecting a raid by the Nazi storm-troopers. We only had three or four revolvers between us, but one of the members of our cell was a plumber, who supplied us with bits of lead pipe. The next day, Németh and I was travelling on a bus, when a large piece of lead pipe fell out from under his jacket and rolled clattering over the floor—fortunately without crushing anybody's feet. In his absentmindedness, Németh had tucked it under his jacket in the morning, probably thinking it was his fountain pen.

When I had left Berlin for Russia, Németh had returned to Budapest, now, a year later, we were again reunited. I found him, as usual, in dire financial straits, living in the small, dark flat of his girl-friend, Juci (pronounced Youtsy). Incapable of looking after himself and of taking any practical initiative, Németh, who was now over forty, had never had a flat or place of his own. He had lived with his mother until he got bored with having to get home every night from Juci's, so now he lived there on a narrow couch. Juci, whom he was to marry a year later, was a small, dark-haired, swarthy-complexioned girl—she looked just like the little mouse into which Németh's mother had turned in the story. In the morning, she darned his socks, from late afternoon until midnight she was away, for she worked as a secretary on the staff of a morning paper. It was an ideal arrangement as Juci did not mind Németh's occasional unfaithfulness, and, I suspect, even took a secret pride in his conquests.

H

The latest of these was a lady of the Hungarian aristocracy of imposing dimensions, called Zsuzsa (unpronounceable). If Juci looked like a nimble grey mouse, Zsuzsa looked like an ornamental baby elephant. Juci loved Zsuzsa. Zsuzsa hated Juci, and was mortally jealous of her. Juci kept sending flowers to Zsuzsa in Németh's name, because Németh always forgot to send them. One day this was discovered by Zsuzsa, who threw a fit and threatened to have Németh thrown into the Danube by her footmen. Németh told me this story, on the day of my arrival, as an example of feminine unreasonableness. Juci, who was making coffee for us, chimed in delightedly:

'. . . And imagine if poor Zsuzsa had known that I not only *sent* the flowers but also *paid* for them.'

'Yes,' said Németh. 'Juci behaved very correctly in this affair, but I am afraid Zsuzsa did not.' 'Correctly' was the *mot juste* if ever there has been one.

Németh took my play to his friend Bárdoss, director of the *Belvárosi Szinház*, which means 'City Theatre'. Bárdoss read it the same evening, and bought it the next day. We decided that Németh was to translate the play into the Hungarian and that we should appear on the bill as co-authors, in the old tradition of 'the firm'. We split the advance that Bárdoss had paid, and Juci, who was always very practical about money, quickly worked out that under a régime of strict economy, both Németh and I could live on it for three months. During these three months 'the firm' was to produce a second play, transfer its activities to Paris, and live happily ever after. We also decided that Németh should leave Juci's cramped room where he couldn't work and, for the first time in his life, set up on his own. So he and I each found a furnished room on the Danube front, at a few minutes' distance from each other, and began to work furiously on the new play. In the evenings, we went to one of the three or four cafés where the various literary cliques gathered, listened to the newest shaggy-dog jokes, and discussed every subject on earth except politics. Within a few days I had met nearly every Hungarian writer and his retinue, for the more prominent were always followed to their cafés by a suite of wives, ex-wives, mistresses, and the wives' and mistresses' boy-friends. The latter were a tribe of extremely correct, nice and well-behaved young men who felt deeply honoured by being admitted to the society of celebrated writers.

It was a strange society, and quite different in atmosphere from literary cliques in Paris, London or Berlin. Post-war Hungary was a dwarf-state, with a population of seven million of whom the majority were semi-literate peasants. Like Austria, it lived in a permanent economic depression, only interrupted by acute crises. But unlike Austria and other small countries, it had no ties, through a shared language, with the cultures of larger neighbours; the Magyars are an isolated ethnic enclave in Europe, and their only relatives are the distant Finns. Hungarian writers could only secure a larger audience by emigrating, and learning to write in the language of their adopted country. But to abandon his native language and traditions means in most cases death to the writer, and his transformation into a nondescript, cosmopolitan journalist or literary hack. Hungary's main export since the first World War had been reporters, scriptwriters, film producers, magazine editors, commercial artists, actresses, and manufacturers of topical best-sellers—the international demi-monde of the arts and letters. They were strewn all over the world by that centrifugal force which is generated when an exceptional amount of talent is cooped up without means of expression in a small country. Though I had the good fortune to be brought up bilingually and to leave Hungary as a child, I have paid the penalty which the loss of one's cultural roots entails through a long time.

Those who remained at home were condemned to write for a small, spoiled, saturated audience. The leading Hungarian poets and novelists of the nineteen-twenties and 'thirties would have occupied an honourable place in the literature of any great nation. The smallness and misery of their country condemned them to eke out their living by writing newspaper columns, and at the same time forced them to live in an atmosphere of mental inbreeding. Writers in larger countries, once they grow out of their juvenile cliques, avoid this by instinct; but the small-town artist is condemned to a lifelong intellectual ghetto. The literary ghettoes of Budapest were the cafés, which were also the headquarters of the warring factions. Many writers worked, read, and received their visitors in cafés. They had their reserved tables, their habits, their courts.

These peculiar circumstances lent the intellectual life of the town a warm intimacy which entirely captivated me. After a year spent in the grim human desert of Russia, I was suddenly thrown upon the bosom of a cosy, incestuous family. I remained a convinced Marxist, and was to stay in the Communist Party for another five years, but I have always been hungry for contrast, for a manner of existence directly opposed to the one I was supposed to be leading. If ever there existed a decadent society, it was here in the cafés of Budapest. For me it was a perfect escapist holiday, and at the same time a confirmation of my belief that bourgeois culture was doomed.

It would be futile to describe personalities; as only a few works of Hungarian literature have been translated into Western languages, the authors and their relationships to each other would mean little to the Western reader. I must nevertheless mention three of them.

Frederick Karinthy was the H. G. Wells and the James Thurber of Hungarian letters, both in one. He was immensely popular and immensely prolific. He wrote novels and plays of a fantastic and Utopian type, and short satirical sketches which appeared three times a week in an evening paper. Some time after my visit he fell ill with a brain tumour. He was operated on, seemed to have completely recovered, but died suddenly, a year or two later, of a cerebral haemorrhage. Before his death he wrote a detailed account of his illness, from the first symptoms—the auditory hallucination of a train roaring past the café every day at 7 p.m. precisely—to partial amnesia and total blindness, culminating in a description of the operation. It was carried out in the approved manner, the patient, fully conscious, lying face down on the operating table, and the surgeon talking to him while operating on the exposed brain.[1] The book is both an autobiographical curiosity and a masterpiece of introspective observation. It

[1] The brain itself is insensitive to touch, and the resection of the scalp and skull is made painless by local anaesthetics.

was published in England under the title *Journey Around my Skull*, but attracted little attention.

Karinthy was the kind of wild literary genius which grows in small countries and provincial towns. He certainly had international stature, but he could neither be translated nor transplanted, for his writing was saturated with the traditions of his country, the idiom of his town, the specific slang of his *milieu*. He was a darkly handsome, stocky, middle-aged man with an air of tolerant melancholia. His gestures, slow and tired, carried a strange authority. His court, which resided at the Café Hadik in Buda, consisted of his wife Aranka; her boy-friend Csuri; his devoted secretary and court-jester Dénes; and two former girl friends, permanently in the throes of some domestic or psychological crisis. Aranka was a now fading classical beauty, and a great lady of considerable intelligence and wit who constantly fought a losing battle against her own innate bitchiness. Some twenty years earlier she had been the muse of Hungary's great poet, Endre Ady, who had drawn a portrait of her as a flapper greedy for life with the face of a saint and the character of a lesser guttersnipe. Her lover, Csuri, was a blasé young man who addressed Karinthy as 'master' and treated him with impudent deference, while Karinthy suffered him as an ageing St. Bernard suffers the antics of a fox terrier. As Aranka refused to keep house, the court took all their meals in restaurants, and Karinthy generally paid for everyone; he was permanently in debt and forced to hack out three pieces a week for *Az Est*, a cheap tabloid paper.

The long evenings spent at Karinthy's table, his air of tolerant resignation as he listened to the chatter and quarrels of his court, gave me the first intimation of the abyss of loneliness in which some artists are condemned to live.

Between Karinthy's operation and his death, Aranka's boy-friend, Csuri, left her. She tried to commit suicide by jumping out of a window, but only succeeded in breaking her hip; she remained permanently lame. The Nazis put an end to her misery. Aranka was of Jewish extraction; she either ended in a death camp or killed herself—I do not remember which.

Two Hungarian writers were particular friends of 'the firm';

the poet Attila Jozsef, and the critic and essayist, Paul Ignotus. Though in his native Hungary Attila Jozsef is post-humously regarded as the greatest poet the nation has produced, his name is still virtually unknown in the West. This may justify the pages that follow—quite apart from my personal feelings for a dead friend.

Attila Jozsef committed suicide at the age of 32; both his work and his personal fate were a terrifying symbol of our time. He was a contemporary Villon, whose life and poetry revolved around the two treacherous poles of this age, Marx and Freud, and who died a victim of both.

Attila was born in 1905, the son of a day-labourer and of a charwoman. His father disappeared when he was three, and until his seventh year Attila was brought up in an orphanage. He earned his living while at school as a movie-usher, newsboy and night-waiter; and at college as a railway porter, Danube sailor, dock-worker, office-cleaner and private tutor.

His first poems were published in the leading Hungarian literary magazine, *Nyugat* ('Occident') when he was sixteen. One year later, in 1922, *Nyugat* printed his poem 'Innocent Song' which caused a nation-wide scandal, and his expulsion from the University of Szeged. 'Innocent Song' was acclaimed as a kind of manifesto of the Central European post-war generation. The translations in this chapter are merely meant to indicate the trend of Attila's poetry.[1]

INNOCENT SONG

I have no God, I have no King,
my mother never wore a ring,
I have no crib or funeral cover,
I give no kiss, I take no lover.

For three days I have chewed my thumb
for want of either crust or crumb.
Though I am twenty, strong and hale—
my twenty years are up for sale.

[1] As mentioned in the Preface, I am indebted to Laurie Lee for his kind and expert help in preparing them.

Should there be none who wish to buy
The Devil's free to have a try;
then shall I use my commonsense
and rob and kill in innocence.

Till, on a rope, they hang me high,
and in the blessed earth I lie—
and lush and poisoned grasses start
rank from my pure and simple heart.

His first volume of poems was published in the same year,
his second volume in 1925, when he was twenty. In that year,
the Maecenas of Hungarian letters, Baron Louis Hatvany, sent
him on a summer vacation to France, and in later years, too,
helped him with small sums. Nevertheless, the whole of
Attila's short life was haunted by poverty; he never achieved
'the monthly two hundred' which became one of his various
obsessions. The 'two hundred' refers to Hungarian pengoe,
and the total of the unattainable dream was the equivalent of
twelve pounds per month.

When I met Attila in 1933, we were both twenty-seven. He
was of pure-bred Magyar, rural stock : of medium height, lean,
sparse, sinewy, he carried his body like a regimental sergeant-
major. He had a narrow face with a high forehead, calm
brown eyes, and calm, regular features to which a certain dash
and enterprise was added by a trim moustache with pointed
ends. It was a handsome and manly, but quite unremarkable
face that could have been a ladies' hairdresser's; nothing in
its unruffled appearance suggested that its owner had spent
several months in a mental hospital, suffering from delusions,
and was heading for the final break-up.

At the time of our friendship he was, in fact, quite normal
except for certain eccentricities and intellectual obsessions.
Dominant among these were psychoanalysis and Hegelian-
Marxist dialectics. Attila had joined the Hungarian underground Communist movement in the late 'twenties, and had
been expelled for Trotskyist leanings in 1930 or '31. But he
had remained a true proletarian and a true revolutionary, who
hated the 'Bonapartism' of Stalin with a Jacobin passion. Intellectually, he was an accomplished acrobat of the Dialectic,

and capable of arguing until three or four o'clock in the morning about some obscure decree of the Paris Commune of 1871, or the Budapest Commune of 1919, analysing its implications with a manic rush of words, and with a chess-player's logical precision (he actually was a passionate chess-player, too). In the early hours of the morning he would go home and, unburdened of these cerebral obsessions, write one of the poems which have since become classics of Hungarian literature. He would read it to Németh and me the next day, over coffee after lunch, and then at once launch again into a dialectical excursion. He fled from poetry into cerebration, from cerebration into poetry. In his work, he achieved a magic synthesis of the two. In his life, the split never healed, either in the metaphorical or in the clinical sense : the disease of his mind was schizophrenia.

We never quarrelled about politics for, though a Party member, I, too, was a born Trotskyist by temperament, and Attila did not challenge me on the point where my faith was most vulnerable, meaning Russia. Attila was not interested in Russia. He was interested in the misery of his own country, which he knew to the bottom of its depth :

'. . . On the rim of the city where I live / when darkness begins to fall / soot-flakes sail the air, like soft-winged tiny bats / and settle everywhere / hardening, thickening, like birds' excrement : / thus weighs this age on our chests . . .'

His songs of the slums show no trace of the dreary naturalism and Socialist Realism that were the vogue of the pink 'thirties; they are pure and fresh and lyrical, even at their most terrifying :

'Oppression, like a swarm of vultures / makes carrion of our hearts, / and misery oozes down the globe / like spittle over the moron's face.'

The unique quality of the poems of his later years lies in their miraculous union of intellect and melody. In this respect I can think of no contemporary poet to whom he could be compared. His most complex and cerebral, Marxist and Freudian poems read like folk-songs, and sometimes like nur-

sery rhymes; 'ideology' is here completely distilled to music
which, whether *adagio* or *furioso*, is always eminently *can-
tabile*. His rhythm almost automatically translates itself into
song; his rhymes are virgin matings or rolling four and five-
syllable words (Hungarian is an inflecting language with
long words, rich in dark vowels, full of rustic sap and juice,
and highly onomatopœic; all of which turns translating into
a nightmare of frustration). One of his last poems, written
while under psychoanalytic treatment, shortly before insanity
set in, is an example of that new branch of poetry that he
created—the Freudian folk-song. It is called 'The Sin' :

> It seems I am a sinner grim,
>   but, thank you, I feel fine.
> It worries me though, why that sin
>   eludes me when it's mine.
>
> I am a sinner without doubt
>   but though I rack my brain,
> that crafty sin turns round about
>   and leaves me without stain.
>
> As treasure-divers in a lake
>   I seek that guilt profound;
> I left my mother for its sake
>   and yet my heart is sound.
>
> One day I'll find it, stowed away
>   in some prim governess—
> but now friends, let's to the café
>   I'm itching to confess.
>
> I tell you : once I killed a man,
>   my father—so I think.
> Before my eyes his red blood ran
>   in a night of curdled ink.
>
> I stuck him with a knife, God's truth;
>   we're human, after all,
> and shall in turn feel murder's tooth,
>   and stabbed, as he was, fall.

So I confess . . . and lingering, wait
   to watch the antic crowd;
to mark those frightened by my fate
   and those who laugh aloud.

Then, just before I turn to stone,
   I catch one kindling eye
which signals : you are not alone
   for all must sin who die . . .

Perhaps my sin is an infant stain
   and really nothing worse;
and soon the world will shrink again
   and I'll ride my rocking horse.

God leaves me cold; so does the devil;
   it was not these who made me.
One day I shall my sins unravel
   and all mankind shall aid me.

At the time of our friendship, Attila was an extremely
amiable and amusing, though somewhat exhausting, companion. He had his moments of exuberance and would write
drinking songs—'O wine, milk of virile men . . .'—though he
drank rarely. He also wrote a congratulatory poem to his own
birthday—the thirty-second and last :

Thirty-two and very wise—
this poem shall be a surprise
   and so pret-
   ty-pretty.

A gift that shall the spirits rouse
of the lonely guest in this coffee-house:
   my-
   self.

Thirty-two, what an event,
and never enough to pay the rent,
   and always hungry
   in Hung'ry . . .

He had moments of a classical and festive mood : his poem of welcome to Thomas Mann, on the occasion of Mann's visit to Budapest, has the beautiful closing lines :

> ... We shall listen to you and some
>   will just gaze at you in joy, for it delights
>   us to see you here : a European among the Whites.

Attila usually got up at midday, and joined Németh and myself for coffee after lunch; and unless we told him that we had to work, he would stay on and talk through the whole afternoon. In a sense he was also a member of 'the firm', for we had commissioned him to write the songs for the Hungarian version of the play. But even during that period of sanity there were occasional frightening flashes on the horizon. One day, twiddling his pointed moustache, he startled us by pronouncing in a casual, conversational voice a phrase of fantastic obscenity, all the more startling as he normally displayed a kind of proletarian puritanism.

On another occasion I found Attila lying on the couch in Németh's room, in a state of obvious depression. I asked whether anything was the matter, and he said yes. I asked what it was and Attila, suddenly sitting up, said, grinning : 'Let's see whether you can find out through *Bar Kokhba*.' 'Bar Kokhba' was a question-and-answer game much in vogue at that time in Budapest, a variant of 'animal, vegetable or mineral'.[1] The dialogue which ensued was roughly on these lines :

I: Is it something that happened today?
A.: Yes.
I: Is it money?
A.: No.
I: A woman?
A.: Yes.
I: Irene?

---

[1] The name of the game is derived from a legendary event: Bar Kokhba, leader of the Gallilean insurrection against Rome, sent a spy to the enemy camp. The Romans caught the spy and cut out his tongue, then let him go. He nevertheless managed to convey what he had seen to his leader, by answering Bar Kokhba's questions with blinks of the eye signifying yes or no.

A.: No.
I: Judith?
A.: Yes.
I: Is it tragedy or comedy?
A.: Tragedy.
I: Has she run away?
A.: No.
I: Has she killed herself?
A.: N-no.
I: Tried to kill herself?
A.: Yes . . .

Thus did I learn that Judith, Attila's wife, had tried to poison herself, and had been taken in a critical state to the public ward of a hospital. Attila was not allowed into the ward, and was waiting for news over the telephone. He loved Judith and was suffering agonies on her behalf; but that did not prevent him from playing that game. In the end Judith was saved. That scene was partly a symptom of his state of mind, and partly an expression of the macabre *Galgenhumor* which saturated the atmosphere of the whole town.

Attila had repeatedly tried to kill himself, the first time at the age of nine, when he swallowed a bar of starch in the belief that it was poison. At fourteen or fifteen, he lay down on the railway track to get himself run over by a goods train which passed through the village every day at a given hour. Time went on, but the train did not come. In the end Attila got up and started walking along the rails to meet it. He then discovered the reason why the train was late : it had killed another person a mile farther up the line. 'Somebody else has died for me,' he used to say afterwards.

From then on trains, in particular goods trains, became another of Attila's obsessions. They keep roaring through his poems, as the ocean 'sick of prey, yet howling on for more' does through Shelley's : until finally they got their prey. In 1937 he spent a few weeks in a mental home. Then, as his condition seemed to have improved, he was handed over into the care of his sisters, who were living in a small village on Lake Balaton. One evening in November, he ambled down to the railway station where a goods train was standing, bound for Budapest. As he was approaching the station, the train slowly began to move. He broke into a run, squeezed through under the lowered barrier, knelt down at the track, and, as the train was gathering speed, laid his right arm in between two carriages on the rail. The arm was later found, cleanly severed and thrown at some distance from the mangled body.

A few days after Attila's death, his family found in his drawer a shirt from which the right sleeve had been cut off with scissors. His guilt-complex had apparently inspired him with the idea that he must have his right arm cut off; and when that was done the train, howling for more, had drawn the rest of his body under the wheels. His death was, fittingly, announced to his sisters by the giggling and spluttering village idiot.

The Hungarian Communist Party, which had excommunicated Attila Jozsef in his lifetime, canonised him after his death. Had he been still alive when Hungary came under Russian rule, he would have shared the fate of all my other friends; so it is just as well that he chose the goods train. If he could come back for an hour, he would twirl his moustache and launch into a dissertation on the proper dialectical timing of one's death.

The third person I have mentioned was our mutual friend, Paul Ignotus. He was a youngish, baldish, humorous and amiable person who had lived all his life in the shadow of a famous and overbearing father. Old Ignotus had been the literary pope of Hungary, founder and editor of *Nyugat*, leader of the 'Western' movement in Hungarian letters. Young Ignotus followed in his father's footsteps as a brilliant literary critic, and co-editor, with Attila and Németh, of a literary magazine; in the late 'thirties he emigrated to England, where he worked during the war in the Hungarian section of the B.B.C. He did not take any direct interest in politics; he was a mild Liberal with vague sympathies for both Socialism and Communism which he regarded as the radical wing of the 'movement towards progress'. After the war the new Hungarian régime offered him the post of Press Attaché at the Hungarian Legation in London, which he saw no reason to refuse.

In 1950 his father died, and Ignotus went to Budapest to

attend his funeral. This was a short time before the trial of the former Minister of Foreign Affairs, László Rajk. Ignotus never returned to his post. A short paragraph in the Hungarian papers announced that he had been sentenced to nine years' imprisonment for high treason and espionage. He was never tried in public. His crime was that he had lived in the West; his tragedy that of the confused and gullible Liberal. During our long post-war discussions in London he had always smilingly reproached me for my 'fanatical' distrust of Stalinite régimes, and had dismissed my warnings not to return to Budapest as the result of an obvious persecution mania.

In writing these pages I have been haunted by the memory of Richard Hillary's book, *The Last Enemy*. At twenty-three, Hillary was the only survivor of a group of young fighter pilots —the flying undergraduates of the Battle of Britain. He called himself 'the last of the long-haired boys' and felt that he was an anachronism, a survivor from another generation. There is a phrase which runs monotonously, like a row of tombstones through his book : 'From this flight Broody Benson did not return'. 'From this flight Bubble Waterston did not return.' 'From this flight Larry Cunningham did not return . . .' He was the only one left, and he had 'to go on paying the tribute; for the survivor is always a debtor.'

A few months before my arrival in Budapest, two Comintern agents, Szállai and Fuest, had been summarily tried and hanged. They had arrived with false passports from Moscow to reorganise the underground party in Hungary, but had been detected and arrested soon after they had crossed the frontier. These executions created a considerable stir, for since the late 'twenties Horthy's régime had settled down to a fairly liberal routine, more or less in the tradition of the late Austro-Hungarian Empire. The leaders of the Commune of 1919 were in exile—some in Moscow, some in Paris; but minor participants such as Németh, and sympathisers such as Baron Hatvany, had gradually been allowed to return, and live unmolested. Freedom of the Press had been restored; the legal opposition in Parliament comprised several parties, including the Socialists, and the *literati* could express pretty well any opinion they liked. Attila Jozsef was free to publish his revolutionary poems, and Lajos Kassák, the doyen of Hungarian revolutionary writers, to edit, at his table in the café, his Marxist quarterly. The police did not bother about Communist *littérateurs,* so long as they remained merely *littérateurs* and had no contact with the one potential enemy, the underground Party. By 1933 that underground Party had been reduced to a handful of intrepid fanatics; the rank and file had deserted them. Szállai and Fuest, two tried and experienced Comintern men, had been sent to remedy this situation and to instil new life into the underground. Their execution—the first political execution for several years—was intended by the régime as a warning example.

My friends in Budapest told me ghastly details about it. The hanging had not been public, but certain notables and privileged persons had been admitted to it. Several ladies of the Hungarian aristocracy had managed to obtain admission tickets. They were females of that loud-voiced, flashy and conspicuous variety who are the despair of Ritz managers all over Europe. When the two men were led to the gallows in the prison courtyard, where a special stand had been erected for the onlookers, the noble ladies broke into screams of hysterical abuse. Szállai and Fuest had both participated in the Commune of 1919, and the ladies were now getting their revenge for the ignominies they had suffered by having refugees billeted in their houses and for the stains they left on the carpets. The two men under the gallows answered back; one sang the 'Internationale' until the trap fell, the other shouted slogans and promised that their death would be avenged. Had they been able to foresee what form that vengeance would take, they would probably have died less bravely.

When I arrived in Hungary, the memory of these events was still fresh. The reader may think that under these circumstances it was a risky thing for me to travel from Moscow straight to Budapest. In fact it was not; but the niceties and ambiguities of a Communist's double existence in those days are rather complicated to explain. It ought to be remembered that, with the exception of Attila and Németh, nobody in Budapest knew that I was a member of the Party. I had never written in Communist papers. In my Party cell in Berlin I had been listed under the alias Ivan Steinberg. To all appearances my record was perfectly proper. I had worked for years for the respectable Ullstein papers, and had been sent to Russia as a correspondent of the equally respectable Duncker Press Agency on behalf of a string of Liberal newspapers. I had never been mixed up in Hungarian politics. I even had a certain reputation in Hungary, for the papers had reported with patriotic pride that the only reporter on the Zeppelin Polar expedition had been a Hungarian. Incidentally, my Palestine passport having expired shortly after that trip, I had reverted to Hungarian nationality, and was travelling with a Hungarian passport. In short, I was a bourgeois journalist who, after many travels in foreign countries, including Russia, had come to visit his aged parents in his home-town.

There was, of course, a remote possibility of some Hungarian agent in Berlin having reported that I had been frequenting Communist circles. But that in itself, and even membership of the German Communist Party (which could hardly be proved), was not a punishable offence, provided that my activities had not been directed against Hungary. At worst, I thought, the police would interrogate me (as they did), and have me shadowed (as I believe they did). But as long as I steered clear of any contact with the underground Party (which I certainly did), I had nothing serious to fear.

This calculation, confirmed by advice that I had gathered in Moscow, proved correct. When I arrived at the Hungarian frontier, the passport officer suffered a slight shock when he saw my Russian visa. Hungary maintained no diplomatic relations with the Soviet Union, and Hungarian papers had no correspondents in Moscow. But when I explained that I was working for German newspapers and showed my credentials, the officer, somewhat doubtfully, let me proceed to Budapest. He kept my passport, however, and told me that I would get it back at police headquarters, whither I should be summoned in due time.

The summons came about a week after my arrival, to my father's address. I went to headquarters without being unduly worried. The sergeant at the inquiry desk was of the jovial, moustachioed type familiar from my childhood; Communist or not, I found it a cosier place than the G.P.U. in

Baku. I was received in a room by three cool and polite plain-clothed officials of the Political Department. On the staircase I had kept repeating to myself : 'DON'T BE ON THE DEFENSIVE. YOU HAVE A CLEAN CONSCIENCE. YOU WORK FOR THE HAPPINESS OF MANKIND.' It was either this auto-suggestion that did the trick, or the journalist's brazenness that I had acquired, for after the first few minutes the atmosphere became quite sociable. The four of us sat around a table; after I had told my story about Ullsteins, Duncker, and so on, they seemed to have run out of questions, and there was a pause. To my relief, they did not inquire about my associations in Berlin. Instead, the man at the head of the table—the Deputy Chief of the Political Department—said softly, in a tone of semi-humorous despair :

'You don't seem to realise that you are the first Hungarian since 1919 to arrive with a legal passport straight from Moscow.'

'I am also the first Hungarian who almost got to the North Pole,' I said.

The obviously least intelligent of the three asked me slyly whether I had 'established contact with Communists in Moscow'. I said that I had interviewed a lot of them, and that all my contacts had been Communists, as the Communists were the Government. 'How did they strike you?' he asked curiously. I said that some of them seemed very clever men indeed. Had I seen Stalin? I admitted regretfully that I hadn't. Whom else had I seen? I mentioned Bukharin and Radek, but before I could go on, the Deputy Chief interrupted in a casual tone : 'And Béla Kun?'

There was a dramatic silence. Béla Kun, dictator of the Commune, had already become a legendary figure in Hungary, a devil with horns. Before I had time to think, I heard myself answer. 'Of course'—which was a lie. I had tried to see Béla Kun in Moscow, but he had been either too busy, or not interested. I am not quite sure why I lied—perhaps an instinct told me that if I denied having met Béla Kun they would not believe me; or perhaps I simply enjoyed a little boasting. At any rate, I had apparently taken the right line, for they all became quite electrified, and asked with naïve curiosity whether it was true that Kun had gone completely bald;

whether he had 'made a career in the Kremlin'; and whether, living among all those Russians, he still spoke Hungarian fluently. My affirmative answers to the last two questions seemed to reassure their patriotic pride. I am sure they resented it when Dimitrov, the Bulgarian, instead of Kun became Head of the Comintern.[1]

In the end they gave me my passport back, and we all shook hands. The Deputy Chief's last, casual question was whether I intended to visit factories and working-class suburbs. I said no, I was working on a play. 'Fine,' he said. 'As long as you stick to the cafés and leave the factories alone, you are all right with us.'

It was a perfect summing up of the Communist Party's own view of its intellectuals.

I left, highly satisfied wtih myself. It did not occur to me, in my self-congratulatory mood, to reflect on the liberalism of this 'semi-Fascist' régime, or to compare the relative freedom which its citizens still enjoyed with the condition of a citizen of the Soviet State.

The play was never produced. Bárdoss's enthusiasm evaporated as suddenly as it had been aroused. His excuse was that he did not like the Hungarian translation. He had only read the German original in a hurry, and on re-reading the play more carefully in his own language he had discovered both its weaknesses as a play, and its ultra-Left tendency.[2]

The other projects of 'the firm' came also to nothing. The second play was abandoned owing to our demoralised condition, though it was nearly finished. The Hungarian Press wouldn't touch my articles on Turkestan; though not directly political, they had an unmistakable pro-Soviet bias. All I managed to sell was a feature story about the harem of the Emir of Bokhara.

[1] Kun was arrested in the great Soviet purge in May 1937, and shot without trial.
[2] I lost the typescript of *Bar du Soleil,* together with other unpublished manuscripts, during my flight from France in 1940. In 1943, I wrote another version around the same basic idea and called it *Twilight Bar.* It had the same theatrical weakness as the original play, was produced in France, America and various other countries, and was nearly everywhere a flop.

Our funds were running out. In the end we churned out a couple of detective stories for pulp magazines, to pay for our rent. We wrote them, sitting back to back at two little tables in our favourite café, having previously parcelled out the chapters. Németh wrote in Hungarian, I in German, but as we were both bilingual this did not matter. It was quite fun while it lasted, yet we had to admit that for the second time— the first time was in Berlin—our literary partnership had ended in failure. Fortunately, I still had my ticket to Paris. Németh talked vaguely of joining me there later on. And so we parted, closer friends than ever.

This last phrase may arouse some scepticism, for the failure of a joint enterprise usually leads to mutual recriminations or silent resentment. The fact is that Németh and I never quarrelled; to the end, our long friendship remained free from any tension, and any resentment of the other's shortcomings. It was a singularly harmonious relationship and, for the irritable and quarrelsome character that I was, quite exceptional. The explanation is, I believe, that though we never talked about it, we were both well aware of the hidden springs and motives of our friendship. On the surface, it rested on the traditional attraction between diametrically opposed natures. I was active, efficient, full of nervous vitality; Németh was lazy, absent-minded, and completely helpless in practical matters. Twice I had revolutionised the dreamy trot of his existence : by getting him to Berlin, and by turning up in Budapest with the play. It was to happen yet a third time; but after each of these interludes he would quietly creep back to hibernate in the twilight of Juci's den. Like all his friends, I took it for granted that Németh was a kind of saintly sponger or sponging saint. Yet all this, as I have said, was on the surface. The real basis of our relationship was a tacit understanding that Németh was a noble failure and that I was a cheap success. This formula was not affected by the circumstance that I had ceased to be a success and had become a penniless exile.

My acquiescence in that rôle was partly due to my chronic inferiority complex, but mainly to the fact that I recognised Németh's superiority as a writer. I knew that Németh was an artist and that I was a journalist. I also knew that his approach to poetry and to music, his complete indifference to the vanities and trivia of existence, were on a plane different from mine. I knew that his lazy and absurd manner of frittering his life away somehow brought him closer to the essence of being than my furious entanglements in the webs of Maya. In *Arrow in the Blue* I have tried to describe the lasting split between the active and the contemplative sides of my character. The contemplative half had been dormant for a long time. In Németh it found its projection and incarnation. I had gone the way of the Commissar; I needed a Yogi as an *alter-ego*.

I have often wondered since whether I had perhaps read more into Németh than the facts justified. By a series of hazards the text of the second play, which we had written together in Budapest, has survived. I re-read it, for the first time in twenty years, when I began writing this chapter. With mixed feelings I found my original notion confirmed. In the three existing acts of the play—the fourth was never completed—Németh had only written two or three scenes, leaving the rest of the donkey-work to me. But these scenes stand out like a group of live visitors in a museum of waxworks.

I left for Paris in September, 1933, a short time after my twenty-eighth birthday. The escapist interlude had come to an end.

XVI. The Crusade without Cross

THE next three years, from the autumn of 1933 to the autumn of 1936, were for me years of extreme poverty and hectic political activity. They were the years of the great anti-Fascist crusade which, with drums and fanfares, advanced from defeat to defeat.

First came Hitler's defiant withdrawal from the League of Nations. Then the defeat of the Socialist insurrection in Austria. Then Hitler's victory in the Saar. Then Hitler's repudiation of the Treaty of Versailles. Then the Anglo-German naval pact, granting Hitler a larger fleet than France's. Then Hitler's march into the Rhineland. Then Hitler's march into Austria. In between Mussolini's conquest of Abyssinia, and the Japanese conquest of Manchuria, and Franco's victory in Spain. And so on, to Munich and Prague, and to the war which we had foreseen and had been unable to prevent.

For seven years, the statesmen and the people of the West failed to see the obvious, failed to understand the threat to their civilisation, and to eliminate it while it could still be done at a relatively small price. This seven-years'-blindness which benighted the West from 1932 to 1939 was one of the remarkable phenomena of History. As if acting under a curse, the various nations and political parties, Right and Left, however opposed their policies were in other respects, seemed to collaborate to bring about Europe's destruction. The attitude of the Conservative forces ranged from inane misconceptions of the nature of Hitler's régime to passive sympathy and active complicity. The various Socialist and Labour parties indulged in rhetorical denunciations of the Fascist danger, and did everything in their power to prevent their countries from arming against it. The Communists exploited the anti-Fascist movement for their own purposes and wound it up with a staggering betrayal. It looked as if they were all partners in a secret European suicide pact.

The only mitigating circumstance the West could plead was of a psychological nature. The West was mentally incapable of believing in the gory tales about Nazi atrocities and in their fantastic plans for world conquest which sounded like something straight out of science fiction. When Hitler was beaten, the same psychological block made its appearance with regard to the Stalinite régime and its plans for conquest; the pattern repeated itself with a perverse and uncanny precision. But then, it required exceptional powers of imagination for people brought up in the traditions of the West to accept and visualise the revival of medieval torture and antique state-slavery. It required an even greater intellectual effort to believe in the reality of the National-Socialist and Communist schemes to enforce the millennium by terror, conspiracy and conquest. This incredulity towards the incredible was the most generalised phenomenon in the Seven Years' Night.

In 1933 and during the next two or three years, the only people with an intimate understanding of what went on in the young Third Reich were a few thousand refugees. In the torture chambers of Columbia House in Berlin, in the newly established concentration camps of Oranienburg and Sachsenhausen, of Dachau and Buchenwald, hundreds of comrades personally known to us were being tortured, murdered, and driven to suicide. For us, the actual deeds and future intentions of this new régime were not a matter of speculation and academic controversy, as they were for the politicians of the West, but an intimate, harrowing reality. This condemned us to the always unpopular, shrill-voiced part of Cassandras. Nobody likes people who run about the streets yelling 'Get ready, get ready, the day of wrath is at hand'. Least of all when they yell in a foreign accent and, by their strident denunciations of the alleged aggressive intentions of Berlin or Moscow (as the case may be), increase international tension and suspicion. They are quite obviously fanatics, or hysterics, or persecution maniacs.

It is doubly painful to write about these seven years at a

time when the mood of Western Europe is bent on repeating the same suicidal errors. The lesson of the 'thirties : that an aggressive, expansive power with a messianic belief in its own mission will expand as long as a power-vacuum exists; that improvement of social conditions, however desirable in itself, is no deterrent and no protection against attack; that the price of survival is the sacrifice of a distressingly large part of the national income over a distressingly long period; and that appeasement, however seductive and plausible its arguments sound, is not a substitute for military strength but an invitation to war—all this should be only too fresh in Europe's memory; yet an astonishing number of British, French, Italian politicians, not to mention millions of common men, seem determined to commit the same errors and re-live the same tragedy again.

'From the danger of war one cannot protect oneself by weapons, one can achieve this only by moving forward into a new world of law. . . . Armaments cannot be fought by piling up armaments; that would be like getting Beelzebub to drive out the devil.'

This sounds like a speech by Mr. Aneurin Bevan in 1953. In fact it is a speech by Mr. Clement Attlee, delivered on March 11, 1935 in the House of Commons, in protest against the Government's proposal for a modest increase in rearmament. When he suggested 'disbanding the national armies' as a brilliant idea to save peace, he was interrupted by shouts : 'Tell that to Hitler.' He brushed the interruption aside, as Mr. Bevan and his French counterparts brush similar irrelevances aside eighteen years later. In the same year, 1935, a Peace Ballot, on the sweetly reasonable lines that disarmament should start at home, obtained eleven million signatures in England —more than half of the total electorate.

Even the slogans the aggressor employed to hypnotise the victim were the same. The *leitmotif* was Peace, Peace, Peace. Hitler, like Stalin, sponsored Peace Congresses and Peace Appeals, and never tired of denouncing 'the conspiracy of the armament manufacturers' and 'the warmongers of Wall Street'. Anti-Nazi refugees who talked about the German concentration camps and Hitler's plans for world-conquest were regarded as fanatics and fomenters of hatred, as their succes-

sors, the East-European refugees and ex-Communists, are regarded today. If only the Cassandras and Jeremiahs would
shut up, we could have peace for our lifetime! After each
act of aggression and defiance, Hitler made a gesture of peace
which was as eagerly taken at face value as similar gestures by
Stalin and Malenkov were later on; and people who warned
against such gullibility were accused of deliberately sabotag-
ing the chances of peaceful settlement.

'It is to be hoped that this speech will be taken everywhere
as a sincere and well-considered utterance. . . . There are no
greater enemies to the peace of Europe than those who would
spread an atmosphere of suspicion. . . .' Is this *The New Statesman and Nation* commenting on a speech by Malenkov, or
The Times commenting on a speech by Hitler? It happens to
be the latter—on May 21, 1935; but the pattern and the
arguments are the same. One of the outstanding features of
neurotic behaviour is the patient's inability to learn from his
past experiences. Behind the shallow truism that 'history re-
peats itself' hide the unexplored forces which lure men into
repeating their own tragic errors.

The scapegoat of the deluded was at that time not the
United States, but the 'militarism' of France. When Hitler
marched into the Rhineland and the French Prime Minister
came to London for consultations, he had the same type of
welcome that American generals have nowadays in Europe,
for it was obvious to all enlightened, peace-loving men that
the real danger to peace came not from Hitler but from the
aggressive French. 'The St. Vitus' dance of Francophobia and
Germanophilia which had seized the Left and the humani-
tarians in England since the conclusion of the Versailles peace
reached its climax.'[1] It was the same unconscious desire to
evade reality which we observe today; it is so much easier to
stand up in a manly way to 'French militarism' in 1936, and
to 'American Imperialism' in 1953, than to the Nazi and
Soviet Empires.

There were also the so-called 'detached political experts'
who disliked the Nazi régime but warned against exaggerat-

[1] Leopold Schwarzschild: *World in Trance* (London, 1943). Schwarzschild's book contains the most concise summary of the Seven Years'
Blindness.

ing its dangers by pointing out that the Germans only wanted to annex German territories such as the Rhineland and the Saar. The Germans, they went on, were far too intelligent to swallow a foreign body such as Czechoslovakia, which they could never digest. Since 1945, the detached experts have used precisely the same arguments regarding Russia's intentions in Central and Western Europe. The result of all this was that by 1936 the Belgians, Rumanians, Yugoslavs, etc., had become 'neutralists' and the system of collective security disintegrated, as the European Defence Community is disintegrating today. The neurotic who each time commits the same type of error and each time hopes to get away with it is not stupid; he is just ill. And the twentieth-century European has become a political neurotic.

To watch this folly; to wait for the catastrophe which one is unable to prevent; to read, as late as October 1938, that 'it is this happy conviction of faith in Herr Hitler's sincerity and honesty which offers the key to European peace'[1]—filled me with a choking, impotent despair. I tried to describe it some years later, during the war, in an article 'On Disbelieving Atrocities'.[2] It is a highly emotional piece, but it reflects the mood :

There is a dream which keeps coming back to me at almost regular intervals; it is dark, and I am being murdered in some kind of thicket or jungle; there is a busy road at no more than ten yards distance; I scream for help but nobody hears me, the crowd walks past laughing and chattering.

I know that many people share, with individual variations, the same type of dream. I believe it to be an archetype in the Jungian sense: an expression of the individual's ultimate loneliness when faced with death and cosmic violence; and of his inability to communicate the unique horror of his experience. I further believe that it is the root of the ineffectiveness of our atrocity-propaganda.

For, after all, you are the crowd who walk past on the road, laughing; and there are only a few of us, escaped victims and

[1] *Evening Standard,* 31.10.1938.
[2] *The New York Times Sunday Magazine,* January, 1944.

eye-witnesses of the things which happen in the jungle who, haunted by our memories, go on screaming at you on the wireless, in newspapers and at public meetings. Now and then we succeed in reaching your ear for a minute. I know it each time it happens by a certain dumb wonder on your faces, a faint glassy stare entering your eye; and I tell myself: now you have got them, now hold them, hold them, so that they will remain awake. But it only lasts a minute. You shake yourselves like puppies who have got their fur wet; then you walk on, protected by the dream-barrier which stifles all sound.

I have been lecturing now for three years to the troops, and their attitude is the same. They don't believe in concentration camps, they don't believe in the starved children of Greece, in the shot hostages of France, in the mass-graves of Poland; they have never heard of Lidice, Treblinka or Belsen. You can convince them for an hour, then they shake themselves, their mental self-defence begins to work, and in a week the shrug of incredulity has returned, like a reflex temporarily weakened by a shock.

Clearly all this is becoming a mania with me and my like. Clearly we must suffer from some morbid obsession, whereas the others are healthy and normal. But the main symptom of maniacs is that they lose contact with reality and live in a fantasy world. So, perhaps, it is the other way round: perhaps it is we, the screamers, who react in a sound and healthy way to the reality which surrounds us, whereas you are the neurotics who totter about in a screened fantasy world because you lack the faculty to face the facts. Were it not so, this war would have been avoided, and those murdered within sight of your day-dreaming eyes would still be alive.

I said: 'perhaps', because obviously the above can only be half the truth. There have been screamers at all times— Prophets, Preachers, and Cranks, cursing the obtuseness of their contemporaries, and the result was very much the same. There are always the victims screaming from the jungle, and the people who pass by on the road. They have ears but hear not, they have eyes but see not. So the roots of this must lie deeper than mere obtuseness.

Amos, Hosea, Jeremiah, were pretty good propagandists, and yet they failed to shake their people and to warn them.

Cassandra's voice was said to have pierced walls, and yet the Trojan war took place. And in our days, the Ministry of Information and the B.B.C. are on the whole doing a quite competent job. For almost three years they had to keep this country going on nothing but defeats, and they succeeded. But at the same time they have lamentably failed to make people aware of the grandeur and horror of the time into which they were born. The people carried on business-as-usual style, except that the routine of this business included killing and being killed. Matter-of-fact unimaginativeness has become a kind of cult with the Anglo-Saxon nations; it is usually contrasted with Latin hysterics and praised for its high value in an emergency. But they tend to forget what happens between emergencies; and that the same unimaginativeness is responsible for the failure to prevent their recurrence. . . .

Against this nightmare background, my doubts and misgivings about Russia paled to insignificance. When you march in a crusade, even in a losing crusade, you are not in a mood for reflection. Reflection only set in some three years later, when the Russian purges began to assume the proportions of mass terror. 1936–37 was the turning-point, not only in my political orientation but in my whole attitude to existence. In the condemned cell of a Franco prison my former life was to be dissolved and recast in a new shape. But that crisis was still in the future, three years ahead.

The mood of these three years is only partly reflected in the dream of the murderous jungle and the indifferent crowd on the road. That nightmarish quality was one half of the truth. For at the same time these were years of single-minded dedication, filled with purpose, relatively free from doubt, and thus, paradoxically, happy years as well as tormented years. During some weeks of extreme penury I was forced to sleep in a hayloft in a Paris suburb and to walk every day several miles on an empty stomach to the Party office where I worked without pay. I was lightheaded with hunger and my shoes were falling to pieces, but I was engaged in a useful activity, anonymously and wholeheartedly, and this knowledge gave me a feeling of spiritual cleanliness, of innocence regained. Work is a powerful drug, and those who become addicted to it develop an almost unlimited capacity for self-delusion. Month after month we assured ourselves that the fall of the Nazi régime was imminent, and this spurious certainty kept us going by dazing us and galvanising us at the same time.

Once again I must remind the reader of the two basic elements of the revolutionary creed: attraction by Utopia and rebellion against a sick society. My years in Russia had made Utopia recede; but when my faith had begun to falter, Hitler gave it a new, immensely powerful impulse. Thus started my second honeymoon with the Party.

XVII. Blind-Man's-Buff

I ARRIVED in Paris in the middle of the Reichstag Fire Trial, which was holding Europe spellbound. The day after my arrival I met for the first time Willy Muenzenberg, Western Propaganda Chief of the Comintern. The same day I started work at his headquarters, and thus became a minor participant in the great propaganda battle between Berlin and Moscow. It ended with a complete defeat for the Nazis—the only defeat which we inflicted on them during the seven years before the war.

The object of the two contestants was to prove that it was the other who had set fire to the German Parliament. The world watched the spectacle with fascination, and with as little understanding of its true meaning as small children have when they watch a complicated thriller on the screen. For the world was not yet accustomed to the stage-effects, the fantastic swindles and cloak-and-dagger methods of totalitarian propaganda. And in this case there was not one producer of the show, as later in the Moscow trials but two, who played out their tricks against each other like rival medicine men before the assembled tribe.

The two medicine men were Dr. Joseph Goebbels and Willy Muenzenberg; but few knew at the time, and know to this day, of the existence of the second. The world thought that it was witnessing a classic struggle between truth and falsehood, guilt and innocence. In reality both parties were guilty, though not of the crimes of which they accused each other. Both were lying, and both were afraid that the other knew more of the actual facts than he really did. Thus the battle was really a blind-man's-buff between two giants. Had the world understood at the time the stratagems and bluffs involved, it could have saved itself much suffering. But neither then nor later did the West really understand the psychology of the totalitarian mind.

The dramatic aspect of the trial was epitomised in three scenes. Their style was somewhere halfway between Shakespeare and Gilbert-and-Sullivan. The first was the duel between Dimitrov and Goering. Georgi Dimitrov, the future Secretary General of the Communist International, was then the secret leader of its Balkan section. Goering was then Prime Minister of Prussia, and Minister of the Interior of the Reich. Dimitrov was one of the five defendants, accused by the Nazis of having set fire to the Reichstag. Goering appeared officially as a witness for the prosecution, in fact as a defendant against the Communist accusation of being the real author of the fire. The Comintern chief in the dock and the Nazi chief on the witness-stand exchanged invective like Homeric fishwives. Never in history had a member of the government of a great power made such a grotesque spectacle of himself in a public courtroom.

Dimitrov: Does Prime Minister Goering know that hundreds of thousands of German workers have found employment thanks to the orders placed by Soviet industry?

Prime Minister Goering: I will tell you what the German people know. The German people know that you are an impudent fellow who has come here to set our Reichstag on fire. In my eyes you are a rascal who belongs straight to the gallows. . . . Wait until I can lay my hands on you outside the sanctuary of this court. . . .

Dimitrov: You are obviously afraid of my questions, Mr. Prime Minister.

Goering: Get out of here, you swindler!

Another witness for the prosecution was Propaganda Minister Goebbels. He spoke at length about the illegal, deceitful and conspiratorial methods of the Communists.

Dimitrov: Is it known to the Herr Reichsminister that in Austria and Czechoslovakia his National Socialist comrades are also [like the Communists] forced to work underground, to employ illegal propaganda methods, false passports, fictitious addresses and coded messages?

Goebbels: I will answer you with a quotation from Schopenhauer : Everybody deserves a glance, but not everybody deserves an answer.

Lastly, there was the fantastic confrontation of the Chief of the Potsdam Police, Count Helldorf, with the chief defendant, van der Lubbe.

Helldorf was a dashing young aristocrat, a Prussian officer, a symbol of the new *Herrenmensch*—the Nietzschean masterman, chosen to rule the world. Van der Lubbe was the psychopathic son of an alcoholic street-hawker in Holland. He was twenty-four, and he had been a plasterer's apprentice, then a waiter, then a valet, then a tramp. He was homosexual and, afflicted with a chronic eye disease, lived in the permanent fear of blindness. He was a compulsive liar, and had a pathological craving for fame. He had joined the Communist Youth League, and later the Party, no less than four times, and each time had left again because he found insufficient scope for his ambitions. He then joined an ultra-Leftwing sect that advocated individual terror, and finally, through homosexual friends, fell under the spell of the National Socialist revolution. He had written a pamphlet and had printed postcards with his photograph on them, announcing that he was undertaking a journey round the world, and he had tried to achieve celebrity by swimming the Channel. Defeated by the water, he took to fire. On the night of February 27, 1933, aided by unknown accomplices, he burnt down the German House of Parliament and became a historic figure.

If Helldorf symbolised the new élite, the Fascist masterrace, van der Lubbe symbolised, in an extreme form, the emotionally unbalanced, mentally unstable generation between the wars, the frustrated and befuddled masses with their latent hysteria, who became the Fascists' dupes and prey.

Count Helldorf, like Goering and Goebbels, appeared in the courtroom for the explicit purpose of refuting the Comintern's accusation that they were the instigators of the fire, and had used van der Lubbe as their tool. Helldorf was confronted in court with Lubbe for the purpose of establishing that they had never met before. This confrontation was one of the climaxes of the trial.

Helldorf was his usual dashing, smiling, commanding self. Lubbe was a horrifying apparition, half man, half beast. Saliva was dribbling from his mouth, and mucus from his nostrils down on to the floor. From time to time his Counsel wiped his face with a paper handkerchief. When standing, Lubbe's hands were dangling down and his head bent on his chest like a chimpanzee's. When sitting, his head hung between his knees like a broken puppet's. He had been kept in chains for seven months before the trial, and during the trial itself. He was in a stupor during the whole proceedings, obviously drugged to prevent him from giving away the show. The symptoms indicated that the drug used was scopolamine, which produces a condition similar to the stuporous form of dementia præcox. It was a clumsy and amateurish method; the technique of processing defendants for show trials was still in its infancy. During the whole trial, this ghost only came to life once or twice, to babble about 'voices in my body', and to ask to be sentenced to death without further ado.

So there they stood facing each other in the courtroom, *Herrenmensch* and *Untermensch*, the racy leader and the slavering dupe :

The President of the Court: Accused Lubbe, step forward. Lift your head, Lubbe, and look the witness in the face. Now lift your head, Lubbe, come on! Come, look the witness in the face.

Translator (in Dutch): You are asked to look the witness in the face.

The President: Come on, lift your head.

Counsel for the Defence: Lift your head, Lubbe.

Translator: You must look the witness in the face. Lift your head.

The President: Come on, lift your head. Lift your head, van der Lubbe.

For three full minutes the President, translator and counsel were trying to coax the comatose figure into lifting his dang-

ling head from his chest. Then, suddenly, Helldorf rapped out
a single short command :

'*Mensch, mach doch den Kopf hoch, los!*'

'*Jerk that head up, man, snap to it!*'

And up went Lubbe's head, like a sleeping dog's when
woken up by his master's voice.

In that scene, not only the whole trial was summed up. It
was a *tableau vivant* representing the new relationship between leaders and led, a new development in European history. Where reasoning and persuasion had failed to move the
entranced victim, the whip-hand had jerked him into action.

Both Nazis and Communists agreed that van der Lubbe was
the tool who had actually lit the fire. Both parties also agreed
that for the formidable task of preparing a conflagration of
that size he must have had several expert accomplices. The
Nazis cited as accomplices four Communist leaders : three
Bulgarians, including Dimitrov, and a member of the German
Reichstag, Torgler. They had been preparing the trial for
seven months, but during the trial itself the frame-up became
so blatantly obvious that the four Communists had to be
acquitted. The acquittal was by implication an indictment of
the true instigators of the act. The facts that had emerged
during the trial, in spite of the court's efforts to efface the
truth, made it clear that the Nazis themselves had burnt down
the Reichstag—as a pretext for the dissolution of the Left-
wing Parties, and the institution of mass terror.

So far so good. But how was it done? Who had persuaded
Lubbe to serve as a stooge, who had conceived the plan, who
had been in the know, and who were his physical accomplices? The incendiaries could only have come through the
underground tunnel which connected Goering's palace with
the Reichstag : this fact and Goering's self-contradictory
statements convinced us that the Prussian Prime Minister was
in the plot. But how could we make the naïve West believe
such a fantastic story? We had no direct proof, no access to
witnesses, only underground communications to Germany.
We had, in fact, not the faintest idea of the concrete circumstances. We had to rely on guesswork, on bluffing, and on the
intuitive knowledge of the methods and minds of our opposite

I

numbers in totalitarian conspiracy.

The 'we' in this context refers to the Comintern's propaganda headquarters in Paris, camouflaged as the 'World Committee for the Relief of the Victims of German Fascism.' I arrived in Paris, as I have said, in the middle of the battle, and my part in it was a subordinate one. I had to follow the repercussions of the trial, and of our propagands, in the British Press and in the House of Commons, to study currents of British public opinion, and draw the appropriate tactical conclusions. For a while I also edited the daily bulletins which we distributed to the French and British press.

When I joined the battle, the first round had already been won; the Nazis were on the defensive. They had been forced to call Goering, Goebbels and Helldorf to the witness-stand in a desperate attempt to whitewash themselves before world public opinion. Their failure, and our final triumph—the sensational acquittal of the accused Communists—was almost entirely due to the genius of one man, Willy Muenzenberg.

Willy was the grey eminence and invisible organiser of the anti-Fascist world crusade. He had escaped from Germany on the night of the fire, had set up his headquarters in Paris and started his campaign, a unique feat in the history of propaganda.

First, he founded the 'World Committee for the Relief of the Victims of German Fascism', with branches all over Europe and America. It was camouflaged as a philanthropic organisation, and had in every country a panel of highly respectable people, from English duchesses to American columnists and French savants, who had never heard the name of Muenzenberg and thought that the Comintern was a bogey invented by Dr. Goebbels.

This World Committee, with its galaxy of international celebrities, became the hub of the crusade. Great care was taken that no Communist—except for a few internationally known names, such as Henri Barbusse and J. B. S. Haldane—should be connected in public with the Committee. But the Paris Secretariat which was running the Committee, was a purely Communist caucus, headed by Muenzenberg, and controlled by the Comintern. Its offices were at first in the Rue Mondetour near the Halles, and later at 83, Boulevard

Montparnasse. Muenzenberg himself worked in a large room in the World Committee's premises, but no outsider ever learned about this. It was as simple as that.

Next, he founded his own publishing house in Paris—'Editions du Carrefour'—and set his staff to compile the famous first *Brown Book of the Hitler Terror and the Burning of the Reichstag*. The *Brown Book* probably had the strongest political impact of any pamphlet since Tom Paine's *Common Sense*.

It was published anonymously. The front page said : '*Prepared by the World Committee for the Relief of the Victims of German Fascism, with an introduction by Lord Marley*.' The book contained the first comprehensive report on the German concentration camps (including statistics and lists of victims), on the persecution of Jews, the repression of literature, and other aspects of the terror. The documentation had been assembled by the Comintern's Intelligence *apparat*. The *Brown Book* further contained the 'complete inside story' of the fire, starting with a detailed biography of Lubbe, unearthed by the *apparat* in Holland, his contacts with the homosexual circles around the Leader of the Brownshirts, Captain Roehm, and ending with a convincing description of how the incendiaries penetrated into the Reichstag through the underground tunnel. Several direct participants in the action were named : Count Helldorf, S.A. Leaders Heines and Schultz.

All this was based on isolated scraps of information, deduction, guesswork, and brazen bluff. The only certainty we had was that some Nazi circles had somehow contrived to burn down the building. Everything else was a shot in the dark. But it went straight to the target. Within a few weeks, the *Brown Book* was translated into seventeen languages and circulated in millions of copies. It became the bible of the anti-Fascist crusade. It was smuggled into Germany in large quantities, bound in the cover of Recklam's cheap classics series, disguised as Schiller's *Wallenstein* and Goethe's *Herman und Dorothea*.

The anonymous author of the *Brown Book* was Muenzenberg's chief lieutenant, Otto Katz, alias André Simon—who was to be hanged as one of the accused in the Slansky trial in 1952. I shall have more to say about him later on.

While the *Brown Book* was being prepared, Muenzenberg branched out into other activities. Always under cover of the philanthropic 'World Commiteee for Relief', he and Katz organised the 'Committee of Inquiry into the Origins of the Reichstag Trial'. It was composed of lawyers of different nationalities and of international repute, among them the former Italian Prime Minister Francesco Nitti; the son of the former Swedish Prime Minister, Senator George Branting; Counsel for the defence of Sacco and Vanzetti, Arthur Garfield Hayes; *maîtres* Moro Giaffery and Gaston Bergery, France; D. N. Pritt, England, and others. On September 14, 1933, the first public session of the Committee of Inquiry was opened in the courtroom of the Law Society of London, by Sir Stafford Cripps. The Committee cross-examined witnesses, sifted evidence, and acted in fact as 'an unofficial tribunal whose mandate was conferred by the conscience of the world' —as Katz, the invisible organiser of the Committee, wrote in the *Second Brown Book*.[1] The proceedings of the Committee came to be known as the 'Counter Trial'. A public shadow-trial of this kind was a novelty for the West and gained world-wide publicity. Muenzenberg had struck on the idea when, in search of a new propaganda stunt, he had remembered the 'secret courts' of Russian revolutionaries in Czarist days.

The verdict in the Counter Trial, which found the Communists innocent and the Nazis guilty, was announced in Caxton Hall, London, on September 20th—the day before the real trial opened before the Supreme Court of Germany at Leipzig. Thus, thanks to Muenzenberg's genius, the Nazis were from the very beginning put on the defensive. The proceedings before the Supreme Court lasted for three months, most of which time was spent in frantic efforts to refute the accusations of the *Brown Book* and the findings of the Counter Trial. The *Brown Book* was actually referred to in the proceedings as the 'sixth defendant'. It was a unique event in

[1] '*The Reichstag Fire Trial*. The Second Brown Book of the Hitler Terror, based on material collected by the World Committee for the Relief of the Victims of German Fascism, with an Introductory Chapter specially written for the book by Georgi Dimitrov, a Foreword by D. N. Pritt, K.C., an Appendix on Murder in Hitler-Germany introduced by Lion Feuchtwanger, and 21 illustrations from original sources, London 1934.'

criminal history that a court—and a Supreme Court to boot —should concentrate its efforts on refuting accusations by a third, extraneous party. Hence the parade of Cabinet Ministers on the witness-stand; hence the fantastic request of the court to the Head of the Potsdam Police, to furnish an alibi for his movements at the time when the crime was committed; hence the incredible self-degradation of Prime Minister Goering :

'The "Brown Book" says that I looked on while the fire was being prepared, dressed, I believe, in a blue silken Roman toga. All that is missing is an allegation that, like Nero at the fire of Rome, I was playing the fiddle. . . . The "Brown Book" is a work of incitement that I have destroyed wherever I find it. . . . It says that I am a senile idiot, that I have escaped from a lunatic asylum, and that my skull has collapsed in several places.'

After the acquittal of Dimitrov, Torgler, *et al*, Muenzenberg's victory was complete. It had far-reaching and lasting political effects. In the public mind, Dimitrov's acquittal became synonymous with the acquittal of Communism in general from the charge of conspiracy and violence. Communist terror was an invention of the Nazis to discredit their main opponents; in reality, the Communists were honest defenders of freedom and democracy, only more courageous and determined than others. To call Dimitrov a 'Comintern agent' was to speak the language of the Nazis. Dimitrov became the symbol of that brave and respectable type of modern Liberal, the 'anti-Fascist'.

Six months later the group of S.A. leaders to which the authors of the fire had in all likelihood belonged—Roehm, Heines, Schultz, etc.—were liquidated in Hitler's 30th of June purge. Thus the precise circumstances of the fire will probably never be established. Both Heines and Schultz had produced fairly convincing alibis, and in some other respects too the guesses of the *Brown Book* had been wide of the mark. But that did not diminish the effect. In totalitarian propaganda details do not matter.

Even more remarkable was the Communists' achievement

in effacing from public memory the fact that for years, in Germany and elsewhere, they had preached violence and armed rebellion. The evidence was there—on the front-page of every Communist paper. But as the Trial had established that they had not planned an armed rebellion on the day of the Fire of the Reichstag, the public regarded it as implicitly proven that they never had and never would at any date.

The most fascinating example of how the world was fooled is the affair of the so-called 'Sofia plot' which played an important part in the Reichstag trial. The Sofia plot was probably the ghastliest single act of terrorism in modern history. On April 14, 1925, the chief of the Bulgarian General Staff was shot dead in Sofia. During his funeral service two days later, the Cathedral of Sofia was blown up by a time-bomb hidden behind the altar. A hundred and fifty people were killed on the spot, and over five hundred seriously wounded. Among the dead were fourteen generals, the Chief of Police, the Mayor of Sofia, over fifty high government officials, thirty newspaper editors and journalists, and so on. The King and leading members of the Cabinet were among the wounded. The idea behind the plot had obviously been to exterminate the Government and leaders of the Bulgarian ruling class in one blow.

The Government's retaliatory measures were even more terrible than the outrage itself. According to official figures, eighty-one trials were held involving 3,537 persons, of whom 300 were condemned to death. According to opposition reports, at least 5,000 were killed or disappeared. Some prisoners were burned alive in the great heating furnace of the Sofia Police headquarters. One of Dimitrov's brothers was killed in Sofia prison. Dimitrov himself, leader of the Bulgarian Communist Party, was condemned to death *in absentia*. He, and the Comintern, naturally denied any responsibility for the outrage and claimed that it was the work of police *agents provocateurs*.

When Dimitrov was arrested seven years later on the charge of having set fire to the Reichstag, the Nazi Press accused him of having also blown up Sofia Cathedral. Dimitrov and the Muenzenberg-Comintern machine shrewdly seized this opportunity to convince the world that, as the communists were innocent of the Reichstag outrage, they were also innocent of the Cathedral outrage. In his famous concluding speech at the Reichstag trial, Dimitrov once more drove home this point :

'My Lords, this is not the first time that such an outrage has been falsely attributed to Communists . . . I would also remind you of the outrage in Sofia Cathedral. This incident was not organised by the Bulgarian Communist Party, but the Bulgarian Communist Party was persecuted on account of it. Under this false accusation two thousand Bulgarian Communists, workmen, peasants and intellectuals were murdered. That act of provocation, the blowing up of Sofia Cathedral, was actually organised by the Bulgarian police.'

The truth of the matter only came out fifteen years later—through Dimitrov's own mouth. On December 19, 1948, at the 5th Congress of the Bulgarian Communist Party, Dimitrov flatly stated that the Sofia Cathedral had, after all, been blown up by the Communist Party, which at that time had been suffering from a Left deviation :

'The Party Executive inside the country, however, proved unable to cope with the ultra-Left deviation, to discontinue in time the policy of armed uprising and to proceed with the re-organisation of the Party's activity in accordance with the changed conditions. The Fascist government continued its terroristic course with even greater ferocity. Taking advantage of the desperate actions of the leaders of the Party's military organisation, culminating in the attempt at the Sofia Cathedral, it started a mass slaughter of active Communists. . . .'

Funnily enough, both quotations appear in the same book : *Georgi Dimitrov—Selected Speeches and Articles,* published by the British Communist Party, with a preface by Harry Pollitt (Lawrence & Wishart, London 1951). The first quotation, in which Dimitrov protests the Party's innocence, appears on page 23; the second, in which he admits its guilt, on pages 202–203. In the first quotation the blowing up of the Cathedral is called by the translator an 'outrage', in the second an 'attempt'; actually Dimitrov used in both cases the same word : '*Attentat*'.[1]

[1] cf. Michael Padev, 'A Bulgarian Dictator', *The Contemporary Review,* London, October, 1949.

After the acquittal, Torgler was taken into 'protective cus-
tody', that is, to a concentration camp, whereas Dimitrov and
his two Bulgarian aides were, despite Goering's repeated
threats, whisked off in a plane to Moscow. Two historians of
the Comintern, Ruth Fischer and Franz Borkenau,[1] have
asserted that from the very beginning of the trial Dimitrov
knew that a secret arrangement had been concluded between
the G.P.U. and the Gestapo, according to which, whatever the
outcome of the trial, he would reach Moscow in safety.

Ruth Fischer's assertion is based on confidential information received by her at the time of the trial from Wilhelm
Pieck, then a member of the German Central Committee, now
President of the Soviet German Republic, and from Maria
Reese, Deputy of the Reichstag and Torgler's girl friend. Ruth
Fischer asserts that Pieck was worried at the time lest Torgler
should learn of the arrangement and spill the beans during
the trial out of resentment at having been excluded from the
deal. Pieck, therefore, 'was busy arranging for a refugee from
underground Germany to arrive in London with the startling
message that Torgler was a traitor to the anti-Fascist cause.
. . . Pieck's courier did go to London and deliver his message
in a loud stage-whisper, but since Torgler never revealed the
arrangement by which Dimitrov was saved, the charge against
Torgler was allowed to peter out.'

I myself have no first-hand information regarding the
alleged deal. I remember, however, that Muenzenberg repeatedly and meaningfully warned us, his staff, 'not to build
up Torgler'. The implication was that Torgler might weaken
or even turn his coat. But this suspicion need not necessarily
have been related to the alleged Dimitrov deal.[2]

If a secret understanding did exist, it was merely one more
link in the chain of underground relations between the two
totalitarian régimes which lasted from the Nazis' ascent to
power until the Stalin-Hitler pact. But even if this were the

[1] Franz Borkenau, *European Communism,* London 1953, and Ruth
Fischer, *Stalin and German Communism,* Harvard, Mass., 1948.
[2] Torgler himself survived the war in a German concentration camp
and is now an official of the Social Democratic Party in a small German
town. His case proves again that the secret of survival in such circumstances lies in colourlessness and self-effacement. Torgler somehow
managed to remain inconspicuous even during his own trial.

case, Dimitrov was running the risk of infuriating the Nazis during the trial to such an extent that the deal would be called off. His personal courage remains wholly admirable. The pathetic rôle he played later on both as Secretary General of the Comintern and during the Stalin-Tito affair, merely proves that a Communist is apt to behave like a lion towards his enemies and like a mouse towards his superiors in the hierarchy.

And so the homeric battle of blind-man's-buff between the two giants ended. It had taught me that in the field of propaganda the half-truth was a weapon superior to the truth, and that to be on the defensive is to be defeated. It taught me above all that in this field a democracy must always be at a disadvantage against a totaliarian opponent. My years with Muenzenberg have made me sceptical regarding the West's chances of waging 'psychological warfare' against opponents like Hitler and Stalin. For to wage effective psychological war the West would have to abandon precisely those principles and values in the name of which it fights.

XVIII. Red Eminence

MY first meeting with Willy Muenzenberg made a strong impression on me. I became deeply attached to him—an attachment which lasted until he was assassinated in 1940.

Willy was born in Thuringia of working-class parents; as a youngster he had been a worker in a shoe factory for six years. When I met him he was forty-four—a shortish, square, squat, heavy-boned man with powerful shoulders, who gave the impression that bumping against him would be like colliding with a steam-roller. His face had the forceful simplicity of a wood-cut, but there was a basic friendliness about it. His broad, cosy Thuringian dialect, and his simple, direct manner further softened the powerful impact of his personality. He was a fiery, demagogical, and irresistible public speaker, and a born leader of men. Though without a trace of pompousness or arrogance, his person emanated such authority that I have seen Socialist Cabinet Ministers, hard-boiled bankers, and Austrian dukes behave like schoolboys in his presence. His only mannerism was to underline a point in conversation by a sudden flashing of his steel-grey eyes under raised eyebrows; and though this was usually followed by a smile, the effect on the interlocutor was rather like lightning. His collaborators were devoted to him, the girl comrades worshipped him, and his private secretary—tall, lean, game-legged, self-effacing young Hans Schultz—was known to work sometimes until three or four o'clock in the morning to get the ideas that incessantly spouted from Willy's fertile brain into shape. For Willy only dictated what he called 'drafts' or 'theses', which all ran something like this :

'Write to Feuchtwanger. Tell him articles received and so

on. Ask him to do a pamphlet for us, ten thousand copies to be smuggled into Germany, upholding cultural heritage and so on, tradition of Goethe and so on, leave the rest to him, love and kisses. Next, Hans, you buy a book on meterorology, find out about highs and lows and so on, find out how the wind blows over the Rhine, how many quarto handbills you can hang on a toy balloon, in which area of Germany balloons released on the French side are likely to come down, and so on. Then, Hans, you contact a few wholesale manufacturers of toy balloons, tell them it's for export to Venezuela, ask them for estimates for ten thousand balloons. Next, Hans . . .'

In the Comintern hierarchy Willy occupied an exceptional position, and this for two reasons. First, he was not a politician but a propagandist, not a 'theoretician' but an 'activist'. He took no part in the battles between factions which, every two years or so, produced a devastating earthquake in the Communist universe. He did not manœuvre for position, and the wrangles about the dialectically correct interpretation of the line left him cold and contemptuous.

Secondly, Willy was the head of a worldwide and powerful organisation, the 'International Workers' Aid' (IWA), known in Party slang as 'the Muenzenberg Trust'. The IWA was run by Moscow as an autonomous body, and not subject to the control of the local Communist Parties. Willy thus enjoyed a greater measure of independence and freedom of action in the international field than any other Comintern leader. Undisturbed by the stifling control of the Party bureaucracy, the Muenzenberg Trust's newspapers, periodicals, film and stage productions were able to exploit imaginative methods of propaganda in striking contrast to the pedantic, sectarian language of the official Party Press. Willy's spectacular successes, his unorthodoxy and ill-disguised contempt for sycophancy and hairsplitting, earned him the heartfelt hostility of the Party bureaucracy. The German bosses in particular—Ulbricht, Pieck, Eisler and Co.,—who now rule the Eastern Zone of Germany, were permanently plotting his downfall. They finally succeeded in 1937, during the Great Purge.

Willy had founded his famous Trust in September 1921 in Berlin. In his youth, after the years in the shoe factory, he had emigrated to Switzerland where he had worked as an assistant in a pharmacy. During the first World War, while in Zurich, he had been drawn into the circle of Lenin, Trotsky and the other Bolsheviks in exile. In 1917, he was expelled from Switzerland, returned to Germany, joined the revolutionary *Spartakus-Bund* and, in 1919, became one of the founder members of the Spartacists' offspring, the Communist Party of Germany. His early efforts as a propagandist were directed at young boys and girls; in 1920 when the Communist Youth International was inaugurated in Moscow, Willy was elected its president. Never have so many and such pretty girls marched in political demonstrations as during Willy's presidency.

A year later, when Russia was ravaged by the great famine that followed the Civil War, the Third Congress of the Comintern launched an appeal for help to the workers and friends of Socialism throughout the world. The appeal was followed by the founding of the IWA, with Muenzenberg at its head. It became at once an enormous success, though not exactly in the way that was originally intended. The original idea was famine-relief, and in the first two years some fifty shiploads of goods of all sorts, from drugs to trucks and sewing machines, were in fact collected and sent to Russia by the IWA. The quantity and the miscellaneous composition of these goods did not mean much to a starving country the size of Russia, but their indirect propaganda value was incalculable. Muenzenberg had hit on a new technique in mass propaganda, based on a simple observation : if a person gives money to a cause, he becomes emotionally involved in that cause. The greater the sacrifice, the stronger the bond; provided, of course, that the cause for which you are asked to make the sacrifice is brought to life in a vivid and imaginative manner—and that was Willy's speciality. He did not, for instance, ask the workers for charitable alms; he asked them to donate one day's wages 'as an act of solidarity with the Russian people'. 'Solidarity' instead of 'charity' became the keyword of his campaign, and the key-slogan of the IWA. Contributors were given IWA stamps, badges, medals, pictures of life in the U.S.S.R., busts of Marx and Lenin—each donation was forged into a link. Willy had found the pattern which he was to repeat in founding the 'World Committee for the Relief of the Victims of German Fascism' and in his various Chinese, Spanish and other relief campaigns : charity as a vehicle for political action.

The 'International Workers' Aid', like its successor the 'World Committee', soon branched into activities which had little or nothing to do with the original philanthropic purpose. The mobile canteens and soup-kitchens which the IWA had organised in famine-stricken Russia made their appearance during the following years in the working-class quarters of countries torn by social strife : in the Germany of the inflation years, in Japan during the 1925 strikes, in England during the 1926 General Strike. Out of the pamphlets issued in support of the relief campaign, grew the Trust's own publishing firms, its book clubs, and a multitude of magazines and newspapers. By 1926, Willy owned two daily papers in Germany with mass circulations, *Berlin am Morgen* and *Welt am Abend;* the *Arbeiter Illustrierte Zeitung*, a weekly with a circulation of one million, the Communist counterpart of *Life*; a series of other publications, including technical magazines for photographers, radio amateurs, etc., all with an indirect Communist slant. In Japan, to quote a remote country as an example, the Trust directly or indirectly controlled nineteen magazines and newspapers. It also financed Communist avant-garde plays which were in great vogue at the time. Finally the Trust was also the producer of some of the best films by Eisenstein and Pudovkin that came out of Russia (produced by *Meshrabpom-Film*, the Russian abbreviation for 'International Workers' Aid').

Within a few years, the Muenzenberg Trust had progressed from soup-kitchens for starving children to the launching of *Storm over Asia*. By the same method, the Paris World Relief Committee progressed within a few months from pious philanthropy to the organisation of the underground resistance movement in Germany, and to an indirect Communist propaganda agency in the rest of the world. As Ruth Fischer has pointed out, Muenzenberg was the original inventor of a new type of Communist organisation, the camouflaged 'front'; and the discoverer of a new type of ally : the liberal sympathiser, the progressive fellow-traveller :

'The success with which the Communist line was propagated among Social Democrats and Liberals during these years, the publication of *Ce Soir* in Paris, and *P.M.* in New York, the thousands of painters and writers and doctors and lawyers and debutantes chanting a diluted version of the Stalinist line—all this had its root in Willy Muenzenberg's International Workers' Aid.'[1]

The official Party bureaucracy hated not only Willy; they also looked with disfavour at his collaborators, who became branded as 'Muenzenberg-men'. This outward pressure moulded the people around Willy into an intimate clique, a kind of Party within the Party. The atmosphere that prevailed among us Muenzenberg-men was a strange mixture of revolutionary camaraderie and of the jealousies of courtiers around a benevolent despot. As usual in the German Party, everybody on the staff, including the office char and the driver (who were also émigré Party members), addressed the boss as 'Willy' and '*du*'. Manners were entirely informal, distinctions of rank or seniority did not—in theory—exist, and everybody, including Willy, drew—in theory—the same pay : the 'Party maximum' of fifteen hundred francs a month. In reality, of course, salaries were differentiated by means of expense accounts, and there existed a strict hierarchy of power, as in any ministry or business enterprise. Though Willy was impervious to flattery and hated every form of toadying, we were wary of contradicting him or incurring his disfavour, and dependent on his moods. And when Willy sauntered into a room, with the casualness of a tank bursting through a wall, we all watched his face for signs of sunshine or thunder, as employees do in any bourgeois outfit.

Willy's 'inner circle' consisted at that time of his wife, Babette Gross; his chief lieutenant, Otto Katz; and the 'Three Musketeers'—Hans the secretary, Emil the driver, and Jupp, the bodyguard and odd-job man.

Babette, *née* Thuring, was one of the two daughters of a Potsdam family. She was tall and distinguished-looking, with a still beautiful face, and efficient in a quiet, polite way. One would imagine that cool, patrician Babette and squat, proletarian Willy clashed in physical appearance; but there existed such a visible harmony between them, and both had so much

[1] Ruth Fischer, op. cit.

dignity in their different ways, that they gave the impression of a perfectly matched couple.

In the wild 'twenties, when the world of their parents had collapsed, the Thuring sisters had broken loose from their moorings, got caught up in the radical bohemia of the inflation years, joined the Communist Party of Germany, and went to live in unmarried union with its two most outstanding leaders : Babette with Willy Muenzenberg, her sister Greta—dark, petite, vivacious and gay—with Heinz Neumann. Willy was assassinated in France in 1940, Heinz Neumann during the Purge in Moscow in 1938. Greta did three years of forced labour in the Soviet concentration camps of Karaganda, was handed over by the G.P.U. to the Gestapo in 1940, and served another five years in the Nazi concentration camp of Ravensbrück. Her autobiographical book *Under Two Dictators* (London, 1949) ranks among the two or three best of its kind. Both Babette and Greta now live in Germany, and are still politically active in the anti-Communist camp.

Next in importance to Babette came Otto Katz. Otto was Willy's right-hand man, and his perfect complement; he had all the abilities that Willy lacked, and vice versa. Willy was a rugged leader, Otto a smooth and slick operator. Willy looked like a master-cobbler in a Thuringian village—one could imagine him sitting on a low stool, with a leather apron, driving tacks into an old boot with the energy of a sledge-hammer. Otto was dark and handsome, with a somewhat seedy charm. He was the type of person who, when lighting a cigarette, always closes one eye, and this habit became so fixed with him that he often closed his left eye while thinking out a problem even when he was not smoking. Willy did not speak a word of any language except German; Otto spoke fluent French, English, Russian and Czech. Willy was unable to write a single coherent paragraph; Otto was a glib journalist who had written and edited several books, all but one anonymously.[1] He came from Prague, had been business manager

[1] *Neun Männer am Eis,* Berlin, 1929. *The Brown Book of the Hitler Terror* (anonymous), London, 1933. *The Reichstag Fire Trial—the Second Brown Book of the Hitler Terror* (anonymous), London, 1934. *Hitler Prepares for War—The Third Brown Book* (anonymous), London, 1936. *The Nazi Conspiracy in Spain by the Editor of the Brown Book of the Hitler Terror,* London, 1937.

of a famous Liberal weekly in Berlin—Leopold Schwarzs-
child's *Das Tagebuch*—then manager of Erwin Piscator's
Communist stage productions; then manager of one of the
Muenzenberg Trust's publishing firms; then manager of
Meshrabpom-Film in Moscow (where I had met him for the
first time); then, during his years in Paris, organiser of the
World Relief Committee, organiser of the Spanish Relief
Committee, director of the Spanish News Agency, and dispen-
ser of the loyalist Government's secret propaganda funds for
French newspapers and politicians. He was the invisible
Willy's roving ambassador, and made periodic trips to Eng-
land and to Hollywood to collect funds, and to organise 'anti-
Fascist' committees. He had political contacts everywhere; he
was attractive to women, particularly to the middle-aged,
well-intentioned, politically active type, and used them
adroitly to smooth his path.

One of Otto's tasks was, of course, to spy on Willy for the
apparat. Willy knew this, and did not care. Willy needed Otto,
but he hardly bothered to disguise his contempt for him. Once,
when I asked Willy where he had first met Otto, he said in
his cosy Thuringian drawl : 'I fished him out of the Landwehr-
canal.' The Landwehr-canal in Berlin was a narrow water-
way, conveniently situated for the dumping of corpses and for
committing suicide. Apparently Otto, in the early 'twenties,
had got himself into some financial jam and told Willy that
Willy must either give him a job, or he would drown himself
in the canal. When Willy broke with the Comintern in 1938,
Otto was the first to desert him—as everybody had expected.
And when fate caught up with Otto in 1952, and he was
hanged in Prague on the absurd charge of being a British spy
and a Zionist conspirator, not a single voice was raised in his
defence among his former friends, associates and political
contacts.

In spite of all his seediness, Otto was, paradoxically, a very
likeable human being. He had the generosity of the adventurer, and he could be warm-hearted, spontaneous and helpful—so long as it did not conflict with his interests. I despised
and liked him at the same time. During my imprisonment in
Spain he let loose an international campaign for my liberation which was quite out of proportion with my importance

to the Party. On my return from prison he stood at the Gare du Nord with a huge bunch of flowers, and our embrace, on that occasion at least, was one of real fraternal warmth. It was also Otto who, moved by a kind of distressed sympathy, made a remark to me that I never forgot, and that I have quoted in *Arrow in the Blue*: 'We all have inferiority complexes of various sizes, but yours isn't a complex—it's a cathedral.'

My most vivid memories of Otto do not relate to politics, but to occasional meetings early in the morning in the food market of the Rue de la Convention. I was then a bachelor who did his own shopping, and Ilschen, Otto's pretty little wife, liked to sleep late in the morning; so in the crowded market of our popular *quartier* I often ran into an unshaven and tie-less Otto, the collar of his jacket turned up, with a net shopping-bag in his hand, bargaining with a fishwife, his left eye shrewdly closed, and displaying the same earnest charm that I have seen directed on other occasions at Miss Ellen Wilkinson, M.P., or Mlle. Genevieve Tabouis, columnist-oracle of the defunct *Oeuvre*. I should add that these relationships were purely functional, Otto's interests being entirely concentrated upon the Popular Front or the fish, as the case may be.

Our friendship, however, only began at a later period. At the beginning we did not get on well, and it was Otto who swiftly and smoothly brought my career as a 'Muenzenberg-man' to an end. Given the atmosphere of court intrigue and favouritism that surrounded Willy, it was inevitable that Otto should regard me as a potential rival. We were both multi-lingual, we both had a bourgeois background and useful contacts in the non-Communist world, and we were both efficient, dynamic and alert. Such types are rare in the Communist Party, for they cannot stand its rigid discipline, and usually leave after a short time. But there the parallel ended, for Otto had political ambitions whereas I had long realised my total unfitness for a political career. As far as the Party was concerned, my only ambition was to serve—to be 'exploited by the Party', as the official slogan had it. This urge for subordination and anonymous usefulness was obviously the reverse of a character consumed by ambition and vanity in other fields; but Otto could not be expected to know of this peculiarity, and to believe in the sincerity of my motives. As for Willy, he knew that Otto would betray him before the Kremlin-cock crowed thrice. But Willy, who had an unerring instinct for character, also sensed the element of puritanism and naïveté in my relationship to the Party—and decided that just because of that I would never become a first-rate, 'Muenzenberg-man'. Engaged in a constant struggle against the bureaucracy, Willy could not afford to have puritans and innocents in his entourage. By the nature of things he had use for only two types : men like Otto about whom he had no illusions and with whom his relations were based upon a calculated give-and-take; and men like Hans and the Three Musketeers, who were blindly and unconditionally devoted to him. A psychological freak of my kind was obviously unfit for the high-powered, streamlined Muenzenberg Trust.

The verdict in the Reichstag Trial was announced two days before Christmas 1933. Once the trial was over, the usual anti-climax set in. The Second Brown Book—*Dimitrov contra Goering*—was being prepared. The newspaper cuttings, documents and pamphlets in our offices had grown to huge bulk, and Willy decided to expand them into an Anti-Fascist Archive, which in turn was expanded into a Free German Library.[1] I was assigned to work in the Archive, which I liked well enough. Yet it was an evident demotion, and I felt that my days as a Muenzenberg-man were numbered.

I could probably have succeeded in neutralising Otto's jealousy and keeping my unobtrusive job in the Archive. But I was faced with a more important problem on a different level. For the first time I had become a professional Communist, a salaried employee of the Party. Officially, of course, I was employed by the 'World Committee for Relief', but in fact I was paid by IWA, that is, with Party money; my situation was that of a Party official delegated to work at a 'front' organisation. And this idea went strongly against the grain. I had never wanted to become a party bureaucrat, and I had a deep aversion to all kinds of political officialdom. It dated perhaps from my Zionist days, when I had learnt to despise

[1] The latter, housed on the Boulevard Arago, was also the headquarters of the illegal French branch of the International Workers' Aid.

the self-important, inflated bureaucrats of that movement. It had deepened when I had come to know the machinery of Comintern politics. I wanted to live for the Party, not off the Party; I wanted to be an amateur Communist, not a professional.

It was an illogical attitude for a Marxist, an expression, no doubt, of 'petit-bourgeois romanticism', and in fact quite heretical in view of Lenin's insistence on the need for 'professional revolutionaries'. But I could not help it. The atmosphere in the Muenzenberg Trust was more liberal and easy-going than in an orthodox Party office, and one need not be afraid that an uncautious remark would be held against one on the day of reckoning. Nevertheless I felt that after a few years as a 'Muenzenberg-man', there would be little left in me of what independence and self-respect I possessed.

I was at a crossroads. Either I must make a career in the Muenzenberg Trust, as I had once done in the Ullstein Trust, and live as a professional Communist; or I must make a living by some other means, and regain my financial independence. I felt that the whole of my future depended upon this choice; and as at every similar turning-point, the decision made itself, without conscious weighing of pros and cons on my part. Early in 1934 I resigned from the one and only salaried Party job that I have ever held, and for the time being, parted company with Willy and Otto, without arguments or bitterness.

XIX. Introducing Dr. Costler

HAVING decided not to make Communism my career, I now settled down and wrote two books in quick succession. One was my first novel and was never published; I shall come back to it later. The other was published under the pen-name 'Dr. A. Costler' and became at once an international best-seller. Moreover—such is the irony of fate—it has remained the only book of mine that met with an unanimously friendly reception. Even critics who find all of Mr. K.'s books detestable, found for Dr. C.'s book nothing but praise. I am quoting some comments in the footnote.[1] The reader will find this self-glorification more pardonable when he learns that the book in question, published under the names of 'Drs. A. Costler, A. Willy and Others', bore the title *The Encyclopædia of Sexual Knowledge*.

It was the first of an anonymous trilogy which in some respects has become a standard work in its field. The full title of the second book was '*Sexual Anomalies and Perversions, Physical and Psychological Development, Diagnoses and Treatment*, a Summary of the Works of the Late Professor Dr. Magnus Hirschfeld, President of the World League for Sexual Reform, Director of the Institute for Sexual Science, Berlin, etc., Compiled as a Humble Memorial by his Pupils

[1] As I have not kept the original reviews, I can anly quote from those which appear on the jacket:

'Lucid, unshocked, eminently sensible' (*New Statesman and Nation*). 'Excellent for Doctors and Psychologists . . .' (*Time and Tide*). 'Covers the ground thoroughly and gives up-to-date information . . .' (*The Listener*). 'Well documented and accurate' (Aldous Huxley). 'Gives all the essential knowledge that any layman (or woman) needs on all aspects of the subject' (*The Schoolmaster*). 'This monumental book may be commended' (*The Medical Officer*).

and edited by Norman Haire, Ch.M., M.B., President, Sex Education Society; Editor, Journal of Sex Education, London. A Textbook for Students, Psychologists, Criminologists, Probation Officers, Judges, Educationalists, and all adults.'

The title of the third book was, in the original French edition, *L'Encyclopedie de la Famille*; it had in England a curious publishing history about which I shall speak later.

The first book contained chapters by two other authors; the second I wrote alone; the third contained chapters by Manes Sperber (who had been a practising psychotherapist before he made his reputation as a novelist).

All three books were written between 1934 and 1939, in the intervals between various political jobs, imprisonments, and the writing of books under my own name.

The Encyclopædia of Sexual Knowledge consisted of six parts. The first dealt with the physical and psychological manifestations of the sexual drives from childhood to maturity; the second with the physiology and psychology of love; the third with pregnancy and childbirth; the fourth with impotence, frigidity and other common disturbances; the fifth with the more common sexual aberrations; the sixth with prostitution and venereal diseases. Parts three and six were written by a German specialist, Dr. Levy-Lenz (whose name appeared in the French edition as 'Lery-Lenz'), and the chapters on prostitution by the publisher (who appeared among the authors as 'A. Willy').

The second book of the trilogy was what its title said, a condensation of the works of Magnus Hirschfeld, during his lifetime the leading authority in his field. The 'pupils' who appear as author was I, but the English edition was considerably enlarged and revised by the editor, Norman Haire.

The third book was a manual of the psychology of marriage, written mainly from the point of view of the Adlerian school (Manes Sperber, Fritz Kuenkel). To this the publisher of the English edition added, without my knowledge (I was in a concentration camp when the book went to press), a rehash of the physiological chapters of the first book and a number of additional chapters; he then published the manuscript under a different title.

My reasons for writing these books were twofold. First, I had somehow to earn a living during the starvation years of exile. Secondly, my passion for writing popular science had never died completely, and, among all sciences, the science of sex is paradoxically the least known.

My first contact with sexology[1] dated back to the days when I was science editor at Ullsteins. In the spring of 1932, a short time before I lost my job, I studied for several weeks the admirable work done in Dr. Magnus Hirschfeld's *Sexual-wischenschaftliches Institut*. In view of the reputation which the *Vossische Zeitung* enjoyed, I was allowed to be present at a number of exploratory interviews and therapeutic sittings with typical patients. To remain inconspicuous, I was given a white overall and introduced as the doctor's assistant—that is how the future Dr. Costler came into being.

The patients were ordinary people who would pass unobserved in the anonymous mass of any great city. I particularly remember a young and pleasant electrical engineer, a huge, jovial railway porter, and a middle-aged accountant. The young engineer was a repressed homosexual who had never heard of homosexuality; he thought himself a criminal or, at least, mentally deranged, had twice tried to commit suicide and suffered from chronic fainting fits. The Herculean railway porter was a pseudo-hermaphrodite. The accountant suffered from *ejaculatio praecox*, a common nervous disorder which had wrecked his otherwise happy marriage. And so it went on. I had read Freud and Adler and Jung and Steckel, but I had never imagined how many hidden tragedies cross one's path every day in the streets; and when it came to statistics, the extent of the sexual mass-misery was quite staggering. Twenty years later, the Kinsey report came as a revealing shock to the American public. But in 1932, the basic data on the modern emotional plague could already be found in Hirschfeld's Berlin institute. The chaotic social conditions in Germany before the Nazis took power, the despair, nihilism, and near-hysteria of large sections of the people, had

[1] There is, curiously, no English expression for 'Sexualwischenschaft'; to avoid the clumsy 'sexual science', I shall use the term 'sexology' which seems legitimate.

naturally deepened the crisis in *mores* and made it appear in an even more lurid light.

I wrote a series of articles whose factual content was so shocking that the *Vossische* did not dare to print them. They carried as a motto the inscription over the gate of the 'Sexualwischenschaftliches Institut'; AMORI ET DOLORI SACRUM— loving and suffering are sacred. I quote a few paragraphs that may serve as a motto to the books that I later wrote on the subject, and as an explanation for my interest in it :

Out of sixty million Germans approximately one and a half million are homosexuals who live in permanent conflict with the law.

In the sixty-million population of Germany, every year more unborn children are illegally aborted than children are born.

Birth control, one of the decisive factors in a nation's destiny, is a clandestine practice. The 'public advertisement and offer for sale' of contraceptives is illegal; the annual sale of ninety million of these appliances represents ninety million more or less veiled offences against the law.

Even these introductory remarks may suffice to let a quite incredible idea dawn on us—the idea that the routine sexual activity of our times has its place outside the law.

The films, the radio and the printing presses tell us that the great cataclysm of 1914 has revolutionised the erotic habits of our age. It is true that the Chinese Wall has collapsed; but its ruins are covered by a jungle that we call the new morality of the post-war era. We are exposed to an inflation of bogus enlightenment; pamphlets circulate by the million with prescriptions for the perfect marriage, life and love; the psychoanalysts and the Salvation Army, nudist prophets and public prosecutors, Lesbian clubs and sex blackmailers are fighting for our bodies and souls. The taboos have been smashed—but they have merely been replaced by half-baked slogans and catch-phrases. And the lonely wanderer in the labyrinth of Eros is lonelier than ever.

In the economic chaos of the pre-war world, millions of individuals were unable to satisfy their hunger. The sexual chaos of the post-war world has shaken mankind to a similar extent, but it has equally failed to answer the problem of millions how to satisfy their instincts, how to resolve the tragic dilemma between artificially over-stimulated desire and the stern limitations of custom and law.

Is there a change, is there an improvement since that much advertised breaking of taboos? Has the revolution in our customs really created a better and healthier state of affairs? There is no evidence for this optimistic belief. The evidence of polls and statistics, the evidence of the cafés, bars and taverns in our towns all point to the opposite conclusion.

I thus became interested in sexology as one of the many facets of the crisis in our civilisation. However, I would hardly have thought of writing a book on the subject (and much less a trilogy of some half a million words), but for the desperate impasse in which I found myself as a Communist exile who did not wish to make a living out of Communism. No French publisher would print *Red Days*, no French theatre would produce 'the firm's' plays, and I could not get a job on a French newspaper as my French, though fluent, was far from perfect. Hence, when a publisher suggested to me that as a one-time science editor, I should write a popular *Encyclopædia of Sexual Knowledge*, embracing everything that the average citizen wanted to know of the subject, I eagerly accepted the offer. He gave me a dozen or so standard text-books and reference works, ranging from Mantegazza's *Die Hygiene der Liebe* to Van de Velde's *Ideal Marriage,* and from these I condensed and distilled the 'Encyclopædia' at a rate of about four thousand words a day.

I wrote the book in six or eight weeks, and was paid for it a flat sum of three thousand francs—at the time approximately forty pounds. This sum included the sale of the copyright; I received no royalties. When the book became a world best-seller, the publisher felt moved to make an additional payment, not foreseen in the contract, of another £20. The latest English edition, dated January 1944, shows the imprint: 'New Cheap Edition 25/- Nett. Over 75,000 copies Sold.' The French, American, Spanish and Italian editions had a similar success; I have no idea in what other languages the book appeared.

The publishing firm in question was owned by two brothers from Budapest. They were actually relatives of mine—this is the one fact in this chapter that I find embarrassing to confess.

In *Arrow in the Blue* I have mentioned that my mother's stuffy and conservative middle-middle-class family had been ruined in the 1890's by the marriage of one of its female members to a villain in the best tradition of Victorian melodrama. The two brothers were the offspring of that marriage. As a child I had known them well; then I had lost sight of them—until the older one turned up as a publisher in Paris and approached me with his offer. I shall call him Theodore, and the younger one Freddie.

The two brothers had contrasting personalities. Freddie had inherited his father's character; he was a typical adventurer from that colourful region between the Danube and the Levant. Dark and handsome, with a faun's face, and eyebrows grown together over a fleshy nose, Freddie was charged with sex like a gypsy fiddler. He was ostentatious in manner and dress, a reckless gambler, a seducer of women, and a generous squanderer of money. He had fascinated me all through my childhood as the embodiment of dazzling villainy, a hero of disreputableness. He was about ten years my senior. When I was five, I admired him because on our country holidays he stole chickens, wrung their necks and roasted them on a spit. When I was ten, he burgled my father's wardrobe to pawn his suits; when I was thirteen, he put my favourite governess in the family way—see *Arrow in the Blue*. Freddie had all the flashy charm of his type; and beyond that, like many people who lie for art's sake and believe in their own lies, he had an almost hypnotic power of persuasion. He was also a hypochondriac with a tendency to hysteria, an aggressive coward, and a man with a desperate need to be liked and admired. In short, a psychopathic character straight out of a textbook, but full of charm and seduction.

Theodore, the older one, was by disposition Freddie's exact opposite. He had started life as an introvert and a bookworm. As an adolescent he had been awkward and complex-ridden, tortured by jealousy for the younger brother who was the darling of his parents and the spoiled genius of the family. Theodore grew up with a kind of Cinderella complex. He studied law without ever exercising his profession, dabbled in journalism, and never got anywhere until Freddie took him into his publishing firm. Had he been a stronger character, he would have grown in the opposite direction to Freddie. But he was weak and ruined his life by trying to imitate his younger brother. Honest and even scrupulous by disposition, he became gradually corrupted by Freddie, who had an uncanny power over him and whom he then tried to outdo in reckless manners and as a lady-killer—parts for which he was pathetically unfit. He lived in a permament cramp, and his forced antics were embarrassing to watch.

Family relationships pertain to a plane where the ordinary rules of judgment and conduct do not apply. They are a labyrinth of tensions, quarrels and reconciliations, whose logic is self-contradictory, whose ethics stem from a cosy jungle, and whose values and criteria are distorted like the curved space of a self-contained universe. It is a universe saturated with memories—but memories from which no lessons are drawn; saturated with a past which provides no guidance to the future. For in this universe, after each crisis and reconciliation, time always starts afresh and history is always in the year zero. This may explain why, after I had been done in by Freddie and Theodore over the *Encyclopædia* as thoroughly and completely as a choir-boy in a gold-digger town, I proceeded, one year later, to write the second book for them; was done in again, and yet, four years later, proceeded to write the third —for which I haven't been paid to this day. It may also explain why, in spite of all this—and in spite of two jovial blackmailing attempts by the late Freddie, threatening to disclose Dr. Costler's identity 'to the world public'—Freddie himself has never lost his fascination for me.

Freddie died, in 1951, completely destitute, in a London hospital. He died of a brain disease. He had played a more important part in my life than our actual relations seemed to warrant. From my early childhood, the dark, cocky, totally irresponsible cousin had served as a bogey in my mother's family. 'Beware of Freddie, my child' and 'never become like Freddie' were her constant admonitions, a refrain that rang in my ears for years. So, of course, Freddie became immensely attractive as the embodiment of forbidden badness, and as a small child I worshipped him—the more so as he took me to football games, taught me chess, dirty words, and how to cheat on my pocket-money accounts. But I soon realised how ruthlessly he betrayed my confidence and used me as a tool, so my adulation of Freddie changed into a mixture of fascination and horror.

Through Freddie, I had my first experience of moral evil. To most sheltered middle-class children 'evil' is an abstraction; through Freddie I came early into direct contact with it and realised that evil is really evil. But since I continued to love Freddie, while morally condemning him, I learned not only to recognise evil, but to understand it with an intuitive, almost tender, comprehension. (Perhaps that is the reason why, later on, I could not help liking Otto Katz.) I recognised that there was a good deal of Freddiness in myself, and a tendency to emulate him as poor Theodore did; but at the same time I also understood that this part of myself was the enemy within whom I had to fight for all I was worth. It was like an infection which forces the organism to develop antitoxins; the reaction against the Freddiness in myself must have played an important part in my early obsession with Utopia, the Perfect Cause, the arrow in the blue.

Through Freddie I also learnt the complexities and contraductions of human character. As a born gambler, he was generous in his private life; during the years of exile when I was unable to support my parents, he often helped them by small loans and gifts. At the same time he seemed to be incapable of meeting his business obligations or repaying debts —an incapacity based on a genuine neurotic inhibition. He had a great affection for me and entertained me lavishly when we met; but this did not prevent him from ruthlessly exploiting and cheating me in our business relations. He was willing at any time to lend me small sums of money, but refused to pay me royalties on the books from which his and his brother's fortunes were mainly derived. When, in the end, I went to my solicitors, he wrote to me with genuine indignation that he had never expected such ingratitude from me.

His last years were like the end of a morality tale. I had broken off relations with him in 1939, and during the following twelve years, until his death, I saw him on only one, un-

forgettable occasion. He had been interned as an enemy alien
in 1941. Unlike other Hungarians in England who were released within a few months when their loyalty had been established, he was kept in internment during the whole period of
the war. In November 1942, I received a hysterical letter from
him asking me to 'use my influence' to get him released at
once, and ending with the usual veiled 'or else'. I tore the
letter up in disgust, and a week later got another even more
hysterical one, asking my forgiveness and begging for help.
The charges against him, according to his letter, were 'leading
an immoral life, publishing pornographic books, dope pedd-
ling, racketeering in wines and spirits, being a Hungarian secret agent, and passing on information to the Nazis'. I believe
that he invented most of these charges himself in order to
make the real charges appear equally absurd; at any rate, he
was never tried on any of them. I did not know what he had
been up to in the years since I had last seen him, and was
careful not to get mixed up in all this, but I sent him occasional food parcels, cigarettes and comforting letters to the
internment camp on the Isle of Man. Then, some time in 1943,
he made the foolish mistake of trying to bribe one of the
officers in the camp, was brought up to London for a special
investigation, and asked me to visit him. That was our last
meeting.

It took place in the Brompton Oratory School which, during the war, had been requisitioned by the Ministry of Home
Security and used as a kind of transit camp for political de-
tainees. I was kept for a while in a desolate waiting-room.
Then the door opened, and an unshaven, collarless figure in
a once too-showy, now stained and crumpled suit was escorted
in by a sergeant. For a fraction of a second I did not recognise
him. He walked up to me with a would-be debonair grin, but
at that moment another door opened, an officer walked
through the room, and the sergeant ordered Freddie to stand
to attention. Freddie jumped to the command and pulled
himself up in the indescribable way old convicts have when
standing to attention in the prison yard : with shoulders
slumped forward, arms dangling to knock-kneed legs. His
stubbled, grey, creased face expressed an abject servility, and
a fear which was quite unwarranted by the circumstances. He

was then allowed to sit down, and we talked across a table in the sergeant's presence. For a minute or so Freddie seemed embarrassed by his preceding humiliation, but soon he became again his cocky, scheming, persuasive self, trying to involve me in the affairs of his firm with the promise of ample rewards after his liberation and 'for the sake of our past friendship'. Our past friendship had ended when my solicitor unsuccessfully tried to serve a writ on Freddie, but he seemed to have genuinely forgotten it. I told him, as gently as I could, that I wished to have nothing to do with his affairs.

'My poor boy,' Freddie said feelingly, 'you have been hopeless all your life. First you were a Zionist, then a Communist, always broke, always shabbily dressed and hungry, except when I bought you a decent meal. Now you write political novels which nobody wants to read. You will never make real money in your life. I was the only one to give you a break and make you a world success with the *Encyclopædia*. And now, when I am down, you snootily refuse to help me with my business, which I cannot conduct from the camp, although you know that I am innocent and detained on entirely arbitrary grounds. But to tell you the truth, I have never expected anything else from you.'

His hypnotic persuasiveness had not lost its effect, and for a moment I felt the embodiment of darkest ingratitude. I asked Freddie timidly whether the last food parcel had been all right. He looked at me with scathing irony from under his dark, joined satyr's eyebrows and remarked that I seemed to believe that he had become a vegetarian. I told him apologetically that rationing made the sending of meat impossible. His irony deepened to amused contempt : '*Rationing*—that's typical of you. I will tell you the name of a shop in Soho where you get as much Hungarian gooseliver-paté and Italian salami as you like.' He added as an afterthought : 'You can send the sergeant a salami, too.' The sergeant, a young chap from the Midlands, changed colour but kept silent.

When the time was up, after Freddie and I had shaken hands for the last time, the sergeant made Freddie stand to attention, and after an 'about turn !', made him leave the room at the 'quick march'. During this humiliating manœuvre, Freddie's face again seemed to fall to pieces.

Stumping out of the room, with the obscene nakedness round the neck of men in town-suits deprived of collar and tie, his eyes dulled with cringing and panic, the hero of my childhood vanished from my life.

How Freddie came to be a publisher I only know by hearsay. It was not he, but Theodore, who commissioned me in the spring of 1934 to write the 'Encyclopædia'. At that time he was not yet Freddie's partner, but his employee at a modest salary. He told me how Freddie, after one of his bankruptcies, had married a girl with a dowry whose parents kept a stationery shop with a lending library in a Hungarian provincial town. After getting rid of his creditors, Freddie had worked in the lending library for a few months. At that time, Professor Van de Velde's *Ideal Marriage* had just been published in German, and had created a great stir by its outspoken treatment of the physiological aspects of conjugal life. On the spur of one of his sudden inspirations, Freddie got into a train, went to see the German publishers in Stuttgart, and bought the foreign-language copyrights of the book. He published it in Hungarian and, I believe, in Italian, and at the same time sent Theodore to Paris to found a French publishing firm.

The firm's name was 'Editions . . .', featuring the surname of the brothers.[1] Its method of operation was different from that of other publishers. Freddie had invented a system by which he sold his books before they were written, and when it was still doubtful whether they would ever be written. (That, Theodore explained to me, was the reason why he could pay me no royalties.) The Paris office—consisting of two dingy rooms, and staffed by one accountant and one typist—sent out large numbers of circulars to professional people, mostly in provincial towns. Their addresses were culled by a statistical sampling system from that series of excellent French address books called the *Bottin Professionel*. The circulars contained an elaborate description, with list of contents, illustrations, etc., of the projected book, pretending that it was in the pro-

[1] Their firm in England ran under the same name until it was dissolved and the copyrights of the Dr. Costler book were ceded to another publisher, under whose imprint they are now sold

cess of printing, and asking for cash payment in advance at a 'preferential price'. If the first batch of 2,000 circulars brought orders from less than one and a half per cent. of the addresses, the idea of the book was dropped, and the cash payments were refunded. (This happened to another contemplated Dr. Costler book, an Encyclopædia of Psychic Research.) If the orders exceeded one and a half per cent., a second batch of 10,000 circulars were sent out. If the orders from these confirmed the percentage of the first batch, the book was commissioned, and the number of circulars was simultaneously increased to 100,000 or 200,000, in the now certain expectation of at least 2,000 buyers, which for a high-priced book and practically no overhead expenses meant an excellent profit. In fact, the *Encyclopædia* sold some 30,000 copies in its first year in France, and if, during the following twenty years, it sold only a further half as many copies, Freddie and Theodore must have made some fifteen thousand pounds out of it in that country alone, compared to my sixty.

The English editions of the three books featured Norman Haire as editor. He was a Harley Street specialist on birth control. I have never met Mr. Haire, but I have looked him up in *Who's Who* for 1946, where he occupies more space than either Winston Churchill or George Bernard Shaw. I am told that he died in 1952.

I was in doubt whether to use a pseudonym, and the halfheartedness of the disguise (with only two letters in the name altered) reflects my hesitations on the subject. But I had no guarantee that the published text would be identical with my manuscript. The publishers had reserved the right to edit the manuscript, and I had reason to suspect that they would cut, alter and embellish it as they saw fit. I had in fact no more control over the book than a film-script writer over the finished product. As matters turned out, the French edition of the *Encyclopædia* followed the manuscript without major distortions, except for its style. I wrote it (as I wrote all my books until 1940) in German, in a sober, matter-of-fact style which the translator changed into the oily and whimsical language of the kind of popular science book which treats the reader as a gentle moron. In the English translation, which was based on the French text, this tendency is even more accentuated and very embarrassing indeed; there are also numerous additions and alterations by editor and translator. In short, I do not recommend the book. People in need of guidance will find more up-to-date works on the subject at a lower price; while those in search of titillation will find the book about as stimulating as a gourmet would find a Salvation Army kitchen. Much the same is true of the second book.[1]

Another reason for preferring a pseudonym was the natural fear of a politically-active person of the odium that still attaches to matters sexual. It is this hypocrisy which turns the publishing of books on sex into a shady business, and which breeds and feeds the Freddies of this world. After all, it can hardly be a writer's ambition to see his name displayed between douches and rubber appliances in the windows of chemist shops in Charing Cross Road. Yet even that seemed preferable, and more honourable, than to earn my living by the political prostitution which the Party demands from its scribes. It is one thing to believe in the ultimate truth of the teachings of Marx and Lenin, but quite another to write to the dictate of the drill-sergeants of the Party bureaucracy, to perpetrate 'hymns to Stalin' (as my friend Johannes Becher was forced to do), to pretend that Trotsky was a Nazi agent, to eat your words and confess your sins in public every six months, vowing repentance and whining like a schoolboy 'I shall never do it again'.

While I was still hesitating whether to accept Theodore's offer, an article appeared in one of the magazines published by Muenzenberg. Its author was a Party hack called Rudy Feistman, and its title *Lenin'sche Dialektik oder Trotzkistisches Nasebohren* ('Leninist Dialectics or Trotskyist Nose-picking'). I was already inured to abuse as a political weapon,

---

[1] The English edition of the third volume of the triology belongs to an entirely different category. It has only 46 pages (pp. 336–382) out of 805 in common with the manuscript that Sperber and I wrote. The remaining 759 pages are a reprint of the first book with a number of additional chapters by various hands. The original title *Encyclopedie de la Famille* has been characteristically changed to *Encyclopaedia of Sexual Practice*. 'Dr. Costler' has been omitted from the list of authors, to which several fictitious names have been added. It is a confused, repetitive and irresponsible compilation, edited, as the preceding volumes, by Norman Haire.

yet somehow the nauseating impudence of the title, however unimportant the article was in itself, decided the issue for me. When I mentioned it to Willy, he simply shrugged without comment. He was as independent as a Comintern leader could possibly be, yet the limits of that independence were all too evident.

Rudy Feistman was one of the young intellectuals, or rather eternal adolescents of the Party, who had never done any serious work in their lives, were incapable of standing on their own feet, and therefore regarded themselves as 'professional revolutionaries'. They had become so completely soaked in the atmosphere of the Party and in the dialectics of the smear, that they regarded slander as a natural and legitimate weapon. Rudy had been a friend of my first wife's and I knew him well; in 1940, after my break with the Party, we were locked up in the same concentration camp, where he insinuated as a matter of course that I must be a Nazi agent. He was tall, gawky and unkempt, with a perpetual, supercilious smirk on his ruddy, thick-lipped face which the Lord seemed to have left unfinished half-way through out of boredom. I loathed him not so much as an individual than as a type.[1] The fact that the Party encouraged hordes of these little intellectual spivs to talk of the creator of the Red Army in terms of 'nose-picking' filled me with a more profound disgust than other events of greater consequence. Confronted with that intellectual sewer, I preferred the fresh air of Charing Cross Road.

[1] Feistman, after getting mixed up in the Soviet intelligence apparatus, was liquidated in 1952 in the Eastern Zone of Germany.

K

XX. Schoolmaster in Maisons Lafitte

I HAD just finished writing the *Encyclopædia*, when Willy Muenzenberg asked me to see him on an urgent matter. Among his numerous enterprises was a Home for refugee children. Officially it was open to the children of needy German refugees of all classes and political parties; in fact its inmates were, with a few exceptions, the children of Communist Party officials who had either been killed by the Nazis, or sent on secret missions into Germany, or were engaged in other confidential Party work which made it impossible for them to look after their families. The Home had run out of money. It housed some thirty children between the ages of two and sixteen in a villa in Maisons Lafitte, near Paris, appropriately called 'La Pouponnière', which a charitable Frenchman had put at the Committee's disposal. Willy asked me to spend a few days in the Home and write a fund-raising pamphlet about it :

'Tell them they can't let the children starve while their parents are fighting for Freedom and so on, five thousand words, and get some photos of the brats, make them look jolly but thin.' The matter, he added, with one of those impressive flashes of his eye, was urgent.

How urgent it was, I realised the next day when I arrived at the desolate villa, a few hundred yards from the forest and from the famous racing track at Maisons Lafitte. Diphtheria had broken out among the children, there was no trained personnel to look after them, and the stocks in the larder consisted of rice, macaroni, cocoa, sugar, cooking fat and nothing else.

The Communist Party has a sound maxim for its writers

and intellectuals : it is called the 'operative principle'. It means that you cannot write about the strategy of Communism without having worked in a factory, or Party cell, or underground organisation. The tenet 'No revolutionary theory without revolutionary practice' dates back to Marx, who spent more time in organising small workers' associations than in writing *Das Kapital*. Similarly, if a Soviet writer embarked on a novel about collective farming, or a motor car factory, he had to spend several months of active work in a *kholkhoz* or a factory to get the 'operative angle', the inside feel of his subject. Thus it was only natural that, though I knew less about children than about Bushmen, I was turned from the moment of my arrival into a schoolmaster, nurse and medical assistant.

Instead of a few days, I stayed in the Home for more than two months. This unexpected experience led to the birth of my first novel. I started writing it on the spot, after I finished the pamphlet. The novel won the second or third prize (I don't remember which) in an international competition of the *Büchergilde Guttenberg*, a Socialist book-club in Switzerland, but was never published. It was called *Die Erlebnisse des Genossen Piepvogel und seiner Freunde in der Emigration* —'The Adventures in Exile of Comrade Cheepy-bird and his Friends'. The title was a homage to an enchanting little boy of four who had learnt the expression 'Genosse' among the first words in his vocabulary, and addressed with it all grown-ups, children and animals. One day, tottering about the garden, he exclaimed, pointing at a sparrow on a tree, 'Look, comrade, there is a comrade cheepy-bird'; hence his nickname which also served as his alias.

All other children and all members of the staff had aliases, for reasons which were only half playful. Their surnames had to be kept secret from the outside world and even, as far as possible, from each other. As some of the children's parents lived under false identities in Germany or elsewhere, the list of names of the children in Maisons Lafitte would have given the Gestapo valuable clues for finding out which functionaries of the Communist Party were engaged in active underground work, and possibly even for tracking them down. The Home had actually been burgled under suspicious circumstances, though whether this had been done by the Gestapo was impossible to know. At any rate, no documents showing any of the children's surnames were kept in the Home, and the children themselves had been taught never to disclose them. They kept to the rule with surprising discipline—helped, of course, by the sensation of participating in an exciting cops-and-robbers game.

The members of the staff were only known by their nick-names. The most striking of these was 'Clysteria' for a psycho-analytically inclined female comrade whose duties included the application of enemas to the smaller children. Collectively the grown-ups were known as the 'Chaldeans'—an expression borrowed from a novel about a Soviet orphanage which was the rage at the Home. Of the 'Chaldeans' there were altogether five, who, between them, had to do the supervising, nursing, cooking and house-cleaning for the entire Home. They were, in order of their importance : Marianne, the cook, a member of the French C.P.; Ferdinand, the 'Chief Trustee', an Austrian comrade of unknown past, with an endearing habit of cursing all day under his breath in soft Viennese; Clysteria, who dispensed the most hair-raising Freudo-Marxian theories about the sexual life of suckling infants with an impish Mona Lisa smile; Thusnelda *das Burgfräulein*—a name with a Wal-ter Scott flavour, meaning something like 'the damsel of the Castle'—who was an energetic young gymnastics teacher, al-ways racing up and down staircases with a chamber-pot in each hand; and Hermann, the man of all jobs, a former mem-ber of the Party's paramilitary organisation in Saxony, who shared my passion for Russian billiards and struck me as the only sane person among the 'Chaldeans'. Before my time the staff had also included a certain 'Pickelchen', which means 'Little Carbuncle' or 'Spot on the Nose'. He was Clysteria's consort, a timid soul, who wrote Marxian essays on the history of art, and had resigned from the staff when the larger child-ren took to beating him up too often. None of the members of the staff had any educational qualifications or experience.

Such discipline as existed in the Home was mainly ensured by a kind of Council of the older children, called 'The Col-lective'. The Collective held daily sessions, sat in court over offenders, and functioned generally as a kind of administra-tive body. Members of the Collective were all children over twelve except for Ullrich, the only boy of upper middle-class origin, who was expelled from it for 'anti-social behaviour'. In short, the Home was a kind of organised bedlam, and its atmosphere similar to that which had prevailed in the early years of the Revolution in the schools of Russia.

The diphtheria outbreak, which coincided with my arrival in 'La Pouponnière', proved of a relatively harmless kind, but it led to the unfortunate result that the Home was put in quarantine by the French school authorities. The bigger children had been attending the local school; now, for several weeks, they were confined to the Home, which made the staff's task even more impossible than it had been before. Accordingly, I was warmly welcomed as a temporary addition to the ranks of the 'Chaldeans', under my old Party name of Comrade Ivan.

Among the various duties which fell to me were : to hold a kind of Class for the smaller children, and to put them to bed; to edit the weekly wall-paper of the Collective, scrub the floors when it was my turn, and give private lessons in the Russian language to the two unquestioned leaders of the Collective : Piet the Great, and Florian the Bonze. Piet was nearly sixteen, a tall, strong and thoughtful youth, the son of a Hamburg stoker who had been killed by the Nazis; Florian the son of a member of the Party's Central Committee (now a member of the East German Govermment), already at fifteen a budding Comintern-bureaucrat. 'Bonze', it will be remembered, was the slang word for Party brass-hats.

Apart from these functions I also acted on two occasions, while Marianne was absent, as a cook. Assisted by the counsels of the Collective, I filled a huge cauldron (it was a dinner for thirty) with macaroni, cocoa and sugar, and let it all hopefully boil for half an hour. As I did not know that one is supposed to drain the starchy water off the macaroni, the contents of the cauldron solidified into a deliciously compact sort of sweet black pudding which, served with molasses, was remembered by all for a long time. My second attempt was a variation of the same recipe, with rice instead of macaroni as the basic ingredient; but this time, guided by a dialectical intuition, I added large quantities of bicarbonate of soda. This dish became known as 'pudding à la Ivan' and secured my admission as an honorary member to the children's Collective.

Children were a new and amazing discovery for me; I was thrown into their alien universe, with its private laws of logic and subterranean sensitivities, like a traveller in Mbo-Mba-Land, without dictionary or guide, reduced to making contacts by gesture and grin. But contact was made easier by the fact that I had actually lived in Russia where none of the other 'Chaldeans' had been, and could give a first-hand account of the domes like golden onions which face the Kremlin walls; and also by my own infantile streak and passion for inventing games, which a frustrated childhood had left behind.

After two months in La Pouponnière, I returned to Paris and finished the novel in the late spring of 1934. The manuscript, which I had thought lost when I had to flee from the Germans, is one of several that escaped the searches of the Gestapo, stowed away in an old knapsack in a Paris cellar. On re-reading it after twenty years, I found it too amateurish and uneven to be published even as a period-piece. Instead, I propose to include here the synopsis, written for the benefit of a prospective publisher. It ran as follows :

The action takes place in a home for German refugee children near Paris; time, the present. The characters are children from 2½ to 16 years, mostly of proletarian origin; parents and staff . . . The thirty émigré children, cut off from their French environment, lead a kind of desert-island existence which undergoes strange transformations, follows its own logic, and reflects in a much more pointed form than is normally the case, the problems of social integration and the crises of puberty. The initial difficulties and disorders in the inadequately staffed and financed Home are overcome by the growing sense of responsibility of the Collective; the stages of this evolution, the shared experiences of the children, occupy the major part of the novel.

In the last part of the book, individuals, characters and destinies begin to take shape. 'Ullrich the Opposition', already at the age of fifteen a typical middle-class intellectual, is incapable of subordinating himself to the proletarian community of the children. His inner conflicts, and clashes with the Collective, lead to an abortive attempt at suicide. The story of his main opponent Piet, son of a Hamburg stoker killed by the Nazis, provides the closing chapters of the book.

The main characters in the novel were, apart from those already mentioned, 'Saucy Gustav', 'Igelchen', and 'Bobo, the Badger'. 'Igelchen' means Little Hedgehog, which sounds rather endearing in German. Igelchen was seven : a very pretty, haughty, husky-voiced and unapproachable proletarian princess, the step-daughter of my Party-guru, Peter. Bobo the Badger, aged eight, was an egg-headed, misshapen humpty-dumpty and an inveterate bed-wetter, whose father worked in the Party underground in Germany. As for Saucy Gustav, aged 13, I shall let the *curriculum vitæ* (authentic) that he wrote for the Committee speak for him :

I was born August 1921 and sent to foster-parents where I stayed six years and was then sent to the Jewish Orphanage which I disliked. For it was like a barracks, and prayers all the time. We were also beaten. One day my mother turned up and took me away. I was then nine. But she couldn't keep me because I am illegitimate. My mother worked in the Jewish Office as an assistant. My mother was a member of the Independent Socialist Party and gave me political enlightenment. But at that time I did not understand much about politics. Later I was sent to a home for Workers children in Berlin and my mother lost her job. Then my mother joined the German C.P. I liked school, we had a teacher who was also a Communist. We also had a group of Communist Pioneers. Then Hitler came and the Pioneers were dissolved. On May 1st somebody made a speech as follows: 'The Marxists want only manual workers in the May-Parade, but we want everybody.' That was Demagogy, because May Day belongs to the Working Class. Because of this argument they locked me into a dark bunker. In the bunker I was afraid and sang the 'Internationale'. Later they arrested my mother, and my uncle brought me to Paris. Later they let my mother go, but she can't get out of Germany because they won't give her a passport. I apply to be admitted to the Home because my mother is a Fighter against Fascism and my uncle without money. Signed Gustav R.

The excerpt which follows is typical of the atmosphere of that singular children's crowd. It is based on a factual incident, and the dialogue is photographically faithful, in the tradition of 'Socialist realism'. A food-parcel belonging to Igelchen, had been stolen by an unknown thief. Amidst general excitement a meeting of the children's Collective is called, to discuss that measures should be taken in the interest of social justice :

. . . The door had hardly closed behind Ullrich, when Saucy Gustav's shrill voice pierced the silence:

'I propose that we hold a Collective Court with respect to the burglar and pass sentence on him.'

'Rot, Courts are a bourgeois hypocrisy,' said Thekla the Goose.

'It isn't rot, in Russia they have Courts, too.'

'But only for counter-revolutionary saboteurs. Not for burglars.'

'You don't say. And what do they do with the burglars?'

'In Soviet Russia they haven't got burglars at all.'

The Gooose always had an answer to everything. That was one of her unpleasant qualities. For the moment, however, nobody contradicted her, because nobody wished to say anything against Russia. In the end Piet said in a measured voice:

'You are all blockheads. The burglars were all honest people to start with. But in pursuance of the capitalist system, and the economic crisis, they had to go on the dole. Thus they became burglars in pursuance of satisfying their economic needs and to care for their innocent wives and children. Thus all burglars, and also all ordinary thieves are a manifestation of capitalism.'

'. . . and in pursuance of the profit-system,' added the Bonze.

'That is correct,' said Piet the Great.

Little Louise asked timidly: 'But when capitalism is finished, will burglars be finished?'

'Burglars will be finished, because in pursuance of the Revolution and of Socialism everybody will have enough to eat and thus nobody will have to be a burglar,' explained Piet.

'But if he wants to?' asked Saucy Gustav.

'He doesn't want to, you idiot!'

'Why doesn't he want to? Maybe he wants to, nevertheless.'

'Why should he want to? If, for instance, you get two pounds of chocolate with every meal, would you want to break into the cupboard and filch Igelchen's parcel?'

Gustav did some hard thinking. 'No—in that case I wouldn't want to,' he said on a tone of surprise.

'So there you are.'

Everybody admired Piet. Then Little Louise asked:

'Do they get two pounds of chocolate with every meal in Russia?'

Everybody laughed.

'Silence,' shouted the Bonze. 'Anybody who laughs will be expelled.'

'Oi declare,' said Saucy Gustav, 'we should now pass on the burglar a sentence of not-guilty in pursuance that he is a victim of the capitalist crisis and system.'

'Hear, hear.'

'Silence,' said the Bonze. 'I agree that we should pass sentence of not-guilty. But before we pass sentence, we must know on whom we pass sentence.'

'That's correct,' said Gustav. 'We must establish the identity of the criminal.'

'Just like a detective story,' whispered Little Louise.

'Silence,' said the Bonze. 'This is not a detective story, but a Collective Court. I now ask everybody present, on their word of proletarian honour, whether he did it.'

Silence.

'Word of honour, it wasn't me,' said Gustav.

The Bonze: 'I haven't asked you.'

Gustav: 'Why not?'

The Bonze: 'Well, who was it?'

Silence.

The Bonze: 'He who did it should speak out without fear, as he is going to be found not guilty anyway.'

Silence.

The Bonze: 'Then I declare: nobody did it. Then it must have been one among the small fry.'

Gustav: 'Oi declare, if it was one of the small fry, we needn't declare him not guilty.'

'Why? Isn't he too a victim of the economic crisis?' pro-

tested the Goose; and she added as an afterthought:

'In America they pour chocolate into the Ocean in pursuance of profits, and we poor refugee children have to go a-burgling for our chocolate.'

'That's correct,' said Piet the Great.

'It isn't chocolate the Americans pour into the Ocean, it's coffee. Mocca. From Brazil.'

'That makes no difference,' said Piet.

The Bonze: 'Whether chocolate or coffee is all the same; our duty is to find the culprit. That is our collective duty. That's all.'

Piet the Great: 'I propose that we appoint a commission.'

'A Criminal Investigating Commission,' whispered Little Louise.

General consent.

They proceeded to vote. Florian and Piet were nominated by an overwhelming majority. The session was closed.

XXI. Down to Rock-Bottom

IN spite of its documentary realism and Socialist uplift, the novel was condemned by the Party as a reflection of bourgeois, individualistic tendencies. This had disastrous consequences for me; and as the e pisode is typical of what Communist writers have to endure, I shall describe it in detail.

The Party was represented in this case by the Communist caucus within the 'Association of German Writers in Exile'. The latter was a kind of cultural centre for the German émigrés in Paris. It held weekly public meetings where German and French writers read from their works, or lectured on some literary subject; this was followed by public discussion. Officially, the Association was politically neutral except for its opposition to the Nazi régime; in fact it was run by the Caucus, a group of Communist writers who determined the policy of the Association, decided whom to invite as speakers, and steered the public discussions into the proper channels. As usual in such 'front'-organisations,[1] the chairman (a second-rate *littérateur* by name of Rudolf Leonhard) was not a member of the Party, but drew a salary and took his orders from it.

The Caucus met privately once a week. Only one of its members was a writer of international standing : Anna Seghers, author of *The Fishermen of St. Barbara* and *The Seventh Cross*, whom I admired, and still admire, both as a novelist and as an attractive and charming woman, but with whom I never found any personal contact. Next in importance came Egon Erwin Kisch ('Egonek' for short), one of the most

[1] Communist-controlled organisations, camouflaged by a neutral façade or front.

popular characters in the international crowd of Communist intellectuals, who during the years of exile was a kind of father-figure for me.

Kisch came from Prague, where he had made his reputation as a young crime-reporter and writer of short stories about thieves and prostitutes. His first book, *Der Rasende Reporter,* became a classic of German journalism, and was followed by a series of travel-books on China, America, Australia and Soviet Asia, all written from the Communist point of view, but sparkling with wit and colour. He was then around fifty, short and fat around the midriff, but with his dark, humorous face and charming manner still very attractive to women. He had a penchant for young girls, whom he held spell-bound by his accomplished art of telling anecdotes, some of which would last for half an hour. He was also an amateur magician, and performed thought-reading tricks with his wife—faithful, complacent, horse-teethed Giesl, who looked like a school-mistress and worked for the G.P.U.

In his attitude to politics, Kisch was a complete cynic. He always avoided getting involved in argument with the stock phrase 'I don't think; Stalin thinks for me', delivered with a straight face; this usually caused a tense silence, followed by a hasty change of subject. He was also the inventor of a parlour-game, a new variation of the kind in which you throw dice and push a little horse along a race-track; only, it was not a race between horses, but between Party officials : instead of falling into a ditch or crashing into a fence, the participants were purged for Trotskyist leanings, expelled for Bukharinist deviations, and so on. How he got away with all this is difficult to explain : partly, I suppose, because he was one of those irrepressible personalities to whom everything is forgiven; partly, because his popularity was an asset to the German Party among intellectuals and sympathisers; and also, perhaps, because Egonek's heresies served as a screen for Giesl's work for the *apparat.*

Hidden behind the mask of the humorous cynic was a tired, disenchanted man, who had no illusions about the Party, but even fewer about the world outside the Party. At any rate, he felt too old to retrace his steps and start afresh. In one of my novels, an elderly Communist remarks : 'Once you have invested all your capital in a firm, you don't withdraw it—not at our age, not after thirty years. It would be indecent, I tell you; positively indecent . . .' Kisch never said this to me in as many words; but when I wrote that line, I heard it spoken in his voice. He died of heart-failure, in his native Prague, under the new Communist régime, a short time before his compatriot and intimate friend, Otto Katz, was hanged.

There were two other novelists in the Caucus; Gustav Regler and Bodo Uhse. Though I respected Regler, particularly for the courageous and distinguished part he played as a Commissar of the International Brigades in Spain, we were never on intimate terms; with Uhse I got on well, on the basis of a somewhat superficial camaraderie. Becher, Willy Bredel and other German writers living in Moscow participated in our meetings when they visited Paris; Manes Sperber, who at that time was not yet in Paris, joined our ranks at a later date. The remaining members of the Caucus (among them Alfred Kantorovicz and Max Schroeder, both former members of my old Party cell in Berlin) had never written a book; they were small Party-bureaucrats whose claim to be writers was based on an occasional article in the Party papers. They were a humourless, fanatical and unpleasant lot, but as they were more important in the Party hierarchy than the real writers, they ran the show.

Only three members of the Caucus have left the Party since : Regler, Sperber and myself. Kisch is dead; the others live in the Eastern Zone of Germany.

When I had finished the novel, I was asked by the Association of German Writers in Exile to read extracts from it at one of their weekly public meetings. The reading was fairly successful, but the next day the Caucus met in conclave and came down on it like a ton of bricks.

The attack was led by one Otto Abusch, alias Ernst Reinhardt, former editor of the *Rote Fahne,* the official Party paper in Berlin. He was the delegate of the Central Committee to the Caucus, with the task of acting as a political watchdog over us unreliable intellectuals, and hence in a position of virtually absolute authority. In a dry, dispassionate voice Reinhardt declared that I had not succeeded in ridding myself of the heritage of my bourgeois past; that instead of Socialist realism, I employed the methods of bourgeois individual psychology; that I represented the turmoils of puberty as a general phenomenon instead of correctly pointing out that such crises only occur in adolescents brought up in a decadent bourgeois environment, but are unknown among the healthy youth of the Soviet Union; finally, that the book displayed a frivolous, critical attitude towards an institution maintained by the solidarity of the international working-class and its anti-Fascist allies, and controlled by responsible comrades of the Party.

This set the key for the debate. Two or three of the Party-hacks followed suit. I retorted in a sharp and irritated tone, and thereby put myself even more in the wrong. None of the writers dared to contradict openly the delegate of the Central Committee. Only Kisch came to my defence by pleading tolerance on the grounds of my lack of ideological training. The discussion was wound up by the chairman of the Caucus—a young man of twenty named Hans Dammert who was not a writer either, but who had shown great courage under Nazi torture. He declared crisply that the deviations and distortions of the novel were of so serious a nature that they called for measures which exceeded the competence of the Writers' Caucus, and that 'other organs of the Party' would accordingly be informed.

The disciplinary action at which Dammert had darkly hinted did not materialise, but there was not much comfort in that. A first novel is as nerve-racking an experience as the first courtship of a clumsy and sensitive fool. I had set the usual high hopes on it, and had awaited judgment with trembling uncertitude. I had sent the manuscript to a German publishing firm in Holland, who had politely rejected it. That had, of course, been a blow; but the condemnation of the Writers' Caucus had the effect of a sledge-hammer coming down on my head. It was not the dashing of my hopes to see the novel published that hurt most, but the cold spite of the bureaucrats in the Caucus, and the indifference of the real writers who had been present.

I no longer had any friends outside the Party. It had become my family, my nest, my spiritual home. Inside it, one

might quarrel, grumble, feel happy or unhappy; but to leave
the nest, however cramping and smelly it seemed sometimes,
had become unthinkable. All 'closed systems' create for those
who live inside a progressive estrangement from the rest of
the world. I disliked a number of people in the Party but they
were my kin. I liked a number of people outside the Party,
but I no longer had a common language with them.

Had my novel been condemned by some literary clique, I
could have left it after a comforting exchange of abuse. But in
this case no such escape was possible. The Caucus met in session once a week, but privately we saw each other all the time,
and its members were my only social circle. How long would
it take for me to live this disgrace down? Would I ever live
it down, or was I always going to remain an outsider, and
treated, at best, with tolerant condescension?

My discouragement was verging on despair. This was the
second book which the Party had rejected. *Red Days* was at
least going to be published, in a mutilated version, for the
benefit of German-speaking Ukrainians. With the novel I did
not even have that meagre consolation. It was fated to wilt
away in a drawer, together with the manuscripts of the two
plays. A drawer full of unpublished manuscripts has about the
same effect as a decaying corpse under the floorboards. Particularly if one is an exiled writer living in a cheap hotel-room
that smells of discouragement anyway. For the first time I gave
myself up to a prolonged period of self-pity.

The hotel room was on the Boulevard de Belleville, where I
had moved since my return from Maisons Lafitte. Belleville,
with the adjoining Menilmontant, had once been famed as the
quartier des apaches, and had since become a dreary working-
class suburb. The sixty pounds that I had earned with the
Encyclopædia had been spent to the last penny. For a while
I lived on the charity of a friendly couple. They had a self-
contained little flat in the same hotel, and were both social
welfare workers, employed in a medical centre in the slums.
As they were busy all day, I scrubbed their kitchen floor, did
the cooking and washing-up, and in exchange shared their
meals. Sometimes they shamefacedly gave me five francs for a
packet of cigarette tobacco or a cake of kitchen soap. The
name of this kindly couple was Grunwald; they helped me

a second time during my flight from France in 1940. He died a few years ago; Hanna Grunwald is now a welfare worker in Harlem.

I was again at a dead end, as I had been eight years earlier, when I had nearly starved in Palestine. But now I was twenty-nine, and I felt rather like the once promising, no-longer-so-young young man of whom it was said that 'he had a great future behind him'. Living on charity, a writer of rejected books and plays, a refugee, and an outsider among my friends and comrades—my self-pity knew no bounds. It was, as I have said, the only prolonged period in my life when I abandoned myself to that vice. It only lasted a few weeks, but it was ghastly—ghastlier than prisons and concentration camps; for if under normal circumstances self-pity is an indulgence, in a crisis it becomes a powerful destructive agent.

I did not leave my room for several days, and one night I stuck scotch tape on the draughty slits of the door and window, and opened the gas-tap. I had placed my bug-stained mattress next to it on the floor, but as I was settling down on it, a book crashed on my head from the wobbly shelf. It nearly broke my nose, so I got up, turned off the gas and tore off the tape. Of all one's failures, a failure in suicide is the most embarrasssing to report. The book that fell on my head was the Second Brown Book, *Dimitrov contra Goering,* with the story of the Reichstag Trial. A more drastic pointer to the despicableness of my antics could hardly be imagined. I must either have kicked the shelf, or it was a case of the Dialectic producing a miracle.

In favour of the miracle theory I should mention that I repeatedly seem to have been saved by things falling on my head. The last time this happened was a few days before the fall of Paris, when I was hiding from the police. Adrienne Monnier, that admirable French woman of letters and friend of Briand, gave me shelter in her flat. I was exhausted, and lay down on a couch with a book that I had taken at random from her shelves. As I was lying on my back, holding the book over my head, a small, flattened object fell from between its pages on my forehead. It was a pressed, four-leafed clover which had been lying in that book for some years. Mademoi-selle Monnier, who saw the clover fall on me, came over to the couch and kissed me between the eyes. 'Now I know,' she said, 'that you will come through safely.'

I told nobody about the stupid incident with the gas-tap, except, some time later, one person, Egonek. Kisch was always fond of grotesque anecdotes, and I told him the story in that vein. It must nevertheless have got round, for twelve years later, when I returned to Paris after the war, and became the target of a concentrated attack by the French C.P., several newspapers articles mentioned 'the traitor Koestler's attempted suicide in a Paris hotel room in the 'thirties' as an additional sinister streak in my character. What puzzles me is that they never came out with the Dr. Costler story which, by one way or another, must have come to the knowledge of the *apparat*. Perhaps the Party thought that it would rather endear me to the girl comrades.

This is a chapter of digressions which I have crossed out and reinstated again. My inability to stick to a straight narrative of that period reveals how painful its memory still is, and how strong the inhibitions are in approaching it. It was one of the most depressing periods in my life—depressing from several points of view : poverty, failure as a writer, isolation within the Party. On top of all this, the girl comrade with whom I lived at the time was going through a harrowing conflict of her own, and was unavailable just at the time when I was in desperate need of moral support.

There was one psychologically very curious aspect to this crisis : it followed almost exactly the story of the novel which was its cause. My conflict with the Writers' Caucus was a repetition of the conflict between 'Ullrich the Opposition', the lonely adolescent intellectual, and the Children's Collective —even to the point of Ullrich's abortive attempt at suicide. It is usual for writers to transform lived experience into fiction; but it struck me as unusual and in fact uncanny, that I should have to re-live as personal experience a fictitious situation that I had invented. The explanation of the mystery is, of course, that Ullrich was a character closely modelled on my own past; I had projected myself back into adolescence. The chapter from the novel which follows was written a few months before the events that I have just described, and which it fore-

shadows in the prophetic ways of the unconscious. My reason
for inserting here what appears as yet another digression is
that these extracts faithfully reflect a mood which I am unable to recapture today, twenty years after the event, when
the faith and despair of my Communist days have gone dead
on me.

Extracts from Ullrich's Diary

April 6, 1934

*At times I feel literally stifled and choked by loneliness. For
instance, I am sitting alone in a room, reading a book. The
others are playing in the garden. I know it, but I don't hear
them. Suddenly I stop reading. The air around me begins to
vibrate. The whole room trembles with loneliness. It is saturated with loneliness like a chemical solution. My nerves swell
with it like capillary tubes. It penetrates into my stomach and
heart like an acid. It pumps tears into my eyes like an acrid
fume. There is a horror in it which cannot be described.*

*Then I want to join the others. I want to warm myself
against their bodies, I want to belong to them, I rub myself
against them like a sheep pressing against the flock. I want to
feel that I am not the only person alive in this world.*

*But I have hardly been two minutes with them, and it is
all gone. They bore me. They are primitive. They are stranger
to me than Hottentots. They don't understand me. I can't
talk to them. I don't have the feeling that they are really alive.
Some are like marionettes on wires, others like figures in a
waxworks. I feel even lonelier in the garden than I did in my
room. I hurry back to my room, and the whole thing starts
afresh.*

April 10

*Today I am sixteen; and it is exactly sixteen days since I
was expelled from the Collective. Talk of numerology . . .*

*As a birthday gift they have generously offered to take me
back to the Collective. The Bonze transmitted the message in
the presence of the whole horde. I refused, of course. It is
clear to me that the offer was inspired from 'above'. Left alone,
they would never have made it. I don't care a damn. I told*

them in the presence of the whole precious Collective that I don't care a damn.

April 11

It drives me mad that my mother should after all have been proved right: I don't belong to them. No profession of faith in Marx and the proletariat can alter the fact. I believe in Marx and I believe in the proletariat, but I can't get accustomed to the smell of Charlie's socks. I am a frustrated Communist. I am frustrated by a pair of socks—the real ones of Sweatfoot Charlie, and the intellectual sweatfeet of Piet and Florian.

April 12

However—if I feel so repelled by them, and they by me, then why does it hurt so much that I don't belong to them? There is a contradiction here.

The same evening.

Whether I feel repelled or not, is beside the point. The point is that I have no other choice. For outside this Home I have nowhere to go. If I can't adjust myself to my present circumstances, the only solution is to hang myself. The contradiction is solved.

April 13

'The spiritually inclined is always lonely,' my father used to say. Rot. My father, the Herr Professor, was a mummy already in his lifetime. My mother is the vestal virgin of a mummy.

No, I don't belong to the sunken world of my parents. But I don't belong to the others either. Least of all do I belong to myself. That mysterious personage is unknown at this address.

April 14

I know that these little Proles can't help being what they are—dumb, callous, primitive, narrow in mind, coarse in spirit. Perhaps I still labour under that contempt for the 'children of the streets' which my parents inculcated into me. But however hard and honestly I try, I can't find the proper tone with them. For it is of course up to me, the privileged and superior party, to find the proper tone. There is an estrangement, impossible to bridge. Before one of them answers my question, I already know the repartee, and the re-repartee, and everything else he is going to say. I do not despise them since I have become a Marxist—but they bore me stiff. They think so slowly that I can hear the grinding of the wheels in their heads, as in an old grandfather clock. In mine, they go tick-tack as in a chronometer.

April 16

I have been reading a beautiful and terrible book by Ernst Glaeser. It has a dialogue between an old professor and a young boy:

'I have come to you,' says the young boy, 'to ask you on which side I stand in this great upheaval, and where I belong.'

'Well, well,' says the professor, 'I believe that you don't belong anywhere.'

Then he goes on: 'The patrician class is dying. We are dying with it. A new class, whose education and philosophy of life is different from ours, has taken the wheel of History in its hands. In twenty years from now it will be alone on the bridge.'

Then the young boy talks some nonsense, and the professor goes on:

'There is a collective destiny, and to revolt against it doesn't lead anywhere. History is not interested in the wishes of individuals. We are individuals. We are condemned to remain individuals. We can never get into the stream.'

'But if we take the plunge and dive into the stream?' asks the boy.

'Then it will deposit us at the next bend like phosphorescent driftwood,' says the professor. 'History has spat us out. We stand between the front lines. We are civilised but useless. If you remain honest, you will spend your life in depressing independence between the fronts. You will see everything and understand everything, you will survive new wars and new revolutions, but you will be alone, without friends, without a roof or a country, without echo and achievement . . .'

When I read this I felt as if I had been clubbed on the head. It sounded like one of those dreadful curses out of the Old Testament. I am still shaking as I write these lines.

No, no, this shall not be my destiny. I don't want to be a piece of phosphorescent driftwood left at the muddy bend. I want to be carried by the stream, in the stream, with the stream, part of the stream. I shall do everything to belong again. I shall go to Canossa. I shall deny myself as I have denied my parents.

I shall write this very day a demand to be accepted again into the Collective.

Here the first part of Ullrich's diary ends. He tries with all his might to make up to the Collective, and in particular to Piet, the son of the martyred stoker from Hamburg, who symbolises in Ullrich's eyes the honest, strong and simple-minded revolutionary working class. But his advances to Piet strike a false, patronising note; instead of a reconciliation there is a row, ending in a fight; Ullrich is knocked out and seriously injured. Piet is reprimanded, and the next day vanishes from the Home without trace. Piet is almost grown-up anyway, he felt out of place among the children and decided to fend for himself. Ullrich is devoured by remorse, and a more unhappy adolescent than ever :

May 11

I shall soon start dreaming of Piet as Brutus dreamt of Caesar after murdering him. What nonsense. I didn't do anything to him. I wanted to be reconciled with him, and he offended and bullied me. But they all behave as if it was my fault that he has left. They hardly talk to me now. The worst of it is that I am unable to rid myself of this unjustified sense of guilt. They avoid me as if I were a leper. This is hardly an exaggeration. Yet I am not a leper, merely a phosphorescent piece of driftwood left on the bend. The river steadily follows its course, and I sit on the bank and throw the pebbles of my idle thoughts at it.

May 17

It really can't go on like this. I ought to leave. But Mother

*hasn't got the money to take me out, and I wouldn't go back
to her anyway. There is no return to where I came from. And
there is no road leading where I want to go.*

May 18
*I have read Ehrenburg's new novel. It is a variation on the
same theme: his Kolya, too, can go neither forward nor back;
he loves Tolstoy and is bored by the Five Year Plan, he is
interested in individual people and not in the timetable of
mankind. Needless to say he commits suicide in the end, a
Werther-case of unrequited love for the proletariat. Ach! the
silly, maudlin Werther. The sound of his name is enough to
make me sea-sick. To die is a great thing; to remain ridiculous
even in death is unthinkable. The Romans used to tie comic
masks over the faces of their prisoners before they let the beasts
loose on them in the arena; they died not as martyrs but as
clowns. Their torturers robbed them of the last shred of their
humanity: the dignity of death.*

The same evening.

*The unimaginable thing about death is that there is no
sequel to extinguish the pain. The moment of death freezes
into an eternal present because it can never dissolve into
memory.* L'ennui sans fin de la mort.

At this point Ullrich's diary ends, and he tries to kill himself by cutting his wrist in a rather amateurish way. After he
has been bandaged, a new member of the staff, Dr. Moll, the
only person in the Home who has a liking for Ullrich, sits
down at his bedside :

*'I became so frightened as it grew slowly darker around me,'
Ullrich said in a feeble voice, which sounded more childish
than usual. 'I suppose I didn't mean it very seriously from the
beginning.'*
'Well, dying needs a lot of patience,' said Moll.
*'I feel so terribly ashamed,' said Ullrich, 'and yet I feel
happier than I have for a long time.'*
*'Don't overestimate that,' said Moll, 'the hangover will come
afterwards.'*

'Why are you always so disagreeable to me?' asked Ullrich.

'I am disagreeable by nature,' said Moll, 'only the others don't notice it so much.'

'Do you also believe,' said Ullrich, 'that History has spat us out and that we can't get away from our past?'

'We can,' said Moll, 'but it is rather difficult.'

'I can't,' said Ullrich. 'I tried but I haven't succeeded.'

'You were too arrogant,' said Moll.

'Only at the beginning,' said Ullrich. 'Afterwards I went to Canossa and was filled with humility.'

'That's only another form of arrogance,' said Moll, 'and the most unappetising one.'

'But how should I set about it?' asked Ullrich.

'It is rather difficult,' said Moll, 'and only a few succeed. It is a kind of hara-kiri. You must saw off the branch on which you sit, and tear out the roots that have nourished you, for their sap is poisoned with the thoughts and images and feelings of a world that is doomed to perish; and you must be able to grow roots in the new earth.'

After a while Ullrich said:

'One can agree to all this and nevertheless feel sad for that which must perish—even if one hates it. For it contains so much that is part of oneself that one cannot imagine living without it.'

'The world of the burghers must perish because it denies and mocks the ideals that have constituted it,' said Moll.

'Everything you say is so harsh and hopeless,' said Ullrich, already half asleep, in his new, childish voice. 'It is like a burden that one must carry. All I want is to live like others, and nothing else.'

'That is a very ambitious wish,' said Moll. 'We all only want to live like the others, and look at the complications to which that leads. Good night, my boy.'

XXII. . . . And Up Into the Hayloft

I WAS saved by an unexpected offer from the Party. It was
the offer of a full-time job, unpaid, but one very much to
my liking, and in which I became entirely absorbed during the
next six or nine months. The idea was to create a centre for
the study of the social structure and inner workings of Fascist
régimes, more scholarly in its approach than the mass-
propaganda methods of the Muenzenberg Trust permitted.
The idea came from my old Party friend and Party-guru, Peter
Maros.[1] He had just returned from a prolonged stay in Yugo-
slavia to Paris, and it was he who asked me to work in the new
set-up. It was called INFA—*Institut pour l'Etude du
Fascisme*.

Peter could not have turned up at a more appropriate moment. I was immensely grateful to him for coming to my rescue
by providing me with work and a new purpose. On his arrival
he had telephoned me and suggested that we meet at the Café
Weber in the Rue Royale. I was taken aback by his suggesting
such a resplendent place, and proposed a cheaper locality.

'Never mind,' said Peter, 'I'll pay for the coffee. It will do
you good to come out of your hole.' So he must have already
heard that I was in a bad way.

It did me good indeed. I had not been near the Boulevards
for weeks, and to save the Métro fare I walked all the way
from Belleville to the Rue Royale. During my first stay in
Paris as a correspondent of Ullsteins, whose offices were in
that neighbourhood, Weber's had been my favourite café.
Now it appeared to me as a place in a foreign country, on the
distant shores of Luxury. It was in the early summer, the ter-

[1] See *Arrow in the Blue*.

race of Weber's was basking in the sun, and the crowd looked as if a swarm of chattering starlings had settled down at the tables, momentarily assuming human shape. So life seemed to be going on, in spite of the Caucus's condemnation of my first novel. Peter was sunburnt, but otherwise quite his former lean, thin-lipped, ascetic-looking self. He gave me his firm and meaningful handshake and, as was his habit, stared at me for a few seconds, without speaking, through his slightly goggly eyes which radiated brotherly love and the stern determination of an important Comrade on the Cultural Front. Then, with his usual enthusiasm and convincingness, he explained to me the project.

The *Institut pour l'Etude du Fascisme* was to be an enterprise off the beaten track of Party life. The Party was to run it, in the person of Peter, but the Institute was to finance itself, and appear to the public as one of the enterprises of the Popular Front. Various French personalities had been approached and had promised moral support and financial contributions—among them Professor Langevin and the Joliot-Curies, André Malraux. Bertrand de Jouvenel, and so on. The French Trade Unions were also interested. But, at the beginning, money was of course slow in coming in. So, for the time being, the Institut was staffed with unpaid voluntary workers. Métro fares were, however, being provided, and also a soup at midday, for the Institute was housed in a flat which included a kitchen. That, said Peter, was all that INFA could offer—except for the truly fraternal atmosphere of a small band of people devoted to an important mission on the cultural front. Would I be prepared, under these conditions, to take over the Institute's Department of Publications? Of course I would—it sounded wonderful. Then I asked who the Department consisted of. 'For the time being,' said Peter, 'of yourself.'

I started work the next day. The Institute's premises were a four-roomed flat at 25 Rue Buffon, near the *Jardin des Plantes*. The staff consisted of Peter; three German women called Rita, Ellen and Lys, who did the clipping, filing and research work; a boy called René, half French, half Russian, who did the translating; a middle-aged man called Max, who was the 'business manager'; and a cleaning woman who also did the cooking of the midday soup. All were Party members, with the exception of René and Ellen, who were merely sympathisers. Strange as it may seem, in spite of months of intimate collaboration, I never knew the surnames and background of most of them, nor even where they lived.

They were an extremely pleasant and devoted bunch of people, and on the whole INFA was the happiest and most decent set-up that I had come across in my whole Party career. It had something of the spirit of the early days of the movement—that was perhaps the reason why, after a year, the Party bureaucracy deliberately wrecked it. We all worked on the average ten hours a day, without pay, and some of us with the midday soup as our main meal. (It was always a thick, purée-like, German soup of lentils, peas or potatoes, occasionally with bits of delicious sausage swimming in it.) There were no jealousies or intrigues until after six months the Party appointed a kind of Commissar, who, within a short time, destroyed the whole enterprise.

Peter's basic idea in launching INFA had been to find out what Fascism really was. Obviously slogans like 'barbarism', 'return to the Middle Ages', 'gangster rule', and so forth, did not provide an explanation. Nor did the so-called 'theoreticians' of our Party—though of course we were careful not to indulge in any explicit criticism. The Party regarded Fascism simply as 'the overt form of the dictatorship of the finance-capitalists', as distinct from the 'camouflaged form of the same dictatorship in the so-called democratic countries'. Thus the only difference between, say, England and Nazi Germany was in the 'external forms' in which the dictatorship of the capitalist ruling class expressed itself, whereas the 'class-content' of both régimes was the same. Also, in Party parlance, everybody who was not on our side was a Fascist. The Socialists were 'Social-Fascists', the Catholics were 'Clerical-Fascists', the Trotskyists were 'Trotsky-Fascists', and so on. Hence at 25 Rue Buffon, INFA resolved to find out what Fascism really was.

Our programme was to start on a modest and scholarly basis. The 'publication department' was to issue a bi-monthly bulletin (of which three numbers were actually published), and a series of pamphlets and books for a specialised audience (several were actually published by writers for whom we provided the research-material). It would also provide progressive cultural organisations and Trade Unions with 'ideological weapons'—that is, documentary material, and furnish, on request, similar material to the French Press.

At the beginning all went well. After a month the first INFA-Bulletin appeared in print. An Italian comrade wrote for it an excellently documented article on 'Conditions in the Ricefields in the Po Valley', which I still gratefully remember because all the rest of the bulletin I had to write myself. I also wrote, under INFA's imprint, a series of six somewhat optimistic articles on 'The Underground Resistance Movement in Germany' for the Paris evening paper *L'Intransigeant*. In spite of my desperate need of money, I had been unable to bring myself to write for the French bourgeois Press; now, as I wrote in the name of INFA, my inhibitions vanished, and I regained my journalistic skill. We all got on extremely well with each other. Peter, in spite of his streak of messianic phoneyness, was an endearing character and very pleasant company. I never felt that he was my boss, and to the end we worked in complete harmony. René was a quiet, efficient, somewhat colourless young man of agreeable manners. Lys was a middle-aged woman who had a charming little daughter. I think she was the widow or divorced wife of a Party bigwig, and that she scraped along on a small Party pension; she never mentioned her private circumstances. Rita was a tall and beautiful girl who lived with a Russian comrade presumed to be working for the *apparat*, and had accordingly even more reason to be discreet. Ellen, the youngest— she was not yet a member of the Party—was the amusing and high-spirited daughter of a Jewish banker from Berlin; she liked to emphasise her exotically piquant features by a barbaric make-up, and looked rather like a Nefertete from the Kurfuerstendamm. Her parents were in despair about her 'getting mixed up in politics' and had cut her allowance, so that she was nearly as poor as the rest of us, which she regarded as a huge joke. She had a golden cigarette case, but never a cigarette in it. She was the only one who, free from the priggish inhibitions of the really poor, always tried to borrow a franc or two from the others. The three women got on miraculously well. Then there was also Greta, the char-cook, a working-class woman from Berlin's red suburbia, who mothered us all.

With the exception of René and Ellen, we were all 'old Party horses'; all of us, I suppose, had at one time or another been caught up between the wheels of the Party machine and carried a hidden scar. Hence we were all glad to live and work in this friendly oasis, under the benevolently goggling eyes of Peter. There was never any explicit criticism of the Party, but there were little silences and quiet shrugs, and the shared knowledge of disappointments and frustrations, which brought us even closer together. When work was finished, some of us always stayed behind, huddled in the kitchen, and talked endless shop. The Institute was our collective hobby and obsession.

There must have existed millions of Communists of every age and nationality like us, an untapped human reservoir of idealism and devotion, vast enough to transform the political desert of this globe. History was repeating the tragedy of the early Church—the spiritual spring-tide that had carried the pure and humble towards the millennium, and had left them stranded in the grip of a debased Papacy; the messianic faith at the beginning of the Crusades and their terrible end.

Why did these frustrated, dedicated millions fail to shake off the grip of the Kremlin Borgias? Those who lived inside Russia were obviously reduced to helplessness; but what about the honest Peters and Lyses and Egons and Arthurs, over whom the G.P.U. could exercise no direct control? There are various answers to this—atomisation, dispersion, the sorry end of all independent Communist splinter-groups who had no Russian money and power behind them. But the basic cause for our paralysis lay deeper : it was the true believer's insurmountable horror of excommunication. Though we trusted each other, we shrank from actually giving voice to our heretical thoughts. A shrug, a silence, were the limits to which we could go without outlawing ourselves before our own conscience :

There was a conviction shared by the best among my friends who have now either left the Party or been killed. Though we wore blinkers, we were not blind, and even the most fanatical among us could not help noticing that all was not well in our

movement. But we never tired of telling each other—and our-
selves—that the Party could only be changed from inside, not
from outside. You could resign from a club and from the or-
dinary sort of party if its policy no longer suited you; but the
Communist Party was something different: it was the incarna-
tion of the will of History itself. Once you stepped out of it
you were extra muros, *and nothing which you said or did had*
the slightest chance of influencing its course. The only dia-
lectically correct attitude was to remain inside, shut your
mouth tight, swallow your bile and wait for the day when,
after the defeat of the enemy and the victory of World Revolu-
tion, Russia and the Comintern were ready to become demo-
cratic institutions. Then and only then would the leaders be
called to account for their actions: the avoidable defeats, the
wanton sacrifices, the mud-stream of slander and denuncia-
tion in which the pick of our comrades had perished. Until
that day you had to play the game—confirm and deny, de-
nounce and recant, eat your words and lick your vomit; it was
the price you had to pay for being allowed to continue feeling
useful, and thus keep your perverted self-respect. (The God
That Failed.)

The only member of the Institute who did not seem to fit into the picture was Max, the business manager. He looked like
a fat, middle-aged travelling salesman in ladies' underwear.
The Party had sent him to us as an 'efficient organiser', but we
all felt ill at ease with him—until one day he vanished in un-
explained circumstances from the Rue Buffon and from
France. I believe that he also took some of our meagre funds
with him, though Peter, and Lys who kept the books, were
flatly non-committal on the subject.

In the ensuing emergency I was given the additional job of
business manager. It consisted mostly in visiting our various
French patrons and asking them for donations. It was in this
capacity that I first met, among other French intellectuals,
André Malraux. I went to see him at his office at Gallimard's,
his publishers, and we talked while walking up and down in
the pretty garden at the back of the Gallimard building. As a
fervent admirer of Malraux's, I was overwhelmed by the occasion, but went on bravely about the great prospects of

INFA, and its even greater need for donations. Malraux listened in silence, occasionally uttering one of his characteristic, awe-inspiring nervous sniffs, which sound like the cry of a wounded jungle beast and are followed by a slap of his palm against his nose. At first this was rather startling, but one soon got accustomed to it. When I had had my say, Malraux stopped, advanced towards me threateningly, until I had my back against the garden wall, and said :

'*Oui, oui, mon cher, mais que pensez-vous de l'apocalypse?*'

With that he gave me five hundred francs, and wished me good luck.

I usually went on my begging tours once a month, for which occasion I put on my one remaining good shirt. (The others were of the short-sleeved French *chemise de sport* variety, made of a kind of net-fabric which betrayed the hairiness of your chest as a darkling shadow.) Among the patrons of INFA whom I visited on these tours were Professor Langevin, bearded and gentle, Frederick Joliot-Curie, young, intense and eager, Louis Aragon, tense with ambition and vainglory, the only one who always gave good advice and never a penny; finally Professor Lucien Levy-Bruhl, whose work on the pre-logical character of primitive mentality had a great influence on my intellectual development and whom I accordingly idolised. Levy-Bruhl was then over seventy, and near his death. A small, fragile figure, sitting erect behind a large desk, his delicate face framed by a white goatee and white mane, he has remained in my memory as the prototype of the great French *hommes de lettres* of the last century.

All these men, and many other French intellectuals were kind and helpful to the anonymous 'anti-Fascist refugee' that I was. Though most of them were not Communists, they gave money to INFA, lent their names to our Committee of Patrons, and gave me letters of introduction to others. Yet there was something withdrawn, impersonal and chilling in their helpfulness; I was grateful for their help, but it depressed me that neither I nor any of my fellow refugees was ever invited to a French house. I knew of course that this reserve was an inherent part of French tradition, and during my previous stay in Paris as a foreign correspondent I had taken it for granted. But poverty and exile make one oversensitive; what a refugee craves most is relief from his permanent feeling of uprootedness. Soldiers abroad have the same craving to escape from their bleak army billets into the comforting warmth of a family around a meal. The British have an instinctive understanding of this need and, for all their apparent shyness and restraint, they have a way of picking up the stranger as if he were a kind of stray dog, carrying him to their houses and making him feel at home; while the French, with their easy affability, embrace him warmly and let him stand shivering in the street, condemned to remain forever a permanent tourist or permanent exile, as the case may be.

Thus the great mass of refugees in France lived cut off from French contacts and led a kind of ghetto existence. They read their émigré papers, frequented their émigré-clubs and cafés, lived immersed in their émigré universe, and its inevitable feuds and intrigues. During my seven years as a refugee in France, I lived entirely in the company of fellow-refugees and continued to write and think in German; yet from the moment when, in 1940, I settled in England, I began to write in English, moved among English friends and ceased to be a refugee. Incidentally, quite a number of writers whose native language was not English have risen to prominence in English and American letters; but I cannot think of a single analogous example of a writer whose native language was not French.

For the story of my remaining years in France, these circumstances have to be borne in mind. It is a story of physical and spiritual exile and, individual crotchets apart, typical of the condition of the political refugee—at that time numbering thousands, and now hundreds of thousands.

To live up completely to the destiny of the refugee, I now became homeless in the literal sense of the word : unable to pay my rent even in the cheap Belleville hotel, I moved to a hayloft which was rent-free. The hayloft was located in an open-air colony of gentle cranks in Meudon-Val Fleuri, half-way between Paris and Versailles. The colony lived in a lovely park which had once been a deer park of the fourteenth or fifteenth Louis, with various abandoned stables, pavilions and summer-houses for the amorous dalliances of the Court.

These buildings, and a number of tents, were now occupied by a motley crowd of vegetarians, nudists, poets, and painters, mostly followers of the Raymond Duncan sect, and by a number of refugees without proper identity papers hiding from the police. It was run by a bearded young man named Paul, who wore sandals and hand-woven garments, and was a secret member of the Party.

I was told about the colony by a comrade, the German writer George Glaser, who was as down and out as I was. George was a very gifted and lovable boy of genuine, blue-blooded, proletarian origin; not a middle-class bohemian, but a real tramp with the gift for fending for himself under the most unlikely circumstances. He lived in a tent, which he had wangled out of some charitable organisation, in a wild corner of the colony's park, and earned the few francs he needed for food by odd jobs in the colony. When he heard in what straits I was, he arranged with Paul that I should be allowed to sleep in the hayloft of one of the summer-houses; for a bed or a tent the colony charged a rent which, though ridiculously small, I could not pay. So, one day in June or July 1934, just before the next rent in the hotel was due, I packed my few belongings into a suit-case, and tramped out with George to Meudon-Val Fleuri.

During the next few weeks I led a life that was almost perfectly happy. At seven-thirty in the morning I started, on an empty stomach, on the three-mile walk from Val Fleuri to the Métro terminal at the Mairie d'Issy, thus saving the train fare which INFA paid me; and on sunny days I saved the Métro fare too. At midday I filled up on thick soup and bread; around six or seven o'clock in the evening I again took the Métro to Issy, or walked all the way home to my loft. In a little shop in Issy I bought my dinner, which invariably consisted of a pound of bread and a few ounces of lard, at a total cost of 50 centimes. Bread and lard were not only the cheapest variety of food if you had no cooking facilities, but also relatively the most nourishing; it used to be the staple diet of the poor in my native Hungary. Often I could not resist eating my dinner while I trudged along the last stretch of the road; this meant swallowing the lard without salt, under which circumstances it is tasteless and indigestible. Yet somehow I could never get myself to carry salt in my pocket.

After dinner I wandered through the park with George or some other people in the colony. I remember one particularly pleasant young man called Luntz, and his equally nice girl (and later his wife), Clairette. Luntz, a Socialist, had spent several years in the notorious prison of Brest Litovsk, where he had contracted tuberculosis; now he was recuperating. He was nearly as poor as I was, yet one evening he bought me a real hot dinner in a *bistro*, the pleasure of which I still remember. I also remember him telling a particularly gruesome story about a fight with rats in a punishment cell in Brest Litovsk, and of prisoners who died of infected rat bites. He was a gentle and sensitive young man, without a trace of fanaticism or bitterness, and happily in love with pretty and gay Clairette. A few years later, they emigrated to America, where Luntz edited an excellent but unfortunately short-lived monthly, *The Modern Review*.

Though I was always slightly hungry, and ravenous on Sunday when there was no INFA soup, I was in excellent health and profoundly contented. Work, and a glowing feeling of comradeship and belonging had burnt every trace of self-pity out of my system. At last, I felt, I was leading the life a Communist should lead, a life of poverty, dedication and obedience.

I was now approaching the landmark of thirty. Though emotionally still unstable and far from being grown up, a change in personality began slowly to crystallise behind all the contradictions and confusions. My earlier years had been a succession of breathless pursuits of the arrow in the blue : the perfect cause, the ideal Helen, the knowing *shaman*, the infallible leader. Now, after a series of disillusionments, the perfection of the cause which I served became gradually less important than the act of serving in itself. Through a long process of trial and error, I began to learn that complete dedication to a cause was for me a physical necessity, my only haven from the nagging sense of guilt which early childhood had implanted, and my only salvation from becoming that typical and boring phenomenon of our age, the neurotic intellectual stewing in his private limbo.

In other words, I began to accept the fact that I was a per-

L

son of the obsessive type. Blessed or cursed with a surplus of nervous energy which demanded excessive outlets, I had to be obsessed with some task if I was not to be obsessed with myself. During the last few months in that hotel room in Belleville, I had evidently been going to pieces. Had that hotel room been in Chelsea or Greenwich Village, the probable sequel would have been spending three hours a week during the next three years on a psychiatrist's couch, to emerge in the end with a more or less successfully patched-up personality. But as I was penniless and could count on no help from outside, I had to fall back once again on 'Babo'—Muenchausen's boastful Baron in the Bog, who pulled himself out by his own hair when on the point of drowning. Hence, instead of that magic couch, I was lying on a hayloft and dreaming of our plans for an International Anti-Fascist Exhibition —a grandiose affair, which would prove once and for all by historical parallels, statistical figures, graphs on rearmament, and so forth, that APPEASEMENT MEANS WAR, and which at the same time would appeal to the emotions by wax-work representations of daily life in a concentration camp, accompanied by the warning that IT WILL HAPPEN HERE.

It can, of course, be said that living in a hayloft and working hard without pay was a sign of a need for self-punishment. Perhaps it was; but if so, it was a constructive form of self-punishment. This leads us back once more to the ambiguity of value-judgments, for the psychiatrist regards every obsession as a disease that ought to be cured, whereas from the historian's point of view the mad obsessions of artists, reformers, explorers, and inventors are the dynamic sources of progress. Even the question whether an obsession is creative or sterile is sometimes impossible to decide, and only posterity will tell whether a man shall be classified as a pioneer or a neurotic crank.

However that may be, it gradually dawned on me that my only happy periods were the periods when I was chasing after the arrow in one shape or another. It was the only form of life which gave me peace of mind—not the prim feeling of virtue of do-gooders and hospital sisters, but the creative joy, the happy furore of building and shaping, of adding a brick to the edifice of that more humane future in which I still believed. It was at the same time an outlet for the chronic indignation which was gnawing at one's guts during the seven years of darkness.

I also discovered that in between the 'dedicated periods' I became depressed, with recurrent suicidal fantasies. In later years, obsession with a cause changed into obsession with the book I was working on; and then the periods between-two-books became hollows of depression. It all sounds obvious in retrospect, but it took many years until I began to understand the pattern, and discern the reasons for these wild ups and downs. It is easy to say 'I happen to be a manic-depressive type', but laborious to discover the individual switch that releases the manic or depressive phase.

Gradually these manic bursts of activity, followed by morbid depressions, levelled out into a relatively stable working discipline which keeps me chained to my desk all the year round for eight or nine hours a day. For an independent writer this is an unusual routine, and the chains are self-imposed; but each time I have tried to break them I had to pay the penalty of being relegated into a limbo of maudlin drunkennesses, tormenting hangovers, and phantom-Helenas. Thus work became my therapy and drug, my compromise with a guilt-ridden ego, and a sacrificial offering to the ghosts of the past. I expect that this condition will last to the end of my days; when my writing has run dry, I shall still sit for eight hours at my desk, growing piles over some boring and meritorious piece of research, as an atonement for an unknown original sin. And over my desk, in a gay frame, shall hang Attila's lines :

> . . . but thank you, I feel fine;
> it worries me though, why that sin
> eludes me when it's mine.

XXIII. Purge in a Teacup

IT was, of course, too good to be true.

Our INFA was an insignificant sideshow of the Communist movement, but the story of how it was destroyed deserves to be briefly told because it contains the whole tragedy of Communism in a nutshell.

Some time in the summer of 1934, the Institute received a valuable addition to its staff in the person of 'Comrade Paul', alias Manes Sperber. A few weeks later the Party delegated a commissar to control our activites. He called himself Jan, but I should rather call him the Invisible Man, for he seemed to possess no personal features or individual characteristics. He was of middling age and middling height; he was baldish, his suit was brownish, his shoulders squarish, his speech slowish, his manners mulish. He was the perfect incarnation of the German Party bureaucrat—wooden-faced and plaster-brained, the interior spaces of his body apparently stuffed with horsehair. And yet he had some formidable qualities. He had been trained in Moscow. I was never to know his name, but I learnt that he had been, among other things, General Secretary of the League of the Godless—an international atheist organisation sponsored by the Comintern and disbanded, I think, in 1934, when the change to the 'People's Front' line was being prepared.

In his long Comintern career, Jan had learnt to master the technique of the 'internal manœuvre' ('*Fraktionspolitik*'). It is a technique difficult to explain to people brought up in the political climate of a democracy, who are used to thinking of political activity in terms of parliamentary debates, appeals to the electorate, the struggles and alliances of parties with a more or less defined programme. In the Marixst camp, ever since the founding of the First International in 1848, the struggles of ideas and personalities were waged by entirely different techniques, initiated by Marx himself. In the small conspiratorial groups of the early years, and in the revolutionary movement which grew out of them, the usual rules of the game of politics did not apply. These rules were replaced, broadly speaking, by revolutionary discipline, and obedience to a quasi-military leadership. The delegates at Party-Conferences and Congresses did not represent the interests of their constituents, or of any specific group of the electorate. Without a proper mandate, the delegates were a diffuse and amorphous gathering, divided into coteries, in Party parlance 'fractions'. Thus these Congresses—which only met at rare intervals, and often under difficult circumstances, for a few days—could never develop into representative parliaments of the Revolution. The 'fractions' were not political parties, but alliances between individuals temporally held together by a common concept of strategy or, more often, a common bid for power. The internal history of the various Communist Parties, including the Russian, is a story of struggles between the various 'fractions', which, in the absence of a democratic procedure, could only be waged by means of intrigue, the springing of traps, the shifting of personal allegiances, and other manœuvres of *'Fraktionspolitik'*. The final decision rested with the Russian Politbureau, and later with Stalin alone, who exercised his power through periodic demotions, expulsions, the liquidation of one 'fraction', and its replacement by another.

Accordingly, the professional Communist politician's concept of 'politics' was fundamentally different from the Western politician's. Principles and ideals, the gifts of public oratory and parliamentary repartee, grasp of reality and knowledge of history, originality, initiative and personal integrity—all these were not assets, but liabilities to the Comintern politician. 'Politics' for him meant the acquisition of techniques and skills which were in almost every respect the direct opposite of the qualities just mentioned. The secret of Stalin's rise to personal power and of his victory over his more brilliant competitors, from Trotsky to Bukharin, is only a secret to the Western observer unfamiliar with the climate and atmosphere of Communism. His lack of any attribute of greatness in the Western sense—the deadly tedium of his writings and speeches, the absence of principles, ideals, originality, his treacherousness towards his associates and deafness to the sufferings of the people, his gross falsifications of history—all this would have made him a grotesque outsider in the House of Commons, and made his incomparable greatness as a *'Fraktionspolitiker'*. True to the dialectics of the Comintern universe, he remained, through the years of manœuvring for position, the perfect Invisible Man; the moment he was established in power, he became the omnipresent god.

Our Jan of the League of the Godless was a pocket-sized Stalin. On the remote peripheries of the Comintern where our INFA lived, the deadly battles of the Olympians were reenacted in more or less harmless, and often grotesque, versions. Jan had no power to liquidate us, to send us to a labour camp, to extract confessions from us. To Communists outside Russia, these things could only be done by ordering them under some pretext to Moscow. If any of us had received the call, he would, of course, have obeyed. But we were far too unimportant for such grand measures; they were only used on leaders and *apparat*-men.

So the battle of the INFA was in a sense a shadow battle; the implied penalties were not death or confinement, only disfavour and dismissal—and in the last resort, of course, expulsion from the Party. But the knowledge of these dangers was quite sufficient to condition us to obedience, and to lend Jan an absolute authority which everybody took for granted.

Jan set to work in a quiet, inconspicuous manner. He never made a harsh remark, he never expressed direct disapproval of anything that was said. It took me at least a month to realise that his aim was the elimination of Peter from the Institute. Since Jan had arrived, we had every week two or three 'official meetings', which took up much time and had the inevitably paralysing effect of a sudden change of atmosphere from friendly informality to bureaucratic solemnity. At these meetings, Jan delivered speeches which lasted from one to two hours, laying down the 'general principles' of our work in orthodox Dugashwilese, such as 'deepening our contact with the masses of toilers', 'broadening our ideological front', 'intensi-

fying the dialectical mastery of our scientific-educational
work', 'remedying our neglect to take sufficient account of the
camouflaged Fascist character of the so-called teachings of the
so-called Austro-Marxist school', and so forth. All this was an
unintentional parody of Stalin's 'directives' and 'theses' addressed to sessions of the Supreme Soviet of the U.S.S.R., and
had no practical relation whatsoever to our actual work. Jan
deliberately avoided getting involved in practical problems,
and thus to assume direct responsibility for anything that was
done. But after a while I began to discover that although his
lectures had no bearing on our work, they had a direct bearing
on personalities. In each of his speeches, he singled out members of the staff for praise in a significant order of priorities—
whereas his exhortations to 'self-criticism' were, in one way or
another, always aimed at Peter and later on, when I had made
it clear that I stood by Peter, at myself. These attacks were
always veiled, and never mentioned any concrete shortcomings in our work; they were couched in the nebulous terms of
'broadening fronts' and 'intensifying efforts', 'deepening contacts', and the like. But they achieved their purpose : the experienced 'old Party horses' on the staff understood that, for
one reason or another, Peter and I were in for it.

In any normal Party office this would have been sufficient to
finish us off. The staff would have taken the hint, would have
denounced us on grounds of inefficiency, Trotskyism or corruption; the Central Committee would have ordered an investigation and would have thrown us out from the Institute
or the Party itself, as the case may be. But the people who
worked in INFA were an exceptional lot. They did not contradict Jan—that would have been a useless and quixotic
gesture and interpreted as mutiny—but they abstained from
attacking Peter or me, and seemed to be deaf to Jan's oblique
hints.

The Party could, of course, have got rid of us by a simple
order. But, according to the principles of Comintern politics, it
is essential to 'unmask', that is, discredit a person or fraction
'in the eyes of the masses' before he or they are liquidated—
hence the infinite and painstaking trouble that is taken to
extract self-incriminating confessions from the victim. The
'masses' in this case were not only the six or eight people on

our staff, but the important group of French intellectuals who sponsored INFA. They would ask questions, and if it came to a scandal, this would one day boomerang back on Jan in the form of an accusation of 'political sabotage'.

So Jan devised a new manœuvre. In the happy days before he had descended on us, the Institute had accepted my project of an International Anti-Fascist Exhibition, and by the autumn we were well launched on it. It was an ambitious project : the Exhibition was to be held in one of the vast pavilions of the annual Paris Fair, at the Port de Versailles. It was to remain open for a month or longer, with public rallies, lectures by the élite of European intellectuals, and so on. It would, of course, cost millions of francs and was far beyond our financial and organisatorial powers. But Peter and I got several progressive bodies interested—such as the League for the Right of Man, the League against Racial Persecution, and some of the leaders of the French Socialist Trade Unions Council. The negotiations were delicate, as each of these bodies pursued its own policy, and they were often at loggerheads. A loose agreement had been reached, according to which INFA should work out the detailed plans and budget of the enterprise, and then we would all get together and appoint a mixed committee for its implementation.

Our small staff was working feverishly on the plans, when one day a new man appeared, introduced by Jan. Jan described him as 'Maurice, a reliable comrade, who is a caricaturist and a designer'. He was to help us with the 'artistic side' of the project.

Maurice was a stocky man in this thirties, with pointedly proletarian manners and a peeved, distrustful expression. I learnt later on that he had worked for the *apparat* in Hamburg, and had occasionally done caricatures for the Party paper. He shook hands with us with an unsmiling, suspicious look in his red-rimmed eyes, and for the next three days never spoke a word. He was installed with his drawing-board in Jan's own room; he asked us no questions about the work of the Institute which was new to him, and took no interest in the plans on which he was supposed to collaborate. Gradually we discovered that comrade Maurice was very nearly a moron, and that his distrustful silence was due to his inability to grasp any subject that was being discussed. Then, one day, we were shown the drawings he had prepared. One was a sketch for a poster on which a giant worker in overalls smashed a pigmy Hitler with a hammer; the other was a sketch for the main Exhibition hall with one wall reserved for 'photographs of the atrocities committed by the Fascist barbarians' and the opposite wall for 'photographs of the Socialist reconstruction in the Union of Socialist Soviet Republics'.

That was just what we had feared most. Any project on undisguised Communist propaganda lines would lead to an immediate snapping of the precarious ties with the persons and organisations on whom the realisation of the project depended. The alternative to be presented to the public must be 'Fascism or Freedom', and not 'Fascism or Communism'. Our only possible line was to stress the defensive community of interest of all parties from the Centre to the extreme Left, including the Socialists, who, regardless of their ultimate aims, were all threatened by a common danger. In short, we could only succeed by adopting a 'People's Front' policy, meaning a broad coalition of all the parties of the Left. It was at this point that the battle of the Olympians had its direct repercussions in our miniature universe.

In 1934, the Communist International went through one of the periods of convulsion and upheaval which accompany each of its reversals of policy. The official line up to the beginning of that year had been one of intransigent radicalism, rejecting any compromise with Socialists and Liberals. The subsequent reversal of policy is summarised by the following quotations:[1]

Maurice Thorez, leader of the French C.P., in Cahiers du Communisme, April 1, 1934:

'Any attempt to forget, to extenuate the rôle of social-democracy [in suppressing the working classes] is more than a mistake, it is a crime against the working class.'

Maurice Thorez in Humanité, April 13:

'All gossip about a marriage between Communists and Socialists is fundamentally alien to the spirit of Bolshevism.

We do not want to unite with social-democracy. Fire and water cannot mix.'

Maurice Thorez in Cahiers du Bolshevisme, July 1:
'We the Communist Party, we are ready to renounce all criticism of the Socialist Party during our joint action. . . . Neither from the lips of any of our propagandists nor from the pen of any of our editors will there be found the smallest attack upon the organisations and the leaders of the Socialist Party while they are faithful to the agreement they will have concluded with us.'

Thus by June 1934, after Thorez had been summoned to a hurried visit to Moscow, the line had been completely reversed. The Socialists who, two months earlier, had been denounced as Social-Fascists, had now become precious allies of the 'People's Front against Fascism'. Bourgeois democracy which, two months earlier, had been regarded as 'Fascism in disguise', was now praised as a guarantee of freedom, and it was now the duty of Communists to 'cherish every scrap of bourgeois democracy'. All revolutionary slogans were eliminated from the Communist vocabulary, and replaced by the slogans of 'freedom, peace and national unity'.

But this spectacular about-turn was as yet only tentative. The new 'People's Front' strategy was being tried out in France as a preliminary to the Franco-Russian military pact of 1935. It only became the official policy of the Comintern a year later, at the Seventh Congress in Moscow, in July 1935. In the meantime, and particularly during the second half of 1934, everything was confusion and hesitation. It seemed quite possible that the French experiment would again be reversed —such things had happened in the past—with woeful consequences for those who had fallen for it. Stalin himself had so far made no pronouncement. Manuilsky, Secretary General of the Comintern (who was soon to be replaced by Dimitrov), was known to be engaged in a bitter fractional struggle against Béla Kun and Piatnitsky, representing the 'Left'. And Jacques Doriot, the most popular figure among the Communist leaders in France and the direct rival of Thorez, had been expelled from the Central Committee (and subsequently from the

Party) as late as April 1934—precisely because he had been advocating the 'People's Front' line a few months before Moscow had ordered it.

Peter and I fell into a similar trap. Owing to our dependence on French Socialist and Liberal sponsors, we would have been bound to adopt the 'People's Front' line for purely practical reasons—even if it had not happened to correspond to our natural inclination and political temperament, which it did. But for Jan, as a member of the Comintern bureaucracy, the situation was not as simple as for us, and fraught with danger. For the German section of the Comintern was in a position entirely different from the French, and was stubbornly opposed to the new line.

In France, where the Communists were relatively weak, they could only gain by an alliance with the Socialists and the progressive middle-class; above all, the impending Franco-Russian alliance made it imperative that France should be united and strong. Exactly the opposite considerations applied to Germany. Here the Communists, as the Nazis' victim number one, had a chance of monopolising the opposition movement; the moderate parties were discredited, and defeat had made the hatred between exiled German Socialists and Communists even more embittered. It was probable that in the end the new policy would be imposed on the German Party too—but it was also possible that the French and German sections would be ordered to adopt different lines, as it sometimes happened in the Comintern. The first alternative was the more likely one, but there was no certainty. Under the circumstances, Jan could only play for time. But Peter and I had acted on the new line ahead of time—just like the unfortunate Doriot. To attack us on these grounds would not have been politic, in case the new line was later confirmed. At the same time, Jan had also to avoid getting involved in the Institute's practical activities, and assuming responsibility for any step on which we decided. Hence all the evasive talk about 'broadening the front'—which could be interpreted as an endorsement of the 'People's Front' line—and of 'deepening our contact with the masses'—which could be interpreted as sticking to the old, revolutionary line.

But if Peter and I were replaced by others, the new men

would, by force of circumstances, be bound to adopt the same
policy we had pursued. It was in this dilemma that Jan proved
his mastery of 'internal manœuvring'. He brought in Maurice
the moron, who spoke no French and would not commit Jan
to anything because he would do nothing at all. What mattered to Jan, and what would have mattered to any Comintern man in his place, was to last through the period of upheaval.

A few days after the arrival of Maurice, Jan called a meeting. After one of his long-winded and nebulous sermons, he
came out with a series of 'proposals for the reorganisation of
the Institute's work in the interest of higher efficiency'. Comrades Peter and Arthur should withdraw from the Exhibition
project so that they could devote their energies to other, un-
specified tasks. The Exhibition project would, in the interests
of efficiency, henceforth be concentrated in the hands of one
person, Comrade Maurice, who would be in charge of all planning, negotiations and administrative tasks.

The proposals were, of course, decrees. Our exclusion from
the Exhibition project meant not only that we were 'politically
liquidated', but the end of the project itself which, by the
nature of circumstances, depended on our work. I believe that
everybody present understood this. The meeting lasted three or
four hours, and ended with my resignation from the Institute;
since I had taken the job voluntarily and not by the Party's
orders, this could not be construed as a direct breach of Party
discipline. Peter, the real target of Jan's manœuvre, was a
better Communist than I; he sat through most of the meeting in silence, staring at Jan with an expression of Christian
love which the latter, for all his horse-hair stuffing, seemed
to find embarrassing. Peter's only contribution to the discussion was an attempt to dissuade me from leaving the Institute.
He spoke very quietly, trying to convince me that some Party
decisions may be hard to face at the time, but that in the end
the Party always proved to be right—an axiom in which he
firmly believed. Yet after a few weeks he, too, was finally
forced to resign.

The other members of the staff spoke in a similar vein. They
did it with so much warmth that it amounted to an implicit
criticism of the purge, and made it even harder for me to

leave. Yet nobody dared to contradict Jan's directives. Such an act of insubordination was unthinkable to them, in spite of their loyalty to Peter and their devotion to our Institute. It did not even occur to any of us to ask for a vote on Jan's 'proposals'. That, too, was unthinkable.

Peter resigned some time during the winter, and after another month INFA closed down.

The Party, or at least Jan, must have foreseen this outcome. Our Institute was an altogether too unorthodox and independent enterprise. It aimed at a study of social phenomena beyond the limits set by the Party's changing slogans, and regardless of these changes. Such an approach must sooner or later lead to deviations from, and conflicts with, the Party line; it fell into the category of 'bourgeois objectivism'. If the Comintern wanted to retain its monolithic ideological structure, such attempts, large or small, could not be tolerated. It was therefore essential to get INFA under closer control by liquidating Peter, who was its creator and moving spirit. If it did not survive the bloodletting, so much the better, as it was bound to remain a permanent headache anyway.

It may seem strange to the outsider that this whole storm in a teacup was aroused, not by a clash of policies, but by a difference in timing—by the fact that Peter and I were a few months ahead of the line. But exact timing is one of the secrets of 'Fraktionspolitik'. Inside a closed universe, whose heroes are periodically unmasked as traitors, and which progresses in a jagged zig-zag of policy-reversals, everything depends on making the proper shift of personal allegiance and political orientation at the exactly proper time. The Comintern politician's fate is not unlike the trapeze acrobat's, whose life depends on letting go of the swinging bar with split-second precision. The prophets and visionaries of the past become martyrs because they were born a century or two before their times. In the Communist movement, a time-lag of a few months was quite sufficient to be crucified.

To change the metaphor : every political system may be compared to a series of sieves or filters through which the politician, manager or bureaucrat who aspires to power must pass. But the pattern of the mesh is different for each political system. In England, for instance, the main quality a politician must possess if he is to pass through the filter is a certain upright and dependable mediocrity; in America, it is some popular quality that appeals to the imagination of the masses; in Latin countries, a gift for oratory and histrionics; in the Communist world, the qualities which I have tried to describe. The filter represents, as it were, the principle of natural selection in a given régime. No politician, however gifted, can pass through it if his personality is not cut to fit the specific shape of the mesh. When, once in a while, a genius succeeds in getting through by busting the filter, the whole structure of the system is apt to change.

My failure as a Communist was not due to any unfortunate hazards, but to a personality-pattern which was unsuited to pass even the lowest filter in the series. It was a first inkling of this which had caused me to prefer the writing of sex books to working in the Muenzenberg Trust. After my experience with INFA, I finally accepted it as a fact. From that time—the end of 1934—my conscious retreat from the Party began. It was to last another three years, for the war in Spain forged new ties with the Party, as the victory of Hitler had done. Without that, I would probably have left when the Great Purge in Russia got under way.

XXIV. Excursion into the First
Century B.C.

THE day after my career at INFA came to an end, I was
    moved by a momentary curiosity to look up the name
'Spartacus' in the Encyclopædia. The German Communist
Party is the offspring of a revolutionary group that called itself 'Spartakus-Bund', and was founded in 1917 by Karl Liebknecht and Rosa Luxemburg. The name 'Spartacus' was accordingly a household word among Communists; but, like
most Communists, I had only the vaguest notion who Spartacus was. I knew that he had led some sort of a revolution in
antiquity, and that was about all. It was one of those blind
spots in one's education which one always means to cure by
looking the subject up, but somehow one never gets round to
doing it.

So I opened Volume II, *Seefeld to Traun*, of *Meyers Lexi-
kon*, and read the following :

'Spartacus, leader of the Slaves' or Gladiators' War 73–71
B.C., a free-born Thracian, was sent, as a Roman prisoner of
war, to the Gladiators' Training School in Capua, fled from
there in 73 with seventy of his comrades, occupied Mt.
Vesuvius, defeated the Praetor Varinius, and saw his following grow to 70,000 men. He now took possession of Southern
Italy and four times defeated the Romans, until in 71 the
Praetor M. Licinius Crassus drove him to the south-western
tip of Italy; he fell at Petelia, together with 60,000 slaves.
The prisoners were crucified, the survivors who had succeeded in breaking through were annihilated by Pompeius
(qv.) in the foothills of the Alps. Bibl. : Hartwig, *Der
Sklavenkrieg.*'

This laconic text took such a hold on my imagination that
I resolved on the spot to add to my four unpublished manuscripts a fifth one, by writing a historical novel. It took four
years to write, involved me in a mammoth research task, gave
me a new outlook on history, and was my first novel to appear
in print.[1] Before I was able to finish it, I was obliged to write
four other books : two more sex books in order to live, a propaganda book for the Spanish Loyalists, and an account of my
imprisonment in Spain. Thus the writing of *The Gladiators*
became something of an obstacle race. By the time the book
was finished, in the summer of 1938, I had broken with the
Party, and the political dialogues in the novel now read to
me like a logbook, reflecting a pilgrim's progress to inner
freedom.

The following weeks I spent mostly at the *Bibliothèque
Nationale*. My material condition had by now slightly im-
proved. Since August I no longer lived in the hayloft in Val
Fleuri; I lived in a little hotel on the Ile St. Louis with
Dorothy, to whom this book is dedicated and who, a few
months later, became my first wife.

I had met Dorothy the previous year, when we had both
been working for Willy Muenzenberg. She was then a girl of
twenty-five, with dark, tousled hair, large brown eyes, and a
pleasant oval face with a shy and earnest expression. She did
not fit into either of the two main categories of women found
in the German Communist Party : the tough, cocky, working-
class girls, and the neurotic Cinderellas of the bourgeoisie.

Dorothy's father had been a Berlin banker; her brother,
Ernie, was a young doctor; her sister, Liesl, was married to
Peter. While still at school, Ernie and his two sisters had
drifted into the Socialist youth movement, and from there,
lured by Russian films, avant-garde plays, and Brecht-Eisler
songs, into the Communist Party. Their father had died several
years before, leaving his money to his widow, my future
mother-in-law. She was a domineering and eccentric woman,
haunted by the fear of poverty, who hated her daughters because they were Communists, and who lived, of all places, in a

[1] *The Gladiators*, London, 1939.

service flat in Shepherds Bush. She paid Dorothy an allowance of five pounds a month, which even in 1934 was a riducu-
lously small sum; when we were married, she sent her, as a
combined trousseau and wedding gift, a pair of woollen
knickers.

So Dorothy was nearly as poor as I. However, after leaving
INFA I wrote occasional articles for Leopold Schwarzschild's
liberal weekly, *Das Neue Tagebuch*, and Dorothy had a part-
time job; so we managed to scrape along, cooking our meals
on a gasfire in the *cabinet de toilette*, and visiting the *cinema
du quartier* once a week.

Our little hotel was a narrow, rickety building on the Quai
d'Anjou, with a misleadingly grand name, Hotel de la Paix.
Each time someone pulled the chain of the lavatory behind the
milk-glass window on the landing, the whole hotel shook with
the gurgling and rushing of Water through the lead pipes, so
that we seemed to live surrounded by a waterfall. But the
traditional shortcomings of the plumbing were compensated
by the lovely view over the Seine from our window, and by a
plane tree whose branches grew almost into our room. It was a
good room to work in, but I felt equally happy at the *Bibliothèque Nationale*, where I spent most of the day, in front of
one of the green-shaded desk-lamps, digging into Roman history, the condition of slaves in antiquity, the regulations concerning gladiators' fights, the folklore of Thrace and Gaul,
the economy of the Roman state, the topography of Mount
Vesuvius, and similar subjects. Thanks to Jan's cunning
manœuvre, I had entered upon the new life just when I was
ready for it. During the next seven or eight months I read
more history than I had done since my school-days, and wrote
the first eight chapters of *The Gladiators*; about one-third of
the book.

From the moment when I had joined the Communist Party
three and a half years earlier, I had been submerged in the
stream of Revolution. Now I was coming up for air, looking
at the stream, wondering where it was leading, and trying to
find out about the nature of the forces that made it move. At
first, my imagination had been caught by the picturesque and
romantic aspects of the Slave War : the circus gladiators who
were its leaders, their camp in the crater of Vesuvius, and by

the fact that the Slave Army came within an ace of conquering Rome and thus altering the whole course of history. But soon my interest shifted from the picturesque façade to the historical and moral lessons of the first great proletarian revolution. There existed some obvious parallels between the first pre-Christian century and ours. It had been a century of social unrest, of abortive revolutions and violent mass movements, starting with the Sicilian Slave Rising which led to the crucifixion of twenty thousand rebels, down to the revolution of Marius and Cinna, the rebellion of Sertorius and the Catiline Conspiracy; and in between, Spartacus, the most important and enigmatic figure of all.

The causes which led to these upheavals had an equally familiar ring; the breakdown of traditional values, a rapid transformation of the economic system, mass unemployment caused by the importation of slave labour and of cheap corn from the colonies, the ruin of the farmers and the growth of large latifundia, a corrupt administration and a decadent ruling class, a falling birth-rate and a spectacular rise in divorces and abortions. Only against this background could it be understood that a band of seventy fugitive circus fighters could grow within a few months into an army of 70,000 men, and for two years hold half Italy under its sway. In fact, it was one of those rare moments in history when all the elements of what Marxists call 'an objective revolutionary situation' were assembled.

Why then did the Revolution fail? And how was it possible that Rome, with its corrupt, parasitic ruling class and anachronistic economy, whose end was declared imminent by its own poets, satirists and philosophers—how could it happen that this doomed Empire survived for nearly another five hundred years? And what about the Marxian dictum in the Communist Maifesto that throughout History 'free men and slaves, oppressors and oppressed, carry on an uninterrupted fight that must end either in a revolutionary reconstitution of society at large, or in the common destruction of both contending classes'? In the first century A.D. there were already twice as many slaves as free men in Italy. The initial success of the Spartacus rising had shown them their own strength, had shown them that Rome was helpless against them once they dared to lift their heads. They never did again; it was not the Roman proletariat who brought the Empire down, but the barbarian invader. Why did the Roman slaves fail 'to take their fate into their own hands' as the Communist Manifesto said? And why, two thousand years later, did the German and Italian proletariat still fail to recognise their own interests, and support the Neros and Caligulas of their own age? Did the concept of 'class-consciousness' have any practical value in explaining history? Was not the psychology of the masses an infinitely more complex phenomenon? Why was this all-important subject a blank on the Marxist map of the world? Why did the 'Party of the masses' ignore the discoveries of Le Bon, Fraser, Durkheim, Levy-Bruhl, Freud and Jung, who all stressed the irrational and affective nature of group-behaviour, so strikingly demonstrated by Fascism and its allied movements? Did the Party's monotonous ravings against the 'traitors to the working class' and 'lackeys of the bourgeoisie' explain why the people refused to follow us? Did the closed universe in which I lived have any relation to the reality around me?

It was not I who asked these questions, it was the material in which I was working. The answers which emerged were tentative and hesitant, and very remote from the doctrinaire certitude of historical materialism. Up to now, I had been critical of the Soviet leadership and the Comintern bureaucracy, but not of the basic teaching of Communism, which I regarded as historically correct, and as self-evident as the axioms of Euclid. Now, the more engrossed I became in my subject, the more questionable became the very foundations of the doctrine, the more cracks appeared in the wall around the 'closed system', and the more fresh air blew in. I wrote the novel in the excited mood of a voyage of discoveries, where every turn opens a new vista. If some critics have called it my best novel, it is perhaps because the passions and angers which contemporary events aroused in me were here projected on a screen remote in space and time, and purified from the topical dross which tends to clutter up my other books.

The original sources on Spartacus turned out to be disappointingly meagre and biased. Even the *Encyclopædia Britannica* remarks that 'his character has been misrepresented by Roman writers, whom his name has inspired with terror down to the time of the Empire'. All the references in Livy, Plutarch, Appian and Florus added together amounted to less than ten pages. They had obviously felt the whole episode to be so humiliating that the less said about it the better—a striking justification of Marx's scorn for 'bourgeois historians' and for his assertion that all history was written with an unconscious social bias. The one exception seemed to have been Sallust, of whose *Historiæ* only fragments survive. An eighteenth-century French historian, Charles de Brosses, had filled in the missing details with much imagination and revolutionary rhetoric, thus providing an opposite, quasi-Jacobin slant.

But although direct references to the Slave Revolt itself were scant, background material on social conditions and political intrigues was abundant. In a similar way, next to nothing was known about the character of the slave leaders and the ideas that guided them, whereas a great amount was known about their opponents: Pompeius, Crassus, Varinius, Gellius Publicola, the Consuls and Senators of 73–71, their friends and contemporaries. This allowed, on the one hand, a wider scope for imagination than a historically well-defined hero would permit; in fact, not only the characters of Spartacus and his lieutenants, but also the details of their campaign and the organisation of the slave community had to be invented. But, on the other hand, the detailed knowledge available about the period provided a pattern or frame from which much could be deduced; so that the filling in of missing details became a problem of intuitive geometry, the piecing together of a jigsaw puzzle.

The sources gave no indication of the programme or common idea that held the Slave Army together; yet a number of hints indicated that it must have been a kind of 'socialist' programme which asserted that all men were born equal, and denied that the distinction between free men and slaves was part of the natural order; there were further hints to the effect that a one time Spartacus tried to found a Utopian colony, based on common property, somewhere in Lucania. Now such ideas were entirely alien to the Roman proletariat before the advent of primitive Christianity. This led to the wild, but fairly plausible guess that the Spartacists had been inspired by the same source as the Nazarenes a century later : the Messianism of the Hebrew prophets. There must have been, in the motley crowd of runaway slaves, quite a number of Syrian origin, and some of these may have acquainted Spartacus with the prophecies relating to the Son of Man, sent 'to comfort the captives, to open the eyes of the blind, to free the oppressed'. Every spontaneous movement eventually picks up, by a kind of natural selection, the ideology or myth best fitted to its purpose. I thus assumed, for the purposes of my jig-saw puzzle, that among the numerous cranks, reformers and sectarians whom his horde must have attracted, Spartacus chose as his mentor and guide a member of the Judaic sect of Essenes, the only sizeable civilised community that practised primitive Communism at that time, and taught that 'what is mine is thine, and what is thine is mine'. In short, what Spartacus needed most after his initial victories was a programme and credo that would hold his mob together; and the philosophy most likely to appeal to the largest number of the dispossessed seemed to be the one which a century later found a more sublime expression in the Sermon on the Mount—and which Spartacus, the slave Messiah, had failed to implement.

In contrast to these speculations regarding the unknown heroes of the tale, I felt the need to draw the known historical background with a strict, indeed pedantic accuracy. This led me into a study of such far-fetched subjects as the nature and shape of Roman underwear, and their complicated ways of fastening clothes by buckles, belts and sashes. In the end, not a word of all this found its way into the novel, and clothes are hardly even mentioned in the text; but I found it impossible to write a scene if I could not visualise how the characters were dressed, and how their garments were held together. Similarly, the months spent in studying Roman exports, imports, taxation and related matters yielded exactly three pages (in which Crassus, the fat banker-politician, explains to the younger Cato the economic policies of Rome in cynically Marxist terms).

Although it was a fascinating adventure, and provided me with a great amount of fun, I decided half-way through the book never again to write a historical novel. There is a basic inertia to imagination which sets limits to one's capacity for projecting oneself into worlds distant in space and time. Every culture is an island. It communicates with other islands, but ultimately it can only experience tragedy and laughter in its own climate. The habits and mentality of, say, a Knight in the Second Crusade have a frame of reference so strange to us that we find it difficult to believe in the reality of the person. The thoughts of a galley-slave or a Thracian captive trained to die in the arena are so unimaginable that the figures are reduced to meek or menacing shadows on a dim screen. There are, it seems, only two possible techniques for the novelist to bring these shadows of history into focus. One is to turn them into silhouettes with sharp profiles, into character-types as entertaining as the shadow-plays of childhood, but without the depth and warmth and luminosity needed to make emotional identification possible. The alternative technique is to cheat; to bring the shadows alive by projecting into them the feelings and ideas of the writer's own period. All historical novels and plays seem to use one of these two techniques, or a mixture of both. In *The Gladiators*, the treatment of characters belonging to the upper strata of Roman society, whose habits are familiar to us, follows the 'modernising' technique of making them speak as if they were slightly eccentric contemporaries of our own; whereas Campanian labourers and Lucanian shepherds, Thracian gladiators and walrus-moustached gloomy Celts had to remain, by the force of circumstances, silhouettes in profile, or coloured bas-reliefs, as it were.

Another headache was the treatment of the crowd-scenes—of the amorphous, inarticulate, semi-barbarian horde which is the real hero of the book, milling down the highways of Italy, sacking its cities, defeating the disciplined legions of Rome. Most novelists avoid mass-scenes like the plague, even where the story calls for them; I was amused in re-reading *War and Peace* how adroitly Tolstoi got round them. The older generation of Soviet writers made a point of manipulating huge crowds in motion, but only two of them—Sherafimovich and Sholokhov—seem to have succeeded. Other examples that come to the mind are Stephen Crane in *The Red Badge of Courage*, Werfel in *The Forty Days of Musa Dagh*, and Flaubert (at his worst) in *Salammbô*. I was influenced by none of these, but by a novel by Alfred Döblin, *The Three Steps of Wang Lun*. It is the story of a mythical mass-rising in China, written in a semi-expressionistic style, and half forgotten to-day even in Döblin's native Germany. *Wang Lun* was my literary bible, and when I tried to visualise the Roman slave horde, Döblin's crowd of ragged Chinese beggars appeared be-fore my eyes. Other 'influences' were Thomas Mann, the early Feuchtwanger, and Thornton Wilder's *The Woman of Andros*. Their different styles popped up in different parts of the book—or so I thought, guiltily, for most readers failed to recognise the models. The novel was first published in Eng-land in 1939, in an excellent translation by Edith Simon. Then the war broke out, the German manuscript was lost during my flight from France, and the German edition which appeared after the war had to be re-translated from the English transla-tion. A similar misfortune befell the next novel, *Darkness at Noon*.

The Gladiators is the first novel in a trilogy concerned with the ethics of revolution, the problem of Ends and Means. In the second, *Darkness at Noon*, the problem is restated in a contemporary setting; in the third, *Arrival and Departure*, it is shifted to the psychological level. Spartacus is a victim of the 'law of detours', which compels the leader on the road to Utopia to be 'ruthless for the sake of pity'. He is 'doomed al-ways to do that which is most repugnant to him, to become a slaughterer in order to abolish slaughtering, to whip people with knouts so that they may learn not to let themselves be whipped, to strip himself of every scruple in the name of a higher scrupulousness, and to challenge the hatred of man-kind because of his love for it—an abstract and geometrical love'. But Spartacus shrinks from taking the last step—the purge by crucifixion of the dissident Celts and the estab-lishment of a ruthless tyranny—and through this refusal he dooms his revolution to defeat. In *Darkness at Noon*, the Bol-shevik Commissar Rubashov goes the opposite way and fol-lows the 'law of detours' to the end—only to discover that 'reason alone was a defective compass which led one such a winding, twisted course that the goal finally disappeared in the mist'; and that he had become guilty of 'having placed the idea of mankind about the idea of man'.

XXV. Ten Little Nigger Boys

I HAD just finished writing the first chapter of *The Gladiators*—it was actually Chapter Five, for I had started writing it in the middle—when the Party ordered me on a new mission. I was to leave immediately for the Saar, to edit a comic weekly paper.

The fate of the Saar territory with its important coal mines and 600,000 German-speaking inhabitants had been left undecided after the first World War (as it was to be left after the second). Clemenceau had originally claimed it for France, but the decision had been postponed for a period of fifteen years, at the end of which it was to be settled by a plebiscite. In the meantime, the territory was administered by the League of Nations.

The date of the plebiscite had been fixed for January 13, 1935. Its outcome would be of symbolic importance, far surpassing the issue of the Saar itself, for here an ethnically German, but politically free population would be passing judgement on Hitler's régime after two years. The various political parties in the Saarland had formed themselves into two camps : the 'German Front', comprising all the pro-Nazi groups, and the 'People's Front', comprising Socialists, Communists and Liberals. I arrived in Saarbrücken in the middle of December, when the propaganda campaign was at its peak. The comic weekly that I was to edit was to serve the interests of the campaign.

The referendum gave the Saarländers the choice between three solutions. They could either vote for the return of the Saar to Germany, or for its incorporation into France, or for the maintenance of the *status quo*—that is, for remaining under the League of Nations' administration. Since the population of the Saar is German, it was obvious that the French alternative had no chance whatsoever. Accordingly, the Socialists (and the Liberals, who numbered few) had been campaigning from the outset for the *status quo* solution. Whereupon, in the earlier phase of the campaign, the Communists had proclaimed that continuation of the *status quo* would indirectly benefit French interests, had denounced the Socialists as 'agents of French imperialism' and launched their own slogan for 'a Red Saar in Soviet Germany' ('*Eine Rote Saar in Soviet-Deutschland*').

'But, comrade,' complained the distressed Saar miners at Party headquarters, 'there is no Soviet Germany as yet, so what do we stand for?'

'We stand, comrade, for a Red Saar in Soviet Germany.'

'But, comrade, there *is* no Soviet Germany, so do you mean we should vote for Hitler?'

'The Central Committee did not say you should vote for Hitler. It said you should vote for a Red Saar in Soviet Germany.'

'But, comrade, until there is a Soviet Germany, would it not be best to vote for the *status quo*?'

'By voting for the *status quo*, comrade, you would align yourself with the Social-Fascist agents of French imperialism.'

'In this case, comrade, would you please tell us who the bleeding hell we *are* to vote for?'

'You are putting the question in a mechanistic manner, comrade. As I told you before, the only correct revolutionary policy is to fight for a Red Saar in Soviet Germany.'

There had been hundreds of discussions on these lines every day.

In 1953, when the Communist Parties in France, Italy, etc., play an important part on the European scene, it is difficult to believe such grotesque episodes from the earlier history of the Comintern. One must bear in mind, however, that before the inception of the 'People's Front' policy in 1935, the European Communist Parties were relatively small, did not enter into coalition governments, and did not participate in the political life of their nations; they were, by and large, revolutionary sects rather than political parties, with a peculiar sectarian jargon and an incredibly twisted way of reasoning. Today, the jargon and the twists are still present, but since the Soviet sphere now embraces one-third of the earth, the peculiarities of Communist language and behaviour are treated with the same kind of embarrassed indulgence as the eccentricities of the rich and the foibles of the powerful. Churchill likes his glass of brandy and Stalin occasionally shoots his friends, for such are the habits of the great. But in 1934, when Russia was weak and frightened, and the Communist Parties in Europe no more than small, beaten, troublesome minorities, the paranoid tendencies inherent in the movement were manifested in stark and bewildering forms. The 'Red Saar in Soviet Germany' slogan was only one example among many. The so-called 'Heckert Resolution' of 1933 was another. It proclaimed that Hitler had not defeated the German working class, which had merely carried out a 'strategic retreat', and this was the gospel of the German Party for two years. Moreover, it declared, Hitler's victory was a good thing because it had 'cured the masses from the influence of the Socialists, and thus accelerated the speed of Germany's march towards the proletarian revolution'.

The Comintern's attitude to the Saar reflected the struggle between the old, radical line and the 'People's-Front' line. The idiotic slogan of the 'Red Saar' had obviously been designed by the German Central Committee for the purpose of evading the issue until that struggle was settled. It was on a par with Jan's nebulous talk about 'widening fronts' and 'deepening contacts'.

When the decision was made in Moscow, the line changed overnight. Before June 1934, everybody who proposed to vote for the *status quo* stood branded as an agent of French imperialism; after June 1934, every Communist's duty was to vote for the *status quo*.

The change of line was made known to the faithful in an article in INPRECORR, the Communist International's official weekly, on June 8, 1934, under the headline 'Leninist Tactics in the Saar Question' by W. Mueller. It seems worth quoting it, as a typical document of the period :

'For the Communists the Saar problem, as a class question, has always been a problem of the German proletarian revolution. With the proletarian revolution in Germany they want at the same time, by means of the revolutionary mass struggle in the Saar, to achieve the social and national emancipation of the Saarland. There Communists were and are even more today of the opinion that the prospects of the proletarian revolution in Germany have become more favourable as a result of the revolutionary upsurge which is taking place. Therefore they were, and are still today, of the opinion that the propaganda and preparation of the masses for the fight for Soviet power also in the Saar district must be continued and strengthened. . . .

'None of the three alternatives on which the vote will be taken—namely attachment to France, return to Germany, or the maintenance of the *status quo,* corresponds to the Socialist aims. Because the Social-Democrats are splitting the working class and preventing their unity on a revolutionary basis, the Communists are still today unable to lead the decisive political class battle in the Saar and to solve the German problem in the sense of their final Socialist aim.

'The interests of the workers and the toiling population demand a decision which shall provide the greatest possibility for the development and extension of the anti-Fascist class struggle. Under the present conditions, and in spite of the hostility of the Communists to the capitalist régime, this possibility is offered by the *status quo.* . . . For the time being the Communists decide for the *status quo* in order the better and more rapidly to develop the revolutionary forces. But their support of the *status quo* will cease the moment the proletariat of Germany takes up the victorious fight for power.'

To appreciate this sample it should be noted that in the plebiscite the Nazis obtained over ninety per cent. of the votes, the anti-Nazis eight per cent., of which probably less than three per cent. were Communist votes. It should also be remembered that it was written at a time when Hitler's power was in rapid ascendancy, and when the Communist opposition in Germany had been completely and finally crushed. Against this background, the first paragraph of the quotation with its bombast about a 'mass struggle' and 'revolutionary upsurge' indicates the schizophrenic estrangement from reality which was so typical of the Comintern of the period—and is still typical of the climate behind the Iron Curtain where the 'closed system' is not only mentally but physically cut off from the rest of the world.

Immediately after the referendum, the Communist paper on the Saar (I think it was called *Volkstimme*) came out with its last issue. The headline across the front page read: 'HITLER'S DEFEAT ON THE SAAR'. The article explained that dialectically the Nazis had suffered a defeat because they had only obtained ninety per cent. of the votes instead of the ninety-eight per cent. which they had boasted they would get. By the time the paper reached the news stands, its staff had fled to France. The editor was Ernst Reinhardt, our commissar in the Writers' Caucus.

My own comic weekly was dialectically a lasting achievement, though mechanistically it only lived for one issue. When that came out, the Party stopped the paper and sent me back to Paris.

It was called *Die Saar-Ente*. (*Ente*=Duck=*Canard*; after the famous French satirical weekly *Le Canard Enchaîné*.) It appeared a month before the plebiscite, and had four pages, with drawings by 'Fritta' and texts by myself. The only features in it that I still remember was an illustrated poem in the manner of the 'Ten Little Nigger Boys'. The ten little nigger boys were Nazi Brownshirts who were liquidated, one after another, in the Strasser-Purge, in the Roehm-Purge, because of a non-Aryan grandmother, and so on; until the last surviving little nigger boy joined the anti-Fascist front.

It never occurred to me that the story could also be applied, *mutatis mutandis*, to the Communist Party—and with even greater justification in view of the almost clockwork regularity of its periodic purges. But it must have occurred to others. Perhaps the sub-conscious mind, that sinister humourist who likes tripping up one's tongue and sticking out its own, had played one of its tricks on me—as it did once later, on a terrible occasion, when in a speech before a Party audience it made me say : '. . . And so, comrades, we shall continue the struggle against the Stalinite tyranny—I mean, of course, against the Hitlerite tyranny.' Luckily, the Party doesn't believe in Freud.

Why exactly the Party stopped *Die Saar-Ente* I have never learnt. Perhaps because of 'The Ten Little Nigger Boys'; perhaps because *intra muros Cominterni* humour was always regarded as a dangerous virus; or perhaps simply because the paper was bad—though in the latter case it could have been continued under another editor. However that may be, I was merely told that the Party lacked the funds for the continuation of the experiment, so would I kindly pack up and go back to Paris.

Yet another of my Party missions had ended in failure. But by that time I had become too hard-boiled to mind, and was only too glad to go back to the first century B.C.

On my return to Paris, I wrote a report on the Saar for Schwarzschild's *Das Neue Tagebuch*. I have unearthed that article in a public library. It appeared a week before the referendum, and ended with what I thought to be a very cautious forecast of its result. One-third of the Saar, I said, was solidly anti-Nazi, another third undecided; thus the vote against Hitler would be somewhere between thirty and sixty per cent. I believed, of course, in this estimate, otherwise I would not have published it. Before I entered the Communist Party I had been a highly paid and fairly successful political reporter; the catastrophic deterioration of political acumen, which this story indicates, is an example of the effects of living inside the 'closed system'. It is typical of the reports which the Kremlin's political intelligence agents send home regarding trends of public opinion in the West.

During my fortnight's stay in Saarbrücken I met again, and for the last time, Paul Dietrich, my jovial Comintern chief of Moscow days. When I left, we shook hands casually; then he returned to Russia and two years later joined the grey host of the millions who vanished behind the Arctic Circle.

I also ran into some other people whom I knew by sight

from Moscow or Berlin without knowing who they were, or in what confidential job they were engaged. Among them was 'Edgar', my first contact in the *apparat*, who was to meet his fate even before Dietrich. They all looked a little greyer, a little more drawn in the face, a little more anonymous, than the last time. Among them was also a young woman with a curiously steady gaze, whom I had not met before, and whom the others called 'Martha'. We spent a long and pleasant evening in a café, in the company of Dietrich and others, without my knowing that she was Babette Muenzenberg's sister, the wife of the fabulous Heinz Neumann who had engineered the Communist revolt in Canton in 1929. The next time I met 'Martha', alias Greta Neumann Buber, was sixteen years later. By that time Heinz Neumann had been shot in Russia, and Greta had survived three years in a Russian, and another five years in a German forced labour camp.

In short, the Saar was a kind of international rendezvous of the 'Ten Little Nigger Boys', the pioneers of the European Communist movement. It was the last but one rendezvous of its kind—the last one was to take place two years later in Spain.

In the background of that rendezvous was an event whose importance I did not understand at the time. But the Dietrichs and Edgars and Marthas had understood it at once, and this was the reason why they looked so haggard and reserved. On December 1, a member of the Russian Politburo, the Party boss of Leningrad, Sergei Kirov, had been assassinated by a man named Nicolaiev. His shots ushered in a new epoch in the history of Russia, and of the international Communist movement. On December 6, 12 and 18, the Soviet authorities laconically reported the execution without trial of a hundred and four persons. A special decree, issued on the day after the murder, deprived the accused of the right of defence and appeal, and ordered that death sentences were to be carried out immediately after pronouncement. Zinoviev, first President of the Comintern, Kamenev, President of the Moscow Soviet, and many other leaders of the October Revolution were arrested and later executed. The Terror had begun.

It had begun with a revolver shot, as if at a prearranged

signal—as the Terror in Germany had begun with the Reichstag Fire. The man who fired them, Nicolaiev, was a young neurotic, a hapless tool as van der Lubbe had been; and the whole bloody sequence of events followed the pattern set by the Nazis—as it was so often to be the case in years to come.[1]

[1] Strangely enough, most writers on the subject seem to have ignored the obvious parallel between the Reichstag fire and the Kirov murder. Conclusive evidence of the fact that the murder was a deliberate 'provocation', instigated by the Kremlin, has been available since 1938: cf. the official report of the trial of Bukharin, Rykov, Yagoda and accomplices, Moscow, March 1938; and, for a comprehensive analysis of the evidence, H. Dewar, *Assassins at Large*, London, 1951.

XXVI. Marking Time

THE terror did not reach its peak at once; nor did it grow in a steady crescendo. Immediately after the murder of Kirov, tens of thousands of Russians were deported to Siberia —they were collectively referred to in Soviet parlance as 'Kirov assassins'. Then an apparent lull set in. While the liquidation of the old guard of the Revolution was being prepared behind the scenes, Stalin's propaganda played up the new Soviet Constitution, 'the most democratic in the world.' The principal authors of the new Constitution were Bukharin and Radek. A year later, they appeared as the principal accused in the third Moscow trial.

This period of gestation lasted from the spring of 1935 to the summer of 1936. It reminds one strangely of the period of suspense in Defoe's *Journal of the Plague Year* between the first appearance of the plague, and its full outbreak several months later. Typical of the secrecy surrounding this period is the fact that Zinoviev, Kamenev, Smyrnov and accomplices, the defendants in what is known to the world as the 'First' Moscow trial, were in fact tried three times within eighteen months for the same crime. The first time they were tried in January 1935, found guilty of 'being politically and morally responsible' for Kirov's assassination without having any actual part in it, and were sentenced to prison terms. The second time the same defendants, plus a host of new co-defendants, numbering in total thirty, were tried secretly on the same charges in the spring of 1935; all that is known of the trial is that another five years were added to Kamenev's prison sentence. The third time, Zinoviev, Kamenev, Smyrnov and accomplices, were tried in August 1936, under the full blast of publicity. It was this trial that became known to the world as the 'First' Moscow trial. This time all the accused were found guilty as the direct instigators of and accomplices in Kirov's murder, were sentenced to death and shot.

During this year and a half of veiled preparations, Soviet propaganda still managed to keep the world in ignorance about the real state of affairs in Russia. The liberal and progressive-minded section of the European public was completely taken in by the propaganda barrage boosting the new Soviet Constitution and the new 'People's Front' policy in Europe. It was during this period that Stalin proved his genius for propaganda by gradually tightening his grip round the people's neck, and at the same time creating the illusion of a more liberal policy.

This period ended with a bang in August 1936. The death sentences in the 'First' Moscow trial marked the transition from camouflaged terror to stark and open mass terror. But by that time the Spanish Civil War had broken out. Franco's revolt made internal events in Russia recede far into the background for the European Left, myself included. On the day when the first reports of the Zinoviev Trial appeared in the European Press, I was already on my way as a Comintern agent to Spain.

This period of transition and suspense, the year 1935–36, was also the last of my adolescence. I was now thirty, but adolescence is not a matter of age; it is a state of character and mind. The story that I have told betrays only too clearly how unbalanced and unstable I still was. I experienced joy and despair, love and hatred with keen intensity, but my emotions were self-centred, and those who inspired them served merely as projection-screens.

The turning point came at the end of this period, with my imprisonment in Spain. The last year before it was both restless and empty. It was divided between Paris, Zurich, Budapest and other places. I was not travelling for pleasure, but like a hobo from one job to another, in search of a living.

The first station in these wanderings was Zurich. Dorothy's brother Ernie had been offered a post as a hospital surgeon in the Volga-German Soviet Republic, and was emigrating with

M

his Swiss-born wife and their little daughter to that country. The lease of their flat in Westbuehl, one of Zurich's modern residential suburbs, ran for another six months. It would be a pity to waste it; Dorothy and I could live there rent-free while I was writing my book, and even have a real bathroom of our own. I think it was the bathroom that decided us, and in January 1935 we installed ourselves for the next six months in Zurich.

Just before we left Paris, I had an unexpected stroke of luck. In a moment of generosity, Theodore, the Sex Publisher, agreed to pay me five pounds a month for a year against the copyright of *The Gladiators*. He was now prosperous, and intended to branch out into 'respectable' publishing—an intention that he never realised, as will be seen. I was, of course, overjoyed by the prospect of being able to concentrate entirely on the novel, and of finishing it within a year.

Ernie's was a pleasant, modern flat; it had three rooms with large windows opening on tidy, suburban lawns; after the cheap Paris hotel rooms it appeared to us as a place of glamour and luxury. We relished the cleanliness of the Swiss, their homely dialect and their honest, gruff manners. The Town Library was well-stocked with works on antiquity, and had the great advantage that up to fifteen volumes could be taken home.

As against these blessings, we found it more difficult to be poor in Zurich than in Paris. Although the largest town in Switzerland, Zurich has an intensely provincial atmosphere, saturated with prosperity and virtue. To be poor on Montparnasse could be regarded as a joke, a bohemian eccentricity; but Zurich had neither a Montparnasse nor cheap *bistros*, nor that kind of humour. In this clean, smug, orderly town, poverty was simply degrading; and, though no longer starving, we were very poor indeed. We had Dorothy's five pounds per month, and I had the same amount; one day we discovered that our joint monthly income was lower than that of a Swiss worker living on unemployment relief.

Nevertheless, these five or six months were contented and uneventful. I worked my regular eight hours, and sometimes we went for long walks around the lake or in the hills. To our great relief the Party forbade us all contact with the Swiss

C.P. The Swiss police were much stricter than the French in supervising the activities of foreigners, and contact with the Swiss Party would have meant immediate expulsion from the country.

Our friends nearly all belonged to the so-called 'Humm Circle'. Jacob Humm is a distinguished Swiss-German novelist, in whose flat a group of writers met once a week for literary readings and discussions. These evenings were very enjoyable, and the friendly, polite tone of the discussions stood in agreeable contrast to the acerbity of our arguments in the Writers' Caucus in Paris. Humm was a tall, gaunt, eccentric man, with the appearance and manners of a Swiss mountain guide, yet with a great tenderness of feeling and a seismographic intuition for other people's troubles. In several respects he resembled George Orwell. He lived in an old-fashioned, rambling flat on Hecht Platz with his quiet and efficient wife Lilly and a host of children of all ages. One of the peculiarities of the flat was that the frosted-glass lavatory door opened straight into the sitting-room. Our high-flown discussions were punctuated by the comings and goings of the Humm children through that door.

More or less regular participants in our discussions were Ignazio Silone, who at that time lived in Switzerland; Bernard von Brentano, the German novelist; Julius Hay, the Hungarian Communist playwright, and several local journalists and young writers. After a few weeks, Peter, now my brother-in-law, also turned up in Zurich on some mysterious new Party assignment, and became a regular member of the Humm Circle. The assignment had something to do with 'broadening the cultural front and establishing new contacts', but he was very cagey about it; so, knowing Peter's harmless foible of giving himself conspiratorial airs, I did not press him and never found out the exact nature of his mission. He seemed entirely undaunted by our INFA experiences, and when I indulged in some bitter and cynical remark, he just looked deeply into my eyes with his saintly stare, half psychiatrist, half priest, and made me feel ashamed of myself.

Faithful to Party tradition, Peter, Hay and I immediately formed a caucus within the Humm Circle. It was a sophisticated group that could not be approached by direct Communist propaganda; it could only be manœuvred by much patience and by imperceptible steps, into a 'sympathising' attitude. The three of us, thoroughly versed in the Marxist theory of literature, had the advantage of all propounders of a logically self-consistent system over opponents with no system at all. Our arguments were cogent and seemed to make sense, even if the axioms on which they were based were one sided and partly nonsense. The Humm Circle did not embody any political power; it was merely one of the thousands of intellectual côteries all over the world who, in their ensemble, create the climate of public opinion; and in each of these there were, during the nineteen-thirties, small caucuses of Peters and Arthurs patiently at work to make this climate favourable, or at least benevolently neutral, to the Great Social Experiment in Russia and its Western extension, the People's Front against war and Fascism.

The third of us, Julius Hay, was a dark, good-looking and easy-going young man. He was a Communist by philosophy, but took no interest in politics, paid his Party dues as one pays income tax, and lived entirely for his plays. One had been produced in 1932 by Reinhardt in Berlin; since then he had been an exile, wandering through Europe with a suitcase full of unperformed plays which represented his capital and future. After the war he returned to Budapest and became the most celebrated playwright of the régime.

Silone attended the circle less regularly, perhaps only two or three times. He was convalescing in the mountains after an attack of tuberculosis, and only came to Zurich at rare intervals. *Fontamara*, his first novel, which made his European reputation, had been published a few months earlier in a German translation. The publishing history of the book is typical of the almost insurmountable difficulties which émigré writers have to face. Silone had offered the manuscript to the then largest Swiss publishing firm, Oprecht und Helbing, whose owner, the late Dr. Emil Oprecht, was a Left-wing Socialist with Communist sympathies. In spite of this, and in spite of the enthusiastic readers' reports, Oprecht refused to publish the work as the cost of translation from the Italian manuscript 'would make the risk too high'. This is the classic argument which condemns the exiled writer to silence and starvation. After a year or two had passed, Silone's friends discovered a Maecenas in the person of a kindly Zurich fur merchant whose wife had literary leanings. The fur merchant gave Oprecht a guarantee against possible losses, and now at last *Fontamara* appeared in print. It became a best-seller at once, and for the rest of his life the publisher basked in the glory of having discovered Silone. The merit, of course, was the fur merchant's, whose name ought to be remembered by posterity; he was called Herr Mayer.

In the course of the last few years before we met in Zurich, Silone had been gradually detaching himself from the Party,[1] but he did not attack it openly, and the Party was still hoping to win him back. I had much admired *Fontamara*, and was looking forward to meeting Silone. I found him a kind but very reserved person, wrapped up in himself, surrounded by a soft but impenetrable cloud of melancholy and depression. To my great disappointment I was unable to find any real personal contact with him.[2]

In March, Dorothy and I got married. The immediate reason was a problem of passports, the refugee's eternal nightmare. Dorothy's German passport had expired and could not be renewed; by marrying me she could obtain a Hungarian passport. Although in Russia the 'new proletarian morality' had resurrected sexual conventions with a vengeance, Euro-

[1] See his autobiographical contribution in *The God that Failed*.

[2] After the Zurich period we did not meet again for thirteen years; but our names were constantly bracketed together by the critics, with André Malraux as the third, in a kind of triumvirate representing the ex-Communist brand of the Continental novel.

In 1948, on our first post-war visit to Rome, Mamaine (my second wife) and I rang up Silone, and arranged to meet for lunch in a restaurant the next day. Silone arrived late, and after addressing a few melancholy words of greeting to us, buried himself into a newspaper for the rest of the meal, without noticing our bewilderment. Later on Darina, Silone's charming and devoted Irish wife, told us in comic despair that after the luncheon she had rebuked Ignazio for his apparent rudeness to us; and that he had answered in surprise: 'But why should I not read my newspaper? The Koestlers are not strangers but my friends.' We did indeed become quite good friends later on—but it has always remained a somewhat frustrating kind of friendship.

pean Communists still clung to their old-fashioned libertinism, and regarded bourgeois marriage with contempt. But there was no other way of getting Dorothy a passport, so, with a joint sigh of resignation, we decided to go through with that archaic ceremony.

A few days before it was scheduled to take place, Dorothy came to my room with an expression of deep gloom :

'I had a letter from the Consulate,' she said hesitantly, 'telling me that my passport can be renewed after all.' 'Wonderful,' I said. 'Now we can call the whole thing off, and live happily ever after.' Dorothy looked at me pensively from under her tousled hair. 'But now I have written to everybody that we are getting married,' she said. 'If we call it off, what will people say?' So we went to the Humms to borrow their wedding rings for the ceremony. Neither of us breathed a word about this new turn of events. To save our self-respect, the marriage had to remain a reluctant passport affair.

Next to his passport, the refugee's main preoccupation is his identity card or *permis de séjour*. The passport proves his right to exist; the permit his right to reside where he does. The third essential document is the working permit which would grant him the right to earn a living. But this he is in most cases unable to obtain.

In Switzerland, every alien who does not belong to the privileged category of tourists is subject to periodical police check-ups. His means of subsistence, his morals and politics are legitimate objects of scrutiny, and the smallness of the country enables the police to supervise the alien's life fairly thoroughly. A week after we had taken possession of Ernie's flat, a plain-clothed policeman called on us. He saw at a glance that we were impecunious, and when it turned out that we were not even married, his manner became gruff to the point of offensiveness. The sharing of a flat by an unmarried couple is not a cause for deportation even in virtuous Switzerland, but prostitution is, and the detective's questions seemed to imply that Dorothy was a 'kept woman'. However, as we were living in her brother's flat, who was a doctor and had married into a respectable Swiss family, the detective had to beat a grumbling retreat.

After our marriage, the same detective came to see Dorothy

again while I was out. He started with the same insinuations. Dorothy showed him our marriage certificate as proof that she was after all not 'a kept woman'. The man thought for a while, then said : 'I suppose this marriage was arranged to cover up the fact that you are working as his housekeeper without a labour permit.'

In the late summer, young Ellen, the 'Queen Nefertete' of INFA days, turned up in Zurich, as gay and irrepressible as ever. She was engaged to marry a young scientist who had been offered a job in Soviet Russia. He had gone ahead to Leningrad to prepare the ground, and she was to follow him in a few weeks' time.

I never understood what exactly Ellen was doing in Zurich. She said she needed a holiday, and as her actions had always been rather unpredictable, we did not question her further. Long after I left Zurich I learnt that she had been arrested by the Swiss and kept in prison for several weeks on a charge of espionage; and that in the end she had been deported to Russia. Another friend of ours, a strikingly beautiful young woman called Helen, was arrested on a similar charge about the same time, and released after a while. To my knowledge both Ellen and Helen were 'sympathisers', and neither of them a member of the Party. I have never found out why they got into trouble, but I believe that both were innocents abroad who had agreed to pass on messages, or the like, in the belief that they were helping the underground in Germany, while in fact they were being exploited by Soviet Military Intelligence or some other branch of the *apparat*. I mention this episode as one example of the ambiguities of the twilight world in which we lived.

The end of Ellen's story conforms to the monotonous pattern running through these pages. A year after her arrival in Leningrad she had a baby, and until 1937 she wrote more or less regularly from Russia. Then the usual silence. Later on we heard that pretty Nefertete and her husband had been arrested; they have since vanished with the rest.

The same fate befell Dorothy's brother, Ernie. He was arrested in Saratov in 1936 on the usual absurd charges, and has never been heard of since.[1] His wife was also arrested, spent seven years in various Soviet Labour Camps, survived and, thanks to her Swiss nationality, was allowed to return to her native country after the war. Their daughter was taken to a Soviet orphanage; in spite of her mother's desperate efforts, backed by Swiss diplomatic representations, she was not permitted to leave Russia. For a while, the child was allowed to write once or twice a year; then no more letters arrived.

I only met Ernie two or three times. He had joined the Party as a matter of conviction, but took no interest in politics. He was a gentle and entirely unremarkable person, a little spoilt and self-indulgent, ideally suited for the part of the trusted family doctor—which in another time he would no doubt have remained till a happy old age of four-score years.

One day in the summer of 1935, Theodore arrived in Zurich on an unexpected visit. He explained, with an embarrassed air, that he was on his way to Budapest to discuss further publishing plans with Freddie. His embarrassment gave us a premonition of disaster. Sure enough, after some beating about the bush, he came out with a proposition that, instead of continuing with *The Gladiators* I should write another sex book. He had thought the matter over and had come to the conclusion that few readers took an interest in the first century B.C., whereas everybody took an interest in sex.

I tried to argue, but his mind was made up. He had lost interest in Spartacus; my monthly five pounds, half our minimum basic budget, would no longer be forthcoming. Despairingly I suggested that I read to him a few chapters of the manuscript, but Theodore said it would only make him sad to hear my undoubtedly beautiful prose when the hard necessities of business life made it impossible for him to help me. 'My dear boy,' he declared in genuine distress, 'you are an idealist. I too was one when I was young, but I have learnt my lesson.' The dreadful thing was that he spoke the truth. Theodore had tried to study law, to go into politics, and to become a journalist, and had always failed. In the end, he had been forced to surrender to Freddie, the rake. He was still Freddie's employee, and entirely dependent on him. I sus-

[1] See *The God that Failed.*

pected that it was Freddie who had decided against *The Gladiators*, and that poor Theodore now played the part of the heartless businessman merely to uphold his own prestige.

As a consolation, he invited us to an excellent dinner. I was too depressed and resigned even to quarrel with him. During dinner he explained the plan for the new sex book. I said I would think it over.

Then Theodore left for Budapest, with the apologetic smile of the locust who has just destroyed the farmer's crop and shattered his hopes.

It was a restless year.

A few months after getting officially married, Dorothy and I agreed to separate as we realised that we were not much fitted for married life, or that I, at any rate, was not. The reasons for this unfitness I have explained in a chapter of the previous volume, called 'Portrait of the Author at Twenty-five'; unfortunately they were still in evidence at thirty, and even at forty. We parted without quarrel or bitterness, and have remained friends to this day. I may add, as a mitigating circumstance, that this is also true of my earlier and later companions.

After Theodore's catastrophic visit I had to return to hackwork, which occupied me through the whole year, left me little time and energy for continuing *The Gladiators*, and even less for the indispensable research that it involved. I have probably never written more in the course of a single year, and to less purpose—if to live from one day to the next can be called a purpose at all. I continued to write articles and book reviews for *Das Neue Tagebuch*, which at least gave me some professional satisfaction; but as a refugee paper, the *Tagebuch* could only pay very small fees. I also wrote a chapter on Paris for an English Continental guidebook (published by Freddie's now extinct firm in London). I wrote the second sex book, *Sexual Anomalies and Perversions*, comprising six hundred and thirty pages, or over a quarter-million words. I translated S. Fowler-Wright's novel *Prelude in Prague* into German for Muenzenberg's publishing firm. I re-wrote one of my plays as a short story for a literary competition—without success. I wrote two film treatments, which I was unable to sell. I wrote a synopsis for another projected Freddie-book, *The Encyclo-pædia of Psychic Research*, but the circulars did not bring in the required one and a half per cent. of orders, so the book was never written.

Finally, I also wrote about half of a satirical novel, called *The Good Soldier Schweik Goes to War Again*. It was to be a continuation of Jaroslav Hasek's classic about Schweik, the Central-European Sancho Panza. About a hundred pages of the manuscript survive and are in parts quite funny, in a coarsely farcical manner. It had been commissioned by Willy Muenzenberg, who always liked unorthodox ideas, to serve the Party's anti-war campaign, but was vetoed by the Party on the grounds of the book's 'pacifist errors'.

Altogether I must have turned out during that year around half a million words. This would represent a good average for any pulp writer, and it may give the impression that I belong to the enviable category of people who write with ease and facility. In fact the opposite is true. I write as a stammerer talks. I sweat out every word in longhand, slowly and pain-fully, cutting and re-writing all the time; the typescript that goes to the printer is usually the third or fourth version, and then I start again on the galleys. This, of course, refers only to 'serious' work, but it includes newspaper and magazine articles. The finished product of this grind inevitably acquires a certain smoothness, which is often mistaken for glibness or natural ease. Over a number of years my average daily output has remained two pages for fiction, three for non-fiction, counting four hundred words to a page. Incidentally, most writers whom I have asked seem to average about the same amount, but with a considerably smaller number of daily work-ing hours.

It would, of course, have been impossible to write the sex books, or the chapter in the guide-book, at this slow rate. I had to set myself a target of ten to fifteen pages a day, and keep to it. This hectic pace deprived me of any professional satisfac-tion, and made me feel a cheap hack. Even so, I only earned with each of these books about a month's living over and above the time spent in actually writing it.

I felt no missionary purpose in writing my second sex book such as I had felt about the *Encyclopædia*. 'Sexual anomalies and perversions' are an uninspiring subject. The artificial over-excitation of the senses by vast industries living on commercialised sex appeal is certainly harmful; and particularly so in a civilisation that encourages the stimuli, and inhibits the response. But the sober case histories of sexual aberrations with their clinical and compressed style have a singularly chilling effect. The description of the case of 'Mr. X., aged fifty, employee of an insurance firm, living in a respectable suburb, arrested for exhibitionistic practices,' does not set you dreaming any more than an anatomical chart; whereas the entirely virtuous heroine on the magazine-cover does.

This paradox was ironically driven home to me while I was engaged in writing the book. Because of the speed with which it had to be written, I dictated it straight on to the typewriter. The typist whom Theodore had found for me happened to be a pretty young woman, married to a psychiatrist. We worked in my hotel bedroom, shut up together every day for eight hours, myself pacing the carpet, Mrs. F. sitting at the desk, her pretty head bent over the typewriter, demurely hammering out the most hair-raising things that a man might do to a woman, or vice versa. Mrs. F. never turned a hair—hair of the colour of ripe chestnuts, smooth and glossy, and known to me, after a week, down to every individual strand and curl. From time to time she would ask me to spell out for her a terrible Latin word—which I did, my face turning crimson. She knew, of course, the meaning of all the Latin words, being married to a psychiatrist; and if she didn't, she was sure to ask her husband over lunch. For pretty Mrs. F. invariably lunched with her husband, and adamantly refused to go out with me even as far as the restaurant around the corner. She knew that as soon as we went out together, the clinical atmosphere would vanish and I would start making advances across the luncheon table; whereas while we were working in my room, she was protected by the ghosts of Jack the Ripper, the Marquis de Sade, and all the balding insurance agents with a passion for committing sodomy with fishes. How can you stroke a girl's smooth hair when you have just finished a chapter on the hair-fetishists who loiter in tube-stations with scissors in their pockets; or squeeze her hand while she thinks of all the dismembered bodies left in suitcases in the cloakroom of Paddington Station; or whisper amorous words having just called a spade a spade, and in Latin to boot? The effect was paralysing. It was obvious that any attempt at a transition from the abstract to the personal, any impulsive gesture, would produce either a piercing scream or the giggles.

The setting of this edifying story was Budapest. When I had given in and agreed to write the book, Freddie and Theodore, who were spending the summer in that town, had insisted that I write it there, so that they could supervise its progress.

It was my last stay in my native country; after Spain I could return there no longer. It was also the last time that I saw Attila Jozsef. In the two years since my previous visit he had written some of his most moving poems, but his nervous condition had already begun to deteriorate. Among other peculiarities, he had devloped an obsession about matches. Before going to sleep, he felt compelled to count and re-count the number of matches left in the box on the bedside table. That could be explained as a common and relatively harmless symptom in a compulsion-neurosis. But he had also fallen into the habit of burning one match after another while we were talking across a café table, until there were none left in the box. He would pull out the first match, light it and, before it burnt out, light the second from it, and so on, gazing absentmindedly into the small yellow flame. On the first occasion when he did this, I innocently asked him to stop that silly game but he only reacted with an absent, blank stare which chilled me. After that I pretended not to notice what he was doing, and his friends acted in the same way. Though there were still hours and days when our relations were as warm as before, I never again felt entirely at ease in his company. Yet I had no premonition that the end was so near, nor of the terrible form it would take.

As for Németh and Juci, our friendship was resumed with the same intimacy as before. They had in the meantime married. This had infuriated Zsuzsa, Németh's aristocratic mistress, and she had avenged herself by publishing a magazine short story whose hero was a plainly recognisable, malicious portrait of Németh. The story was called 'The Angel', and it dwelt lovingly on a certain aspect of Németh's character which I have described as that of a 'saintly sponger or a sponging saint'. Németh took the whole thing in a truly saintly manner, and Juci would read aloud passages of the story, interrupting herself with appreciative giggles. The publication of 'The Angel' was the main scandal and delight of the literary world of Budapest at about the time when Mussolini marched into Abyssinia.

We again spent all our evenings together, but 'the firm' as a literary enterprise was not resurrected. During my absence, Németh had published a beautifully written pot-boiler—a romanced biography of the Empress Marie Thérèse—but he had done next to no serious work. When I tried to admonish him about it, he brushed me off with the remark that Cervantes wrote *Don Quixote* when he was past sixty, and that no writer should be allowed to publish anything before he was fifty. He was serenely determined to fritter away his life and gifts as the last of the bohemians. He did it with so much grace and detachment, and he was so delighted with the absurdity of the existence he led, that preaching to him seemed pedantic and futile. Again I felt that, with all his sloth and indolence, he lived closer than I to the things that really mattered, and that, in some devious way, his passive acceptance made more sense than my strugglings and kickings in the net.

XXVII. The House on the Lake

THE only relief from this pointless existence was a period of three or four weeks spent in a house on the Lago di Lugano. It belonged to a strange personality who had invited me to stay with her so that I could work undisturbed on my novel.

The house stood in the village of Caslano, on a wooded slope, overlooking the Lake. It belonged to a rich, middle-aged woman, the widow of the famous German film-actor, Eugen Kloepfer. Maria Kloepfer[1] was a benefactress of impecunious Communist writers whom she invited to her house, one at a time, for a month or two. Among those who had enjoyed her hospitality were Johannes R. Becher, Ludwig Renn, and my brother-in-law, Peter. She also contributed generously to the various committees and front organisations of the Party.

On our first evening in her house, she explained to me that she was attracted by Communism as a new way of social life, but equally by Buddhism and Theosophy as ways of spiritual life, and that she regarded psychoanalysis as a bridge between the two. This might have sounded like the gushings of a frustrated society woman who feels the change of life approaching, but Maria was not that type. She was just the opposite.

I remember her best in her white bathing suit. She was tall, with a lean, sinewy body, with small breasts and long limbs, her skin the colour of baked clay from constant swimming and sunbathing. Stretched out in the grass, she looked like a stranded, ageing mermaid, waiting for the flood to call her back. The only discordant feature was her teeth, held together by conspicuous metal braces.

[1] See *Arrow in the Blue*.

Maria lived alone in her house with an elderly maid and an ageing mongrel dog called Ricky. On the second evening, she asked me whether I believed in ghosts. I answered with a joke, and Maria dropped the subject. A little later she said casually, in her well-bred manner, that if at night I heard knocking on the walls I should not worry; she had all her life been plagued by poltergeists, but they were harmless.

I never heard the poltergeists, but I had some experiences with Maria which, though less dramatic, were of a sadder and more harrowing nature. But I can better explain these by anticipating the end of the story. Maria Kloepfer died, a few months after I had left her house, in a mental home. Strangely enough, neither Becher nor Peter—in whose joint company I had first met her a few months earlier—had any intimation of her condition, otherwise they would have warned me.

It was a small house of two floors, and I had the whole upper floor to myself. In the morning we usually went for a swim, then I worked most of the day, but occasionally I accompanied Maria on a walk. About seven in the evening we would have some *grappa*, either in the garden or in the local *trattoria* which consisted of a few wooden benches in front of a cave in the rock. Then we would dine on the terrace of her house, watching the sun set over the lake, with a *fiasco* of red wine in front of each of us. After dinner, we would continue to drink wine until midnight; most of the time we talked, but sometimes Maria played the piano. It sounds like an ideal existence.

The first tension arose in connexion with our occasional visits to the *trattoria*, and had a rather squalid cause. I had arrived in Caslano again literally without a penny—I think I was waiting for some money due to me from Freddie and Theodore, which did not arrive. Thus, whenever we went to the *trattoria*, Maria had to pay for our *grappas*, of which she sometimes ordered several rounds. This I found embarrassing, as the local people in the *trattoria* must obviously take me for a gigolo. So one day I summoned my courage and told Maria that if she insisted on going to the *trattoria*, it would be preferable to bow to the prejudices of the world by her lending me the necessary coins beforehand—which I would repay as soon as my money arrived.

Maria got quietly angry, explained to me that as a Communist I should be above such prejudices, and insisted on continuing to visit the *trattoria* and paying for me. These visits then became rather a torture; I thought everybody's eyes were on us.

The situation was made more sordid by the fact that whenever I needed postage stamps or a tube of toothpaste, I was obliged to borrow the money from Maria. It would have been easier if she had lent me ten francs in one sum, but she never made the suggestion. I resented this, and I resented even more resenting it. She was a generous host, and I felt not only a sponger but an ungrateful one too.

In a tangled human relationship, all the apparently silly surface tensions have their interior roots. The visits to the *trattoria* grated on my sense of inferiority, and to ask for small sums of money was like a regression to the scenes of childhood. Perhaps Maria unconsciously desired that. I was reminded of an incident which Peter had related to me. One day, in Paris, he had met Maria in a café. She had noticed that Peter's only suit was getting threadbare, and packed him into a taxi and bought him the most gorgeous suit he had ever possessed.

Peter, who was a genuine Communist, and Németh, who was a true bohemian, felt no embarrassment about scenes like that, and would have been perfectly happy while Maria bought the *grappas* in the *trattoria*. They had a complete disregard for money, and accepted it, when offered by richer friends, with good grace as a matter of course. But I, bundle of loosely tied complexes that I was, did not possess that grace. I could lend money, but I could not borrow it; I sometimes went to great trouble to render a service to a friend, but if the reverse happened, I felt ashamed and guilty, and broke into abjectly profuse thanks. For a long time I believe that these were signs of an unselfish and noble character. Until one day Maria remarked drily across the breakfast table : 'You have the vanity to give, but you lack the generosity to take.' She often threw off casual remarks like that which flew like darts into the bull's-eye, while sitting primly upright in her sleeveless white linen suit. It set off her brown arms and chest, which had remained pathetically young.

On another occasion she remarked, also at breakfast on the

sun-flooded white terrace : 'You have been kicked about so much that your whole inner surface is raw and sore, and when something touches you, you wince. But the real kick is still in store for you. It is coming soon though, I can feel it.'

During the second week of my stay with Maria, we went for a walk in the woods. Ricky, the old mongrel, was ambling a few yards ahead of us. Suddenly Ricky stopped, rooted to the mossy ground, and gave out a growl which then changed into a plaintive, long-drawn howl. Maria also stopped and grabbed my arm—that alone gave me a start, for she normally avoided, and shrank away from, any physical touch or contact. Her face had changed colour in the undefinably painful manner of a person growing pale under a sunburnt skin, and the braces on her beeth became very visible. The wailing dog's hair was actually bristling, and the whole scene was so eerie that I felt suspended between horror and the giggles. Maria turned on her heel and hurried back along the narrow forest path towards the house, striding so fast on her long legs that I could hardly keep up behind her; yet I could see that she needed all her grim determination not to break into a run. The dog now kept running at her side, now and then licking her hand as if to comfort her. When we got home, Maria said curtly : 'Don't leave me alone, please.' I followed her to a balcony which she rarely used, and which opened on the back of the house, overlooking the woods from which we had come. Mary, the maid, brought up a carafe with *grappa*, giving her mistress a suspicious look, but left us again without saying a word. Maria drank a couple of small glasses, and I asked stupidly : 'What happened?' She was not yet quite herself and said unguardedly with a shrug : 'Ricky saw the uncle approaching us. He sometimes sees him first, and warns me.' On that afternoon, I learnt part of Maria's story.

From time to time, Maria had a hallucination. She saw an uncle, who had died of *dementia praecox* when she was three, advancing on her simultaneously from three directions, from the right, left and front. The frontal image was slightly over life-size, the two lateral images were smaller. Before he could reach her, she was usually seized by a fit. 'Don't get frightened,' she said, 'if you see me rolling on the floor and grinding my teeth—just leave me and call Mary. I don't like people to see

it.' When the hallucination started, Ricky always behaved as
he had today. But sometimes the dog sensed the approach of
the uncle before she saw him, and warned her. He had not
turned up for the last few weeks, and she had already hoped
that she had got rid of him for good. Now she was no longer
sure. Anyway, something was bound to happen during the
next few days—a sign.—What sort of sign?—Oh, nothing
frightening. Just a sign. I would see.

After dinner I learnt more of the story. Maria had suffered
one or two nervous breakdowns earlier in her life. She had
been for a long period under psychoanalytical treatment. The
analyst was a well-known orthodox Freudian whose name was
at the time familiar to me, but I have mercifully forgotten it
since. He had brought back to her the memory of a previously
repressed and forgotten, early traumatic shock. As an infant
between the age of two and three, she had been left alone for
a few minutes with the deranged uncle, who had committed
a sexual assault on her. But the revival of this memory did not
cure Maria. On the contrary : it was after the conjuring up of
the uncle's ghost that the hallucinations started. Before that
she had not even known that the uncle had ever existed, for
he had never been mentioned by her parents. She had then
broken off the treatment, against the analyst's warning, for
fear that if she continued with it she would go insane. About
the same time she divorced her husband, who seems to have
treated her abominably. The analyst was the last link with her
former world. When that link snapped she had retired to the
house on the lake. She wanted no more grave-diggers to work
in her brain. She knew everything that lay interred there, even
the symbolic meaning of the trinity in her hallucination : the
two pocket-editions of the uncle on either side, the large erect
one in the centre, advancing upon her. But the knowledge did
not help, and she wanted to know no more. She wanted to
swim in the lake and get cleaned and tanned by the sun
through skin and flesh down to the bones—an ageing, psychic
mermaid, stranded upon 'the tedious shore of Lethe'.

While Maria was talking, first on the balcony overlooking
the woods, and then on the terrace facing the sea, I had a
strong feeling of listening to the *langage du destin*, as Malraux calls it. That demented uncle seemed to have stepped

straight out of the book on Perversions that I had just
finished. At moments, an absent look of Maria's reminded me
of Attila watching a match burn down between his fingers.
There was also that third parallel : the fatal breaking-off of a
treatment, which Attila had also done—escaping from the
operating table with only a hand pressed against the open
gash. I had a feeling of being under a spell, experienced by
the spiritual viscerae, as it were. Serial coincidences of this
kind had often pursued me when I was passing through a
crisis; gradually I have come to regard them as a warning in
the symbolic code of the 'language of destiny'—see the closing
pages of *Arrow in the Blue*.

At some point during that evening, I said to Maria,
attempting to joke, that in the matter of being 'sore and kicked
about' she certainly took precedence over me. She repeated,
unsmiling, what she had said before, that the worst kick was
still in store for me, and that it would be coming soon.

After that evening, the 'uncle' was never again mentioned
between us. But the next day, or the day after that, another
incident occurred. While we were sitting at lunch, there was
a sudden loud crash. A large, heavily-framed picture which,
an instant before, had been peacefully hanging on the wall
that I was facing, had crashed down on to the sideboard that
stood beneath it. It made me jump, whereas Maria, who sat
with her back to the picture, did not move a muscle. On the
sideboard had stood a row of tumblers filled with milk in
various stages of curdling into yoghourt. Maria had a hobby
of making her own yoghourt; every morning two glasses of
fresh milk were added to the left end of the row, and two
glasses of finished yoghourt were taken off the right end. Now
most of the glasses were broken; the row looked like a line of
soldiers in whose middle a grenade had exploded, and half-
curdled milk was splashed all over the sideboard and the floor.

'How on earth did that happen?' I asked, walking over to
the battlefield. Maria shrugged, and said nothing. I looked at
the back of the picture : the wire was not broken, and the two
picture-hooks were still in the wall, solid and undamaged. In
fact, I was able to hang the picture back in its former place,
where it came again to rest as firmly and innocently as if it
had always stayed there. Maria rang the bell, and Mary the

maid came shuffling in to clear up the mess. 'What happened?' she asked. Maria said quietly :

'*Es spuckt.*'

'*Schon wieder?*' said Mary. 'Now Ma'am will have to go without yoghourt for a whole week.'

When we had settled down again, Maria said gently, as if talking to a child : 'Was the wire broken?'

'No,' I said, 'but *please* don't ask me to believe in miracles.'

'There is no reason to get irritated,' said Maria, 'but I told you something of the kind would happen.'

'What does it mean?' I asked, even more irritated.

'It is a sign,' she said, again shrugging.

'A sign of what?'

'I don't know. Please let us drop the subject.'

Maria rarely used the rhetorical 'please'. When she did, it had a strangely helpless, pathetic ring—it carried an echo of a frightened child saying 'please' to a maniac with whom she had been left alone in a room.

There were no more spooky events during my stay. Occasionally Maria talked to me about the doctrines of Mahayana Buddhism, the Four Noble Truths concerning pain, and the Eightfold Path. She also gave me a German translation of the Pali Scriptures to read. As a prim little materialist, I was fascinated and repelled, as if I had been dragged inside a metaphysical brothel furnished with lotus flowers, pot-bellied sages, transparent ascetics and little white elephants.

Discussing the Twelve Causes, I would tell her with exasperation : 'But it's all tautological, for God's sake.' Then Maria would say : 'Isn't all science also tautological?' I would say : 'Perhaps; but the juggling with concrete mathematical symbols does get you somewhere.' 'Where?' she would ask languidly.

Once or twice, on Maria's quiet but insistent demand, we tried table-lifting without success. 'You are hopelessly unpsychic,' she said, half resentful, half relieved, with a little laugh. She laughed rarely, and it had a charming sound. The previous sultry tension between us now changed into occasional angry quarrels; they were like cloudbursts that are followed by a smell of moss and mushrooms in the air. Quarrelling openly, like fishwives, was a new and delightful experience for Maria who, brought up in a patrician family, was terribly well-bred and well-behaved. Reconciliation usually took the form of a casual proposal to go for a swim.

We had got into the habit of having long races in the water —breast-stroke, back-stroke, side-stroke, and so on. Neither of us had mastered the crawl, nor a proper style, so that after a race to our usual target, a little island half a mile away, we were completely exhausted. Lying on her back, breathless and panting after a victory, Maria had moments of the mysterious, sudden transfiguration of a noble ugly face into one of pure beauty—quickly withdrawing again, as if frightened by its own possibilities, into the safety of its self-made unattractiveness. After such moments, her face shrank and closed, as shutters are closed against a dazzling glare, and her upper lip lifted like a rabbit's, baring the metal brace on her long, yellow teeth.

Maria was fighting what seemed to be a winning battle against the powers of insanity. I did not realise it at the time, and I was unaware of the part that I was playing in it. I thus missed a possible opportunity of saving her. For a brilliant and hyper-sensitive young man I was remarkably stupid where others were concerned.

My hostess was so grimly well-bred and brave, that to give any indication of the situation which had developed was completely unthinkable for her. The situation was that Maria had come to depend on me as a protection against the uncle, the poltergeists and other dangers. Whether she foresaw what would happen when I left, I do not know for certain. The chances are that she did, as will be seen. Yet, when I announced my intention to leave, and the date on which I would be leaving, she did not permit herself a word or gesture beyond the conventional expression of regret that I could not prolong my stay. She walked into insanity with the pose of a woman stepping into the lift at Harrods.

How this situation had developed is rather difficult to explain. Physical attraction in the traditional sense played no part in it, though in a devious sense it did. We shared a passion for the water. Swimming side by side in the chill of the early morning, we were separated and united by a few inches of the transparent liquid, without the direct physical contact

which Maria feared and I did not desire. The panting races
had their meaning, too, like the hectic shadows moving across
the cave of Plato's parable : the real figures outside the cave
were perhaps a Maria ten years younger, and myself ten years
older, and both sane. And then, lying side by side in the grass
a yard apart, there were those flashes of a transfigured face,
almost terrifying in its unrealised beauty—glimpses of the real
person swiftly moving past the entrance of the cave.

It often happens to me in writing these pages that I am
unable to visualise my past self. Then I take a photograph
from a drawer and say—well, here he is. But even that isn't
quite reassuring for I know that that face, with the plastered-
down hair and the fatuous smirk is phoney, the product of
growing a false personality, whose genesis I have described
earlier on.

From the first time we met, Maria instantly saw through
the smirk and the brilliantine; she saw whatever honest substance there was behind it—and behind that honest substance,
the ultimate, gaping emptiness : the void of the nineteenth
century's scientific materialism, the world as a clockwork
mechanism which, once it had somehow been wound up,
would forever follow its course predestined by Newton's laws.
But at least in this mechanical universe there were no gaps for
poltergeists and uncles appearing in triplicate, announced by
a wailing mongrel. It was a trite, aseptic universe, but infinitely preferable to one inhabited by demons. If the world
was a tale told by an idiot, at least it was not a tragedy devised by a raving lunatic. Atoms, electrons and protons were
nice, clean, harmless little things. If God did not enter the
picture, neither did the devils, incubi, succubi, and the remaining zoo of demonology. This was another reason why my
presence in the house was a reassurance and a protection. Of
course, not every member of the Communist Party or the
Rationalist League would have served the same purpose. But
I was a budding writer, and so full of self-contradictions that
I could enter Maria's point of view, and combat it from the
inside, as it were. Also I liked swimming and *grappa*, and in
a way I could be quite nice. Except for abiding with a human
being in a desperate predicament.

But then, I was fighting a rearguard battle of my own, defending my reassuring formulae and equations and ratiocinaions against the invisible writing that had appeared on my horizon, and was closing in on me as the uncle was closing in on Maria. And here Maria was on the side of the invader. She was sick, but she had the gift of occasionally reading fragments of the writing. She knew, if only a few words, of a language to which I had been deaf. I was beginning to discern the sounds, though the meaning was incomprehensible to me. Maria was, without knowing it, gradually converting me to her point of view; and I, without knowing it, was converting her to mine. That kind of situation is, of course, quite common; in a marriage it often happens that the partners change their parts. We were playing a mixed game of blind-man's-buff and musical chairs. It was not a highbrow pastime though, but a game for real stakes, for a year later Maria was dead and I was sitting in a condemned cell. So if I use adjectives like 'desperate', they are here in their proper place.

The difference between us was that I deserted Maria, and that Maria would never have deserted me or anybody else. But that too was implicit in the situation, for she could read the commands of the invisible writing, and I was only just beginning to realise that such a thing existed.

I did not 'suffer' during this mental crisis as one suffers from a toothache. But I was in a kind of chronic inner turmoil, which, though it concerned seemingly abstract matters, made me cry out in my sleep, and the nature of which I can best illustrate by a digression.

In 1952, I met in Princeton an old friend, the late Hans Reichenbach, a leading mathematical logician and Professor of Philosophy at the University of California. I had not seen him for nearly twenty years. He had aged and become partly deaf; instead of a modern hearing aid, he used an old-fashioned ear-trumpet. He asked me what I had been interested in lately, and I told him that I had become interested in Rhine's work on extra-sensory perception. He said that it was all hokum, and I said that I did not think so—at least the statistical evaluation of the experiments seemed to show relevant results (meaning that they seemed to confirm the existence of telepathy and kindred phenomena). Reichenbach smiled and asked : 'Who has checked the statistics?' I said : 'R. A. Fisher in person.' (Fisher is one of he leading contemporary experts in probability calculus.) Reichenbach adjusted his trumpet. 'Who did you say?' I yelled into the trumpet : 'Fisher. *The* Fisher.' At that moment an extrordinary change took place in Reichenbach's face. He went pale, dropped his trumpet and said : 'If that is true, it is terrible, terrible. It would mean that I would have to scrap everything and start from the beginning.' In other words, if extra-sensory perception exists, the whole edifice of materialist philosophy crumbles. And for a professional philosopher that means the crumbling of his life's work.

The rearguard battle that I fought against Maria was of a similarly abstract, and yet deeply emotional nature. I was younger than Reichenbach and not a professor; yet to accept the existence of another plane of reality, inaccessible to the rational mind, nevertheless meant a minor spiritual death-and-rebirth. My already shaky Communist creed was merely the brittle edge of my beliefs. But behind it stood everything that I had thought and believed from my early schooldays, based on the proud achievements of three unequalled centuries, from the Renaissance to the triumphant nineteenth. Behind it stood the conquest of obscurantism and superstitition, the great disinfection of the human mind, the belief in reason and progress, the draining of the marshy lands of mysticism, the feeling of hard solid rock under one's feet. Now everything seemed to give way, as at the slow beginning of a landslide. Maria thought that my soreness was the result of being kicked around; but it was rather the result of inner kickings, a kind of cramp or convulsion of the spiritual viscarae, which can be very frightening.

This condition led to some absurd scenes in the house on the lake. One day, we were again facing each other across the luncheon table in the blaze of noon on the terrace. We had been out swimming, and I could still feel the ripples of water around me, and the circles of silence over the lake. I remarked to Maria that if I did not watch out I would spend all day in the lake, and the novel would never be finished. It was the wrong thing to say. Maria never drew me away from my work and hardly ever set foot on the upper floor. On that day, quite exceptionally, she had knocked on my door and had timidly suggested that I go swimming with her. It must have been hard for her to do that; she must have felt unusually lonely or afraid. In my obtuseness, I had not been aware of this.

She said coolly : 'If you wanted to go on working you only had to say no.'

At last I realised that Maria was hurt. I tried to turn the matter into a joke and said that I had never been able to say no to temptation. But Maria, with one of her infuriating transitions from mermaid to schoolmarm, remarked that temptations could be resisted by means of the Free Will. Soon we were launched again on one of our unending, embittered discussions on Determinism versus Free Will.

On this occasion the argument became particularly acrimonious. Determinism was already a lost position in my crumbling world. Modern physics had several years before abandoned the concept of a strictly determined universe regulated by causal laws. But to abandon Determinism in the sense in which classical science had understood it did not necessarily mean that one had to accept the postulate of Free Will. There were several ways out, such as replacing the laws of causality by laws of probability, and interpreting the latter in a smugly rationalistic manner. For, to accept the concept of Free Will meant to accept ultimate responsibility for all one's actions, past and present, conscious or otherwise. It meant to accept an unbearable load of guilt and shame—without the comforts of an ethically natural science, which allowed one to regard oneself as a chemical machine, without freedom and responsibility, blindly obeying the stresses and pushes of the internal and external environment. I was not ready to accept the burden of freedom.

Accordingly, I became more and more irritated, and began shouting Maria down. Maria reciprocated by throwing her deadly little darts. The more I shouted, the more coolly polite her manner became. Then, suddenly, I had a beastly inspiration.

We were eating cold fruit-soup. The soup was served in a huge tureen. It was a beautiful piece of china, and Maria was particularly fond of it. She hated things being broken, even a Woolworth tumbler. The veranda was surrounded by large, polished panels of glass. I got up, by now trembling with anger, and lifted the tureen up from the table. I said :

'Look, Maria, let us settle this problem in an empirical way, once and for all. If you continue to assert that I have a Free Will, you will thereby enrage me to a point when I cannot help smashing this tureen against the window-pane, for my actions are determined by your words. If you recognise that there is no such thing as a Free Will, the tureen will automatically be safe. But what is a tureen compared to the problem we are trying to settle?'

'It is *my* tureen,' Maria said, watching my hands with anguish.

'I give you ten seconds to decide.' I started counting—one-two-three, in a cold rage. The rage was increased by my realisation that to Maria the tureen mattered more than the problem that was tormenting me. I felt that Maria was a sham, and hated her all the more for it. A well-bred, rich woman, living in comfort, getting a kick out of silly hallucinations, chit-chatting about Communism and Free Will to pass the time. What did she know about lousy hotel-rooms, and living in a hayloft, and having to ask her for half a franc for toothpaste? I was counting on aloud, determined to smash the tureen at the sound of ten, relishing in advance the shattering crash against the huge window-pane, in a frenzy of resentment, vulgar envy, meanness and cruelty. Years of frustration seemed to well up, and disgorge themselves like a mud-volcano. At the count of nine, Maria said :

'All right, you win, put it down.'

'You admit that I have no Free Will?' I asked, to make quite sure.

'*You* certainly haven't.'

'And you?'

'Oh, me'—suddenly Maria began to cry. I had never seen her cry and I had not imagined that she was able to cry. Her face became like a wrinkled baby's. She got quickly up and walked out of the room.

The atmosphere in the house on the lake became altogether too much for me. I found it difficult to concentrate on my work; sitting at my desk, I felt the tensions and stresses emanating from Maria's room a floor lower down, as a Geiger-counter indicates the presence of radioactivity. I reacted to it with chronic irritation and resentment, but these were merely the surface ripples over an undercurrent that drew me towards her, of an attraction which I could not explain to myself because it was different from any other that I had experienced before. It was neither a physical attraction not an intellectual one, for I always got the better of her in argument. Yet these scorings of points were as meaningless as my victory with the soup-bowl had been, and had no bearing on that different kind of reality, or different frame of experience, from which I felt excluded, and toward which I yet felt, reluctantly yet irresistibly, attracted. It was the attraction of a secret whose very existence I denied.

But whereas my verbal victories left me frustrated, Maria seemed to derive a secret satisfaction from her defeats. I had thought that after the scene with the tureen she would be angry or sulking, but over dinner she was in higher spirits than I had seen her for some time. If this fool of a guest was capable of throwing a tureen full of soup at the window, he was perhaps capable of putting the uncle to flight.

Nevertheless, it was evident that this *tête-à-tête* could not go on for much longer. I had often talked to Maria about Németh, for I felt that there existed certain deep affinities between these two, and one evening when Maria was playing the Bach Quadruple Fugue which I had also heard played by him, I said :

'I wish old Németh were here.'

Maria closed the piano, and said : 'Why don't you send him a wire and ask him to come? Or, even simpler, let's ring him up.' So we put through a call to Budapest, got Németh about midnight in Juci's flat, and I explained to him that his presence was urgently needed to help us with table-lifting and interpreting the *bhagavad ghita*. 'But of course,' said Németh. 'It sounds a very reasonable idea. I am glad that you are through with Hegel and so on, because, you see, that contradiction between Voluntarism and Determinism is just too childish . . .'

'What does he say?' whispered Maria.

'He is demolishing Hegel . . . Németh, when are you coming? Tomorrow?'

'Yes, why not? There are trains, I suppose? Have you read Karl Barth?'

'Németh, have you got the money for the fare?'

'No, not really. You could send me the train ticket, I suppose?'

So the next day, Maria wired the money, and Juci wired back that Németh would arrive the day after that at 4.30 p.m. in Lugano. At four o'clock we drove into Lugano, greatly excited. As we were approaching the station, Maria said:

'He is not on the train.'

I said: 'He always misses trains, but now Juci is looking after him and you can rely on her.'

Maria said: 'He is not on the train. There is trouble in his family.'

It had now become an established convention that I would be mockingly sceptical regarding Maria's second sight; but I knew that Németh would not be on the train. He was not. We went to a café near the station and had some *grappas*. When we got out an hour later, there was Németh, standing on the empty, sunny square, a lonely unkempt figure, with a battered fibre suitcase next to him on the pavement.

'What is the trouble in the family?' I asked, after introductions. 'Oh, you know that?' Németh said with his habitual absence of surprise. 'My sister had a miscarriage, but it doesn't matter.' As for the train, instead of taking the Arlberg Express to Zurich, he had started half a day earlier and had come by a series of slow trains via Italy, changing four or five times—a feat that must be unique in the annals of travelling between Budapest and Lugano.

On the drive home, I chatted away. Maria and Németh said little; there was no need for it. They had exchanged a glance, not of scrutiny but of recognition, and now they could sit back and relax, good-naturedly tolerating my existence, which had become so irrelevant that I had to chatter away even more vigorously to prevent myself from evaporating into thin air.

When we got back to the house, Németh put his suitcase down on the veranda, absent-mindedly drank two *grappas*, then went to sniff at the music on the piano. While I was volunteering to show him to his room, Németh and Maria were already playing the Double Concerto; so after I had carried his suitcase upstairs, I sat behind them, watching the movements of their backs, and getting occasional glimpses of their profiles. Németh, with his inward-turned, bulging eyes between the sharp nose and the softly-rippling hair, looked more than ever like an Egyptian scribe of the Third Dynasty. Maria simply looked ten years younger, a parched mermaid put back in her element. The brace over her teeth had vanished between half-parted lips. It had never occurred to me before that Maria's lips, too, were equipped with mucous membranes. Sitting side by side on the petit-point piano-stool, their arms parallel and their fingers dancing on the ebony keys, their profiles sometimes turned toward each other with a silent 'Dr. Livingstone, I presume.' I represented the native tribes.

Shivering with envy and jealousy, I yet had to admit that two or three reincarnations ago, Maria and Németh had been brother and sister somewhere at the foot of the Himalayas, living in enviable incest. Or perhaps Németh was the little white elephant. and Maria the dying lotus flower, her stem invaded by nibbling dark insects. I comforted myself by being cynical about it. The fact remained that they had a common language which I did not share, or rather, in which I could only bellow and stammer. The Greek word for the stammering foreigner is, as we know, 'barbarian'.

I stayed for another week; then my money arrived on a Monday and I told Maria that I would have to leave on Wednesday. She expressed polite regret.

On Tuesday night we all got slightly drunk. There was a full moon, and after dinner we went out in a boat on the lake. I was rowing, then I passed the oars to Németh and jumped into the warm lake in my flannels and sandals. There was a milky mist over the water, and as I swam behind the boat, wallowing in the pains of jealousy, I noticed to my sudden horror that it was unfounded. Németh and Maria sat in the boat facing each other like strangers, Németh splashing awkwardly with the oars, Maria sitting in the stern, hunched and shivering. Presently they changed places, and she took over the oars. Moonlight oozing through the mist over the water has the trick of making a face either very beautiful or like a corpse's, according to the angle of the shadow which it casts over the eyes, and Maria suddenly looked dreadful. Were they both phoneys after all, and did the secret language only exist in my imagination? Had I been taken in by a tendency to romanticise, to glorify a neurotic female and an elderly, sponging *littérateur*? What about detachment and the Eightfold Path, if it wasn't worth a soup-tureen? I crept back into the boat, dripping, greeted by both with silent relief.

My train left in the afternoon the next day. At lunch, Maria looked like a shrivelled old woman. We had a last, embittered argument. I had said something about my dread of another hack-job that was waiting for me. Maria said acidly : 'If you hate it, why do you do it, instead of going on with your novel?' I quoted, venomously, Maria Antoinette's 'Why don't they eat cake?' But it was useless. Maria believed in Communism as a 'new way of life', and deplored the existence of poverty in the abstract, but she was quite incapable of understanding the concrete economic facts of life. So, in a different way, was Németh. 'Frankly,' he said with gentle boredom, 'I have never understood this dreary obsession of the Marxists with economics.' The previous day he had absent-mindedly borrowed fifty francs from Maria—and yet that previous day I had almost agreed with him. Now I was longing to hear the word 'Comrade' again, even from Jan, to repent of all my deviations and swear eternal allegiance to the Party. I felt as if I were suspended on a pendulum gone wild, swinging from one extreme to the other.

It swung violently back again in the afternoon, when I said goodbye to Maria. Again the three of us were walking across the square in front of the railway station. We were talking desultorily. Suddenly Maria stopped in the middle of the square. It was the second and last time that I saw her crying. But this time she put her long, thin arms round my neck and her face against mine. For a moment she stood like that, trying to control her trembling. Then I felt the cool touch of her metal brace against my temple, and I had the instant sensation of infinite peace, as if a faith-healer had laid his hand on me. The next moment, Maria and Németh were gone.

The train journey to Paris was not unlike the crossing of the Caspian after I had left Baku. The encounters with Nadeshda and with Maria had, on their different planes, both touched me to the core. Both had lived under the threat of their destinies, and when it was closing in on them, I had failed them both. In each case there had been mitigating circumstances which one could plead before a court, but not before oneself. In both situations cleverness of the mind had been no help against blindness of the heart. I believed that, with Németh in the house, Maria would no longer be lonely and afraid. I did not see that Németh, who was also a refugee from reality, and lived in the same world as Maria, could not protect her for precisely that reason; whereas I could, because I was a mocking sceptic and a stammering barbarian. But Maria knew or felt it; that was why, at the moment of parting, she had lost control over herself. Then she had pulled herself together, accepting what was to come, and giving me absolution with that single, soothing touch of her lips.

There is little left to tell. A week after I left, the uncle appeared on the veranda, where Maria and Németh were taking their aperitifs. She had a fit worse than any before. A few days later, Németh had to return to Budapest, leaving Maria in a doctor's care. A few weeks later, she was taken to an institution. A few months later, she was dead.

XXVIII. Homage to a Spy

FOR a few months during that year I also had a part-time job in a press agency, run by one of the most remarkable personalities I have met. He was Alexander Rado, a Soviet agent who, during the war, became the director of the Red Army's European espionage network in Switzerland. The history of the network and the tragic end of Alex Rado had been described in detail by his deputy and successor, Alexander Foote.[1]

Alex Rado was by profession an expert in cartography, and as such a member of several geographical societies. He was short, rather fattish, with a round, gentle, scholarly face. He was kind and warm-hearted by nature but very shy and inhibited in personal relations, as true scholars sometimes are, and also rather absent-minded and awkward in his movements, so that he always reminded me of that pathetic character, the Fat Boy in school, bad at games and the good-natured target of practical jokers.

There were no sinister over- and undertones in Alex Rado's character. He was the modern, Puritan type of spy, motivated entirely by idealism and devotion, like Richard Sorge or Ignatz Reiss. He was a Hungarian like myself, and I had known him for years, though I cannot remember whether I first met him in pre-Hitler Berlin or in the Paris exile.

At the time when I worked under him, Alex was in his middle forties. His wife, Lene, came from a Berlin middle-class family and was also a long-standing and trusted member of the Communist Party. Lene had the slim good-looks, the caustic humour and quick wit of the typical *Berlinerin*; she

[1] A. Foote, *Handbook for Spies*, London, 1949.

excelled at impudent repartees, which was not considered good manners in Party circles. I once ran into her by chance in the Luxembourg Gardens. My fortunes were then at their lowest ebb, and I was shambling along dispiritedly in a pair of crêpe-soled tennis-shoes, because those were the cheapest you could buy and I had no others. Lene took my arm and burst out laughing : 'My poor Arturo,' she giggled, 'you have no idea how silly you look. You may become a tramp, but never a class-conscious proletarian.'

It was the ideal marriage of contrasts—Lene, slim, nimble, coquettishly malicious; Alex, round, slow and awkward, with a heart of gold under tissues of fat. They had two young children, and a charming old lady living with them who was either Alex's or Lene's mother. They lived in a little house in the hilly suburbs near the *observatoire* of Bellevue. Now and then they invited me to dinner; these occasions have remained in my memory, for the Rado's house was a haven of peace for me. They were practically the only family among the Communist émigrés who led a normal life and had a real home— not a hotel room or furnished apartment, but a house with their own furniture, including a dining-room with children and a granny around the table. Their closest friends and neighbours were the writer Anna Seghers and her husband, Dr. Radvany, who had an apartment in Bellevue or Meudon. They, too, were of course Communists and, by a curious coincidence, Radvany too was a Hungarian married to a German wife.

All I knew about Alex, apart from his overt professional activities, was that in Party circles he was rumoured to be vaguely 'connected' with some *apparat* or other. But that meant very little. There were lots of different *apparats*, and lots of different ways of being connected with them. Since it is the duty of every Party member to pass on any relevant information which happens to come his way, most Communists who occupy a position of some consequence in their professional life have some 'connexion' with one *apparat* or another— usually the political, or industrial intelligence branch of their national Party, or of the Comintern. The conspiratorial etiquette of the Party requires, however, that such relatively harmless contacts should be kept just as scrupulously secret as espionage in the strict sense of the word. Thus when I thought of Alex's rumoured activities as an *apparatchik*, I imagined that they were more or less of the nature of my political reports to Edgar in the Berlin days.

There was also another reason why it never entered my head that Alex might be engaged in real espionage. People who were working on that kind of line were never open members of the Party, and were strictly cut off from any contact with the Party. It was, therefore, quite reasonable to assume that although many of my Party comrades had some '*apparat* contact', none of them could occupy any position of importance in one of the 'real' underground *apparats*—the Red Army network, or the G.P.U. network—for the simple reason that if they did, I would not have known them.

This rule held in fact good, and only two exceptions have come to my knowledge later on. One was Alex Rado; about the other, and its unpleasant consequences for me, I shall speak later.

At the end of 1935 or the beginning of 1936, Rado opened a press agency in Paris. Its exact name I have forgotten—I think it was called '*Agence d'Information Inter-Continentale*', or something like that. It occupied two rooms in the *Immeuble Elysée*, an office building in the rue du Faubourg St. Honoré. One day, Alex telephoned me and offered me a half-time job in this agency, which I accepted at once. The salary was small, but under the circumstances it meant much to me. I believe that Alex offered me the job out of simple kindness, without ulterior motive—perhaps as a result of my chance meeting in tennis shoes with Lene.

The news agency had an editorial staff of three : Alex, 'Volodya' and myself. Volodya's full name was Vladimir Posner. He was a good-looking young man of Russian origin, who had, I believe, become French by naturalisation and was a member of the French C.P. Whether he was in any way connected with Alex's underground activities, I do not know. I remember that a couple of years later he was on the point of leaving, or had actually left, the Party, but he eventually rejoined the fold. He has since written several books and has contributed articles to the Communist Press, including some violent attacks against me.

My work in the agency was simple and pleasant. We produced three or four stencilled broadsheets a week in French and German, which were sent to French, Swiss and Austrian newspapers. Volodya did the French version and I the German; we culled the material from the foreign press, and from information which Alex gave us. The latter, I assumed, came from the Comintern's political intelligence branch. Most of our news items dealt with the situation in the Far East, and in particular with the war in China, on which Alex's private sources were most abundant. Our main task was, of course, to boost discreetly the importance of the Communist forces in China, and to present them as a popular movement of agrarian reformers hardly distinguishable from English Liberals. I took it for granted that the agency was founded for this purpose, and was indirectly supported by the Comintern. It struck me, however, as slightly odd that I did not know exactly which newspapers were our subscribers. I asked Alex once or twice, but each time he answered casually that the agency was still in its trial period, and that we were sending the bulletin to a great number of prospective subscribers on approval. I thought he had a reason not to disclose the business aspects of the agency, and among Party members one never presses a question.

I was also a little puzzled by Alex's rather detached attitude to the whole enterprise. When I turned in my sheets to him at the end of the day, his invariable comment was : 'Excellent job'. But then, Alex was an exceptionally nice person, and I knew my job; so why should he quibble? He was shy and scholarly, and not the type of boss who would look for pretexts to assert his authority. I finally came to the conclusion that Alex had been ordered to rig up this rather pointless agency, that he knew there was no future in it, and was simply carrying out his orders with an inward shrug. I thought that he was not very interested in politics, and only happy when he was drawing a map in Mercator's projection. The Hungarian Communist Party has provided the Comintern with a number of eminent 'theoreticians' : Varga the economist, Lukács the philosopher, Gábot the literary critic, and others. I regarded Rado as a typical representative of this illustrious crowd of Magyaro-Marxist academicians.

I was confirmed in this opinion by a curious little episode. One day, I went to see Michael Kolzov, who was at that time the most brilliant and influential journalist in the Soviet Union; it was general knowledge that he was a confidant of Stalin. He had come to Paris to cover some international diplomatic conference for *Pravda*. Head of the Russian delegation to the conference was Maxim Litvinov, then People's Commissar for Foreign Affairs.

Kolzov was a short, thin, insignificant-looking man, with a quiet manner and pale eyes, the exact opposite of the conventional idea of a famous reporter. He arrived, Russian fashion, half an hour late at our appointment, which was in the early afternoon.

'Forgive me,' he said with his pale smile, 'but I have a good excuse. I have been to a cinema.' 'At lunch-time?' I asked, surprised at such frivolity. 'Yes, we were very naughty. We were playing truant. You will never guess who else.' I didn't. The other two lunch-hour movie visitors had been Litvinov, incognito, and Alex Rado. Kolzov then explained that the three of them had been students together at some Swiss University—Geneva, I believe—and had remained friends ever since. At the University they had been called 'the triumvirate'. Since then they only met rarely, and always celebrated such occasions by some stag-outing.

I was much amused at the time by the idea of the Soviet Union's Foreign Minister sneaking away from a diplomatic conference to go to a movie with Alex and Kolzov. Yet a year or two later, Alex became the head of the Soviet espionage network operating from Switzerland, which means that he must have already been an important agent at the time of which I am speaking. That he nevertheless risked being seen in public with the Russian Foreign Minister was a capital offence against the conspiratorial code, yet somehow typical of Alex Rado. It is in keeping with my image of him as the fat boy being caught secretly smoking cigarettes in the school lavatory, and confessing it with an awkwardly apologetic smile.

My job came to an end after a few months. Whether the agency closed down, or whether it merely dropped the German edition, I do not remember. Nor do I know to this day whether it had simply been one of the stillborn enterprises of the Comintern, or whether it had served at the same time as a cover-address, or rendezvous place, for couriers of the network. If this was the case, I must have been completely fooled, for I never noticed any strange visitors enter Alex's room, nor any other suspicious goings-on.

I lost sight of Alex a short time later, when the Spanish war broke out. The rest of his story is told in Alexander Foote's book. In brief outline it is as follows.

Rado arrived in Geneva in 1937 to take up his post as director of the main (and later, the only), Red Army intelligence network operating from Switzerland. His official position was that of a partner in an old-established and respectable firm of Swiss map-makers. When the war broke out, most of the strategic maps that appeared in Swiss newspapers were drawn by Alex. Foote describes him as 'very short and fat and speaking six languages fluently.' He goes on to say : 'Rado ... lost his nerve in the end, but "Mary" [Lene] was never affected, and ... it was her influence that prevented Rado from breaking down earlier.' This I can well believe, though Foote, who was Alex's successor and, according to his own statement, the direct cause of Alex's eventual liquidation in Moscow, does not hide his dislike for his former chief.

Despite this obvious bias which runs all through Foote's book, Rado's achievement comes out as simply fantastic. Through one of his agents, 'Lucy', alias Selzinger, Alex succeeded in establishing direct contact with the German High Command. He was able to provide Moscow, through his short-wave transmitters, with the 'up to date, and day to day, order of battle of the German forces in the East'; and even to give on request the position of individual German divisions of which the Russians had lost sight. It was an invaluable contribution, which directly affected the course of the war on the Eastern front, and enabled the Russians to make their successful stand before Moscow.[1]

---

[1] Since the above was written, the secret surrounding the incredible 'Lucy' has been lifted in the course of a trial before the Swiss Federal Tribunal in Lucerne. 'Lucy's' real name was not Selzinger, but Rudolf Roessler; he was a former German citizen. I am quoting from the *Manchester Guardian*'s report on the trial : 'Roessler was one of the main wartime "contacts" of Admiral Canaris, the head of German

Foote unintentionally makes it clear that all this was due to Rado's personal courage and initiative : 'The Centre [i.e. Moscow] was extremely suspicious, and at first advised Rado to have nothing to do with it [with Lucy's sources]. Even after Lucy had disclosed the date of the German attack on Russia some two weeks in advance, and checkbacks had shown that the information was correct, the Centre [in Moscow] still refused to accept the information, and insisted that it must be some kind of plant. Despite the Centre's attitude, we continued to "plug" Lucy's information over to Moscow. Rado, in one of his few independent gestures of the war, was paying Lucy without prior sanction from Moscow and insisting that this information was valuable, indeed vital, to the Russian cause. . . . In the end, we managed to convince Moscow that this information was, to say the least, extremely valuable to them. . . .' The 'we' in this case is hardly justified, since at that time Foote only occupied a subordinate technical function in the network.

Throughout the war, Alex pleaded with his superiors in Moscow, unsuccessfully and at great personal risk, for a sincere collaboration with the Western allies, particularly with England. He had, as I remember, always admired the British. The following quotation from Foote is relevant in view of what happened later on. It refers to 1943, when the German *Abwehr* (counter-espionage) and the Swiss police were closing in on the network, when several of its members had already been arrested, and Rado himself been forced to go into hiding :

'Rado therefore suggested that the best thing for the network and himself would be for him to take refuge in the British Legation (there was, of course, no Soviet representation in Switzerland, and the nearest Soviet official was in Ankara or London). Once there, and safely inside the hedge of

Intelligence, and of the anti-Nazi group of officers. He was publisher of the *Nova Vita* in Lucerne, but his actual function was to supply daily battle orders and other vital military intelligence to the Swiss. Without their knowledge, however, he also kept in touch with the Soviet network operating from this town, and he is said to have given warning to Moscow three weeks before the German invasion . . .' (The *Manchester Guardian*, November 6, 1953).

diplomatic immunity, the network could continue functioning as before, with the one difference that the British would have to be brought into the picture. Rado himself was not in touch with the British, but "Pakbo", through his cut-out "Salter", the Balkan Service attaché, made the approach, and Rado received the reply that the British were prepared to harbour him if necessary. The Swiss end of the deal was therefore settled and he had only to square the Centre. I therefore passed on to the Centre Rado's request that he should be allowed to retire from the world and take refuge with the British. Almost by return transmission I received a most emphatic "No". The Centre added that they could not understand how such an old hand as Rado could even think of making such a suggestion, as "the British would track down his lines of communication and use them for themselves".

'This idea of Allied co-operation rather shook Rado, but it was not in the least inconsistent with the attitude that the Centre had adopted on previous occasions. Once, in 1942, Rado had had in his hands certain documents and plans which would have been of great value to the British as well as to the Russians, but the material was so bulky that it was impossible for us to pass it over the air. He therefore had suggested that it be handed over to the Allies—through a suitable and secure cut-out, of course. The Centre's reaction was immediate. Rado received instructions to burn the information at once.'

Rado then remained in hiding until, after the liberation of France, he and Lene managed to get to Paris. Foote was arrested in 1943 by the Swiss, spent ten months in prison, and then also went to Paris. Here both Rado and Foote got into touch with the Soviet Military Mission, neither of them knowing that the other was in Paris. For a fortnight they were separately questioned by Soviet Intelligence, which kept each of them in the dark about the other's presence. They gave different accounts of the causes which had led to the eventual breakdown of the ring. Foote accused Rado of having embezzled part of the network's funds—a charge which in view of Alex's character and past history I find impossible to accept. Foote further accused Alex of gross negligence of the *apparat*'s security rules—a charge based mainly on the fact that the ring's code-book had fallen into the hands of the Swiss police when they arrested one of Alex's collaborators. Alex himself was not informed of these charges until it was too late.

On January 6, 1945, both Rado and Foote were sent off to Moscow in the first Soviet plane that left France after the liberation. Officially the plane was carrying Soviet citizens who had been prisoners-of-war in Germany and were now being repatriated to Russia. Both of them were travelling with Russian repatriation certificates.

The plane travelled via Cairo, where the passengers spent two nights. Alex and Foote were sharing the same hotel room, and it was only here that Alex became aware of the accusations that Foote had levelled against him. In Paris they had only met on one occasoin—at a dinner at the Russian Embassy, during which no business had been discussed. At that dinner Rado had been a little drunk, and had afterwards remarked that it had been the first occasion for many years when he had drunk more than one glass of spirits at one time.

I now quote from Foote's account of what happened in Cairo :

'We were due to spend two nights in Cairo. . . . Accommodation . . . was short, and the manager said that we would have to share rooms. Rather to my surprise, Rado spoke up; it was almost the first time that he had opened his mouth since we had left Le Bourget, and said that he would share with me if I was agreeable.

'I cannot say that he was a lively room companion. The first night he hardly said a word, and declined to come out with me into Cairo for a final fling. On my return from a pleasant and convivial evening he was asleep—or pretending to be. The second evening he was, if possible, even more depressed, but did become somewhat loquacious. He said that he feared we were in for a difficult time in Moscow, and compared our situation to that of a captain who has lost his ship. No explanation would convince the Director that it had not been our fault that we had lost the sources which the Centre valued so highly.

'I attempted to reason with him and calm his fears. I

pointed out that my arrest and the consequent breakdown of communications had been entirely the fault of the Centre. . . .'

Foote, according to his account, then informed Rado of certain developments in Switzerland of which Rado had not known, and which in fact did not incriminate Rado at all. What else Foote might have said during that conversation in the Cairo hotel room we do not learn, but during that conversation the unsuspecting Alex must have suddenly, and for the first time, realised that Foote was his enemy; for the account goes on as follows :

'The information really startled Rado and he became more depressed than before. He bewailed the fact that he had not discussed the matter with me in Paris. Rather unkindly I pointed out that he had only himself to blame, as I had given him my address after our first meeting at the dinner and he had not bothered to come round. It was entirely his own fault that he was going to Moscow unaware of the true state of affairs, and as an old hand at the game he must know the danger of putting in reports without bothering to see if they tallied with the facts.

'There was a long silence after this while Rado sat tapping his fingers on the small hotel table, lost in thought. Then he got up and left the room without a word. I never saw him again. The plane left next morning without him, and his hat, coat, and luggage remained in the hotel bedroom uncollected, mute evidence of a spy who had lost his nerve.'

Six months later—i.e. in July 1945—Foote was informed by his superiors in Moscow that 'Rado had been brought by force to Russia from Cairo and that I might be confronted with him. In fact this never occurred.' Foote was further informed that Rado 'would be shot for negligence in allowing his cipher to fall into the hands of the Swiss police, for falsely reporting that the network in Switzerland was liquidated, and for embezzling some fifty thousand dollars'.

So much for Mr. Foote's account of Alex Rado's end. There only remains one episode to be filled in regarding Alex's stay in Cairo, based on my own, unfortunately sketchy information.

Rado had, of course, embarked on the journey to Moscow of his own free will. He was worried because the discovery of the cipher by the Swiss was in fact partly and indirectly his own fault. On the other hand, this was a relatively minor offence compared to the invaluable achievements of Alex, for by the time the Swiss Police closed in on it, the network had virtually completed its task. Needless to say, if the embezzlement charge had been true, Alex would never have left for Moscow.

Only in Cairo did he realise that he was walking into a death-trap. When he stepped out of the hotel, leaving his coat and luggage behind to avoid suspicion, he had hardly any money on him. The documents he carried on him identified him as a Soviet citizen, and it was on these grounds that the Russians eventually obtained his arrest and extradition by the Cairo police.

Yet after leaving the hotel, Alex had cabled to Lene in Paris, instructing her to get in touch with the British authorities, to acquaint them with all the facts, and to obtain their protection against his being handed over to the Russians. The British were, of course, virtually in charge in Cairo, and they could easily check Rado's record through the British Legation in Switzerland. Yet even if, for one reason or another, they were not interested in Rado's fate, they ought to have prevented his illegal extradition to the Russians, as Rado was not a Soviet citizen and his repatriation papers were a fake.

I don't know for how many weeks or months Alex stayed in Cairo, nor whom on the British side he approached in Cairo, and whom Lene approached in Paris. I only know that Lene's frantic efforts to save him were in vain. This is perhaps the most nightmarish aspect of the story. Yet it is only one detail in the vaster nightmare of the Western Democracies' bungling of their relations with Russia during the later period of the war, and the early post-war years. These political errors are now a matter of history; but the fact is rarely mentioned that thousands of Russian deserters and ex-prisoners of war were forcibly handed over by the Western powers to the Soviet authorities, and thus delivered to the firing squad or the forced labour camps. Alex Rado, the gentle, lovable, scholarly master-spy, was one of the victims of the Occident's guilty ignorance and homicidal illusions.

Part Four

THE INVISIBLE WRITING

1936–40

*On n'est jamais si heureux, ni si
malheureux qu'on s'imagine.*

LA ROCHEFOUCAULD

XXIX. A Confidence Trick

O^N July 18, 1936, General Franco started his insurrection. I was at that time writing the continuation of *The Good Soldier Schweik* in a seaside village near Ostend, called Breedene. The advance that Willy Muenzenberg had paid me on the projected book enabled me to spend two months at this small Flemish resort where one could live cheaper than in Paris, and where a colony of German émigré writers had assembled, among them Joseph Roth, Irmgard Keun and Egon Ervin Kisch.

After a week, it became clear that Franco's revolt would lead to a civil war of long duration, and with possible European complications. Spain was the first European country in which the new Comintern line, the People's Front, had been tried out and had led to a resounding victory for the Leftwing coalition; and also the first country in which the workers and the progressive middle class had jointly taken up arms to resist a Fascist bid for power. It was, from the beginning, a symbolic contest.

A fortnight after the Spanish war had started, I returned to Paris and went to see Willy Muenzenberg.

Since the beginnings of the People's Front, Willy's enterprises had become truly dazzling. In breathless succession he had produced a dozen or more International Congresses, Rallies and Committees. Among them were a Writers' Congress in Defence of Culture, a Committee of Vigilance and Democratic Control, and, most successful of all, the so-called 'Amsterdam Peace Rally against War and Fascism'—forerunner of the Stockholm Peace Appeal. The part of Pablo Picasso was then played by the equally innocent Henri Barbusse. Barbusse's pacifist novel *Le Feu* was the forerunner of Picasso's 'Dove', and Barbusse's book on terror, *Faits Divers,* the forerunner of Picasso's 'Guernica'. The main task of the 'Peace Rally' was to advocate rearmament against Nazi Germany and to fight the pacifism of the British Labour Party—which was being exploited by the rival 'Peace Offensive' of the Nazis.

In his capacity as head of the Comintern's West-European AGITPROP Department, Willy was now in charge of the propaganda campaign in favour of the Spanish Loyalists. He had just formed the 'Committee for War Relief for Republican Spain', with a 'Spanish Milk Fund' added to it—imitating the pattern of the 'Relief Committee for Nazi Victims' and using, as before, a philanthropic cover for political operations. Soon the 'Committee of Inquiry into the Reichstag Fire' was to be duplicated by a Committee of Inquiry into Foreign Intervention in the Spanish War', whose public hearings followed the pattern of the Reichstag Counter-Trial. Willy produced Committees as a conjurer produces rabbits out of his hat; his genius consisted in a unique combination of the conjurer's wiles with the crusader's dedication.

Willy told me that the Party had 'raised certain difficulties regarding the Schweik project'—which meant that the book was off. He did not care, and I was rather relieved, for the real purpose of my visit was to ask Willy to help me to join the Spanish Republican Army (the International Brigade was not yet in being). With this in mind I had brought my passport along. It was a Hungarian passport, and in it was my press card as a correspondent of the *Pester Lloyd*. I had never written a line for the *Pester Lloyd* from Paris; but old Vészi, the editor, had, for old time's sake, provided me with a press card, which was useful in dealings with the *Préfecture de Police,* and for obtaining occasional free theatre tickets.

Willy showed no enthusiasm for my plan. He measured human actions by their propaganda value, and saw no point in journalists wasting their time in the trenches. He thoughtfully fingered my passport, and my press card from the ultra-Conservative, semi-official Hungarian Government paper. Then he had an idea.

'Why don't you make instead a trip for the *Pester Lloyd* to

Franco's headquarters?' he suggested. 'Hungary is a semi-Fascist country. Franco will welcome you with open arms.'

I have already described Willy's habit of suddenly flashing his eyes at the person to whom he was talking, and then to efface the startling effect with a reassuring smile, as if he had just said 'Boo!' to a child. Nevertheless, these flashes left a lasting memory on visitors. This time Willy produced the optical 'blitz' when he started to speak, but he brought out the suggestion itself in a casual manner, watching my reactions.

I agreed at once, somewhat to his surprise. Then we began to discuss technical problems. After a few minutes, Willy called in Otto Katz and informed him of the idea. Otto closed one eye and cocked his head to the other side, as was his habit when thinking. Once or twice he looked at me with an expression which I could not make out at the time. Later I understood that it was meant to convey a private warning to me to back out of the project while there was still time.

The purpose of my visit to enemy headquarters was to collect evidence proving German and Italian intervention on Franco's side. How this was to be done, was not discussed. Willy merely said, with his broad smile, that it would be fine if I could get there and 'have a good look around'. The rest of the discussion was concerned with technicalities. The insurgents refused to allow correspondents of Left-wing newspapers into the territory held by them. The *Pester Lloyd* would be a good cover, but there were several snags. The *Pester Lloyd* would, of course, never agree to sending me to Spain, and if Franco's intelligence department were to check on my credentials, the game would be up. But we agreed that in the confusion of a civil war it was unlikely that anybody would bother to inquire in Budapest whether the *Pester Lloyd* correspondent was genuine or not. Secondly, other foreign correspondents might find it strange that a small Hungarian paper was sending a special war correspondent to Spain instead of relying, as usual, on agency reports. It was therefore necessary to get an additional assignment from some other newspaper which would make the journey more plausible. This was less easy than it sounds, for a Left-wing paper would not serve the purpose, and if I were to approach a conservative French newspaper with the suggestion that they should send me to Franco's headquarters, I would immediately arouse suspicion. In the end, Otto suggested, *faute de mieux*, the London *News Chronicle*. The *Chronicle* was Liberal and anti-Franco, but Otto had friends on the paper's staff who would get me an accreditation without difficulty and delay. We then worked out a cover story on the following lines. I would travel as a correspondent of the *Pester Lloyd*, and would only mention the *News Chronicle* if this became unavoidable—that is to say, if a colleague or press official should show signs of suspicion. In this case, I would confidentially admit that, though my sympathies were the same as the god-fearing *Pester Lloyd*'s, I had been forced for financial reasons to accept a second assignment from a London newspaper whose editors were unfortunately prejudiced against General Franco; but they had given me a free hand to report the facts objectively, and thus a chance to influence British Liberal opinion in favour of Franco. It sounds complicated, but it worked.

Finally, there was a danger that one of the German war correspondents in Spain would recognise me as a former Ullstein man and a Red. Against that there was no protection; I just had to trust my star and take the risk. It was, in retrospect, a foolish risk to take, for I was actually recognised the day after my arrival at Franco's headquarters in Seville.

When all was settled, Otto went out of the room and rang up London. To whom he talked I did not ask and do not know. Less than an hour later London rang back to say that everything was fixed up, and that my letter of accreditation as the *News Chronicle*'s special correspondent with General Franco's forces in Spain was ready for me at the paper's Paris office. All I had to do was to call there and pick it up. I asked Otto whether the *Chronicle* was willing to pay my travelling expenses. Otto said I need not bother about that; the 'Committee' would pay for the journey. We rejoined Willy, who had left us a while ago, in his office. 'All fixed?' he said, and then, turning to Otto : 'How much do you think he will need for the trip?'

'Lots,' said Otto. 'To start with, if Arturo is going to be a Fascist, he needs a decent suit.'

'*Ganz recht*,' said Willy. 'Do you think you can manage on

two hundred pounds?' I was overwhelmed by the sound of such an astronomical sum, and started to protest. Willy was bored. 'Never mind,' he said, 'you can refund what's left over when you come back. Good luck and keep your eyes open.'

On August 22, I embarked at Southampton in the S.S. *Almanzora*, bound for Lisbon. Franco had not yet conquered the Basque coast, his temporary capital was still Seville, and the only access to insurgent territory was through Portugal.

When we arrived in Lisbon, the passport control officer discovered that though my Portuguese visa was in order, the validity of my passport had expired during the journey. In the excitement of my hurried departure, I had forgotten about the expiry date. This gross negligence was to turn unexpectedly to my advantage. After some argument, the Portuguese police agreed to let me land on condition that I went at once to the Hungarian Consul at Lisbon and had my passport renewed. This was very annoying, for I was anxious to avoid calling the Hungarian authorities' attention to me.

The Consul, however, turned out to be a most charming person. He was merely an Honorary Consul and not even a Hungarian, but a huge, jovial Danish export trader. He received me with great friendliness because, as he explained, the only Hungarians he had so far seen had been stranded sailors, and vagabonds in trouble with the police. He extended my passport for a year with a brand-new looking rubber stamp; and when I asked him how I should set about getting an entry permit into Insurgent Spain, he told me to join him after dinner at the Casino in Estoril, where he would arrange everything. He also advised me to move into the Hotel Aviz which served as headquarters for General Franco's emissaries in Portugal. The Consul then presented me to his equally charming wife, who was a member of the Portuguese aristocracy, staunchly Fascist in sentiment, and on intimate terms with the whole Franco bunch in Lisbon.

The same night at the Casino, I was introduced by the Consul and his wife to several members of that illustrious crowd. Everybody seemed to be a marquis or a duke, and I felt very grateful to Otto for my presentable new suit. They all had wonderfully melodious names in copperplate writing on their visiting cards, and I felt so thrilled buying drinks out of Comintern funds for the Marques de Quintanar and the Marques de la Vega de Anzo, that I momentarily forgot all my worries. Later in the evening, a subscription list for General Franco's hospitals was discreetly handed around, and I made a contribution out of the same funds.

It was a strange evening. The drinks, the glamorous atmosphere of the Casino, and the feeling of two hundred pounds of traveller-cheques in my pocket after all these years of poverty, had rather turned my head. I found that all these Fascists were friendly and charming people, and thus quite genuinely forgot that I was playing a confidence trick on them. I found myself suddenly back again in the atmosphere and mood of my pre-Communist, foreign correspondent days. My reports on the Graf Zeppelin's Polar expedition had actually been serialised in the Spanish Press, and some of my new acquaintances vaguely remembered them, or at least pretended to do so; I thus became a potentially valuable asset to Franco's propaganda department. Somebody drank a toast to the Hungarian Regent, Admiral Horthy, and I reciprocated by drinking the health of General Franco. My honest Danish friend, the Consul, beamed with pleasure.

The next day, at the Hotel Aviz, the fraternisation continued, and I was introduced to the two heads of the Franco conspiracy in Lisbon : the Catholic leader, Gil Robles, and a gentleman who called himself Fernandez d'Avila, and was in fact Nicholas Franco, the General's brother. On the same evening, thirty-six hours after my arrival in Lisbon, I left for Insurgent territory, carrying on me two priceless documents : a Safe-Conduct, describing me as a reliable friend of the National Revolution, signed by Nicholas Franco; and a personal letter of recommendation from Gil Robles to the Commander of the Garrison of Seville, General Queipo de Llano.

XXX. The Return of Ahor

THE train to the small Spanish frontier town of Ayamonte
—at that time the only route open to rebel territory—
leaves from the southern bank of the Tagus estuary, which is
reached from Lisbon by boat. The boat started late at night;
most of the passengers on board were bound for Rebel Spain,
and not in a talkative mood.

There were only thirty or forty of us—mostly, I supposed,
volunteers for the Rebel Army, armament dealers, and perhaps some German and Italian officers in mufti. I sat huddled
on the deck, watching the lights of Lisbon fade over the dark
water, and with it the euphoria of the last twenty-four hours.
It was replaced by a growing feeling of anxiety which was
partly due to a justified apprehension of what lay ahead, but
partly quite irrational; and which gradually became so intense
that I caught myself shivering in the warm, scented night. It
was accompanied by an oppressive feeling of guilt, due to my
perfidious betrayal of the friendly Consul's trust—though of
course it had been done in the interest of the Cause. Mixed
into this was the fear that he would find out about me, and
would warn the Spaniards. Maybe he had found out already,
and I was running into a trap. Could they shoot me in that
case? Legally not; in a civil war, perhaps. This led up to the
puzzling question whether I was a spy or not. I was certainly
a paid agent, travelling under false pretences; on the other
hand, I was not working for any military organisation, merely
for a propaganda department—though it was the Comintern's.

But the crux of the matter was that, whether or not I was a
spy, I certainly felt like one. When young von E., in the dis-

tant Berlin days, had threatened to shoot himself, he must have felt the same way; but this time it would be less easy to explain matters away harmlessly. It was now nearly five years since I had joined the Party—five years lived in a twilight-world of ambiguity and deception. Franco's Foreign Legionaries and Moors were even worse than Hitler's Brownshirts, and the mass-shootings in the bullring of Badajoz surpassed in horror any crime the Nazis had committed up to that date. Why then did I feel so guilty for taking in that guileless, jovial Dane? And having accepted the risks from the beginning, why did I feel this subterranean anxiety that was so much more harrowing than real fear?

'Ahor'—the anxiety-neurosis which had plagued my child-hood—burst into full dark bloom again during that crossing of the Tagus. There had been occasional slight relapses during the last years—the night before crossing the Caucasus, for instance; but this was the real thing, the terror of the child locked up in a dark cellar.

Before we got into the train at Barreiro, I bought two litres of red wine and, with it, Dutch courage. It helped on this and on many future occasions; for during the next four stormy years, until my escape to England in November 1940, I lived in a chronic anxiety-neurosis in the clinical meaning of the term. Acute attacks, mostly not motivated by any external threat, would alternate with periods of relative quiet. But even during the latter periods I was dimly aware of a kind of floating haze of anxiety-*cum*-guilt, like morning mist hovering over a lake.

Anxiety, as distinct from realistic fear, is an irrational and capricious scourge; it did not prevent me from behaving quite rationally in a crisis. This is less paradoxical than it sounds, for anxiety is not caused by any known danger; it is the fear of the unknown, and is ultimately rooted in an unsolved inner conflict. It is the rumbling echo of a subterranean war, the dread of punishment for an unknown crime, a sensing of danger that emanates from the inner world.

The only anxiety-free periods were, again paradoxically, those spent in prison—perhaps because here guilt was being atoned for, and the expectation of punishment fulfilled.

The adventures of the months that followed should be

understood against this mental background—which must remain a background, as it would be tedious and repetitive to go on harping on it.

The trip to Rebel Headquarters, though cut short in a drastic fashion, was on the whole a successful one. In Lisbon, I had already found ample proof of the Portuguese authorities' connivance with the insurgents. In Seville, evidence of Nazi intervention on Franco's side could literally be had in the streets, in the shape of German airmen, walking about in the white overalls of the Spanish Air Force, but with a small swastika between two wings embroidered on their blouses. I was able to ascertain the names of several German pilots and (through a young Englishman who had volunteered for Franco's air force and then got fed up with it) the types, markings and approximate numbers of German aircraft delivered to Franco. Finally, thanks to Gil Robles' letter, I obtained an exclusive interview with General Queipo de Llano —the most popular, owing to his radio-speeches, of Franco's Generals—who, believing that I was in sympathy with his side, made some highly indiscreet statements referring to foreign aid. The Civil War had only just entered its second month, and non-intervention was still a carefully maintained fiction; Hitler kept denying that he was sending help to Franco, and Franco denied receiving it. Against this background, the material that I brought back was worth the trouble.

My sojourn in Rebel territory was brought to a sudden end on my second day in Seville. I have to describe the incident that ended it in some detail, as it is necessary for the understanding of some later chapters.

I had found out from the porter in my hotel that all German officers were billeted at the Hotel Christina. He had warned me against setting foot in the Christina for, he said smilingly, all strangers entering that hotel were liable to be taken for spies. The porter also told me that a French journalist had been arrested at three o'clock that morning in our own hotel. The next day a newsreel man of Pathé Gazette was arrested, and subsequently held for three months on the suspicion of having filmed the massacre of Badajoz. The remaining French journalists were, during my stay, under a kind of house arrest. The atmosphere in Seville was not exactly favourable to newsmen—not even genuine ones.

I decided nevertheless to go to the Hotel Christina and to have a closer look at the Nazi pilots. With Nicholas Franco's Safe-Conduct in my pocket, the worst that could happen was, I thought, that they would politely turn me out.

As I was entering the lounge of the Christina, which was nearly empty, I saw four uniformed German air force officers sitting at a table in the company of a fifth person in civilian clothes. I sat down a few tables further on, and ordered a sherry. After a while, the man in civilian clothes walked past my table. We recognised each other instantly. He was Herr Strindberg, a former colleague of mine from Ullstein's in Berlin, and, incidentally, the son of the great August Strindberg. The only explanation for his presence was that he acted as a war correspondent for the Ullsteins, who were now a Nazi trust. Strindberg knew of course that I was a Communist.

He acted as if he had not seen me, and I acted in the same way. He rejoined the table of the Nazi airmen. For a minute or two I was too paralysed to think, and only felt that this was the point in the nightmare where I should wake up. After a while Strindberg and one of the Nazi pilots got up and began pacing up and down the lounge; another airman went to the porter's lodge and made a telephone call. By then I had sufficiently recovered to order another sherry and to decide, more by instinct than by reflection, that my only hope was to take the initiative and to act the innocent. I downed the sherry, then got up and shouted in German, as naturally as I could make it, across two empty tables :

'Hello, aren't you Strindberg?'

They both stopped dead, and Strindberg murmured in an embarrassed voice :

'Excuse me, but I am in conversation with this gentleman.'

I had by now walked up to them and, again following my instinct, which told me that if I retreated now I was lost, I asked Strindberg in a loud and arrogant voice what reason he had for not shaking hands with me. This was obviously the course which a really innocent person would take; moreover, by now I felt genuinely angry. At that point, the German pilot at Herr Strindberg's side stepped in. With a stiff little bow, he introduced himself—'von Bernhardt'—and demanded to see my papers. I grew even angrier and asked on what authority he was acting; von Bernhardt said that as an officer of the Spanish Army, he had the right to ask any suspicious character to identify himself. Considering that he spoke in German and wore a swastika on his blouse, it was a sweet statement. I protested indignantly against the word 'suspicious', disclosed my status as a war correspondent of the London *News Chronicle* accredited with Captain Bolín, head of the Press Department, found the whole incident *unerhört*, and asked to be put into communication with Bolín, to lodge a complaint.

I had mentioned the *News Chronicle* and not the *Pester Lloyd*, for I felt that an English newspaper, even a Left-wing one, would impress them more with the implied threat of diplomatic complications. This was indeed the case. We went on arguing, but von Bernhardt's voice sounded a shade more doubtful, particularly as I insisted that we jointly telephone Captain Bolín. I had told Captain Bolín my *Pester Lloyd—News Chronicle* double-decker story, so he was bound to bear me out on the telephone—and that, I hoped, would enable me to get out of the Christina. I gave no thought to what would happen afterwards—only to getting out of the hotel. I have often noticed that in moments of emergency reasoned planning is automatically replaced by this type of step-by-step thinking.

At that moment, Captain Bolín entered the hotel like a *deus ex machina*. He was a tall, weak-faced, tough-acting officer of Scandinavian descent, who had already become famous for his rudeness to the foreign press. It was Bolín who had ordered the arrest of the French newsmen, and had threatened one of them with a revolver held under his nose. But Bolín had also seen my papers from Gil Robles and Nicholas Franco, and had personally arranged my interview with Queipo de Llano; so he was certainly not prepared to believe that I was a spy. My interest was, of course, to confuse the issue and prevent a reasoned argument by making a scene; so I rushed up to Bolín and launched into an agitated complaint against the indignities that I had suffered, demanding that Strindberg and von Bernhardt should apologise on the spot. Bolín was at first bewildered, then furious, declared that he refused to have anything to do with the whole silly business, that there was a war on, and that he didn't give a damn whether two damned journalists shook hands or not. His rudeness was my salvation. He told us all to go to hell, and ended the scene by turning on his heel. I walked out of the hotel in a huff, prevented by nobody. I have so often walked off in a huff after a quarrel that it looked quite convincing.

I felt now reasonably certain that I had gained a few hours before the truth was sorted out. I drove straight to Queipo's headquarters, where I said that I had been urgently recalled by my paper, and obtained without difficulty my exit permit, still on the Franco-signed Safe Conduct. Then I drove back to my hotel to collect my passport and arrange for a car to Gibraltar, which was the quickest way out. While waiting for it, a French colleague came to my room, told me that news of my row with the Nazi pilots had already got round, and advised me to beat it as quickly as I could. I thanked him earnestly, and let myself be persuaded that everything was not as it should be in Franco's Spain.

I crossed the frontier to Gibraltar one hour before the warrant for my arrest was issued in Seville, as I learnt later on from colleagues. They also told me that Captain Bolín had been black with rage, and had sworn 'to shoot K. like a mad dog if he ever got hold of him.'

It was Captain Bolín who arrested me five months later, when the Insurgents took Malaga.[1]

---

[1] The story of my meeting with Herr Strindberg in Seville was first published in *Spanish Testament* in 1938, and contained some unfriendly comments on his person. I have not seen him again. Ten years later, however, in July 1948, I received a letter from Mrs. Strindberg (whom I have never met) in which she gave a different interpretation of the facts. According to her letter, Strindberg himself, though a Nazi correspondent, had fallen under suspicion because a few days earlier, on his way to Spain, he had been seen in conversation with a British correspondent in Gibraltar. 'On his arrival in Seville,' the letter continued, 'he was arrested and threatened with summary execution as a spy. At his urgent request, however, a cable was sent to Berlin to confirm his credentials. . . . In this critical moment you entered on the scene—another representative of an English paper, and

a Communist to boot! The result was that in the confusion of the moment, he simply disowned you. . . . This disowning of you at the moment of your meeting was the only error he committed towards you. He had nothing to do with your arrest and—this you certainly didn't know—it was through his help or intermediary that you reached Gibraltar!'

The letter was obviously sincere. It was written, Mrs. Strindberg pointed out, without her husband's knowledge, with the intent of clearing him from the charge of denunciation. The suggestion that Herr Strindberg was instrumental in helping me to get to Gibraltar was probably due to a confusion in her memory ten years after the event. The letter also mentioned that during the last years of the Nazi régime Mr. and Mrs. Strindberg did at various times hide Jews in their flat from the Gestapo, at considerable risk to themselves.

XXXI. In Dubious Battle

O<small>N</small> my way back from Gibraltar, I stopped for a day in London and visited, for the first time, the *News Chronicle* building in Bouverie Street. My Seville adventures had made front-page news, and Norman Cliff, the foreign editor, gave me a friendly welcome. On my return to Paris, I went straight to the Muenzenberg office on the Boulevard Montparnasse.

Walking up the familiar steps, I had a warm feeling of safety and home-coming. Hans, Jupp, and the rest of the gang greeted me as if I were Ulysses returning from the island of the Cyclop, then ushered me into the presence of the chief. Willy was in conference with Otto, who was sitting on the other side of the desk, head rocked on one side.

'Nice little trip,' said Willy, grinning.

'He looks rested and sunburnt,' said Otto thoughtfully.

'Now we have gossiped enough,' said Willy. 'You are going back to London to put steam behind that new Committee. The English comrades suffer from sleeping sickness.'

The new committee was the 'Commission of Inquiry into Alleged Breaches of the Non-Intervention Agreement in Spain', which I have already mentioned. It was an offshoot of the Spanish Relief Committee, and was preparing to hold a public show trial, following the example set by the Reichstag Counter-Trial. The Committee was composed, as usual, of a panel of distinguished and unsuspecting personalities—Philip Noel-Baker, Lord Faringdon, Eleanor Rathbone, Professor Trent, and others; but its two secretaries—Geoffrey Bing and John Langdon-Davies—were at the time both members of the C.P., and the active force behind it was a Communist caucus.

This consisted of Ivor Montagu, Isabel Brown, Dorothy Woodman, Bing, Langdon-Davies, and Otto Katz—the latter representing Willy, that is, the West Bureau of the Comintern. Just before my return to Paris, the Home Office had put Otto on their black list, and he was either refused a visa to England or turned back at Dover by the immigration officer— I don't remember which. The Committee, deprived of Otto's periodic visits, felt cut off from the Paris centre; it now became my task to act as liaison, and also to testify about my trip to Franco at the Committee's public hearings.

My next few months were divided between Paris, London and Spain. I now belonged to Willy's 'inner circle'; Otto was no longer jealous of me, realising that I had no political ambitions, and that I willingly accepted his guidance.

Since I had left INFA, I had taken no part in any political activity. Only now, being once more brought closer to events, did I realise how profoundly the People's Front strategy had changed the atmosphere and outlook in the Party. Russia's entry into the League of Nations, and her efforts to conclude a military alliance with France and Czechoslovakia, demanded that Communists in the West should present a New Look of utter respectability. They had to defend 'bourgeois democracy', and support national unity against the common enemy; all revolutionary slogans and references to the class-struggle were relegated to the lumber-room. Even the word 'Communist' was, as far as possible, avoided by Communists, who instead referred to themselves as anti-Fascists and defenders of peace. The Communist Parties in the West acquired a new façade with geranium-boxes in the windows, and a gate wide open to all men of goodwill. On the Committee for Spanish Relief, for instance, the Conservative Duchess of Atholl, the Liberal Sir Walter Layton, and the Communist J. B. S. Haldane, sat side by side. In Paris, the apotheosis was reached in a scene on Bastille Day 1935 in the Salle Bullier where, acclaimed by a delirious crowd of many thousands, the veteran Communist leader, Marcel Cachin, embraced the Social-Fascist reptile Leon Blum, and kissed him on both cheeks, while half of the audience wept and the other half sang first the Marseillaise, then the Internationale.

The background of these developments is illustrated by an

anecdote which the French Socialist Deputy, Grumbach, told some years later at a party. Grumbach had accompanied Laval on his visit to Moscow after the signing of the Franco-Soviet pact in May 1935. The communiqué issued at the end of the visit said, *inter alia*, that 'M. Stalin understands and fully approves the policy of national defence followed by France, in order to maintain her armed forces at the level required by her security'. This signified that the French C.P. would now have to stop voting against military credits, and drop its campaign against the proposed extension of the period of military service—which, of course, the French C.P. promptly did. But Laval could not foresee this complete reversal of the French C.P.'s line, and during one of their conversations, he asked Stalin what the latter advised him to do if the Communists continued to make trouble regarding national defence. Stalin looked at Laval with a smile of jovial irony, took a puff at his pipe, and said : 'Hang them.' Laval did not believe his ears, so Stalin, with a broader smile, repeated his words, dragging a finger across his throat to avoid any possible misunderstanding.

Thus, in retrospect, the memories of those days are tainted with the knowledge of the cynical insincerity behind the façade. But while it lasted, the People's Front had a strong emotional appeal, and the fervent *mystique* of a genuine mass movement.

The same ambiguity applies to memories of the Spanish War. Today we know the aftermath : Russia's refusal to grant asylum to the survivors of the International Brigades, and the liquidation of every Russian and Spaniard who took a leading part in the civil war and knew too much of what had happened behind the scenes. We know how Russia prolonged the agony of Spain by sending just enough supplies to keep the war going until agreement with Nazi Germany was in sight; we know how she used Spain as a convenient killers' lane to get rid of Anarchists, Trotskyists, and other political undesirables. When the war started, the Communists were an insignificant little party, with less than two hundred members in the whole of Catalonia; yet, as the war progressed, they succeeded in gradually transforming the country, through blackmail, intrigue and terror, into an obedient satellite of the Kremlin.

All this we know today, but did not know then. We now know that our truth was a half-truth, our fight a battle in the mist, and that those who suffered and died in it were pawns in a complicated game between the two totalitarian pretenders for world domination. But when the International Brigades saved Madrid on November 8, 1936, we all felt that they would go down in history as the defenders of Thermopylae did; and when the first Russian fighters appeared in the skies of battered Madrid, all of us who had lived through the agony of the defenceless town felt that they were the saviours of civilisation.

For Madrid (how remote this sounds today!) was the first European capital subjected to aerial bombardment on a large scale. During the four weeks from October 24 to November 20, about a thousand people were killed, three thousand injured, and one third of the city was laid in ruins. The impact of that experience lay not so much in its physical horror—though air bombardment without aerial defences is horrible enough—but in the realisation that it marked the beginning of a new and problematical epoch in history, when the age-old distinction between soldiers and civilians would be abolished, and death would strike indiscriminately from the sky—an age of total war and total fear. Typical of this apocalyptic premonition, shared by all who had lived through those days, is the following outburst at the end of the chapter describing the bombardment of Madrid in *Spanish Testament* :

An air-raid, while it lasts, is not a political event in the mind of the person experiencing it, but a natural catastrophe like an earthquake or the erruption of a volcano. On August 16, General Franco declared that he would never bombard the capital of his country, and on August 28th, he began to bombard it. He is a liar. He has turned his compatriots into cattle for the slaughter. This is not a political act, it is a challenge to civilisation.

Anyone who has lived through the hell of Madrid with his eyes, his nerves, his heart, his stomach—and then pretends to be objective, is a liar. If those who have at their command printing machines and printer's ink for the expression of their opinions, remain neutral and objective in the face of such bestiality, then Europe is lost, and it is time for Western civilisation to say good night.

Compared to Germany, Spain was a small and peripheral country, and yet Franco unleashed a wave of more passionate indignation throughout the world than Hitler during the initial stages of his régime. The Nazis' acts of terror were at least hidden behind the walls of prisons and concentration camps. But the massacre of Badajoz, the bombardment of Madrid, the dead children of Getafe, the razing of Guernica, were public events to which the public reacted with a spontaneous convulsion of horror. There were other elements in the Spanish War which touched directly the collective archetypes of European memory : once more the Moors were let loose behind the Pyrenees—but this time as defenders of the Church. The shadows of the Middle Ages seemed to have come alive, the gargoyles were spouting blood, Goya's Disasters were made to look like topical records; once more a mercenary horde, the Foreign Legionaries of the Tercio, killed, raped and plundered in the name of a Holy Crusade, while the air smelt of incense and burning flesh.

Spain caused the last twitch of Europe's dying conscience.

The international propaganda campaign through which that conscience expressed itself was a mixture of passion and farce.

On the one hand, Spain became the rendezvous of the international Leftist bohemia. Bloomsbury and Greenwich Village went on a revolutionary junket; poets, novelists, journalists and art students flocked across the Pyrenees to attend writers' congresses, to bolster morale on the front by reading their works from mobile loudspeaker-vans to the militia-men, to accept highly-paid, though short-lived, jobs in one of the numerous radio and propaganda departments, and 'to be useful', as the phrase went, on all kinds of secret, undefinable errands. Stephen Spender has described, with disarming self-irony, how he and a friend were sent by the British Communist Party on a wild-goose chase after the crew of a Russian ship which the Italians had sunk in the Mediterranean. The search took the young poet to Marseilles, Barcelona, Alicante, Gibraltar, Tangiers and Oran; and was terminated by an inquiry at the Italian consulate, which promptly disclosed the interned crew's whereabouts—'an obvious step', Spender ruefully remarks, 'which could easily have been taken without our leaving London.' Thus a good historical time was being had by all.

There were other grotesque episodes. A famous lady of London's smart set of the 'twenties, who in the 'thirties had taken up the liberation of all coloured peoples, was arrested as a spy in her Madrid hotel room because she was found there in the company of an African native, an anti-Fascist comrade whom the police mistook for one of Franco's Moors. Otto Katz, who had now adopted the alias 'André Simon', was conducting British Parliamentary delegations through a Potemkinised Spain, explaining to them that the burnt-down churches of Catalonia had been destroyed by air bombardments, which had never taken place. Louis Aragon threatened to resign from the War because another writer, Gustave Regler, was appointed to drive the culture-dispensing loud-speaker van, but became reconciled when Regler joined the International Brigade and was shot through the stomach. John Jagger, Labour M.P., ran into trouble with the British Customs because he was carrying in his suitcase, as evidence for our Committee, a German aerial bomb which he had picked up in Madrid, and which was found to be alive and liable to blow up at any minute. 'I believe I have seen you in Madrid' became an opening gambit at Left-wing cocktail parties, Lorca became the most read poet in Europe, and fried octopus the intelligentsia's favourite dish.

On the other hand, there were Ralph Fox, Julian Bell, Christopher Caldwell, John Cornford, and others, who had enlisted straight away in the International Brigade and were killed. And there were George Orwell, Gustave Regler, Alfred Kantorowicz, Humphrey Slater, Tom Wintringham and other writers, who fought under greater hazards and with less reward than in a normal war. And André Malraux, who organised a flying squadron of volunteers in the Republican Air Force, then wrote his masterpiece *L'Espoir*, and finally directed its transformation into one of the greatest films ever made—thus performing a kind of hat-trick by uniting in his person the normally incompatible gifts for action, art and propaganda.[1]

Thus, like other wars, the Spanish War was a mixture of vanity and sacrifice, of the grotesque and the sublime—only more so, because 'ideological' wars are somehow more artificial, confused and absurd than the old-fashioned wars between nations.

After the hearings of the Committee of Inquiry in London —which were as successful as a tactical victory in a strategically lost diplomatic battle can be—I was sent back on a special assignment to Spain. It was an interesting, and somewhat surprising assignment. When Franco's insurrection had failed in Madrid, several Right-wing politicians had fled in a hurry, leaving their correspondence files and private archives behind. I was to search these for documents proving that Nazi Germany had taken a direct hand in preparing Franco's rising, and was to bring the material to Paris. The documents were urgently needed as evidence in support of the Spanish Government's case at the League of Nations, and for purposes of international propaganda.

The surprising thing was, of course, that instead of having somebody from the Spanish Foreign Office search the archives, they wanted a foreigner for this task. But Otto explained to me that it was Del Vayo himself, the Spanish Foreign Minister, who had asked Paris to send a skilled political journalist to do the job. A few days later Del Vayo turned up on a visit to Paris, and invited Otto and myself to tea. Otto was at that time the unofficial chief of the Spanish Government's propaganda campaign in Western Europe, and had large funds (partly of Spanish, partly of Comintern origin) at his dis-

---

[1] It is interesting to compare in this context Malraux and Hemingway, who were both involved in the Spanish War and have both immortalised it, each after his fashion. Their art is so different that it can almost be said to occupy two opposite poles within the novelist's range; their outlook is similar in so far as they both regard physical courage and a life of adventure as supreme values. But these same values are expressed in contrasting attitudes and idioms. Courage, in Hemingway's world, has an embarrassingly exhibitionist, adolescent, dumbhero quality. Courage, in Malraux's world, is lucid and intelligent bravado, with a discursive Gallic flourish.

posal. These funds played a considerable part in securing the sympathy of influential French journalists, and of entire news-papers for the Loyalist cause. In fact, Otto was the grey emi-nence of the propaganda war, and was treated as such by everybody in the Spanish Embassy, including Del Vayo him-self.

Del Vayo asked me to leave for Madrid as soon as possible. Half of his own staff was at the front, the other half over-worked, and he could spare nobody for a full-time job of this kind, which would require several weeks. As I only had •a smattering of Spanish, I would be provided with an inter-preter, a car and every other assistance that I needed. I still did not understand why he did not get a Spanish journalist on the spot to do the job.

'You will understand when you start on the job,' said Del Vayo. 'In Madrid everything is confusion, and everybody is trying to do five different things at the same time. Besides, there are jealousies; some of the fugitives' houses which you will have to search are occupied by the Anarchists, others by the Socialists, and they would all object to letting any Spaniard who does not belong to their party snoop around and take documents away. For an outsider who is sent as an expert from abroad specially for this task, it will be much easier. Since you got around Franco, you will, with God's help, also get around our Anarchists.'

I actually found that he was right. To sift the various archives, and eventually to get the documents out of Spain before one of the parties grabbed them to sit on them till the end of the war, proved a more difficult task than getting into Seville.

I left the next day, provided with a Spanish passport (made out, however, in my own un-Spanish name) for some compli-cated reason of frontier controls which I have forgotten. I had instructions to keep my assignment secret as far as possible, for if it became known that important documents were going to be taken out of Spain, one party or another was sure to start a scandal. All this sounds odd, and can only be understood against the background of internal strife, intrigue, and cloak-and-dagger methods behind the Spanish front, which, a few months later, were to lead to the Anarchist rising in Barcelona, and to civil war within the Civil War. Apart from all this, the Government was secretly envisaging the possibility of the fall of Madrid, and was anxious to remove whatever could be saved without this becoming known. The gold reserves of the Bank of Spain were being shipped to Russia, and the archives to Paris; but it all had to be done in an underhand way.

Typical of this atmosphere was the manner in which the Foreign Office in Madrid communicated with its Embassy in Paris. The only remaining telephone line ran through the main telephone exchange in Barcelona, which was in the hands of the C.N.T., the Anarcho-Syndicalist trade union. It was, of course, essential that diplomatic communications be kept secret, and the Anarchists could be trusted never to keep a secret. Fortunately, the Spanish Ambassador in Paris was at that time Louis Araquistain, Del Vayo's brother-in-law. He and Del Vayo had married two sisters of Swiss-German origin, who had been brought up in one of the *Schwitzer-Dütsch* mountain dialects. The Catalan Anarchists could be trusted to crack a code, but they couldn't learn *Schwitzer-Dütsch*. So confidential messages were passed on between besieged Madrid and the outer world by Mrs Del Vayo, twittering in that strange language over the telephone to her sister in Paris. This idyll ended when Del Vayo and Araquistain fell out because Del Vayo had become too pliant to Moscow's will, while Araquistain fought for a minimum of independence, was duly accused of being a Trotskyist and dismissed from his post.

I stayed in Madrid for three or four weeks, until the search was completed. Del Vayo had kept his promise and provided me with a car, a driver and an interpreter. That car was, to my unending embarrassment, a huge Isotta Fraschini, with a body specially designed and built for the former Prime Minister, Don Alexandro Lerroux. Lerroux had apparently been one of those enviable grand old men who remain a danger to maidenhood to the age of Methuselah. His correspondence files yielded, apart from the richest political material of all the archives that I searched, a wealth of passionate and romantic correspondence with various señoritas, up to fifty years younger than Don Alexandro, on pink and pale-blue sheets, some of which still retained a faint aroma of scent. I put them piously back into their boxes—to Otto's great disappointment, who thought that a little sexing-up of the war could do no harm.

As for the car, it had lavender-coloured curtains, not only on the windows but also over the glass partition between the driver and the seats in the rear—which could be combined to form a couch. It had, moreover, a series of push-buttons on a panel inside the rear door, by means of which Don Alexandro could give his orders to the driver. The signals were 'Faster', 'Slower', 'Stop', 'Turn back', and 'Lights Off'. But there was one more button, hidden from sight. When that was pressed, a red light went on over the driver's seat. The driver then choked the engine, got out, opened the hood, messed about with the carburettor, and reported that the car had broken down, that he was obliged to walk to the next village, five miles away, to get help, and that fortunately there was some champagne left in the picnic basket for Don Alexandro and the Señorita to while away the time. I got the explanation for the red-light button from Lerroux's driver, whom I had taken over together with the Isotta Fraschini. He was a former police inspector, and as inseparable from the car as a Cossack is from his horse. I cursed both of them because they made me the laughing-stock of the journalists in Madrid. I felt that never had a smaller man travelled in a bigger car.

I shall say nothing about life in Madrid under the bombardment; the subject has been covered in a number of books from every conceivable angle. I left Madrid during the first week of November, when Largo Caballero's Government fled to Valencia and the capital was considered lost. We expected from hour to hour the Moors to appear on the Puerta de Sol, for before the International Brigade went into action on March 8, the town was virtually defenceless. The major part of the population, fed on the usual optimistic communiqués, was unaware of this; but those who knew how matters stood were terrified, including myself, and made hasty arrangements to follow the Government to Valencia. This was not quite easy because the Anarchists, furious about what they called the Government's desertion, had armed patrols on the main roads who stopped cars coming from Madrid, requisitioned them at the point of the gun, and arrested the passengers.

Occasionally people were also shot during such incidents, and Madrid was full of rumour and latent panic.

I still had the Isotta Fraschini which I had to return to the Foreign Office, now in Valencia; but I needed some kind of escort for my precious documents which filled two large suitcases. I shuddered at the thought of what would happen to them, and to myself, if some half-illiterate patrol were to open a suitcase and find it full of letterheads displaying the swastika and the arrows of the Phalange. In the end, the Party put me in touch with comrades on the Malraux Squadron. They were anxious to find transport for a wounded pilot who had to be evacuated to Valencia, and for two French pilots, both Party members, who had to fetch two newly-bought planes from France. So it was decided that the four of us should travel together.

It was a strange and burlesque journey. We set out late at night, all of us secretly frightened of running into a column of rebel tanks, or a bellicose Anarchist patrol, but frightened most of all by Don Alexandro's driver, who raced the huge Isotta at ninety miles per hour over the winding roads of Castile. I carried in my various pockets a Safe-Conduct from the Foreign Ministry, another from the Communist Party, and a third which the pilots had obtained from an Anarchist leader. It was rather like travelling in Russia with my two sets of documents had been. Fortunately, the armed patrols which stopped us every half an hour wore huge Party badges on their caps and lapels, so all I had to worry about was to reach into the correct pocket. I did not count the number of times we were stopped, but Dr. Junod of the International Red Cross, who travelled about the same time through Spain, counted altogether one hundred and forty-eight patrols and roadblocks between Madrid and Valencia.[1] Our main protection was the wounded pilot. He had one leg in plaster, and a nearly-healed cut over his eye, but as we thought that the effect was not sufficiently dramatic, we took the plaster-patch off the cut and replaced it with a bloodstained bandage. He was instructed to moan heartbreakingly each time we were stopped, and to curse Franco with delirious '*muertas*'. It proved so effective that my suitcases were never opened, and

[1] Dr. Marcel Junod: *Warrior Without Weapons*, New York, 1951.

we reached Valencia without trouble. I felt profoundly ashamed for having panicked, and this feeling of shame became the direct cause of my falling into Franco's hands three months later.

As disciplined Party members, the French pilots never inquired after the nature of the mysterious documents in the suitcases. Several years later, one of them looked me up in Paris. The Spanish War was over, and he was on his way to China to fight the Japanese. After a few drinks, he asked me with a wink whether I had safely delivered 'the documents'. Now, of course, I could explain to him what it had all been about, and as I did so, his face fell : he and his comrade had been convinced that the 'documents' were gold bars from the vaults of the Spanish National Bank, which we were carrying to safety in this inconspicuous way. He also confessed, to my horror, that they had decided among themselves, in case the Anarchists tried to lay hands on the suitcases, to shoot it out with their service guns.

When the famous documents were examined in Paris, it turned out that the contents of most of them were either already known through different sources, or had been made obsolete by events. Some of the material was published in a book by Otto, which appeared in England under the title *The Nazi Conspiracy in Spain—by the Editor of The Brown Book of the Hitler Terror*. The opening page of the book contains my one and only original research contribution to the diplomatic history of Europe, of which I am duly proud. It reads :

On October 5 and October 10, 1915, the Spanish Foreign Minister, the Marquis of Lema, received the German Ambassador in Madrid. The content of this discussion was embodied in manuscript notes by the Foreign Minister: if Spain would come into the war on the side of the Central Powers, Germany offered Spain Gibraltar and Portugal.

A month later, on November 17 and November 19, 1915, the Spanish Ambassador in Berlin received the same offer from the Wilhelmstrasse. He reported it to his Foreign Minister in a cipher telegram and a letter. The offers were repeated. On March 11, 1916, the Spanish Ambassador was again subjected to pressure at the German Foreign Office. The pearl of Gib-

raltar and the possession of Portugal were described to him in seductive terms.

The notes of the Marquis of Lema and the cipher reports of the Spanish Ambassador in Berlin have been preserved in the archives of the Madrid Foreign Office.

These important facts, which we publish for the first time ..., etc.

Here Otto had gone wrong. The cipher reports were in the Foreign Office, but the notes of the Marquis de Lema I found in the archives of Lerroux. They were the mouse which the labouring mountain bore.

My friendship with Otto and Willy had now grown into real intimacy. I took over Otto's flat at 10 Rue Dombasle, which had become too small for him, and I saw him nearly every day. He had a prodigious capacity for work without ever looking harassed or hurried, and his warmth and charm were such that I no longer noticed his seamy side. His head cocked on one side and blinking with one eye, badly shaven and with a crumpled tie, he looked like the nonchalant impresario and idea-man of the great Comintern variety show.

During the last months of 1936, Otto and I were both writing propaganda books on Spain, which were designed to complement each other. Both were published by Willy's *Editions du Carrefour* in German and French, and by Victor Gollancz as Left Book Club choices in London. Otto's book dealt entirely with the part played by Nazi Germany in preparing and fomenting Franco's revolt. Mine started with my journey to Rebel headquarters, and gave an account of the historical background and the first few months of the war. The title for the German edition, which was published first, was suggested by Otto : *Menschenopfer Unerhört.*[1] In exchange, I suggested the German title for Otto's book, *Spione und Verschwörer in Spanien.*

Willy was impatient to get the books out. He would burst into my flat—a thing which he never used to do before—to see

---

[1] From Goethe's 'Opfer fallen hier
            'Weder Ochs noch Stier
            'Sondern Menschenopfer unerhört.'

how mine was getting on. The Spanish War had become a personal obsession with him as with the rest of us. He would pick up a few sheets of the typescript, scan through them, and shout at me : 'Too weak. Too objective. Hit them! Hit them hard! Tell the world how they run over their prisoners with tanks, how they pour petrol over them and burn them alive. Make the world gasp with horror. Hammer it into their heads. Make them *wake up* . . .' He was hammering on the table with his fists. I had never seen Willy in a similar state.

He believed in atrocity propaganda. The first *Brown Book* had created a world sensation through the horrors that it disclosed, and he wanted me to use the same formula. I argued with him, pointing out that Hitler's was a one-sided terror, whereas in a war the atrocity stories of both sides cancel each other out. But it was difficult to argue with Willy. He insisted on adding to the book a supplement of horror-photographs on glossy paper. The photographs showed the mangled little corpses left after the bombardment of the children's home in Getafe, each one on a separate page. They showed the charred bodies of prisoners allegedly burnt alive, and the dismembered corpse of a captured Republican pilot, which a Franco plane had dropped behind the lines, wrapped in a parcel, with the pilot's name attached on a label. It showed civilian prisoners being led to execution, roped together on a cord, and then the actual shooting. When I myself became a prisoner a few weeks later, I had these photographs before my mind's eye.

I could not prevent the photographs from going into the book, but in the text I cut down the part dealing with atrocities to a dozen pages. In the main, this part was based on the memorandum of Franco's deeds of terror during the first days of the insurrection, drawn up by the Madrid Faculty of Law, and published by its President, Ortega y Gasset. But there were also some less well authenticated items from doubtful or unidentified sources which Willy had received through the *apparat* and passed on to me. My misgivings about these were brushed aside by him with the argument that, as we both knew the allegations to be true, the details did not matter and had sometimes to be 'interpolated'—I remember this conversation vividly, for Willy otherwise never used such scientific expressions. If I still retained scruples, these were dispelled by the unscrupulousness of Franco's propaganda. In England and France, Franco relied on the hoary story that the insurrection had started just in time to forestall a Communist rising. In Germany, the line taken was simply that it was the Spanish Government who began the Civil War by bombarding the Army's barracks in Madrid without any provocation. Compared with the enormity of these lies, our propagands was, in the early stages of the war, relatively honest.

What astonished me was not only the malignity of Franco's propaganda, but the abyss of ignorance and stupidity that it revealed. Goebbels was a formidably intelligent opponent, but the stuff that Burgos turned out looked as if it were concocted by illiterates. To show up the contradictions in the enemy's propaganda was a task that I enjoyed, and thought more effective than the listing of atrocities. Willy held the opposite opinion; and in the medium of mass propaganda he was, of course, right. 'Don't *argue* with them,' he kept repeating. 'Make them stink in the nose of the world. Make people curse and abominate them, make them shudder with horror.' And he handed me a cutting from the Nazi paper *Berliner Nachtausgabe*, dated Madrid, November 4, which ran: '. . . The Red militia issue vouchers to the value of one peseta. Each voucher is good for one rape. The widow of a high official was found dead in her flat. By her bedside lay sixty-four of these vouchers . . .'

'That, Arturo, is *propaganda*,' said Willy.

What infuriated us most was that Franco, like Hitler before him, pretended that he had staged his coup just in time to forestall a revolution of ours. As we were openly advocating revolution, we had no reason to wax indignant, except on the technical grounds that we had not been planning a revolution in that particular country and at that particular time. But a professional burglar would, I imagine, be equally indignant if charged with a burglary he did not happen to commit. It was humiliating to serve as an involuntary midwife at the birth of one Fascist dictatorship after another.

The German edition of the book came out at the beginning of January. The French translation, under the title *L'Espagne*

Ensanglantée, was at the printers when I got the order to return for the third and last time to Spain.

The Loyalist Government had at last managed to set up an international news agency—a thing which should have been done months earlier, but had been delayed by the eternal wrangling between the various political parties. It was called 'Spanish News Agency' in England, and *Agence Espagne* in France. The European head office was in Paris, directed by Otto, the London office was run by Geoffrey Bing. The first two war correspondents to go to Spain for *Agence Espagne* were Willy Forrest, formerly of the *Daily Express*, now of the *News Chronicle*, and myself. Forrest was to cover the central front from Madrid, and I the southern front from Malaga.

I had known Willy Forrest during my previous stay in Madrid, where I had found him the most congenial among the foreign correspondents. He was, I believe, the first Scotsman whom I have met, and he impressed me with his rolling r's, his dry humour, his upright bearing which was more a soldier's than a journalist's, his generosity in buying rounds which contrasted with my Continental ideas of the Scottish, and above all by the fact that though he worked for that counter-revolutionary monster, Lord Beaverbrook, Forrest was a member of the British Communist Party, and made no bones about it. Also, he never used words like 'dialectical', 'concrete', or 'mechanistic', whereas he used expressions like 'decency', 'fairness', 'that wouldn't be right', and the like. He was a new phenomenon to me. A Communist who is a Puritan; a Puritan who drinks; who drinks and doesn't get drunk. I suspected him of secretly believing in God. Odd fish, these British comrades.

Before leaving Paris, I also obtained an additional assignment from the *News Chronicle*. So Willy Forrest and I were both working for the *Agence Espagne* and for the *Chronicle* at the same time, and we were both in the Party, and in all other respects we were as different as two human beings can be; which may be the reason why we got on so well. When we parted in Valencia, I was heading straight for prison; fifteen years later we met again in Paris and celebrated our reunion so thoroughly, that I went straight to prison again for punching a policeman's nose. I hope the next time it will be Willy's turn.

XXXII. Arrest

FORREST and I spent a few days together in Valencia, to discuss with various Government departments matters relating to the Spanish News Agency. It was difficult to find accommodation in the overcrowded town, but Michael Kolzov —the *Pravda* correspondent, whom I have mentioned in an earlier chapter—took us in with Russian hospitality; so the first night Willy and I slept on the floor of Kolzov's hotel room. When we had turned out the lights, and I was on the point of falling asleep, Kolzov's voice suddenly rose in the silence, uttering these words on a curiously flat note—after which he fell into silence again :

'*Attenzione*, Agence Espagne. Tomorrow, in Moscow, starts the trial of Piatakov, Radek, Sokolnikov, Muralov, and accomplices; we are all expected to report the reactions of the Spanish working class.'

This clipped announcement sounded so eerie in the dark room that both Forrest and I still remember the scene. The date was January 22, 1937.

Three days later, the night before I left Valencia for Malaga, a small cosmopolitan crowd of a peculiar kind was assembled in the Hotel Victoria. Present were Michael Kolzov, Wystan Auden, Basil Murray, a Roumanian pilot from the Malraux Squadron with a game leg, a Norwegian girl-journalist, Gerda Grepp, and myself. That party has remained memorable to me because I had an acute attack of anxiety, accompanied by a premonition of doom, which in this case proved justified. Among the guests at that party, Auden is the only one who has escaped unscathed, and he and I are the only ones who survived. The Roumanian pilot was shot down in combat in the course of the next few days. Basil Murray died, also a few days later, from an overdose of drugs. A fortnight later, I was in a condemned cell in Seville. Kolzov was in due time recalled to Russia and shot. Gerda Grepp, who lived with me through the agony of Malaga, contracted tuberculosis and died during the war. I only met Auden again twelve years later, yet he too still remembered that party, and its strangely oppressive atmosphere. It had originally, I think, been created by the pilot who, when we all got a little drunk, kept repeating that he knew he was going to die, hopped around excitedly on his game leg, and had to be carried to bed.

At this point a major difficulty arises with this autobiography, for which I must ask the reader's indulgence. The next six months formed the most decisive period in my life, its spiritual crisis and turning-point. Yet the detailed story of that period I have already written and published fifteen years ago under the title *Dialogue with Death*; and I have no other choice but to refer the reader to it. In this book I must confine myself to a summary outline of events, and to the elaboration of certain aspects of the experience which could not be treated in the earlier book.[1]

Dialogue with Death was written in the late autumn of 1937, immediately after my release from prison, when the events were still vivid in my memory. It was based mainly on my prison diaries, which I had succeeded in smuggling out. When I started on this autobiography, I intended to incorporate *Dialogue with Death*, with a few cuts, into the present volume. But this did not prove feasible. The book is written in a different style, and from an entirely different perspective, by a man fifteen years younger, still under the impact of a shattering experience, and while the Spanish War was still on.

---

[1] In all foreign editions, including the American, *Dialogue with Death* appeared as a self-contained book. In the original English edition, however (Gollancz and Left Book Club, 1937), it formed the second part of *Spanish Testament*, the first part of which consisted of the earlier propaganda book on Spain that I had written for Muenzenberg. *Spanish Testament* is (and shall remain) out of print; *Dialogue with Death* has been reissued in England under that title, in the form in which it was originally written.

The last-mentioned circumstance was responsible for a deliberate under-playing of the spiritual side of the experience, as it would have been frivolous to indulge in introspective reflections while my comrades fought and died in Spain—or so at least it seemed to me at the time. Also, the transformation that I underwent during that experience was at first an unconscious one, and it took some time before it seeped through and altered my conscious outlook; thus, for instance, I only broke officially with the Communist Party nine months later.

In short, the incorporation of the earlier book into the present one would have amounted to grafting a foreign body on to it, disrupting its unity. It would, in fact, read like a very long quotation in a foreign language—and in more than one sense, for it dates from the period when I still wrote in German, and the English version is a translation. Thus *Dialogue with Death* must stand, for what it is worth, as a document on its own, and as a separate volume of this autobiography.

Gerda Grepp and I left for Malaga on January 26, in a car put at our disposal by the Press Department of the Spanish Foreign Office. We shared the car with a Polish journalist who went back a couple of days later and plays no part in this story.

Gerda—who appears as G.G. in *Dialogue with Death*—was a rare mixture of courage and fragility, efficiency and charm. She was the daughter of a former Norwegian Labour Minister, but she had some Italian blood and did not look at all Scandinavian : she was petite, with a full, soft body and a soft face which, when alert, looked like an intelligent child's, and when tired, like a sleepy kitten's. On our journey she was mostly tired, and I enjoyed fussing over her, ghosting her dispatches for the *Arbeiderbladed*, and generally spoiling her as far as the circumstances permitted. Her frail, sweet presence made me feel strong and protective, and held my anxiety at bay.

We arrived in Malaga on January 27 and stayed there together for ten days, visiting the various front-lines, all of which were only a few miles away. The town was cut off from supplies of food and ammunition, half starved, in a state of near-chaos, and practically defenceless. We had made friends

with the Military Commander's aide-de-camp. We asked him
how long he thought we could hold out if the rebels started
an offensive. He looked at us and said :

'Three days.'

The offensive started on February 4; Malaga fell on February 8, and I was arrested on February 9. On the 6th, I
packed Gerda into a car, tucked the rug around her legs and
sent her back to Valencia, along the only road that was still
open.

My decision to remain in the doomed city was due to a
variety of confused reasons. I must now try to disentangle
these, otherwise the story would make no sense.

The main reason was the presence in Malaga of a newly
acquired friend, Sir Peter Chalmers-Mitchell, who refused to
leave the town. He was then seventy-two, but looked no more
than sixty—tall, white-haired, agile in his movements, and
without a trace of a stoop. An eminent zoologist and former
secretary of the London Zoological Society, he will be remembered by future generations of animal lovers as the creator of
the Whipsnade Zoo—his life-work, realised after thirty years
of effort. He had retired in 1934 to his delightful house in
Malaga. It was called the Villa Santa Lucia, and lay at a few
minutes' walk uphill outside the town, with a beautiful ter-
raced garden overlooking the sea. Gerda and I had visited Sir
Peter with a letter of introduction from the late Philip Jordan, and we had made friends with him at once. I have to call
him 'Sir Peter', for even during the dramatic moments through
which we lived together I used the formal address—partly because of our difference in age, partly because of my un-
familiarity with English custom—and that is how he still lives
in my memory.

Sir Peter explained to us that he intended to stay in Malaga,
because all the foreign consuls had left and he thought it important that a responsible neutral observer should remain in
the town to see what happened when it was captured. We tried
to persuade him to leave, as he had compromised himself by
publicly expressing his sympathies with the Loyalist Government in a letter to *The Times* and at public meetings in England; yet he stuck stubbornly to his resolve.

On the day when Gerda left, all hotels in Malaga closed

down, and I moved to the Villa Santa Lucia. It had a large Union Jack floating from its roof, and so far both parties in the Spanish War had, by and large, avoided interfering with British citizens and British property. I was, of course, not a British citizen, but the house and flag and the dignified old man living in it gave me a spurious sense of security. Now it was Sir Peter's turn to try to persuade me to leave; but I imagined that there was in his voice an undertone of hope that he would not be left to face the ordeal alone. I thought that if we remained inconspicuous during the first few days, until things calmed down and the British Consul came back to Malaga, he would somehow manage to get us both across the nearby frontier to Gibraltar. Never before had a foreign journalist in Spain witnessed what happened when the insurgents took over a town; from the point of view of the newly founded 'Agence Espagne', this prospect seemed worth the risk. Besides, in view of General Queipo's repeated threats of a 'terrible retribution against the Anarchist stronghold' (which Malaga in fact was), we both had the irrational and rather silly conviction that the presence of two 'neutral observers' would have a restraining influence on the behaviour of the insurgents when they entered the town. There is a passage in *Dialogue with Death*, quoting Sir Peter as he explains to me that the rebels would probably shoot fifty thousand people in Malaga without anybody ever knowing what had happened, whereas if he stayed, they might only shoot forty thousand. I had sent with Gerda an urgent message to the *News Chronicle* (Malaga's communications were already cut off), asking them to use their influence with the Foreign Office to get Sir Peter appointed at the last minute as acting honorary consul, 'to mitigate the impending massacre'.

On the day before Malaga fell, however, I almost changed my mind. I went, for the last time, to military headquarters and was in the Commander-in-Chief's room when the report came in that the spearhead of the Rebel army's tanks was less than five miles from the town centre, and that resistance had collapsed. The Commander, Colonel Villalba, then got into his car, and without further ado drove off to Valencia (where he was courtmartialled and, I believe, shot for desertion). The staff officer, Colonel Alfredo, with whom Gerda and I had

made friends, got me almost by force into his car, already
crammed full of weeping women—his mother, sisters and
relatives. The chaos and panic in the town were now complete, and I thought that if we drove up to the Villa Santa
Lucia, Sir Peter might after all still change his mind. But we
could not get through—the roads were crammed with refugees, and the driver pretended that the *camino nuevo* leading up to the Villa was already cut off. We drove on, with the
refugee stream, towards Valencia.

But all this time I had the memory of Madrid on my mind,
which I had also left in a panic, believing the town lost, though
it was afterwards saved. On that occasion I had at least accomplished my mission; but now I was running away without having said good-bye to Sir Peter, leaving even my typewriter and manuscripts behind. Besides, perhaps the road was
already cut off at the bottleneck at Velez, and I would be
much safer at the peaceful Villa Santa Lucia. In the end, as
we approached the city barrier, I jumped out of the moving
car which Alfredo refused to stop, and walked back on foot to
Sir Peter's house. He was sitting at his writing-desk by the
light of an oil lamp (the electricity supply had long been cut
off), completely oblivious of what was going on outside, and
slightly piqued because I was late for dinner. When I told him
the news, he said that I had been a perfect fool not to leave.

He was, of course, right. There could be no doubt that
Malaga was lost, that after my Seville adventures I would
not have much of a chance if caught, and that my presence in
Chalmers-Mitchell's house, instead of being a help, would
merely endanger his safety. I have tried to explain the reasons,
or rationalisations, which had prompted me to stay nevertheless. In *Dialogue with Death*, these reasons are slurred over
because at the time when I wrote it I myself was still unable
to understand them. I could not yet face the fact that inverted
cowardice, the fear of being afraid, had played a major part
in my actions; nor understand the tortuous ways of the death-
wish.

Sir Peter has subsequently published his personal recollec-
tions of the Spanish War under the title *My House in Malaga*.
The last but one chapter of the book is called 'Koestler and I

are Arrested', and in the following pages I shall let my late friend take over the narrative. It will, I hope, be a relief to the reader (and to myself) to hear somebody else's voice for a change, and to look at the author from a different and detached point of view. It will save me the necessity of repeating my own account from *Dialogue with Death*, and give the reader an opportunity to compare two independently written autobiographical versions of an experience which the writers underwent together. So far as facts are concerned, the two narratives only differ in small details—smaller indeed than one would expect, considering the general unreliability of memory where experiences under violent emotional stress are involved.

For the understanding of Sir Peter's narrative, an explanatory remark is required. It will be remembered that the head of Franco's Press Department, whom I had fooled in Seville and who had promised to shoot me 'like a mad dog' if he ever laid hands on me, was an army Captain by the name of Louis Bolín. By a remarkable coincidence the house neighbouring Sir Peter's belonged to Captain Bolín's uncle, Don Tomas Bolín. At the outbreak of the Civil War, Don Tomas, who was a Monarchist, had taken refuge with his whole family in Sir Peter's house. The family consisted of Tomas, his wife Mercedes, his mother, and five daughters. For a while Don Tomas had been imprisoned by the Loyalist authorities in Malaga, but Sir Peter had obtained his release, and in the end he had smuggled out the whole Bolín clan, at the peril of his own life, to Gibraltar. How this astonishing feat was performed is described in detail in *My House in Malaga*.

Some of the Bolíns' luggage had remained in the Villa Santa Lucia. We were hoping that when the rebels entered Malaga, Don Tomas would soon return from exile, and would then intercede with the Franco authorities in favour of the man who had saved his life and the lives of his family.

Tomas Bolín did in fact return the day after the Rebel Army entered Malaga, but he was furious because some furniture in his house had been damaged, kept brandishing a huge revolver, and was little inclined to show his gratitude to Sir Peter. Sir Peter's narrative starts on the morning after

Malaga had surrendered to Franco. Up to this point we had not been molested :

. . . Perhaps half an hour afterwards, Tomas's messenger came for the field-glasses and the valises of his master. I was in the outside dining-room handing over the glasses and a valise which I had brought down from upstairs, when Lola came running to tell me that a car had stopped below the garden gate. . . . I came into the *sala* from the passage and as I entered it three men in uniform rushed in at the front door with revolvers in their hands pointed at me. One of them, whom I judged to be in command, spoke perfect English, was tall with a weak face, trying to look resolute. Of the others, one was large and plump, the third young and almost frightened, whether from fear of what he thought I might be going to do, or of what they were going to do, I don't know. I said :

'You know you have no right to come into an English house, protected by the British flag, and behave as you are doing. But put down these,' pointing to the revolvers : 'have a cigarette and tell me what you want.'

The three still kept their revolvers pointed at me, and the English speaker barked out :

'I know all about you; I am not the kind to be bribed by a cigarette. Up with your hands ! I've just seen what you and your friends have done to my people's house.'

I knew in a flash. It must be, as it was, Luis Bolín, nephew of Don Tomas, Press agent and staff officer of Franco, and the special enemy of Koestler, as of every British or other foreigner who was not wholly on the side of the rebels, willing to be spoon-fed with propaganda by him. I tried to temporise :

'Please remember that you are doing a very serious thing in behaving in this way to a British subject. So far as my Government is concerned you are only rebels, although I've been helping your people.'

He flared into fury, but I thought was just a little shaken and he held down his revolver; the other two, however, not understanding English, keeping theirs pointed at me.

'Much good the British Government is going to do you; they know all about you !'

Unfortunately at that moment there was a noise just behind me, and I saw Koestler dragging a large valise, one of the Bolíns' which he had kindly carried downstairs and was about to hand over to the man Tomas had sent. All three advanced a step and now pointed their revolvers at Arthur.

'Who is that man, and what is he doing here? You there, up with your hands and come forward.'

'He is the correspondent of a London newspaper, and he is my guest who came to my house, just like your friends, because he had nowhere to sleep.'

'He is a spy; I know all about him. How do you come to know him?'

'He is not a spy; he came to me with a letter from a friend of mine on the staff of the newspaper.'

'What friend? You're lying.'

'Please behave yourself. If you wish to know, the friend was Philip Jordan.'

'Philip Jordan? I know all about him too.' (Luis Bolín was a man of clichés rather than of conversation). Then the other two stood close with their revolvers almost touching Arthur over whom Bolín passed his hands, took some papers out of his pockets and shouted :

'I was sure I knew him,' and then to the others : 'Tie his hands.'

Poor Koestler could do nothing except submit, making, however, an energetic protest. Seldom have I been more thankful than when I remembered that, on general principles, I had refused to let Koestler bring a revolver; the discovery of it would have given them precisely the excuse they wished.

My servants were now standing in horror and fear at the back entrance to the *sala*. Pointing with his revolver to one of them, Bolín ordered her to bring some cord. Then I thought that possibly the presence of Tomas might help; he could not stand by and see us in extreme peril, in the room in which his wife and daughters had been sleeping for many weeks. I called out to Lola to run across for him. He must have been lurking quite near, for he came almost at once and stood, also revolver in hand, whilst the two men were binding Koestler's wrists together with a piece of electric wire. I looked hard at him. He flushed, beckoned to Luis and they had a few whispered words. I suppose I owe my life to him; even he could not face having to go back and tell his wife and his five daughters and his mother-in-law that he had done nothing to save 'Sir Peter' from being shot. I turned on Luis savagely :

'You are behaving abominably to tie the hands of an un-armed man. I dare you to tie my hands,' holding out my wrists.

'I am an officer and have to obey orders.'

'I also was an officer in the British Army, and I know about orders. But you can try to be a gentleman.'

But that I think was beyond him. Meantime Tomas had slunk away.

I asked Luis if I were a prisoner.

'It is necessary for us to take you both away. I am going to lock up your house. We shall come later on to search it.'

The two servants were ordered to go. I insisted that they must be allowed to take their personal clothing and the poor meal that was cooking on the kitchen stove. The villa was locked up, and Koestler and I were ordered to go down to the waiting motor car. Koestler was put in the front seat, his hands still tied, between the armed driver and the younger officer, with his revolver in his hand. I was placed uncomfortably in the back seat between Luis Bolín and the fat man, each with revolvers ready. And so I left the villa, perhaps for the last time, the garden drenched with the scent of jasmine, the bougainvillea hanging down in purple glory, the servants, as always when I left, grouped at the top of the steps, but this time sorrowfully.

We drove up the lane, past my garage, the doors of which were still locked, and turned down into the Camino Nuevo. As we reached the first wide curve, the car stopped and was at once surrounded by a mob in untidy uniforms of all descriptions among which the Requete caps were the most striking. They peered into the windows, yelled 'Red', brandished weapons, shook their clenched fists. No order, no discipline. Simply a herd united by ferocious glee. Against the wall to the right I saw, still as huddled bodies, but whether dead or still alive, I do not know, the men I had seen thrown there in the morning. Clearly an execution ground. Luis Bolín got out and an officer came forward, and they talked for some minutes. I expected that at any moment we were to be dragged out and shot, and I still think that that was the prepared plan, but something, possibly the presence of Tomas, had interfered with it. There could be no doubt about the intention to be rid of us, and no one except they themselves would have known what had happened. A couple of extra unidentified bodies are not noticed in the middle of wholesale executions, and in a time like that the disappearance of Koestler and myself could have been explained in many ways.

But presently Bolín came back, and to the disappointment of the rabble the car drove off with us, down the Camino to the main street, and so along to the centre of the town.

The car stopped at a large building between the Alameda and the market. Its doors were closed, but sentries were pacing in front. Bolín and the fat man got out; Koestler, his wrists still bound, was made to stand up outside and was photographed from every point of view. Then he was ordered back into the car. I was told to stay in the back seat, both of us still guarded by the armed driver and the younger man who kept his revolver in his hand. I lighted cigarette after cigarette, and gave them to Koestler, and also got the two guards to take one each. I suggested that it was nonsense for them to keep Koestler's wrists bound, and showed them a red, raw mark where the wire was chafing. The driver was prepared to agree, but the other said he could not disobey orders. We talked in English, Koestler, in the kindest way, continuing to say that he was sure I at least was safe. I did my best to comfort him, but I was terribly anxious. We waited and waited. The street gradually filled with Civil Guards and Requetes, and nuns and priests stalked about, all having come in with the troops or having emerged from where they had been sheltered. The shops were still shut, and I saw my own grocer standing in front of his shuttered windows, arguing excitedly with two or three Guards. He must have seen me, because the car with two guarded prisoners was conspicuous, but I took care to avoid his eye in case of compromising him. . . .

It was now two o'clock; we were worn out and hungry. Bolín and the fat man suddenly reappeared. We were ordered out and stood in the street for a few minutes, again under drawn revolvers. Then Koestler was marched off.

XXXIII. The Hours by the Window

THE chronological sequence of events during the next four months was as follows.

I was arrested on February 9, kept for four days *incommunicado* in the prison of Malaga, and was transferred on February 13 to the Central Prison of Seville. I was kept in solitary confinement for three months, and during this period was on hunger strike for twenty-six days. For the first sixty-four days, I was kept *incommunicado* in my cell and not permitted exercise. After that I remained in solitary confinement but was permitted two hours exercise a day in the company of three other prisoners. I was exchanged against a hostage held by the Valencia Government on May 14, after ninety-five days of imprisonment.

I was neither tortured nor beaten, but was a witness to the beating and execution of my fellow prisoners and, except for the last forty-eight hours, lived in the expectation of sharing their fate.

I was never officially informed that sentence of death had been passed on me. The Franco authorities made ambiguous and contradictory statements, with the apparent intention of confusing the issue. The only authentic information that I was able to obtain later on is the account published by Dr. Marcel Junod, delegate of the International Committee of the Red Cross, who negotiated my exchange, and who had been officially informed that I had been sentenced to death by General Franco.[1] On the other hand, a few days before the exchange was agreed upon, the British Consul in Seville was allowed to visit me in prison and told me that the Foreign

[1] Dr. M. Junod, op. cit.

Office had asked General Franco for an assurance that I would not be shot, which the latter had refused on the grounds that my case was still *sub judice*. I was only interrogated once, immediately before my release, on the capital charge of 'complicity in a military rebellion', but that interrogation was obviously a formality.

The only direct communication regarding my fate that I received while actually in prison, reached me on the eleventh day after my arrest. On February 19, three officers of the *Phalange*, one of them a young woman, visited my cell, identifying themselves as members of General Franco's Press and Propaganda Department. They informed me that I was or would be (the alternative was left in suspense) sentenced to death for espionage, that General Franco might, however, commute my sentence to life imprisonment as an act of clemency. This was followed by an invitation to make a statement concerning my feelings towards General Franco. In momentary weakness I dictated a statement which said that I believed General Franco to be a man of humanitarian outlook whom I could trust implicitly; but when it came to signing it, I had sufficiently recovered to cross the statement out and substitute another to the effect that if General Franco granted a commutation of the sentence I would assume that he was acting from political considerations, and that I would continue to believe in a Socialist conception of the future of humanity.[1] According to yet another version which Burgos gave out (either to the *News Chronicle* or to a British parliamentary delegation), sentence of death for espionage had already been passed by court-martial in Malaga before I was transferred to Seville.

I have put these contradictory versions down for the record although they were mostly unknown to me at the time; if I had known the details they would only have confirmed me in my expectation that some night or other I would be taken out of my cell and stood against the cemetery wall. During the first few days after the fall of Malaga, prisoners in that town were taken out in batches and shot at any hour of the day; later on in Seville, things settled down to a more orderly rou-

[1] For the text of the statement, see *Dialogue with Death*. It was never used by Franco's Propaganda Department.

tine, and executions were carried out three or four times a week between midnight and 2 a.m. During March, altogether forty-five men from our prison were shot. During the first thirteen days of April, there were no executions, but during the next six nights, between Tuesday, April 13 and Monday the 19th, fifty men were executed, the greatest number in any single night being seventeen (on April 13). After that I lost count as I had worked out a technique of sleeping through the critical hours.

The proceedings were as a rule smooth and subdued. The victims were not forewarned, and mostly too dazed or proud to make a scene when they were led out of their cells by the guards, accompanied by the priest, to the waiting lorry. A few of them sang, some wept, muffled cries of 'madre' and 'socorro' were frequent. Sometimes I saw the whole procession—the priest, the guards and the victim—quickly pass in front of my spyhole, but mostly I only heard them, ear pressed against the cell door. Sometimes the victims were fetched from the mass detention cells on the second floor, or from a different wing; sometimes from among the incommunicados of the death row where I was housed; it was impossible to discover the system. On one night, Thursday, April 15, the inmates of cells 39, 41 and 42 on my left and right were all marched off, with only my own cell No. 40 spared, after the warder had put his key, no doubt, by mistake, into my own lock, and then withdrawn it.

Most of the victims were recently captured militiamen on whom a membership card of the Anarchist or Communist Party or Trade Union, or some other compromising document had been found. They had appeared for a few minutes before a court-martial, and had then been taken back to prison before sentence was passed. The sentence was mostly death by shooting. This was in a number of cases commuted to long-term imprisonment, in which case the prisoner was officially informed, and transferred to a penitentiary. If, on the other hand, the sentence was confirmed, the prisoner only learnt it when they came to fetch him at night. Sometimes his uncertainty lasted several weeks or months. The record was four and a half months, held by a militia Captain.

Another form of execution which Franco had revived, as

Hitler had revived the Axe, was the *vile garotte*, the strangling machine familiar from Goya's drawings. The victim, tied to a post in a sitting position, was slowly choked to death between an iron collar round his throat and a vice being turned through the post against the back of his neck. The man who in *Dialogue with Death* is called 'The Consumptive' was executed by this method a few days after I was released. He was one of the three men with whom I took my exercise, the former leader of a group of *vigilantes* in Madrid, Garcia Attadel. I know of no other case of execution by the *vile garotte*. It was Garcia who told me that the garotte had been revived, but he pretended not to believe that it was actually used.

Nobody was tortured or beaten within the prison of Seville during my stay: these practices were confined to police stations and *Phalange* barracks. The guards were on the whole humane, the food adequate and, except for those of us who were kept *incommunicado*, the prisoners were permitted during most of the day to take exercise and play games in the open patio.

This, I believe, is about all that I need to repeat here regarding the external conditions and events of the period covered by *Dialogue with Death*, and I can now proceed to those internal developments which I have not discussed in the earlier book.

Firstly, during the whole period of solitary confinement in Seville (though not during the previous four days in the prison of Malaga), the anxiety-neurosis and the accompanying feeling of guilt were suspended. I was, of course, often apprehensive and fearful, but it was a rational and, as it were, healthy fear, not the obsessional and morbid variety. I slept well, except on the nights when I listened to my comrades being led to execution, and even on these nights I found sleep later on. I had consistently pleasant dreams, often of Grecian landscapes and beautiful but sexless women, although under normal conditions my dreams range from the unpleasant to the nightmarish. I had hours of acute despair, but these were hours, and in between were entire days of a newly discovered peace and happiness.

This paradox may perhaps be explained as the effect of a

satisfied craving for punishment. The neurotic type of anxiety is the irrational anticipation of an unknown punishment for an unknown crime. Now retribution had come in a concrete, tangible form for a concrete tangible offence; the cards were on the table. Whether I was technically guilty of espionage or any other crime before the law was beside the point; I had gained entry to the enemy camp through deception, and I had done everything in my power to damage their cause. My condition was thus a logical consequence of a consciously taken risk, the whole situation was clean, proper and equitable.

Two years after Spain, I was interned for six months in a French concentration camp, and another year later detained for several weeks in an English prison. These later imprisonments involved no danger of life, and regarding privileges and physical comfort, conditions were less harsh than in Seville. Yet on these later occasions I knew that I was innocent and that my confinement was stupid and unjust; this knowledge made these relatively comfortable detentions mentally unbearable and spiritually sterile. In Le Vernet and in Pentonville I knew that I would eventually get out and resume life. In cell No. 40 in Seville the best I could hope for was commutation of the death sentence, and an amnesty after three or five years in a penitentiary; yet I was much happier and at peace with the world and myself in cell No. 40. I am stressing this contrast because it seems to indicate that the craving for justice is more than a product of rational considerations; that it is rooted in layers of the psyche which a pragmatic or hedonistic psychology cannot penetrate.

It could not even be said, I mused, while pacing up and down cell No. 40, that the punishment was out of proportion with the offence. A civil war, like a revolution, applies harsher standards than international law. The deception I had used in Lisbon had been a particularly infamous one. In *L'Espagne Ensanglantée* I had accused the opponent of committing certain atrocities though I doubted the authenticity of the documentation that I used; it seemed quite proper that I should now be called to verify the missing evidence through firsthand experience. The chapter in the book on General Queipo de Llano, based on a fraudulently obtained interview, was a portrait drawn with a poisoned pen. Now it formed part of the dossier against me on General Queipo de Llano's desk, on whose jurisdiction my fate depended. There was in all this a neat, symmetrical design. A design, however, does not necessarily presuppose a designer. The symmetry of crystals is the product of electro-chemical forces. Nature favours symmetry, tends organically towards symmetry. Justice is a concept of ethical symmetry, and therefore an essentially natural concept—like the design of a crystal.

Thus justice began to assume in my musings a new, double significance as a biological need and as an ethical absolute based on the concept of symmetry. It was independent of utilitarian considerations, but equally independent of any theological assumptions. The notion of 'divine justice' appeared as a lamentable caricature of it, with its dangling carrot and its whip—the ultimate, unconscious source of all *angst*. I congratulated myself on the disappearance of anxiety, and attributed it to this newly discovered concept of justice as an inherent dimension of the space-time continuum. Some die with their boots clean, some with their minds clean; I did not want any mystic mud splashed over the mind's polish. The memory of the house on the lake, and of Maria's end was not a tempting one. Even less tempting was the thought of Dostoievsky's sudden conversion in front of the firing squad. That classic episode came, of course, often to my mind; I regarded it as an example of the cowardly surrender of the intellect, not to divine grace but to the trembling fear of the flesh, and compared my own reactions to it. My prison diary in *Dialogue with Death* contains this half-serious prayer :

'Grant me, O Lord, the right to continued discontent, to curse my work, not to answer letters, and to be a trial to my friends. Am I to swear to grow a better man if this cup is let to pass from me? We both of us know, Lord, that such vows, extracted under duress, are never kept. Do not blackmail me, Lord God, and do not try to make a saint of me; Amen.'

The reflections that I have put down so far were all still on the rational level; they form only one aspect of the process under discussion, and its most superficial one. But as we proceed to others in an inward direction, they will become more embarrassing and more difficult to put into words. They will also contradict each other—for we are moving here through strata that are held together by the cement of contradiction.

I shall now speak of a series of experiences of a different type. These were caused by certain incidents which I must first relate.

On the day when Sir Peter and I were arrested, there had been three occasions when I believed that my execution was imminent. The first time in the *sala* of the Villa Santa Lucia, with three guns digging into my ribs, when Bolín had called for a rope in such a threatening voice that I thought he needed it to hang me (though he only wanted it to tie my hands); the second time, when the car had stopped on the improvised execution ground on the Camino Nuevo; the third time, a few hours later when, after Bolín had told me that I would be shot at night, they took me out of the police station at nightfall and put me into a lorry, with five men behind me, their rifles across their knees; so that I thought we were driving to the cemetery, whereas we only drove to the prison.

On all three occasions I had benefited from the well known phenomenon of a split consciousness, a dream-like, dazed self-estrangement which separated the conscious self from the acting self—the former becoming a detached observer, the latter an automaton, while the air hums in one's ears as in the hollow of a seashell. It is not bad at all; the unpleasant part is the subsequent reunion of the split halves, bringing the full impact of reality in its wake. Much worse was another episode on the same day : being photographed for the rogues' gallery against a wall in the street, hands tied, in the midst of a hostile crowd. This time the anæsthetic of self-estrangement did not get to work; instead, a painful childhood memory was suddenly revived. I felt as helpless as at the age of five when, in a doctor's surgery, I was without preliminary warning tied with leather straps to the operating chair, then held down and gagged by way of preparation for a tonsillectomy. I have described this scene in *Arrow in the Blue*, and have explained how the sensation of utter helplessness and abandonment to a hostile, malign power had filled me with a kind of cosmic terror. It had been my first conscious acquaintance with

'Ahor', and a main cause of the anxiety-neurosis.

As I stood against the wall in that street in Malaga, equally defenceless and exposed, obediently turning my head at the bellowed commands of the photographer, that trauma was revived. This, together with the other events of the same day, and of the next three days with their mass executions, had apparently caused a loosening up and displacement of psychic strata close to rock-bottom—a softening of resistances and rearrangement of structures which laid them temporarily open to that new type of experience that I am leading up to.

I met with it for the first time a day or two after I had been transferred to Seville. I was standing at the recessed window of cell No. 40 and, with a piece of iron-spring that I had extracted from the wire mattress, was scratching mathematical formulæ on the wall. Mathematics, in particular analytical geometry, had been the favourite hobby of my youth, neglected later on for many years. I was trying to remember how to derive the formula of the hyperbola, and was stumped; then I tried the elipse and the parabola, and to my delight succeeded. Next I went on to recall Euclid's proof that the number of primes is infinite.

'Primes' are numbers which are not divisible, like 3, 17, and so on. One would imagine that, as we get higher in the numerical series, primes would get rarer, crowded out by the ever-increasing products of small numbers, and that finally we would arrive at a very high number which would be the highest prime, the last numerical virgin. Euclid's proof demonstrates in a simple and elegant way that this is not so, and that to whatever astronomical regions we ascend in the scale, we shall always find numbers which are not the product of smaller ones, but are generated by immaculate conception, as it were.[1] Since I had become acquainted with Euclid's proof at school, it had always filled me with a deep satisfaction that was aesthetic rather than intellectual. Now, as I re-

---

[1] For the benefit of amateurs, here is the proof:

Assume that P is the hypothetically highest prime; then imagine a number equal $1 \times 2 \times 3 \times 4 \ldots \times P$. This number is expressed by the numerical symbol $(P!)$. Now add to it 1: $(P! + 1)$. This number is obviously not divisible by P or any number less than P (because these are all contained in $(P!)$). Hence $(P! + 1)$ is either a prime higher than P or it contains a prime factor higher than P.—Q.E.D.

called the method and scratched the symbols on the wall, I felt the same enchantment.

And then, for the first time, I suddenly understood the reason for this enchantment : the scribbled symbols on the wall represented one of the rare cases where a meaningful and comprehensive statement about the infinite is arrived at by precise and finite means. The infinite is a mystical mass shrouded in a haze; and yet it was possible to gain some knowledge of it without losing oneself in treacly ambiguities. The significance of this swept over me like a wave. The wave had originated in an articulate verbal insight; but this evaporated at once, leaving in its wake only a wordless essence, a fragrance of eternity, a quiver of the arrow in the blue. I must have stood there for some minutes, entranced, with a wordless awareness that 'this is perfect—perfect'; until I noticed some slight mental discomfort nagging at the back of my mind —some trivial circumstance that marred the perfection of the moment. Then I remembered the nature of that irrelevant annoyance : I was, of course, in prison and might be shot. But this was immediately answered by a feeling whose verbal translation would be : 'So what? is that all? have you got nothing more serious to worry about?'—an answer so spontaneous, fresh and amused as if the intruding annoyance had been the loss of a collar-stud. Then I was floating on my back in a river of peace, under bridges of silence. It came from nowhere and flowed nowhere. Then there was no river and no I. The I had ceased to exist.

It is extremely embarrassing to write down a phrase like that when one has read *The Meaning of Meaning* and nibbled at logical positivism and aims at verbal precision and dislikes nebulous gushing. Yet, 'mystical' experiences, as we dubiously call them, are not nebulous, vague or maudlin—they only become so when we debase them by verbalisation. However, to communicate what is incommunicable by its nature, one must somehow put it into words, and so one moves in a vicious circle. When I say 'the I had ceased to exist', I refer to a concrete experience that is verbally as incommunicable as the feeling aroused by a piano concerto, yet just as real—only much more real. In fact, its primary mark is the sensation that this state is more real than any other one has experienced before—that for the first time the veil has fallen and one is in touch with 'real reality', the hidden order of things, the X-ray texture of the world, normally obscured by layers of irrelevancy.

What distinguishes this type of experience from the emotional entrancements of music, landscapes or love is that the former has a definitely intellectual, or rather noumenal, content. It is meaningful, though not in verbal terms. Verbal transcriptions that come nearest to it are : the unity and interlocking of everything that exists, an inter-dependence like that of gravitational fields or communicating vessels. The 'I' ceases to exist because it has, by a kind of mental osmosis, established communication with, and been dissolved in, the universal pool. It is this process of dissolution and limitless expansion which is sensed as the 'oceanic feeling', as the draining of all tension, the absolute catharsis, the peace that passeth all understanding.

The coming-back to the lower order of reality I found to be gradual, like waking up from anæsthesia. There was the equation of the parabola scratched on the dirty wall, the iron bed and the iron table and the strip of blue Andalusian sky. But there was no unpleasant hangover as from other modes of intoxication. On the contrary : there remained a sustained and invigorating, serene and fear-dispelling after-effect that lasted for hours and days. It was as if a massive dose of vitamins had been injected into the veins. Or, to change the metaphor, I resumed my travels through my cell like an old car with its batteries freshly recharged.

Whether the experience had lasted for a few minutes or an hour, I never knew. In the beginning it occurred two or even three times a week, then the intervals became longer. It could never be voluntarily induced. After my liberation it recurred at even longer intervals, perhaps once or twice in a year. But by that time the groundwork for a change of personality was completed. I shall henceforth refer to these experiences as 'the hours by the window'.

Religious conversion on the deathbed or in the death-cell is an almost irresistible temptation. That temptation has two sides.

One plays on crude fear, on the hope for individual salvation through unconditional surrender of the critical faculties to some archaic form of demonology. The other side is more subtle. Faced with the Absolute, the ultimate *nada*, the mind may become receptive to mystic experience. These one may regard as 'real' in the sense of subjective pointers to an objective reality *ipso facto* eluding comprehension. But because the experience is inarticulate, has no sensory shape, colour or words, it lends itself to transcription in many forms, including visions of the Cross or of the goddess Kali; they are like dreams of a person born blind, and may assume the intensity of a revelation. Thus a genuine mystic experience may mediate a *bona fide* conversion to practically any creed, Christianity, Buddhism, or Fire-Worship.

I was thus waging a two-front war against the concise, rational, materialistic way of thinking which, in thirty-two years of training in mental cleanliness, had become a habit and a necessity like bodily hygiene—and against the temptation to surrender and creep back into the warm protective womb of faith. With those nightly, muffled '*madres*' and '*socorros*' in one's ear, the latter solution appeared as attractive and natural as taking cover from a pointed gun.

The 'hours by the window', which had started with the rational reflection that finite statements about the infinite were possible—and which in fact represented a series of such statements on a non-rational level—had filled me with a direct certainty that a higher order of reality existed, and that it alone invested existence with meaning. I came to call it later on 'the reality of the third order'. The narrow world of sensory perception constituted the first order; this perceptual world was enveloped by the conceptual world which contained phenomena not directly perceivable, such as gravitation, electromagnetic fields, and curved space. The second order of reality filled in the gaps and gave meaning to the absurd patchiness of the sensory world.

In the same manner, the third order of reality enveloped, interpenetrated, and gave meaning to the second. It contained 'occult' phenomena which could not be apprehended or explained either on the sensory or on the conceptual level, and yet occasionally invaded them like spiritual meteors piercing the primitive's vaulted sky. Just as the conceptual order showed up the illusions and distortions of the senses, so the 'third order' disclosed that time, space and causality, that the isolation, separateness and spatio-temporal limitations of the self were merely optical illusions on the next higher level. If illusions of the first type were taken at face value, then the sun was drowning every night in the sea and a mote in the eye was larger than the moon; and if the conceptual world was mistaken for ultimate reality, the world became an equally absurd tale, told by an idiot or by idiot-electrons which caused little children to be run over by motor cars, and little Andalusian peasants to be shot through heart, mouth and eyes, without rhyme or reason. Just as one could not feel the pull of a magnet with one's skin, so one could not hope to grasp in cognate terms the nature of ultimate reality. It was a text written in invisible ink; and though one could not read it, the knowledge that it existed was sufficient to alter the texture of one's existence, and make one's actions conform to the text.

I liked to spin out this metaphor. The captain of a ship sets out with a sealed order in his pocket which he is only permitted to open on the high seas. He looks forward to that moment which will end all uncertainty; but when the moment arrives and he tears the envelope open, he only finds an invisible text which defies all attempts at chemical treatment. Now and then a word becomes visible, or a figure denoting a meridian; then it fades again. He will never know the exact wording of the order; nor whether he has complied with it or failed in his mission. But his awareness of the order in his pocket, even though it cannot be deciphered, makes him think and act differently from the captain of a pleasure-cruiser or of a pirate ship.

I also liked to think that the founders of religions, prophets, saints and seers had at moments been able to read a fragment of the invisible text; after which they had so much padded, dramatised and ornamented it, that they themselves could no longer tell what parts of it were authentic.

In *Dialogue with Death*, there are only a few allusions to all this; partly, as I have said, because at the time when I wrote it the war in Spain was still on and I was reluctant to indulge in introspection; and partly because I was still too shattered and confused to give a clear account, even to myself, of what had happened in cell No. 40.

When, after sixty-four days in the cell, I was for the first time allowed out for exercise and made my first contact with other prisoners, there were three of them in the patio : Garcia Attadel; his former secretary, a Cuban; and a young Andalusian peasant. The peasant was called Nicholas : he was short, thin, with a stubby face and gentle eyes. He was illiterate, spoke to the three of us in a shy, deferential voice, and explained that he had hoped, when the war was over, to learn to read and write. He had been in the Anarchist militia, and had been captured a few days before on the Almeria front. The next day when I was let out into the patio, Nicholas was no longer there; he had been shot during the night.

From then on I lived in the constant fear that on the next occasion Garcia and the Cuban would also have vanished. Garcia was gaunt, with a narrow and fierce Castilian face; the Cuban was dapper, round-eyed, and had the swaggering gait of a dandy. The three of us were exercised during the siesta hour, between one and three, when the other prisoners were locked in their cells. As the morning progressed and the hour of exercise drew nearer, I would become more and more anxious and worried. I was tempted to pray for them, but that would have been another surrender. And yet, in a completely irrational manner, I felt convinced that their fate partly depended on me, and that my willingness for sacrifice could somehow protect them.

I then began to probe into myself to discover the exact amount of sacrifice that I was willing to make. This led to quite grotesque reflections : I found that I was willing to give one limb for each, but only in the form of one leg and one arm and not both of the same kind; that under torture I would soon break down and forsake them; and that I was willing to give my life for their joint lives, but not for a single one. Already in Malaga I had become prone to strange preoccupations of a similar kind. There, people had been marched off to execution at any hour of the day; and when I heard the familiar oily voice read out the lists, I felt an obsessive urge to share in imagination the fate of those who were taken out, to live and re-live the scene of their execution in every detail —for I was convinced that this act of solidarity and identification would make death easier for them.

No doubt, a cunning and childish hope made me unconsciously believe that so much altruism and nobility of feeling would be recognised and duly rewarded by some superior power. But this explanation is, I believe, only true in part. For there was another, and more genuine element in these self-probings and purification rites. There came, for instance, a day when I found that I was ready to give my life for either Garcia or the Cuban, not two against one, but one for one, and without bargaining conditions. Moreover, I felt that this would neither be a noble act nor a sacrifice, but something perfectly easy and natural, like sharing our last cigarettes. I could now no longer understand that I had ever thought or felt otherwise. For it struck me as self-evident, in the manner of twice two being four, that we were all responsible for each other—not only in the superficial sense of social responsibility, but because, in some inexplicable manner, we partook of the same substance or identity, like Siamese twins or communicating vessels. I knew that all these comparisons were awkward and false, and the experience nevertheless true. When I had broken my last cigarette into halves and shared it with little Nicholas, he never thanked me because he knew that his pleasure in inhaling the smoke was mine, that to give was to take, because we were all attached to the same umbilical cord, and were all lying together in the same pulsating womb of transition. If everybody were an island, how could the world be a concern of his?

I was quite aware of the fact that solitary confinement is a spiritual hot-house. On the other hand, my predicament was merely an extreme form of the predicament inherent in the human condition. The difference, whether measured in terms of freedom, or fear, or of life-span expectation, was a difference in degree, not in kind. The metaphysical problem of the nature of the bonds which united me with my fellow prisoners reflected—though in a more naked, concentrated form—the basic problem from which all systems of social ethics are derived. And my seemingly absurd and overstrung preoccupations had, I felt, a desperately direct bearing on the state of our society and on applied politics.

My Party comrades, for instance, would say that the question whether A should sacrifice his life for B, depended entirely on the relative social value of A and B. If Comrade Arturo was more useful in the struggle against Fascism than little Nicholas, then, in a concrete situation, it would be for Nicholas to lay down his life for Arturo, but not the other way round. Moreover, if the latter, led by mystic sentimentality, were to sacrifice himself for Nicholas, this would weaken the cause he was serving, and would constitute an objectively harmful, anti-social act. From there it followed that not only one, but a thousand or a hundred thousand Nicholases could and would be sacrificed if the cause was supposed to demand it. For in this view Nicholas existed merely as a social abstraction, a mathematical unit, obtained by dividing a mass of ten thousand Militiamen by ten thousand.

But that equation did not work :

The Party denied the free will of the individual—and at the same time it exacted his willing self-sacrifice. It denied his capacity to choose between two alternatives—and at the same time it demanded that he should always choose the right one. It denied his power to distinguish between good and evil— and at the same time it spoke accusingly of guilt and treachery. The individual stood under the sign of economic fatality, a wheel in a clockwork which had been wound up for all eternity and could not be stopped or influenced—and the Party demanded that the wheel should revolt against the clockwork and change its course. There was somewhere an error in the calculation; the equation did not work out.—(Darkness at Noon).

I remembered a phrase of Malraux's from *Les Conquérants* : '*Une vie ne vaut rien, mais rien ne vaut une vie.*' In the social equation, the value of a single life is nil; in the cosmic equation it is infinite. Now every schoolboy knows that if you smuggle either a nought or the infinite into a finite calculation, the equation will be disrupted and you will be able to prove that three equals five, or five hundred. Not only Communism, but any political movement which implicitly relies on purely utilitarian ethics, must become a victim to the same fatal error. It is a fallacy as naïve as a mathematical teaser, and yet its consequences lead straight to Goya's Disasters, to the reign of the guillotine, the torture-chambers of the Inquisition, or the cellars of the Lubianka. Whether the road is paved with quotations from Rousseau, Marx, Christ or Mohammed, makes little difference.

I feel that this present account gives a far too tidy and logical description of a spiritual crisis with its constant ups and downs, advances and relapses; its oscillation between new certainties and old doubts; its sudden illuminations, followed by long periods of inner darkness, petty resentments and fear. My stay in cell No. 40 was a protracted, compulsory sojourn on the 'tragic plane' where every day is judgment day. When I got out, the process continued. It had started at the unconscious foundations, but it took many years till it gradually altered the intellectual structure.

I do not believe that anybody, except a very primitive person, can be reborn in one night, as so many tales of sudden conversions will have it. I do believe that one can suddenly 'see the light' and undergo a change that will completely alter the course of one's life. But a change of this kind takes place at the spiritual core of the subject, and it will take a long time to seep through to the periphery, until in the end the entire personality, his conscious thoughts and actions, become impregnated with it. A conversion which, after the first genuine crisis, saves further labour by buying a whole packet of ready-made beliefs, and replaces one set of dogmas by another, can hardly be an inspiring example to those who cling to a minimum standard of intellectual honesty. Nor do I believe that a true spiritual transformation can be the result of a process of conscious reasoning, working its way downward as it were. It begins on the level where the unconscious axioms of faith, the implicit premisses of thinking, the innate standards of value, are located. It starts, as it were, in the boiler-room, at the fuse-boxes and gas-mains which control life in the house; the intellectual re-furnishing comes afterwards. Some eminent converts of our time seem to have left it all to the decorators; and the Christian love they show their neighbours is about as convincing as a Communist peace offensive.

It was easier to reject the utilitarian concept of ethics than to find a substitute for it. Perhaps the solution was to be found in a reversal of Bentham's maxim :—the least suffering for the smallest number. It sounded attractive—up to a point. But beyond that point lay quietism, stagnation and resignation. To change from Lenin's way to Gandhi's way was again tempting, yet it was another short-cut, a toppling over from one extreme to the other. Perhaps the solution lay in a new form of synthesis between saint and revolutionary, between the active and the contemplative life; or perhaps we lived in an era of transition comparable to the last centuries of the Roman Empire, which admitted of no solution at all.

In the years that followed I wrote a number of books in which I attempted to assimilate the experiences of cell No. 40. Ethical problems had hitherto played no part in my writing; now they became its central concern. In *The Gladiators*, two-thirds of which was written after Seville, and *Darkness at Noon*, which was the next book, I tried to come to intellectual terms with the intuitive glimpses gained during the 'hours by the window'. Both novels were variations on the same theme : the problem of Ends and Means, the conflict between transcendental morality and social expediency. The next novel, *Arrival and Departure*, was a rejection of the ethical neutrality of science as expressed in the psychiatrist's claim to be able to 'reduce' courage, dedication and self-scarifice to neurotic motives. The hero, who has been made to see on the psychiatrist's couch that his beliefs 'in big words and little flags' have been illusions, his courage vanity, his self-sacrifice the effect of repressed guilt, is apparently cured of all these unreasonable attitudes. Yet after the cure he once more volunteers for a dangerous and self-sacrificing mission, driven by an urge that emanates from his untouchable core, beyond psychological causation and beyond the grasp of reason. Finally, in *The Yogi and the Commissar*, I tried once more to digest, in the form of essays this time, the meaning of the solitary dialogue of cell No. 40. This book, written in 1943, closed the cycle; it had taken five years to digest the hours by the window.

I have said before that, while in prison, I felt free of guilt and neurotic anxiety. Soon after I had regained my freedom and no longer had concrete reasons for fear, both guilt and anxiety returned. The feeling of guilt centred on certain self-accusations concerning my conduct in prison. I found myself guilty on three counts, which I feel I ought to mention as a psychological curiosity for, in the light of reason, they do not appear very grave, and yet they pursued me for a long time with an intense feeling of shame.

The first episode concerns a single phrase that I used, and that still rings in my ear. One day, after the evening soup had been doled out, Don Ramon, a friendly warder, lingered behind at the door of my cell and asked wonderingly how it came about that as an educated person I got mixed up with the *rojos* (Reds). I answered: 'But I no longer am a *rojo*.' I had spoken the truth, but with the intention of telling a lie. Inwardly, I no longer was a Communist, but the break was neither conscious nor definite; and my intention in uttering that phrase was, of course, that Don Ramon should report it.

Now my line of defence, if I were interrogated, could only be to persist in my denial that I was a member of the Communist Party—a confession in front of a Franco court-martial would not only have been suicide, but a betrayal of everybody who was involved in the affair: Willy and Otto, the *News Chronicle*, Chalmers-Mitchell, and so on. So it would have been quite in order had I persisted in my rôle by saying to Don Ramon: 'I never *was* a *rojo*.' But the phrase that had slipped out said: 'I *no longer* am a *rojo*.' It was not only stupid and self-incriminating (that is not the point, and Don Ramon did not report it anyway); it was a self-abasement, the revelation of an unconscious craving to curry favour with the enemy, to come to terms with the executioners. I can still see the perplexed and embarrassed expression on Don Ramon's face; he had the Castilian's proud sense of honour, and had caught the meaning of the nuance; he turned and closed the door of the cell without a word.

The shame of this episode has haunted me for years, as a companion-ghost to that of Nadeshda's figure on the quay at Baku. I kept telling myself that after all it was merely a matter of a phrase blurted out when I was caught unawares, and that it was redeemed by the fact that I had refused to sign the statement in favour of Franco. But such lawyers' arguments carry no inner conviction—as demonstrated by a recurrent dream that kept plaguing me until recently. I saw myself alone in an empty house, attacked by a gang of robbers. For a while I kept shooting at them without much conviction from a window, but seeing that the position was hopeless, I walked out through the gate and, by a little wheedling, made friends with them and was accepted into their gang, comforting myself with the thought that they were not as bad as all that. At this point, I would wake up and remember the dream with shame and horror. But I only discovered the obvious relation of the dream to that 'I no longer am a *rojo*' as I was writing the present chapter. With that, the feeling of guilt on this particular count began to dissolve, and I began to take a more detached view of the incident. All of which goes to show how a feeling of guilt may appear exaggerated in relation to its apparent cause, and yet reveal the real culpable tendency behind it—in this case an unconscious tendency to betrayal, precariously held in check by a sustained conscious effort.

This motive of a potential betrayal which is never consummated and is only known to the subject himself, crops up in two of my novels. In *Darkness at Noon*, Gletkin tells how, when he fell into the hands of the enemy, they tied a burning wick to his shaven skull to extract certain information. A few hours later, his comrades re-captured the position and found him unconscious; the wick had burned down to the end, and Gletkin had kept silence. 'That's all bunk,' he explained, 'I did not give in because I fainted. If I had stayed conscious another minute, I would have spoken. . . . When I came to, I was actually convinced that I *had* spoken. But the other prisoners established that this was not the case. So I got a decoration.' In *Arrival and Departure* there is a similar incident. But just as I did not realise the origin of the dream about the robbers, so in writing these fictitious episodes I was not aware of the motive behind them.

The incident raises the question whether one is ever justified in dismissing guilt-feelings—however unwarranted they may appear—as merely 'neurotic symptoms'. I am inclined to think that explanations which trace the subjective origins of guilt to an exacting super-ego acquired in early childhood are more or less correct as far as they go, but that they beg the question of the ethical significance of guilt, and of its creative aspect. Regarding the latter, I believe that if properly canalised, the consciousness of guilt may become a powerful and constructive driving force; and that the anguish which accompanies it should be regarded as income tax paid in emotional currency.

The second incident occurred towards the end of my imprisonment and can hardly be called an incident at all.

The British Consul in Seville had at last obtained permission to visit me. He was a quiet, reserved man, and naturally a little distant in his manner, for the case of this Hungarian correspondent of a British newspaper, accused of spying for the Spanish Reds, must have struck him as rather fishy. I had, of course, to stick to my part as a *bona fide News Chronicle* correspondent, arbitrarily detained because he had expressed his sympathies for the Loyalist Government in his writings. This brought up the subject of *L'Espagne Ensanglantée,* and the Consul asked, somewhat hesitantly, whether I had proof of all the allegations in the book. It was as if the dentist had touched an exposed nerve with his drill. My pretended self-assurance was suddenly deflated, and I answered meekly that the authenticity of some of the material concerning atrocities was somewhat doubtful. The impression I made at that moment must have been lamentable; I saw it mirrored in the Consul's eyes. He said nothing, and shortly afterwards took his leave with a murmured encouragement and a limp handshake.

Here again, guilt had become focussed on a secondary event —the admission made to the Consul—whereas its real source was the uncleanliness of the propaganda work I had been engaged in, and all the deception and fraud in which I was plunged up to my neck. My self-deflation in front of the quiet and reserved Englishman who was doing his duty in coming to my assistance, yet could not hide his silent revulsion, had acquired the power of a symbol. It reflected the clash of two worlds: the world of straight, intellectually limited, unimaginative decency, based on traditional values, and the twisted world of ruse and deceit in the service of an inhuman Utopia. It had ended with the humiliation and defeat of the second.

The third count on which I found myself guilty was in failing to fulfil a vow made in cell No. 40 : if ever I got out alive I would write an autobiographical essay where truth would be carried to the point of self-immolation, done with the ruthless sincerity of an X-ray photograph that would make Rousseau's Confessions look like a conventional oil print. I kept postponing this undertaking for fifteen years, and when I started on it I soon realised that the book would never conform to the original intention. Some of the reasons for this are mentioned in the chapter 'The Pitfalls of Autobiography' in the previous volume. I would like to add to it a few words.

Take, for instance, the pitfalls of sex. It is usual in our time to measure the 'sincerity' of an autobiography by its outspokenness in matters of sex. Thus the fame of Rousseau or Cellini rests largely on certain notorious passages. This attitude is not entirely unjustified. Since in these days confessions regarding his sex life expose the author to infamy or ridicule, courage in this particular field may indeed be regarded as a measure of his sincerity.

On the other hand, this kind of repression always breeds over-emphasis. The pious memoir-writers of the Victorian Age gave such preference to the spiritual over the carnal, that a reaction was inevitable. Yet once the pendulum has been permitted to swing to the opposite extreme, it is legitimate to strive after a balanced position where sexual experiences are treated frankly, but only in so far as they are relevant to the evolution of the character and the story. If I have failed to make Rousseau blush in his grave, I like to believe that this is due not to a lack of sincerity, but to the lack of an appropriately blush-making aberration. Admissions of character-defects in other fields, though no less embarrassing, will not be found wanting in these pages.

I also became aware, in trying to live up to that vow, of the danger of sincerity degenerating into exhibitionism. There is, of course, no literature and no art without a catalytic grain of exhibitionism. The danger-point, in so far as memoirs are concerned, seems to be reached when episodes that should be embarrassing and painful to tell are told with a wallowing gusto. Whenever I noticed symptoms of this kind, I always felt that something had gone wrong; on re-reading such passages I generally discovered that they sounded exaggerated, obsessional and strident, and had to be thrown out.

Finally, the notion of an 'X-ray self-portrait' is obviously a fallacy. Not only because the object is identical with the observer, which fact alone excludes photographic objectivity. But also, because in the realm of psychology no concrete, objective truth exists, only an almost infinite number of levels of truth. In describing the motives of any action we are not making a precise statement of fact, but only an approximation on a certain level. In which direction and on which level the explanation moves is, of course, a matter of a highly subjective choice. *Dialogue with Death* is an autobiographical sketch written at the age of thirty-two; the present chapter is an 'explanation' of the same events, written at the age of forty-seven. I wonder what shape and colour they would take if I were to re-write them after yet another fifteen years have elapsed. Yet in intent each of these versions represents the truth, based on first-hand knowledge of the events and intimate acquaintance with the hero.

A concluding remark on that neglected subject, sex. It was indeed neglected in cell No. 40 : from the first day to the last I had no erotic dreams or day-dreams; a fact that I find difficult to explain. When I wrote the book on sexual aberrations I had read enough about sex life in prisons to know that auto-erotic indulgences may quickly become an addiction in solitary confinement, and I resolved to refrain from anything of the kind in thought and deed. But such virtuous resolves always break down, unless they receive powerful support from the regions of the unconscious. The nature of that support is unknown to me. I am convinced, however, that without self-imposed abstinence, the hours by the window would not have borne fruit.

XXXIV. Back to the Trivial Plane

IN the hall of the Hotel Ingles in Valencia, writes Dr. Junod of the International Red Cross in his autobiography,[1] I had often seen a very beautiful woman go in and out. Her bearing was proud and a little disdainful. She was a typical representative of the old aristocracy of Seville.

'Muy guapa,' a waiter whispered to me, 'a highly placed hostage.'

I learned that she was the wife of a Spanish Nationalist airman. Although she was being held as a hostage, she had been spared imprisonment, and she lived in the hotel under close police surveillance. Her charm and her beauty certainly had something to do with the preferential treatment she was receiving.

At the Ministry José Giral[2] spoke to me about her. He had just received through the British Embassy a list of twenty-one names of Spanish Republicans imprisoned in Seville. General Queipo de Llano had generously offered to exchange them all against this one woman. Giral smiled knowingly.

'Queipo would like to tempt us, but I'm not playing. Make a counter-proposal for us. I'm interested in one man. He's not a Spaniard, but he's a friend of the Republic. His name is Arthur Koestler.'

'Koestler? I don't know him.'

'He's a Hungarian, a journalist who has been sentenced to death by Franco for sending reports to a British newspaper. I should be obliged if you would send an urgent telegram off to Geneva on the matter because his life is in danger.'

[1] Op cit.
[2] The Minister for Foreign Affairs.

'I will do so as soon as I get back. . . .'
Koestler against the beautiful woman from Seville?
Yes, Salamanca was agreeable.
Negotiations proceeded for the carrying out of the exchange
. . . Gibraltar was informed by wireless, and the obscure Hun-
garian journalist Franco had intended to shoot was released.

I was flown from Seville to the frontier town of La Linea
by the husband of the beautiful hostage for whom I was being exchanged. Her name was Señora Haya. Her husband was
one of Franco's most famous fighter pilots.

On my arrival in London I learnt of the events that had led
up to my release.

After we had been separated, Sir Peter was taken to a hotel
and kept there under police surveillance. Twenty-four hours
later a British destroyer, H.M.S. *Basilisk* arrived in Malaga.
Her commander intervened with the local authorities, and Sir
Peter was allowed to proceed to Gibraltar. As I was not a
British subject, nothing could be done about me directly.
However, Sir Peter informed the *News Chronicle* of my arrest
over the *Basilisk*'s wireless, and this set into motion the public
campaign through which I was saved.

I can speak about this extraordinary campaign without appearing to be immodest, for it was in no way connected with
my person or merits. The majority of the individuals and organisations who sent telegrams and letters of protest to Franco
I did not know, and they had previously not even known my
name. Among them were fifty-eight members of the British
House of Commons, nearly half of them Conservatives;
authors' and journalists' associations; bishops and clergymen;
political and cultural organisations of every variety and
shape. Even the Hungarian Government intervened.

L'Espagne Ensanglantée had only appeared in French and
German, and many of those who interceded on my behalf
must have disapproved of its contents—provided that they had
read it at all. In England, the centre of the campaign, no book
had been published to that date under my name, which was
entirely unknown. So much so that the Foreign Secretary, Mr.
Eden, in answering a Parliamentary question, declared that
H.M. Government had intervened on Mr. K's behalf 'in spite

of the fact that he is a Czechoslovak citizen'. All that the British public knew was that one among thousands of newspapermen, the correspondent of a Liberal paper was threatened with death by the newest dictatorial régime. So far, neither Hitler nor Mussolini had dared to victimise members of the foreign press, except by expelling them from their territory. Franco's threat was therefore regarded as a further step towards the abolition of intellectual freedom in a tottering Europe. To that extent the case of the unknown *News Chronicle* correspondent had become a symbolic issue.

That the innocent victim happened to be a disguised Communist was, of course, not known to the public. But this ironical twist to the affair was equally characteristic of the days of the People's Front, when Communists were the driving force behind all similar campaigns. Liberals all over the world signed appeals demanding the liberation of Thaelmann, the Communist leader imprisoned by Hitler; not one in a hundred felt the same urge regarding the Communist leaders imprisoned and shot by Stalin. Yet this was the time when the Great Purge was ravaging Russia, a modern version of the Black Death—beginning with the execution of the leaders of the Revolution, ending with the execution of the executioners, and carrying off on its way more than ten per cent of the nation to slow death in the forced labour camps.

I hope not to appear either cynical or ungrateful in pointing out this paradox in the mentality of the liberal public to which I owe my life. The men of goodwill of that era fought clearsightedly and devotedly against one type of totalitarian threat to civilisation, and were blind or indifferent to the other. Such one-sidedness is perhaps unavoidable; it seems to be almost impossible to mobilise public emotions for an ideological two-front war. Yet when I learned about the fuss that had been made about me, and compared it with the unsung end of my friends in Russia (nearly all of whom were at that time already under arrest), I became increasingly aware of a crushing debt that must somehow be repaid. *Darkness at Noon*, which I started writing the next year, was the first instalment towards it.

I also found that, unknowingly, I had incurred another debt, of a personal nature, that could not be repaid. The organiser and driving force of the campaign had been Dorothy, from whom I had been separated for the last two years, but who was legally still my wife. The day when the news of my arrest had appeared in the French papers, Dorothy had peremptorily asked the Party to be sent to London for the purpose of initiating a public protest. The Party was sceptical, and thought that in view of the unsavoury facts that might come out, the less said about me the better. The only person who backed her up was Otto Katz.

Willy's position was already badly shaken. Moscow had re-called him 'for consultations'. Willy, knowing what that meant, was postponing the journey under various pretexts, and Otto, who during all these years had informed on Willy for the *apparat*, was gradually taking over his functions. He was betraying his chief and benefactor, as we all, including Willy, had known that he would when the moment came. Yet once one accepts the basic tenet of Communist ethics that loyalty to the Party overrules personal loyalty, Otto had no other choice; and the attitude he took towards Dorothy proves that in the midst of that struggle for survival, conducted ac-cording to inhuman rules, he tried to preserve a vestige of humanity. By-passing the Party bureaucracy, he authorised Dorothy to go to London on behalf of the Muenzenberg out-fit, and paid her expenses out of the Spanish propaganda funds he handled. Moreover, Otto periodically launched fic-titious news about me in the Press : 'Koestler kept in chains in dark underground dungeon', and the like. It was all in the tradition of similar campaigns, in which Otto was an old hand, the purpose being to provoke a denial and thus to ob-tain some indication of the prisoner's whereabouts.

Thus Dorothy went to England, a country where she had never been before, to mobilise public opinion for her husband, of whom nobody had ever heard before. Her task was all the more difficult as even my official employers, the *News Chronicle*, knew next to nothing about me. I had only met two members of its staff personally : Norman Cliff and Willy Forrest. I had never met the editor, and all in all the paper had published perhaps half a dozen despatches by me. Though the *Chronicle* did everything in their power to help Dorothy, they were naturally handicapped by these facts. Yet

Dorothy, whom I knew as a shy and inhibited young woman, suddenly revealed the qualities of a fighting Amazon. She was tireless and ingenious, tactful and dogged. She spent sixteen hours a day collecting signatures from politicians and men of letters, lobbying in the House of Commons, interviewing Dukes and Archbishops, engineering petitions and protest-resolutions. Her tongue-tied manner achieved more in England than eloquence could ever have done; her sincerity was instantaneously convincing; the fact that she spoke as the distressed wife of a husband in prison was more effective than any political argument. There were many who helped, but it was Dorothy who saved my life.

Dorothy's brother Ernie was arrested in Russia about the same time as I was arrested in Spain. She was, of course, willing to do everything to save him as she had saved me. But public opinion and diplomatic pressure, which still carried some weight with Fascist countries, carried no weight whatsoever with the Soviet régime. Thus I could be saved though I was an enemy of Franco's rule and guilty according to its laws; whereas Ernie, who was innocent and a loyal supporter of the Soviet Union, was shot.

While she was campaigning for me as my wife, Dorothy had, of course, not mentioned that in fact our marriage had broken up several years before. Thus for the sake of appearances, after my return we had to live together for a while. Nothing can bind two human beings more firmly to each other than the kind of experience that Dorothy and I had shared; and we now had a unique opportunity to make a fresh start. For a while we enjoyed the hospitality of Lord (then Sir Walter) and Lady Layton in their house on Putney Hill (Layton was Chairman of the Board of the *News Chronicle*); then we took for the rest of the summer a little house in Shepperton-on-Thames, where I wrote *Dialogue with Death* in two months —most of the book was dictated straight into the typewriter to Dorothy. All the circumstances were propitious; yet my neurotic inability to settle down with a partner for life again proved distressingly stronger than affection and gratitude. I have discussed this painful subject before, and shall not return to it. Our friendship remained, but our ways, a few months later, parted again.

It was also necessary to keep up appearances in another field. After all the public protests against the arbitrary imprisonment of a Liberal journalist, the disclosure that he was, in fact, a member of the Communist Party would have been highly embarrassing, and not only to the *News Chronicle*; it would have made all who had helped out of human kindness look like fools. It would also have been grist to the mill of Franco's propaganda which took the line that all democratic opponents of his régime were disguised Reds. Thus by the logic of circumstances the fiction of the *bona fide* Liberal journalist had to be maintained, first in the account of my prison experiences that appeared in serial form in the *News Chronicle*, and subsequently in *Dialogue with Death* which appeared a few months later. A deception, once started, has the compelling momentum of a rolling stone.

However, during this first prolonged stay in England, when for the first time I met people from every walk of life, a form of existence which required continuous deception became almost unbearably odious. On the Continent things were different. There conspiratorial cunning and underhand methods were in keeping with the political atmosphere created by Hitler, Mussolini, Franco and Metaxas. By force of contrast, England appeared an island of innocence, where plotting was confined to memories of Guy Fawkes and to Victorian melodrama, and where fair play was taken for granted even by members of the ridiculously small and provincial C.P. To be a Communist in disguise in Shepperton, Middlesex, with a retired naval officer for a neighbour whose daughters came over for tennis and tea on the lawn, seemed as grotesquely out of place as the proverbial Yankee at the Court of King Arthur.

Fortunately, I was never asked either in public or in private, except on one occasion, whether I was a Communist— under the circumstances a sign of an almost extravagant discretion. The one exception was Katharine, Duchess of Atholl, whom my publisher, Victor Gollancz, had asked to write an introduction for *Spanish Testament*. Katharine Atholl was President of the Spanish Relief Committee and dedicated to the cause of the Loyalists; a Conservative by conviction and party, she often spoke for Spain on the same platform with Ellen Wilkinson, the Socialist, and Isabel Brown, the Communist. She was then in her middle fifties, with a distinguished career in public welfare to her credit, her tireless energy hidden behind the manner of a mild public librarian. At our first meeting, she asked me whether I was a member of the Communist Party in the casual voice of asking whether I liked playing tennis. I had no choice but to answer 'No' out of a constricted throat; she said : 'Your word is enough for me.' Although denials of this kind are an elementary duty for Party members and become almost a conditioned reflex, I did not feel like an undercover revolutionary but like a schoolboy telling a particularly odious fib. But it was now almost for the last time.

The aged eighth Duke seemed to be rather unhappy about his wife's latest political activites. I have only met him once, for a few minutes. I was lunching alone with Katharine Atholl in their house in Chelsea when the Duke, a tall figure bent by age, shambled into the room, wagged his finger at me, remarked, 'You naughty boy, you are leading Katharine into bad ways,' and shambled out again.

Spanish Testament, incorporating *Dialogue with Death* and several chapters from *L'Espagne Ensanglantée*, was published in the beginning of 1938. It became a Left Book Club choice, was translated into several languages, and had a modest success. Thus, at the age of thirty-three, I was at long last launched on my course as a writer.

I finished the book in the first days of September. By then, I had used up the advance that Gollancz had paid me, and was back on earth, returned from the tragic to the trivial plane. I could not resume my job with the *News Chronicle* and the Spanish News Agency, for, as a condition of my release, I had been obliged to sign an undertaking not to return to Spain for the duration of the war. Lord Layton, who did not know that I was a Party member, tentatively offered me the post of the *News Chronicle*'s correspondent in Moscow; but Gerald Barry, the editor, who did know it, vetoed the project. Instead, it was agreed that I should do a few weeks' tour for the *Chronicle* through Palestine and the Middle East.

The tour was to start with Greece, and I travelled by land, across the Continent. My first stop was Paris where Otto greeted me at the Gare du Nord, most incongruously and touchingly equipped with a huge bouquet of roses. We must have looked like a couple of gangsters out of an American film carrying a wreath at a funeral.

The next day I was submitted to a formal interrogation by two delegates of the Party regarding my conduct in prison. One of them was Paul Merker, who after the war became a member of the East German Government and who has since been purged; the identity of the other interrogator is unknown to me.

It is a tradition in all secret revolutionary movements, and especially in the Communist Party, to regard any member of the organisation who has been imprisoned and subsequently released, as *ipso facto* suspect. He might have been bullied or bribed into becoming an enemy agent; or he might have given away his comrades. Accordingly, a Communist released from prison must undergo a thorough investigation by the security organs of the Party, and in countries where the Party leads an underground existence, he will for a considerable time be 'put on ice'—isolated from any contact with other members. As it is often impossible to establish with certainty whether the person is still 'sound' or not, many tragedies were caused in the German underground Party, and later in the French Resistance, by persistent, lingering suspicions which the victim was unable to dispel.

In my own case, the proceedings were quite harmless, and more in the nature of a formality. I had no underground contacts in Franco Spain whom I could have given away; I had been exchanged by an international deal which gave my captors no opportunity for forcing a bargain on me; and that I should have voluntarily become a Franco agent was unlikely. The meeting took place in a little café near the Bastille. Merker, a broad-shouldered, burly man with a slow and thoughtful manner, cross-examined me for about an hour in a neutral but not unfriendly voice, while the other man watched me without speaking. He was a smallish, colourless person, with small, hard grey eyes, who spoke German with a foreign accent that I could not place. In the end Merker said that he had finished with me—but perhaps the Comrade would like to ask some further questions? His voice, in addressing the other man, was slightly deferential. The other shook his head, looked at his watch and got up. The only words he had spoken during an hour were his opening phrase when Merker introduced us, 'I have heard about you'; and his closing words, 'Good-bye'.

The two of them left together. In observance of an old Party rule regarding meetings with members of the *apparat*, I had to stay behind in the café for another five minutes. No verdict had been announced and no comment on my conduct made; yet I had a feeling that all had gone well—though I no longer cared much about the Party's favour or disfavour, anyway.

However, once the interrogation was over, I had a sudden, intense attack of anxiety, and I noticed how unsteady my hand was as I lifted the cup of cold *café au lait*. This was the autumn of 1937; a few weeks earlier Marshal Tuchachevsky and eight top-ranking Generals of the Red Army had been shot after a secret trial; every day we heard of new arrests, accompanied by incredible and frightening accusations. The harmless interrogation of a moment ago carried a terrifying echo. It was impossible not to think how helpless one would be facing that taciturn, hard-eyed man, not at a Paris café table, but across the Prosecutor's desk in the G.P.U. building in Baku or in the Lubyanka. For instance, I had said nothing about that fatal phrase 'I no longer am a *rojo*'; but I knew that under different circumstances that phrase would eventually have come out, that its motives and implications would have been wrested from me step by step, and that alone would have been enough to finish me off. By these standards, which had once been my own standards, nobody was without guilt. The Terror was roaring across Russia, like a tidal wave drowning everybody on its way, and even a small, distant ripple of it made the cup tremble in one's hand in a Paris café. Before my stay in cell No. 40, the words 'prison' and 'execution' had only brought to my mind some abstract cliché like Fascist Terror, or the Dialectics of Revolution. Now the same words had a different ring, they echoed the muffled cries of *madre* and *socorro* which could not be dislodged from the ear, like an insistent tune that drives one crazy. I thought of Nadeshda and Werner, Alex and Eva, Ernie and Paul Dietrich, and there was always the same muffled refrain of *socorro, socorro.*

My next stop was Switzerland, where I had arranged by correspondence a meeting with Thomas Mann. It was my first and last personal meeting with the author of *Buddenbrooks* and *The Magic Mountain,* whom I had admired more than any other living writer in my youth. The meeting itself was a rather cruel disappointment, but the event that caused it is worth recounting, as it seems to involve a striking example of telepathy.

To explain it, I must again hark back to Seville. During the first three weeks of solitary confinement, before I was allowed books from the prison library, my only intellectual nourishment had been the remembrance of books read in the past. In the course of these memory exercises, a certain passage from *Buddenbrooks* came back to me and gave me great spiritual comfort—so much so, that at times when I felt particularly dejected, I would have recourse to that scene as if it were a pain-soothing pill. The content of the passage, as I remembered it, was this. Consul Thomas Buddenbrook, though only in his late forties, knows that he is about to die. He was never given to religious or metaphysical speculation, but now he falls under the spell of a book which for years has stood unread in his library, and in which he finds explained that death is nothing final, merely a transition to another, impersonal form of existence in the All-One. ' . . . He felt that his whole being had been unaccountably expanded and . . . there clung to his senses a profound intoxication, a strange, sweet, vague allurement . . . He was no longer prevented from grasping eternity . . .' The book to which Consul Buddenbrook owes his revelation is Schopenhauer's essay *On Death, and its Relation to the Indestructibility of our Essential Selves.*

The day after I was set free, I wrote Thomas Mann a letter (I knew that he lived in Zuerich-Kuessnacht), in which I explained to him what I have just explained, and thanked him for the spiritual comfort that I had derived from his work. The title of Schopenhauer's essay was expressly mentioned in my letter, which was dated from the Rock Hotel, Gibraltar, May 16 or 17, 1937.

Thomas Mann's answer reached me a few days later in London. It was a handwritten letter which I lost, together with all my files, on my flight from France in 1940. I cannot, of course, remember its actual text, only its content which, for the sake of simplicity, I shall paraphrase in direct speech :

Dear Sir,
Your letter arrived on May. . . . On the afternoon of that day I was sitting in my garden in Kuessnacht. I had read Schopenhauer's essay in 1897 or 98, while I was writing *Buddenbrooks*, and had never read it again as I did not want to weaken its original strong impact on me. On that afternoon, however, I felt a sudden impulse to re-read the essay after nearly forty years. I went indoors to my library to fetch the volume. At that moment the postman rang and brought me your letter. . . .

After this startling prelude, I looked forward to my meeting with Thomas Mann with even greater trepidation than I would have felt in any case. In the train from Paris I read his speech delivered on the occasion of Freud's eightieth birthday, and derived a curious impression from it. The subject of spiritual reincarnation (in a literal sense, and then again not in a literal sense—in his essays Mann is difficult to pin down) kept recurring as a *leit-motif*. In his fastidiously ironical and elusive style, which had become more elusive and mannered in his later work, Mann seemed to suggest that he considered himself a kind of spiritual reincarnation of Goethe—Mann's preoccupation with Goethe's personality is much in evidence in his work. With an uncomfortable feeling I asked myself whether the great man really believed that he was Goethe, or whether he only believed it metaphorically—for, since he received the Nobel Prize in 1929, Thomas Mann had been the unchallenged *Dichterfuerst* of German letters.

The meeting took place in a Swiss holiday resort (I think in Locarno, but I am not sure), where Dr. Mann and his wife were staying at the time. From the moment I arrived, everything went wrong. There is a character in *The Magic Mountain*, the semi-educated Frau Stoehr, who is always trying to be refined, and always gets her expressions wrong. She has, for instance, a dreadful habit of saying '*wenn es Ihnen konveniert*' (roughly, 'if it conveniences you' for 'if it is convenient to you'). When I arrived at the hotel where the Manns were staying and where I had booked a room, I rang up Dr. Mann as arranged. He said : 'Well, when would you like to come over to my room?' I was so excited that I blurted into the telephone, just like Frau Stoehr :

'Whenever it conveniences you, Herr Doktor.'

There was a bewildered silence in the receiver, then a faint cough. 'Well, hm,' the Olympian voice said at last, 'I shall be pleased if you will join me on my little morning walk tomorrow at eleven o'clock.'

As it was six o'clock in the afternoon, and our rooms only separated by a few yards across the corridor, and as I had come all the way to Switzerland to pay homage to the Master, I found this reception slightly chilling. But what else could one expect if one said 'conveniences you' like the semi-illiterate Frau Stoehr? Mann must have thought that I was trying to be dreadfully facetious. I would have liked to bite my tongue off, chew it, and spit it into the cuspidor.

The walk next day did not yield much comfort. We talked mostly of the *Joseph* trilogy, of which the second volume had, I believe, just been published. Mann had read a huge amount of ancient history and mythology, and been influenced by the theories of certain German anthropologists. I asked him whether he had read Levy-Bruhl, and when he answered in the negative, I said impulsively : '*Ach*, but you must.' Mann shook his head : 'I feel that I have read enough in that direction. If you know too much about a subject, it cramps you.' It was the only remark Mann made during the day that impressed me. The remainder of the talk was desultory; I could not help feeling that Thomas Mann was talking for the record. It was not a dialogue, but a series of ponderous statements such as : 'I do not hold with dictators; however, if choose one must, I am inclined, as a humanist, to prefer Herr Stalin to Herr Hitler, as the lesser evil.' There was never a moment of personal contact. This was no doubt partly due to my paralysing timidity and gaucherie in the master's presence; on the other hand, Mann did nothing to put me at ease. He asked no questions regarding my prison experiences, nor any other question betraying any interest in my person; I was treated half as a visiting journalist, half as a casual Eckerman who would, it was to be hoped, note down every word of the conversation in his diary and preserve it for posterity. The air was full of echoes of Weimar; I had an uncanny premonition that as I was now made to play Eckerman, that name would be explicitly mentioned within the next hour.

On our return to the hotel, we met in the garden Mrs. Mann who asked me to join their table for lunch. There was also present a friend of the Manns' whose name I have forgotten : a pleasant and exquisitely courteous man of about forty who made a visible effort to put me a little more at my ease. The moment that I had been expecting with a mixture of dread and curiosity came between the first and second course. I hardly knew what I was eating, nor what the conversation was about, when I heard Thomas Mann's voice come booming across the table, at the end of a sentence to which I had not listened :

'(boum-boum-boum)—as Goethe had occasion to remark to Eckerman.'

And a few minutes later, turning to me :

'(boum-boum-boum)—as I had occasion to remark during our little walk.'

It was so depressing that I almost quoted Frau Stoehr again. I left the same evening.

Since that unhappy meeting, I have re-read a substantial part of Thomas Mann's early work. Much of it has lost its original impact on me, but it has retained its grandeur and subtlety, its poetic irony, its universal sweep and range. Most of his later work I find mannered to the point where it becomes unreadable. But *Buddenbrooks* and *The Magic Mountain*, the stories and essays (excluding the political essays), and indeed the major part of his work up to and including the first volume of *Joseph*, remain as a monument of the early twentieth century, and Germany's most important single contribution to its culture. Thus personal disappointment did not diminish my admiration and gratitude for Mann's work. It did seem to provide, however, an explanation for a certain aspect of Mann's art which had always puzzled me : I mean the absence of human kindness. There has perhaps never been a great novelist so completely lacking the Dostoievskian touch of sympathy for the poor and humble. In Mann's universe, charity is replaced by irony which is sometimes charitable, sometimes not; his attitude to his characters, even at its most sympathetic, has a mark of Olympian condescension. It makes the reader feel that he is really just another Frau Stoehr.

The only exception to this is Mann's treatment of children and dogs; perhaps because here condescension, the gesture of bending down, is implicit in the situation. The title of his only story about dogs is, revealingly : *Herr und Hund*. Which does not prevent it, however, from being a masterpiece.

Thus Mann's 'humanism'—his favourite word for describing his philosophy—is something rather abstract, a *Weltanschauung* in rarefied air. In our age, the term has lost its once well-defined meaning, but its very ambiguity makes it eminently suitable for the elusive style of Mann's philosophical essays. The result is a humanism without the cement of affection for the individual human brick, a grandiose, but unsound edifice which was never proof against the nasty gales and currents of the times. This may explain a series of episodes in Mann's public career which were exploited by his opponents and embarrassed his admirers—such as his support of Prussian imperialism in the first World War; his hesitant and belated break with the Nazis; his silent endorsement of the new despotism in Eastern Germany, and his acceptance of the Goethe Prize from a régime which banned and burned the books of his compatriots and fellow-authors. They were not so much political mistakes, to which every mortal is liable, but symptoms of a bluntness of moral perception, of a defeat in ethical sensitivity caused by the absence of *charitas*. They do not affect Mann's greatness as an artist, but they have defeated his claim to the cultural leadership of the German nation. It is impossible to be angry with Picasso for believing that Stalin was the greatest benefactor of mankind, for one feels that his error is the result of a naïve and warmhearted passion. But it is not so easy to forgive the moral *faux pas* of the ironically dispassionate Olympian.

XXXV. An S.O.S.

My next stop was Belgrade, where I had arranged to meet my parents. It had by now become too risky for me to visit them in Budapest. Closing time was approaching for Europe, one by one the doors of the countries of one's youth were being shut in one's face. They are still closed today, though for other reasons, and guarded by other dictators. There ought to be a new word coined for the benefit of twentieth-century Europeans : Stepmotherland.

It was the last time I saw my father. Since our previous meeting, only two years back, he had suddenly become an old man. On that earlier occasion he had been sixty-six, but so full of zest and vigour that people generally took him to be in his early fifties—a fact of which he was very proud. Men who look and feel much younger than their age often seem to break down suddenly and without transition, as the night falls in the tropics. He still talked of his 'colossal' and 'grandiose' projects, but now his voice had a pathetic ring, and his eyes often shone with the sad tortoise-wisdom of our race. He was on a milk diet for what he called a 'slight acidity', and which was in fact a cancer of the stomach. But to celebrate the occasion he insisted on having his favourite dish, Hungarian goulash with sour cream and paprika and dumplings and a glass of wine; and for once my mother let him have his way.

My mother was unchanged—resolute, temperamental, caustic and irritable, as I had always known her. I discovered to my amazement that my father had managed to keep her in ignorance of the fact that I was in prison until the very day when I was released. He had read the news of my arrest and presumed execution in Malaga in the evening paper, while sitting with friends in a café. He had fallen off his chair in a faint, and had spent the next two hours in a telephone booth, warning all my mother's relatives and friends to keep the news hidden from her. My mother only read one paper, the *Pester Lloyd*, and mostly only the headlines; during the month that followed, whenever there was a reference to me in the *Lloyd*, my father tore out the page before my mother had seen the paper, or pretended that it had not been delivered. It was an extraordinary *tour de force*, in the imaginative tradition of the envelope-cutting machine and the radio-active soap. To the end, my mother had noticed nothing—except that her bridge-partners sometimes looked at her in a funny way and showed her more consideration than before, which she took as a sign of her superior skill at the game.

Apart from this, the subject of my imprisonment was not mentioned between us. To my father, who had carried the burden of knowledge and anguish alone, the topic was still too painful, to my mother too embarrassing. For her generation, prison signified eternal dishonour to a family, and the politics of remote Spain provided no excuse; thus no reference to that scandalous episode was ever made between my mother and me.

The last time I saw my father he was waving farewell through the window of the night train from Belgrade to Budapest. He died in 1940, while I was making my escape from France, when communications with Hungary were interrupted. I only learnt of his death several years later. When my mother rejoined me in London after the war, I gathered that they had both thought I had fallen into the hands of the Nazis, though they never admitted their fears to each other. On the day before he died, my father had asked her to take my photograph away from his bedside table. 'I can bear it no longer,' he said quietly, and those were his last words referring to me.

The Middle Eastern trip had been discreetly intended by the *News Chronicle* as a sinecure for me, but it became, in fact, an assignment to another region of terror and guerilla warfare. The first country to be covered on the tour was Greece, where I had meant to spend a quiet fortnight; but after a few days in Athens a cable from London instructed me to proceed at once to Palestine where the Arab rebellion had suddenly flared up again.

Even the few days in Athens had been far from peaceful. Greece, too, lived under a quasi-Fascist dictatorship, the régime of General Metaxas who had seized power by a *coup d'état* in 1936. It was one of the nastier, and probably the silliest, dictatorship in Europe, illustrated by the fact that it had put Plato's *Republic* on the list of banned subversive books. The élite of the progressive intellectuals had been put into prison or deported to an island-camp in the Ægean. It was a monotonously familiar story. Before I left Paris I had got in touch, through the Party, with Greek refugee circles who had given me an address in Athens and a password. I was thus able to establish contact with some members of the underground opposition, both Communists and Liberals. I don't remember who they were, and hardly anything of what they told me, except that it had the same, familiar ring : arrests at night, beatings, frame-ups, summary judgments. One story stuck in my memory : the torturing by the police of a young Communist girl, with details too sickening to relate. In the Balkans, police brutality was an old tradition, but Fascism had given it a new zest; and since Malaga I had become physically allergic to that kind of thing. Wherever one travelled in Europe, one could not escape it. Mussolini, Hitler, Dollfuss, Metaxas, Franco : the Continent was lousy with dictators. I remembered a disgusting boy at school who had suffered from furuncles and accepted bets as to where on his body the next one would break out. Would it be the turn of the Rexists in Belgium, or of the *Croix de Feu* in France? I wrote two pieces on the Metaxas régime so savage that even the *News Chronicle* would not print them.

There was no direct line from Greece to Palestine, so I travelled via Alexandria where, to remain true to style, I ran into some riots—it was either the Greenshirts or the Blueshirts demonstrating either against the Government or against the British. I had just time to watch an autobus being turned over by the rioters and set on fire, before I had to catch the train for Kantara.

In Kantara, which is on the Suez Canal, one changes trains for Palestine. The station was crammed with British troops, reinforcements for Jerusalem. On the previous day, the British had arrested the entire Arab High Committee in Palestine and deprived its leader, the Grand Mufti, of his functions; nobody knew what would happen next. The Arab shoeshine boy in the station bar warned me gleefully not to take the troop train : 'There is at least a ton of dynamite under the tracks, *hawadja.*' But as it turned out, the Arabs of Palestine, deprived of their leaders, were for the moment paralysed; the dynamiting of trains and ambushing of motor cars only started a fortnight later.

I stayed in Palestine for a month and a half. During the first, relatively quiet fortnight, I saw a number of friends and colleagues from Berlin who had managed to escape from the Nazis. They had all been compelled to take up new professions : a former editor of an Ullstein paper was a cloakroom attendant in the King David Hotel; a woman lawyer had become a cook in a boarding-house; my former chief, Dr. Magnus, head of the Ullstein's international news service, was now space-salesman for an obscure little Polish gazette. It was another chapter in the story of the liquidation of Europe's intellectual élite. These men had survived, but they were rooted in German culture, knew no Hebrew, had never been Zionists, and were thus condemned to a pointless and sterile existence in a country to which they had been driven by force and not by inner choice.

My Zionist friends of the old days belonged to an altogether different category. In a convulsed world, they were doggedly hanging on to their tiny strip of promised land. They had transformed the desert into a bitter oasis drenched with their sweat, throbbing with their anguish and passion. In the streets of Haifa and Tel Aviv, in the settlements of Sharon and Galilee, they went about their business with the calm, slow motions imposed by the heat, but underneath they were all fanatics and maniacs. Each of them had a brother, parent, cousin, bride, or in-law in the part of Europe ruled by the assassins. It was no longer a question whether Zionism was a good or bad idea. They knew that the gas-chambers were coming. They were past arguing. When provoked, they bared their teeth.

When the Arab terror campaign was resumed on October

15, one of the first victims was a young orthodox Jew who had recently escaped from Germany. He was stabbed in the back on the holy Sabbath while walking through a street in Jerusalem reading his Bible. Another victim was a twelve-year-old child in Ness Ziona, one of the oldest settlements, built on the so-called Hill of Dreams. He was shot in his sleep. It was typical of the pointless, senseless character of the terror. Though everything here was on a smaller scale, in a sense it was even worse than Spain. There at least one had known where the enemy's frontline was, but here both camps were mixed together, and no one knew when he was going to be knifed in the back, or where the next home-made bomb was going to explode.

Mostly they exploded in crowded buses and train-compartments, or on the railway tracks. The oil pipeline from Mosul was set on fire, the airport in Lydda burnt down, British soldiers were ambushed, Jewish settlers sniped at in the fields, girls were raped, then stabbed to death. For a few days there was a curfew in Jerusalem. At five-thirty the streets were crowded with people hurrying home; a quarter of an hour later they were deserted, all doors and windows closed, and only the rattle of an armoured car on patrol or the whine of a sniper's bullet broke the ghostly silence—the silence of Malaga, the last night before its fall.

After a week, things calmed down a little; another week later it started all over again. The Jews were still holding back, swallowing their bile. It took some time for the tailors from Warsaw and the lawyers from Prague and the Talmud-students from Jerusalem to acquire a taste for throwing gelignite bombs. A year later they had acquired it, with a vengeance.

Eleven years had passed since I had set out for Palestine the first time, a romantic young fool, to work in a collective settlement at the foot of Mount Gilboa; eight years since I had left Palestine, disillusioned by the narrow chauvinism, the limited horizon of the Zionist settlers. During these eight years I had believed that the small and irksome Jewish question would eventually be solved, together with the Negro question, the Armenian question and all other questions, in the global context of the Socialist revolution. So I had left the old Promised

Land for the new land of promise, and had found it an even more bitter disappointment. Now, on my way out of the Communist Party, I had come back.

But it was not a coming full circle. It was a return on a different level of the spiral: a turn higher in maturity, but several turns lower in expectation. I no longer believed that this small and bitter country held out a messianic promise, an inspiration for mankind at large. I no longer believed that the artificial revival of the archaic language of the Bible would produce a cultural renaissance, a return of the age of the Prophets. And I also knew that my roots were in Europe, that I belonged to Europe, and that if Europe went down, survival became pointless, and I would rather go down with her than take refuge in a country which no longer meant anything but a refuge. This resolution was actually put to the test when France fell, and when, instead of heading for Palestine or still neutral America, I made my escape to England—which led to another stretch of solitary confinement in a London prison during the blitz. Yet even that prison-cell in Pentonville meant Europe, my home.

On the other hand, there were six million doomed people in Germany and Eastern Europe who had no such freedom of choice, and for whom Palestine meant their only chance of survival. Whether they were welcome or not, whether the climate and culture suited them or not, were irrelevant questions when the alternative was the concentration camp, the ghetto and finally, the crematorium. In this limited, resigned, and utilitarian sense, I was still a Zionist.

In the early days, I had been a member of Jabotinsky's maximalist party which aimed at the transformation of the whole of Palestine into a Jewish State with an Arab minority. In the light of the intervening years, this programme had proved to be unworkable and utopian; Jews and Arabs were too profoundly divided by religion, culture and social pattern to live harmoniously together in the measurable future. I had thus become gradually convinced that partition of the country, as proposed by the Royal Commission under Lord Peel, was, though not an ideal solution, yet the only possible solution. The serial that I wrote for the *News Chronicle* on my return ended with an urgent plea for carrying out the partition scheme, and a warning of the horrors which further procrastination would entail :

> *The prospects for the future of the Holy Land are one colossal nightmare. Perpetual insecurity is ruining the country's economy; fear and hatred grow daily as murders and vendettas link up into an endless chain. The implacable savagery of this petty guerilla war threatens to destroy slowly but surely a historically unprecedented experiment.*
>
> *Britain must act, and act quickly. This is an S.O.S. for Palestine.*[1]

In 1937 partition could have been carried out with relatively little trouble and less bloodshed. The representative Jewish bodies were prepared to accept it. The moderate Arab leaders would have yielded to diplomatic pressure. The most influential among them, King Abdullah of Transjordan (whom I revisited in Amman during a lull in the riots) gave me an interview which, in somewhat veiled terms, amounted to an acceptance of partition. The Government of Neville Chamberlain, however, refused to implement the Royal Commission's plan, and for the next ten years British policy in Palestine was plunged into a dark night of indecision, error and prejudice. Partition was finally endorsed, after a decade of needless torment and bloodshed, by the United Nations, and implemented by force of arms in the Arab-Jewish war.

From 1942, when the mass-extermination of European Jews began, until the consolidation of the Jewish State in 1948, Palestine became once more my main preoccupation. I spent during this period altogether a year and a half in that country, wrote two books (*Thieves in the Night* and *Promise and Fulfilment*), several pamphlets, countless articles, made speeches, and sat on committees—all the time pleading the case of partition, as the only means to end the horror and save those who could still be saved. Of the various crusades in which I had been engaged this was the most harrowing and painful, a penance for the political vagaries of the past. It involved me in an acute conflict between conviction and inclination, for I have had my fill of terror and violence, and was yet compelled to explain and defend the cause of the Jewish terrorists. Dur-

[1] 'An S.O.S. for Palestine', *News Chronicle*, 15.12.1937.

ing these long sojourns in Palestine, the poisoned atmosphere of the country, the bombings, the hangings, the all-pervading savagery and hatred were active fuel for my anxiety neurosis, and for a while alcohol was the only remedy.

When the war against Hitler was at long last won, I had meant to settle down to a stable and peaceful existence. I had made England my permanent home, wrote in English, thought in English, and had become attached to the country and the people; with approaching middle age, I watched with satisfaction the branching out of my roots. I had applied for British citizenship, and was awaiting the day when I would again have a nationality, a country and a passport. The most wretched moment in this conflict-torn period came when my application was on the point of being granted, yet I felt unable to take the oath of allegiance at a time when Englishmen and Jews were virtually at war. This, too, was part of the penance, but it had its reward. When, at the end of 1948, the State of Israel was safely established and the agony and conflict had come to an end, it gave me much satisfaction to know that my becoming a British citizen was the result of a free choice, and the end of a long and difficult journey.[1]

I have not revisited Israel since 1948. But I felt an equally deep satisfaction when it was reported to me that several members of the United Nations Commission of 1947, which made the historic Recommendation for the establishment of a Jewish State, had gone to the trouble of reading *Thieves in the Night* and that this book had had some influence on them. It is the most satisfactory reward that a writer can hope for, and represents (together with a second incident to be reported later) my main solace when, in hours of depression, I ask myself whether in forty-eight years full of sound and fury, I have achieved anything worth while.

---

[1] In 1951, British and American newspapers erroneously reported that I had become by Act of Congress an American citizen. The fact is that I have never been given, and have never applied for, American citizenship. The misunderstanding arose during a two years' stay in the U.S.A., which was made possible by an Act of Congress. The Act in question exempted me from the provisions of the McCarran Law (which denies access to U.S.A. territory to former Communists) and gave me the right of residence, but had no bearing on the question of nationality.

XXXVI. 'What is this Thou hast done unto Me?'

THE story of my final break with the Communist Party is a story of last-minute hesitations and confusions, which I find difficult to get into focus.

At the beginning of 1938, after my return from Palestine, I made a four weeks' lecture tour through England for the Left Book Club, which at the time was at the peak of its popularity.

The Club's monthly 'choices' were selected by a three-man jury : Victor Gollancz, Harold Laski and John Strachey. The majority of the Club's sixty-five thousand subscribers sympathised with the C.P., but they were English in the first, Communists in the second place, and I found it difficult to take them seriously. Their meetings, compared with those on the Continent, were like tea parties in the vicarage; they put decency before dialectics and, even more bewilderingly, they tended to indulge in humour and eccentricity—both of which were dangerous diversions from the class struggle. After two or three weeks of lecturing up and down the country, from Newcastle to Bournemouth, from Liverpool to Cheltenham, I came to the tentative conclusion that the majority of English Communists were not revolutionaries but cranks and eccentrics, and that they were certainly closer to the Pickwick Club than to the Comintern. I was constantly reminded of a famous story about Lenin. He was shown a newspaper-cutting referring to a strike in England, which said that police and strikers had played a soccer match that the strikers had won. Lenin promptly declared that the English would never make a revolution, and cut the subsidy of the British C.P.

The lectures were on the political and military situation in Spain. About my personal experiences I did not speak—the hours by the window were not a proper subject for the Left Book Club. Questions were asked, but there was rarely any proper discussion. The eagerness and innocence of the audiences was very moving. The Spanish Loyalist Army had come to be regarded as the rearguard of European democracy, and commanded the passionate sympathy of all. At nearly every meeting I was asked whether I had happened to come across comrade so-and-so, a relation or friend of the questioner who was fighting with the International Brigades. The exploitation of the war by Moscow for its own purposes, the activities of the G.P.U. and SIM behind the front-lines, did not enter the picture. Any mention of these subjects would have met with incredulity and indignation.

At almost every meeting there was for me one critical moment. It came when somebody in the audience asked a question about the P.O.U.M.

The *Partido Obrero Unificado Marxista* was a small Leftist splinter group which, in the tradition of such dissident sects, called itself grandiosely the *united* Marxist workers' party. Because of its Trotskyist leanings, the P.O.U.M. was at the time treated by the Communists as enemy number one, and its members were fair prey for the G.P.U. in Spain. It had been made the scapegoat for the anarchist rising in Barcelona. Its leader, Andres Nin, formerly Minister of Justice in the Caballero government, had been denounced as an agent of Franco and arrested, together with a group of his associates. Nin had once been a leading member of the Comintern, but had sided with Trotsky against Stalin; the Spanish war had provided the G.P.U. with an opportunity to settle his, and a few hundred similar accounts. One day Nin and several other P.O.U.M. leaders were fetched out of prison by an unidentified group of men, taken for a ride towards Madrid, and shot without trial and ceremony. Officially their bodies were only found when a British parliamentary delegation came to Spain to investigate the circumstances of their disappearance.

At the time of the lecture tour, Nin and his comrades were already in prison, but had not yet been assassinated. The men of the P.O.U.M. had fought with great bravery and self-sacrifice at the front in Aragon (George Orwell had been wounded while serving as a volunteer in their ranks), and there was no doubt in my mind that the accusations against them were absurd and perfidious. But for a Party member to say this in public meant expulsion, with the inevitable sequel of being himself denounced as a Trotskyist agent of Franco or the Gestapo. That is why questions referring to P.O.U.M. put me in a critical position.

The first time it was asked, the question took me unawares. It had not occurred to me that it would be asked; among German or French Communists this would have been unthinkable. For a moment, my mind was a blank. The correct line to be applied to this and similar cases was that any faction or group that caused a split in revolutionary unity played into the enemy's hands, and that accordingly Nin (or Trotsky, or Zinoviev, or Radek, as the case may be) must *objectively* be regarded as an agent of Franco (or Hitler, or the British Intelligence Service), whereas the *subjective* motives of his actions were historically irrelevant. This answer was part of the catechism for the advanced classes, and I had used it *ad nauseam* in arguments with others and myself. But at that moment my mind remained a blank, and the familiar answer just did not occur to me. Then, without conscious reflection, I took a plunge and said what I really thought. I said that I disagreed with the policy of the P.O.U.M. for a number of reasons which I would be glad to explain, but that in my opinion Andres Nin and his comrades had been acting in good faith, and to call them traitors was both stupid and a desecration of their dead. I was listening to my own voice with curiosity, as if it had been a stranger's.

Their was a short, embarrassed silence. A single voice, probably a Trotskyist or member of the I.L.P., said : 'Hear, hear'. Then the chairman asked for the next question. After the meeting one or two Party members mildly reproved me in private for what they called my exaggerated leniency toward the P.O.U.M. We argued for a while, then changed the subject, and that was all. It was the same at the other twenty or more meetings. Every time the question cropped up I gave the same answer, and every time it was received with the same embarrassed silence, which I could only interpret as tacit consent. Those who disagreed, in public or private, did it half-heartedly, on the grounds that civil wars and revolutions follow their own laws. At this point their thinking apparently stopped; the rumours and whisperings about the unmentionable aspects of Spain that had reached them were as thoroughly repressed and relegated to the unconscious as are the Facts of Life by the clergyman's daughter.

To my great surprise, there were no consequences for me. Even among the lotus-eaters of the British C.P. there must have been some who wrote reports to higher quarters; yet I was not called to account. It had been an abortive suicide, or series of suicides. At every meeting I pressed a figurative revolver to my head, pulled the trigger, heard a faint click, and found to my astonishment that I was still alive and a valued comrade of the Communist Party.

I felt both disappointed and relieved. I lived through my last months as a member of the Party like a person who knows that there is a painful and critical operation waiting for him which is being postponed from week to week. The less one thinks about it the better. And, strangely enough, during this last period I did not give much conscious thought to the matter. I have already said that I had ceased to be a Communist long before I knew it. Now the inner change that had taken place in cell No. 40 was gradually percolating through to the surface. I no longer needed to worry about my attitude to the Party; it was taking care of itself.

After the lecture tour I went back to Paris. A couple of months passed. In March the trial of the so-called 'Anti-Soviet Block of Rightists and Trotskyists' took place in Moscow. It surpassed in wild absurdity and horror everything that had gone before. The defendants were: Nikolai Bukharin, whom Lenin had called 'the darling of the Party', President of the Communist International in succession to Zinoviev who had been shot two years earlier; Christian Rakovsky, former head of the Ukrainian Soviet Republic, former Soviet Ambassador to England and France; Nikolai Krestinsky, predecessor of Stalin as General Secretary of the Communist Party of the Ukrainian Soviet Republic, former Soviet Ambassador to Germany; Alexei Rykov, successor of Lenin as President of the Council of People's Commissars. Finally Yagoda, organiser of the previous Moscow trials, People's Commissar of the Interior, Head of the G.P.U. in succession to Medjinsky whom he confessed to have poisoned together with Maxim Gorky, the author.[1]

To fathom the depths of absurdity reached in this trial one should bear in mind that it made the Purge and the preceding trials appear as the work of a poisoner and degenerate; that all the traitors had been appointed to their key positions in the Soviet State by the wise and vigilant Stalin; and that the Communist International was, during the first fifteen years of its existence, headed by agents of the German and British Intelligence Services.

At about the same time as these major events, a minor scandal was brewing in our writers' circle in Paris. Most of us had for many years known a girl comrade of Anglo-German origin called Judy. She was an attractive girl with an upper-class English background who talked German working-class slang, and was engaged to marry a German Communist serving a five-year sentence of hard labour. In the spring of 1938, the fiancé, Hans, arrived in Paris, having completed his sentence and then illegally crossed the frontier. A few days later, the photographs of Hans and Judy appeared on the front page of the German Communist Party's weekly paper in France, with a caption that denounced them both as Gestapo spies.

I knew that Judy was no more a spy than I, or my brother-in-law Ernie, or Alex and Eva. Hans had worked, until he was arrested, directly under Kippenberger, head of the German C.P.'s military intelligence branch. While Hans was serving his prison term, Kippenberger had been recalled to Moscow and shot in the purge.[2] When Hans arrived in Paris, he did not know about this—nor did Judy, unversed as she was in *apparat* matters. He asked the Party to be put in touch with Kippenberger, and when told that the latter was 'not avail-

[1] Yagoda's successor Yeshov was liquidated as a saboteur of Soviet justice in 1939; Yeshov's successor, Beria, was liquidated as a degenerate saboteur of Soviet justice in 1953. Thus all the heads of the Russian State Police during the last twenty-five years happened to be poisoners, spies and traitors.

[2] The reason for Kippenberger's liquidation was apparently his refusal to get rid of deviationists in the underground German party by the customary G.P.U. method of denouncing them to the Gestapo. See Erich Wollenberg, 'Der Apparat: Stalin's Fuenfte Kolonne,' *Ostprobleme*, May, 1951.

able', he named two other leaders of his outfit who had shared the same fate—as Hans himself would have done, had he not been in a German prison. Hence the notice in the paper.

Hans appealed to the Party, demanding that his case should be investigated by the Central Committee. He received no answer. He and Judy were boycotted by all their friends— Hans by that time half-crazed, and Judy on the verge of a breakdown. Egon and Giesl Kisch had been like second parents to Judy during Hans' imprisonment; now they too turned their backs on her. I wrote a letter to the Central Committee protesting against the public denunciation of two comrades without giving them a hearing, and stating my conviction that they were innocent. I received, of course, no answer, but the Party took no further action against them, nor against me. In the end Hans and Judy managed to get emigration visas to a British dominion, where they were married and have started a new life under a different name.

My siding with the alleged Gestapo agents had been another suicidal gesture that had gone off at half-cock. While I had been in jail, Communist propaganda had used me as a martyr, and some months must be allowed to lapse before I too could be denounced as an agent of Franco or the Mikado. The logical course would have been simply to resign from the Party. But this idea did not occur to me for quite a while. I knew that sooner or later I would be expelled, and this was to me the only conceivable manner of leaving the Party; to take the initiative myself seemed unimaginable. One may cease being a practising Catholic, but one does not send a letter of resignation to the Church.

A short while after this, Eva Weissberg suddenly arrived in London. She had been expelled from Russia after eighteen months in the Lubyanka prison. From her I heard the first authentic details, based on her own experience, of the G.P.U.'s methods of obtaining confessions.

Eva, it will be remembered, was a ceramist by profession. She had been arrested in April 1936. The charges against her were that she had inserted a concealed Swastika pattern into her designs for mass-produced tea-cups, and that in addition she had hidden under her bed two pistols with the intent of killing Comrade Stalin at the next Party Congress. During her year and a half in the Lubyanka, the G.P.U. had tried to brief her for the part of a repentant sinner in the forthcoming Bukharin trial. She had tried to commit suicide by cutting her veins, was saved, and ultimately released and expelled from the country, thanks to the extraordinary exertions of the Austrian Consul. Her experiences provided me with part of the background material for *Darkness at Noon*.

I had known Eva since I was five. We had been to the same Kindergarten, and had in later years remained close friends in Paris, Berlin, and Kharkov. Now she had been rescued from a Communist, I from a Fascist, prison. We had been pacing up and down our respective cells in Moscow and Seville at the same time, and at the same rate of four miles an hour. So we could exchange some modern traveller's tales.

Eva was safe. But Alex, who had been arrested a few months after her, was not. I shall return to his story later.

Among my last memories of life in the Party are two meeting of the Writers' Caucus.

On the first occasion we had to discuss a new slogan of the Soviet Writers' Federation which had just been transmitted to us. The slogan was : 'Write the Truth'. It was an eerie discussion; I wish it had been taken down on a tape-recorder as a document of our times. We knew the truth, that day after day the leaders of the Revolution and our own comrades in Russia were being shot as spies, or vanished without trace. And there we all sat, Kisch and Anna Seghers and Regler and Kantorowicz and Uhse, in a private room of the Café Mephisto (as our meeting-place was appropriately called) earnestly discussing how to write the truth without writing the truth. With our training in dialectical acrobatics it was not even difficult to prove that all truth was historically class-conditioned, that so-called objective truth was a bourgeois myth, and that 'to write the truth' meant to select and emphasise those items and aspects of a given situation which served the proletarian revolution, and were therefore 'historically correct'.

On the other occasion we were visited by a woman comrade from Moscow who exhorted us to exercise more revolutionary

vigilance, and took for her text another slogan : 'Every Bolshevist must be a Chekist'. We took it as quietly as if she had
said : 'Grow your own vegetables, the Nation needs them'.

The end came as another anti-climax.

Some time during that spring of 1938, I had to give a talk
on Spain to the Association of Exiled German Writers' in
Paris. Before the talk, a representative of the Party asked me to
insert a passage denouncing the P.O.U.M. as agents of Franco.
I refused. He shrugged, and asked politely whether I would
care to show him the text of my speech and to discuss it 'informally'; I refused.

The meeting took place in the hall of the *Société des Industries Françaises*, on the Place St. Germain des Prés, before
an audience of two or three hundred refugee intellectuals, the
majority of them Communists. It was my first public appearance in Paris since I had returned from Spain, and I felt that
it would be my last as a member of the Party. I had no intention of attacking the Party while the Spanish War was still
being fought, and the idea of attacking Russia in public still
carried the horror of blasphemy. On the other hand, I felt the
need to define where I stood, and not to remain a passive
accomplice of my friends' executioners. Although I usually
speak extempore, I wrote and rewrote the end of that speech
several times. It was a decisive occasion, and I wanted to
choose my ground carefully. I finally decided on three simple
phrases with which to conclude the speech, each in itself a
pious platitude, and yet a capital heresy for a Stalinist. The
first was : 'No movement, party or person can claim the privilege of infallibility'. The second was : 'It is as foolish to
appease the enemy, as it is to persecute the friend who pursues
the same end as you by a different road'. The third was a
quotation from Thomas Mann : 'In the long run, a harmful
truth is better than a useful lie'.

The effect was about the same as if one had told a Nazi
audience the startling news that all men are born equal. When
I had finished, the non-Communist part of the audience ap-
plauded, the Communist part sat in stony silence, most of
them with demonstratively folded arms.

I went home alone. While I was waiting for the train in the

métro station at St. Germain des Prés, a group of my comrades who had attended the meeting came down the staircase. They walked past to the other end of the platform without a glance, as if I were the invisible man.

That journey home in the métro was a foretaste of months and years of loneliness to come. It was not a physical loneliness, for after the break with the Party I found more friends than I have had before. But individual friendships could never replace the knowledge that one belonged to an international brotherhood embracing the whole globe; nor the warming, reassuring feeling of a collective solidarity which gave to that huge, amorphous mass the coherence and intimacy of a small family.

A few days later, on an evening that I was spending alone at home, it suddenly occurred to me that I might just as well end the agony of waiting, take the initiative and resign from the Party. Although I had been on my way out for a long time, this solution did not appear to me as a logical consequence of the situation, but as an entirely novel and reckless idea. A Communist expelled from the Party is regarded by his comrades as a fallen member of the family; one who leaves in voluntary defiance puts himself outside the human pale. Yet at the same time the idea filled me with the wild elation that I had experienced every time that I had burned my bridges : on that night in Vienna when I had decided to abandon my studies; and on that other night, seven years ago, when I had decided to throw up my career and join the Communist Party.

I worked on my letter of resignation all night. It was, I believe, a good letter, and I am sorry I have no copy of it. And yet that letter, too, was an anti-climax; I still did not have the courage to go more than half the way. It was a farewell to the German C.P., the Comintern, and the Stalin régime. But it ended with a declaration of loyalty to the Soviet Union. I stated my opposition to the system, to the cancerous growth of the bureaucracy, the terror and suppression of civil liberties. But I professed my belief that the foundations of the Workers' and Peasants' State had remained solid and unshaken, that the nationalisation of the means of production was a guarantee of her eventual return to the road of Socialism; and that, in spite of everything, the Soviet Union still represented 'our last and only hope on a planet in rapid decay.'

I clung tenaciously to this belief for another year and a half, until the Hitler-Stalin pact destroyed this last shred of the torn illusion. A faith comes into life through an apparently spontaneous act, like the bursting out of a butterfly from its cocoon. But the death of a faith is gradual and slow; even after the seemingly last flutter of the tired wings, there is yet another twitch, and another faint convulsion. Every true faith displays this stubborn refusal to die, whether its object is a Church, a Cause, a friend or a woman. Nature's horror of the void applies also to the spiritual sphere. To avoid the threatening emptiness, the true believer is ready to deny the evidence of his senses, to excuse every betrayal like a cuckold out of Boccaccio; and if the illusion can no longer be maintained in its original integrity, he will adapt and modify its shape, or try to save at least part of it. That is what I did, in the company of millions of others in the same predicament.

The theory that the Purges, the Slave-camps, the disfranchisement of the people, were merely surface phenomena and temporary expedients on Russia's road to Socialism, is a typical last-ditch rationalisation of this kind. It is connected with the notion that a planned State economy must be itself, regardless of the country's political régime, lead in the end to a free and happy Socialist society. In *The Yogi and the Commissar* I have dealt at length with this fallacy,[1] but arguments are of little avail against the power of illusion. The belief that the Soviet régime, in spite of its admittedly repulsive traits, is nevertheless the only basically progressive country and the great social experiment of our time, is a particularly elastic and comforting one. It permits one to shrug off reality with an all-embracing reference to 'temporary expedients' and 'emergency measures'. It is particularly suited to well-meaning and confused Progressives of all shades, who dislike Communist practices in their own country. For all these reasons, last-ditch illusions of this kind are still as prevalent today as they were in my time among an immense number of people all over the world.

Every period has its dominant religion and hope, and 'Socialism' in a vague and undefined sense was the hope of the

[1] pp. 180 ff. 'The doctrine of the unshaken Foundations'.

early twentieth century. So much so that German 'National-Socialists', French 'Radical-Socialists', Italian 'Christian-Socialists' all felt the need to include the fetish-word into their names. In the Union of Socialist Soviet Republics this hope seemed to have found its incarnation; and the magic worked, and still works, with varying degrees of intensity, on a considerable portion of mankind. The realisation of the full truth about the régime which now rules one-third of the world : that it is the most inhuman régime in human history and the gravest challenge that mankind has as yet encountered, is psychologically as difficult to face for most of us as an empty heaven was for Gothic man. The difficulty is almost the same for the illiterate Italian peasant as for a highly literate French novelist like Sartre, or for a highly realistic politician like the late President Roosevelt—who sincerely believed that Stalin's régime was a kind of uncouth, Asiatic New Deal; that after the war America would 'get on very well with Stalin and the Russian people', and that the only threat to post-war peace would come from Britain's imperalistic designs. That the great American President could believe this, in spite of all the available evidence about Communist theory and Soviet practice, that experienced democratic politicians all over the world could believe this, not to mention scientists, scholars and intellectuals of every variety, is an indication of the deep, myth-producing forces that were and still are at work.

If my hesitations before and immediately after the break with the Party show the tenacity of the hope-sustaining illusion, my experiences in later years reflect another aspect of the irrational forces at work. While I was a Communist, I felt surrounded by the sympathy of progressive-minded people who did not like Communism, but respected my convictions. After I had broken with Communism, the same class of people treated me with contempt. The abuse that came from the Party conformed to pattern; but behind the resentment of those who had never been Communists I felt a different kind of unvoiced reproach. Ex-Communists are not only tiresome Cassandras, as the anti-Nazi refugees had been; they are also fallen angels who have the bad taste to reveal that heaven is not the place it is supposed to be. The world respects the Catholic or Communist convert, but abhors the unfrocked priests of all faiths. This attitude is rationalised as a dislike of renegades. Yet the convert, too, is a renegade from his former beliefs or disbeliefs, and quite prepared to persecute those who still persist in them. He is nevertheless forgiven, for he has *'embraced'* a faith, whereas the ex-Communist or the unfrocked priest has *'lost'* a faith—and has thereby become a menace to illusion and a reminder of the abhorrent, threatening void.

A sad example of this was the way in which my relations with Sir Peter Chalmers-Mitchell came to an end, in spite of the respect and affection that I felt for him. We continued to see each other until 1941. A short time after *Darkness at Noon* had been published, we lunched in Soho, with a mutual friend, Daphne Hardy, the translator of the book. After lunch the three of us travelled together in a tube towards Kensington. We had drunk some wine and were in high spirits. Suddenly Sir Peter, leaning across Daphne who sat between us, said to me : 'Frankly, I did not like that novel of yours. What a pity that you sold yourself for thirty pieces of silver.' I thought at first that he was joking, but he was not; the wine had made him reveal his true opinion of me. We had to talk rather loudly in the rattling train, across Daphne who was quite petrified. I said : 'Please, take that back, or we won't be able to see each other any more'; but he wouldn't. In the end Daphne and I go out off the train—and that was the last I saw of Sir Peter. He was run over by a bus in 1945 and killed. He had never been a Communist. He had been a warm-hearted and generous friend to me. He did not like Stalin's pact with Hitler. But he liked people who changed their Clubs even less.

Whenever I met with this attitude among the naïve, kind and progressive-minded, I felt that the unconscious source of their resentment was not that I had been a Communist but that I had ceased to be one; not that I had fallen into error, but that I had fallen out of it. This may explain why the democratic public in the West reacts with indifference toward Communists convicted of endangering the security of their country and homes, and detests former Communists who denounce the traitors. Incidentally, among the vast number of ex-Communists only a few found themselves in the painful situation of having to denounce their former comrades; not more than a handful of former *apparat* people in the West had relevant information to disclose. The voluminous literature written by former Communists, from the days of Ciliga, Gide, Silone, Serge, to those of Kravchenko, Weissberg, Sperber and Neumann Buber, is a denunciation of conditions, not of individuals, and the main source of the West's knowledge of its opponent. Yet in the public eye the ex-Communist remains an informer and warmonger. It is an understandable attitude, and as human as the ancient custom of hanging the messenger who brings news of a disaster, and endangers our necessary and cherished illusions.

I was twenty-six when I joined the Communist Party, and thirty-three when I left it. The years between had been decisive years, both by the season of life which they filled, and the way they filled it with a single-minded purpose. Never before nor after had life been so brimful of meaning as during these seven years. They had the superiority of a beautiful error over a shabby truth.

Seven years is the span of time for which Jacob tended Laban's sheep to win Rachel his daughter; 'and they seemed unto him but a few days for the love he had for her'. But the morning after the nuptials in the dark tent, he found that he had spent his ardours not on the beautiful Rachel but on the ugly Leah. And he said to Laban : 'What is this thou hast done unto me? Wherefore hast thou beguiled me?'

One would imagine that he never recovered from the shock of having slept with an illusion. We are told, however, that he did obtain the real bride at the price of another seven years of labour. And again they seemed to him but a few days; for, glory be, man is a stubborn creature.

XXXVII. Darkness at Noon

IT is during the critical period after the break, when he becomes an outcast from the party of outcasts, and lives in a state comparable to the mystic's dark night of the soul, that the ex-revolutionary is tempted to go over to the opposite political extreme, or to become a religious convert. Those of my friends who have resisted the temptation and succeeded in retaining their intellectual and emotional balance, are nearly all men with a continuous interest—writers or artists or scientists—which provided them with an independent purpose, a centre of gravity.

When I had returned to Paris at the beginning of 1938, I had brought with me a precious document. It was an agreement with Jonathan Cape in London for the publication of *The Gladiators*, my first novel to appear in print. Cape had paid me an advance of, I believe, a hundred and twenty-five pounds; though I had to pay the cost of translation, it left me with just enough for six months of Spartan living. Thus I was at last able to finish this book which I had been forced to abandon time and again, either because I had run out of money or under pressure of political events. I finished it in July 1938, four years after I began it.

After each of these more or less dramatic interruptions, the return to the first century B.C. had filled me with peace and relief. During the months before and after the break with the Party, it became an occupational therapy. It gave me a sense of continuity which tided me over that period of outer loneliness and inner emptiness. Before the break, I had thought of myself as a servant of the Cause, and of writing as a means of serving it. Now I began to regard myself as a professional writer, and writing as a purpose in itself. As soon as I had finished *The Gladiators*, I began to write *Darkness at Noon*.

The novel, as outlined in a short synopsis that I wrote for Cape, was to be about people in prison in a totalitarian country. There were to be four or five characters who, under sentence of death, find themselves transferred from the trivial to the tragic plane of existence. They re-value their lives and each one discovers that he is guilty, though not of the crimes for which he is going to die. The common denominator of their guilt is having placed the interests of mankind above the interests of man, having sacrified morality to expediency, the Means to the Ends. Now they must die, because their death is expedient to the Cause, by the hands of men who subscribe to the same principles. The title of the novel was to be *The Vicious Circle*.

When I began writing the book, I had no notion of the plot, and only one character was established in my mind. He was to be a member of the Old Bolshevik guard, his manner of thinking modelled on Nikolai Bukharin's, his personality and physical appearance a synthesis of Leon Trotsky and Karl Radek. I saw him as clearly as a hallucination—short, stocky, with a pointed goatee, rubbing his pince-nez against his sleeve as he paced up and down his cell. The next problem was to find a name for him. Rummaging in the lumber-room of memory, I stumbled upon the name 'Rubashov' without remembering where it came from. I liked it because it sounded like *roubashka*, the high-necked, embroidered Russian shirt in which I sometimes dressed him up for a Sunday. Actually, Nikolai Salmanovich Rubashov was the name of the editor of *Davar*, the Palestine Labour Party's daily paper, but I had forgotten this. I had never met the real Mr. Rubashov, but his name was well-known to me during my years in Palestine. Incidentally, the second name, Salmanovich (Solomonson) made my hero a Jew, but neither did I notice this, nor has any reader ever pointed it out to me.

The opening sequence seemed quite obvious. When his own people come to arrest him, Rubashov is asleep and dreaming about the last time when he was arrested in the enemy's country; sleep-dazed, he is unable to decide which of the two hostile dictators is reaching out for him this time, and which of the two omnipresent oil-prints is hanging over his bed. Curiously, this symbolic assertion of the basic sameness of the two totalitarian régimes (which returned as a *leit-motif* in the last lines of the book) was written at a time when in my conscious thinking I was still a Soviet sympathiser, a year before the Hitler-Stalin pact, and when I would still have indignantly rejected the suggestion that there was nothing to choose between Soviet Russia and Nazi Germany.

Once the opening scene was written, I did not have to search for plot and incident; they were waiting among the stored memories of seven years, which, while the lid was down on them, had undergone a kind of fermentation. Now that the pressure was lifted, they came bubbling up, revealing their true essence and colour. Nadeshda, little Werner, the two *nachalniks* in Baku, and a multitude of episodes, single phrases or gestures which, during all these years had been prevented by the inner censor from falling into their proper pattern, did so now of their own accord. I did not worry about what would happen next in the book; I waited for it to happen with fear and curiosity. I knew, for instance, that in the end Rubashov would break down and confess to his imaginary crimes; but I had only a vague and general notion of the reasons which would induce him to do so. These reasons emerged step by step during the interrogations of Rubashov by the two investigating magistrates, Ivanov and Gletkin. The questions and answers in this dialogue were determined by the mental climate of the closed system; they were not invented but deduced by the quasi-mathematical proceedings of the unconscious from that rigid logical framework which held both the accused and the accuser, the victim and the executioner in its grip. According to the rules of the game they could only argue and act as they did.

To the western mind, unacquainted with the system and the rules, the confessions in the Trials appeared as one of the great enigmas of our time. Why had the Old Bolsheviks, heroes and leaders of the revolution, who had so often braved death that they called themselves 'dead men on furlough', confessed to these absurd and hair-raising lies? If one discounted those who were merely trying to save their necks, like Radek; and those who were mentally broken like Zinoviev; or trying to shield their families like Kameniev, who was said to be particularly devoted to his son—then there still remained a hard core of men like Bukharin, Piatakov, Mrachkovsky, Smirnov, and at least a score of others with a revolutionary past of thirty, forty years behind them, the veterans of Czarist prisons and Siberian exile, whose total and gleeful self-abasement remained inexplicable. It was this 'hard core' that Rubashov was meant to represent.

The solution that emerged in the novel became known as the 'Rubashov theory of the confessions', and was the object of a long public controversy. I have taken no part in this controversy. In this autobiography, fifteen years after the novel was written, a few comments regarding the question of its historical authenticity may be justified.

The three flash-back episodes in the novel—Richard, Little Loewy and Arlova—are stylised versions of factual events. The technical side of the G.P.U.'s method of interrogation, such as depriving the accused of sleep by the 'conveyor' system, of making him stand upright for one or several days, the use of the glare-lamp, the threat of execution without trial in case he refuses to co-operate, the alternation between 'hard' and 'soft' treatment, have been confirmed in detail by subsequent reports. As for the central problem : the reasoning by which one type of accused—the 'hard core' type—is induced by logic to confess to the absurd, I must try the reader's patience by two long quotations. The first is a key-passage from the novel; the second a factual account of the interrogation of one of the chief accused in the First Moscow Trial, which has subsequently come to light.

The quotation from the novel is taken from the concluding part of Rubashov's interrogation by Gletkin. Rubashov protests that, though he has opposed the policies of the Leader, he has acted neither with counter-revolutionary intent nor as the agent of a foreign power, but in good faith, according to his conscience. To this, Gletkin answers by a quotation from Rubashov's own writings : *'For us the question of subjective good faith is without interest. He who is in the wrong must pay; he who is in the right will be absolved. That was our law . . .'* In the verbal duel which ensues, Gletkin continues to base his arguments on Rubashov's own writings and speeches; and Rubashov is helpless against them. Gletkin quotes from Rubashov's diary: *'It is necessary to hammer every sentence into the head of the masses by repetition and simplification. What is presented as right must shine like gold; what is presented as wrong must be black as pitch. . . .'* When Rubashov is at last physically and mentally worn out, Gletkin rams the final argument down his throat:

'Your faction, Citizen Rubashov, is beaten and destroyed. You wanted to split the Party, although you must have known that a split in the Party meant civil war. You know of the dissatisfaction amongst the peasantry, which has not yet learnt to understand the sense of the sacrifices imposed on it. In a war which may be only a few months away, such currents can lead to a catastrophe. Hence the imperious necessity for the Party to be united. It must be as if cast from one mould—filled with blind discipline and absolute trust. You and your friends, Citizen Rubashov, have made a rent in the Party. If your repentance is real, then you must help us to heal the rent. I have told you, it is the last service the Party will ask of you.

'Your task is simple. You have set it yourself: to gild the Right, to blacken the Wrong. The policy of the opposition is wrong. Your task is therefore to make the opposition contemptible; to make the masses understand that opposition is a crime and that the leaders of the opposition are criminals. That is the simple language which the masses understand. If you begin to talk of your complicated motives, you will only create confusion amongst them. Your task, Citizen Rubashov, is to avoid awakening sympathy and pity. Sympathy and pity for the opposition are a danger to the country.

'Comrade Rubashov, I hope that you have understood the task which the Party has set you.'

It was the first time that Gletkin called Rubashov 'Comrade'. Rubashov raised his head quickly. He felt a hot wave rising in him, against which he was helpless. His chin shook slightly while he was putting on his pince-nez.

'I understand.'

'Observe,' Gletkin went on, 'that the Party holds out to you no prospect of reward. Some of the accused have been made amenable by physical pressure. Others by the promise to save

their heads—or the heads of their relatives who have fallen into our hands as hostages. To you, Comrade Rubashov, we propose no bargain and we promise nothing.'

'I understand,' Rubashov repeated.

Gletkin glanced at the dossier.

'There is a passage in your journal which impressed me,' he went on. 'You wrote: "I have thought and acted as I had to. If I was right, I have nothing to repent of; if wrong, I shall pay".'

He looked up from the dossier and looked Rubashov fully in the face:

'You were wrong, and you will pay, Comrade Rubashov. The Party promises only one thing; after the victory, one day when it can do no more harm, the material of the secret archives will be published. Then the world will learn what was in the background of this Punch-and-Judy show—as you called it—which we had to act before them according to history's text-book. . . .'

The material of the secret archives, to which Gletkin consolingly refers, has not yet been published. But some of it has leaked out, as it was inevitable in the long run. I shall quote here only one line of evidence : General Krivitsky's account of the method by which Mrachkovsky, one of the accused at the first show trial, was induced to confess.

General Walter Krivitsky was the head of Soviet Military Intelligence (Fourth Bureau of the Red Army) for Western Europe till he broke with the régime in 1937. It was the first case of desertion of a top-ranking official in the Soviet Union's foreign intelligence network. On two occasions the G.P.U. tried to assassinate him in France; on the third, in the United States, they succeeded. His death was made to appear as suicide. General Krivitsky was found shot through the head, apparently by his own hand, in a room in a small Washington hotel where he had never stayed before. He had repeatedly warned his family and friends never to believe, if he were to be found dead, that he had committed suicide. There is an old G.P.U. saying : 'Any fool can commit a murder, but it takes an artist to commit a natural death.'

I have never met General Krivitsky; those of my friends

who knew him admired his courage and integrity. His book *I was Stalin's Agent* was published in December 1939—at a time when I had finished *Darkness at Noon* except for the last, post-interrogation part, 'The Grammatical Fiction'. I actually read Krivitsky's book only several years later, for when I had finished *Darkness at Noon* I became allergic, for a long time, to the whole subject. As Krivitsky's book is out of print and may not be reprinted for years to come, I am obliged to quote the relevant passages.

First, this short summing up of the problem in a chapter of his book called *Why did they Confess?* :

How were the confessions obtained? . . . A bewildered world watched the builders of the Soviet Government flagellate themselves for crimes which they never could have committed, and which have been proved to be fantastic lies. Ever since, the riddle of the confessions has puzzled the Western world. But the confessions never presented a riddle to those of us who had been on the inside of the Stalin machine.

Although several factors contributed to bringing the men to the point of making these confessions, they made them at the last in the sincere conviction that this was their sole remaining service to the Party and the revolution. They sacrificed honour as well as life to defend the hated régime of Stalin, because it contained the last faint gleam of hope for that better world to which they had consecrated themselves in early youth. . . .

Krivitsky proceeds to point out, that this explanation applies only to a certain type of accused (whom I have called 'the hard core'); and then gives the following account of the way Mrachkovsky was persuaded to confess :

Mrachkovsky had been a member of the Bolshevik Party since 1905. He was the son of a revolutionist exiled to Siberia by the Czar. He himself had been arrested many times by the Czarist police. During the civil war, after the Soviet Revolution, Mrachkovsky organised in the Urals a volunteer corps which performed wonderful feats in defeating the counter-revolutionary armies of Admiral Kolchak. He acquired the reputation of an almost legendary hero in the period of Lenin and Trotsky.

By June 1935, all the preparations for the first show trial had been completed. The confessions of fourteen prisoners had been secured. The leading characters, Zinoviev and Kamenev, had been cast for their rôles and had rehearsed their lines. But there were two men in this batch of marked victims who had failed to come across with their confessions. One of these was Mrachkovsky. The other was his colleague Ivan N. Smirnov, a founder of the Bolshevik Party, leader of the Fifth Army during the civil war.

Stalin did not want to proceed to the trial without these two men. They had been grilled for months, they had been subjected to all the physical third degree practices of the Ogpu, but still refused to sign confessions. The chief of the Ogpu suddenly called upon my comrade, Sloutski, to take over the interrogation of Mrachkovsky, and to 'break down' this man—for whom Sloutski had, as it chanced, a profound respect. Both of us wept when Sloutski told me of his experience as an inquisitor.

'I began the examination cleanly shaven,' he said. 'When I had finished it, I had grown a beard.

'When he was first led into my office, I saw that he limped heavily from the effects of a leg wound he had received in the civil war. I offered him a chair. He sat down. I opened the examination with the words: "You see, Comrade Mrachkovsky, I have received orders to question you!" '

Mrachkovsky replied: 'I have nothing to say! In general I do not want to enter into any conversation with you. Your kind are much worse than any gendarmes of the Czar. Suppose you tell me what right you have to question me. Where were you in the revolution? Somehow I do not recall ever hearing of you in the days of the revolutionary war.'

Mrachkovsky caught sight of the two Orders of the Red Banner which Sloutski was wearing, and continued:

'I never saw your type at the front. As for those decorations, you must have stolen them!' . . .

Mrachkovsky rose, and with one swift motion removed his shirt and exposed the scars of the wounds he had received in battles for the Soviet régime.

'Here are my decorations!' he exclaimed.

Sloutski continued his silence. He had tea brought in, and offered the prisoner a glass and some cigarettes. Mrachkovsky seized the glass and the ashtray which was put before him, threw them on the floor, and shouted:

'So you want to bribe me? You can tell Stalin that I loathe him. He is a traitor. They took me to Molotov (the Soviet Premier) who also wanted to bribe me. I spat in his face.'

Sloutski finally spoke up:

'No, Comrade Mrachkovsky, I did not steal the Orders of the Red Banner. I received them in the Red Army, on the Tashkent front, where I fought under your command. I never considered you a reptile and do not regard you as one even now. But you have opposed and fought against the Party? Of course you have. Well the Party has now commanded me to question you. And as for those wounds, look at this.' And Sloutski bared part of his body, exhibiting his own war scars. . . .

Then he said: 'I was connected with the revolutionary tribunal after the civil war. Later the Party switched me to the Ogpu administration. I am now only doing my assignment, carrying out orders. If the Party orders me to die, I shall go to my death.' (Sloutski did exactly that when, eighteen months later, it was announced that he had committed suicide.)

'No, you have degenerated into a police hound, into a regular Okhrana agent,' broke in Mrachkovsky. Then he stopped, hesitated, and continued: 'And yet, apparently, all the soul has not yet gone out of you.'

For the first time Sloutski felt that some spark of understanding had been generated between him and Mrachkovsky. He began to talk about the internal and international situations of the Soviet Government, of the perils from within and without, of the enemies within the Party undermining the Soviet power, of the need to save the Party at all costs as the only saviour of the revolution.

'I told him,' Sloutski reported to me, 'that I was personally convinced that he, Mrachkovsky, was not a counter-revolutionist. I took from my desk the confessions of his imprisoned comrades, and showed them to him as evidence of how low they had fallen in their opposition to the Soviet system.

'For three full days and nights we talked and argued. During all this time Mrachkovsky did not sleep a wink. Altogether I snatched about three to four hours of sleep during this whole period of my wrestling with him.'

There followed days and nights of argument which brought Mrachkovsky to the realisation that nobody else but Stalin could guide the Bolshevik Party. Mrachkovsky was a firm believer in the one-party system of government, and he had to admit that there was no Bolshevik group strong enough to reform the Party machine from within, or to overthrow Stalin's leadership. True, there was deep discontent in the country, but to deal with it outside the Bolshevik ranks would mean the end of the proletarian dictatorship to which Mrachkovsky was loyal.

Both the prosecuting examiner and his prisoner agreed that all Bolsheviks must submit their will and their ideas to the will and ideas

of the Party. They agreed that one had to remain within the party
even unto death, or dishonour, or death with dishonour, if it became
necessary for the sake of consolidating the Soviet power. It was for
the Party to show the confessors consideration for their acts of self-
sacrifice if it chose.

'I brought him to the point where he began to weep,' Sloutski
reported to me. 'I wept with him when we arrived at the conclusion
that all was lost, that there was nothing left in the way of hope or
faith, that the only thing to do was to make a desperate effort to
forestall a futile struggle on the part of the discontented masses. For
this the Government must have public "confessions" by the opposition leaders.'

Mrachkovsky asked that he be allowed to have an audience with
Ivan Smirnov, his intimate colleague. Sloutski had Smirnov brought
from his cell, and the meeting of the two men took place in his office.
Let Sloutski describe it:

'It was a painfully disturbing scene. The two heroes of the revolution fell on each other's necks. They cried. Mrachkovsky said to
Smirnov: "Ivan Nikitich, let us give them what they want. It has to
be done" . . .

'By the end of the fourth day he signed the whole confession made
by him at the public trial.

'I went home. For a whole week I was unfit for any work. I was
unfit to live.'

When I read this account, years after *Darkness at Noon* was
written, I had a sickening feeling of *déjà vu*. The resemblance
in atmosphere and content to the first interrogation of Rubashov by Ivanov in the novel was indeed striking. The simi-
larity between Ivanov's and Sloutski's line of argument was
easy to explain : both the novel and the real event were determined by the same framework of ideas and circumstances. But
there were similarities of detail and nuance which went beyond that. In both cases the interrogation opens with accuser
and accused indulging in sentimental reminiscences of the
civil war; in both cases the accuser has served under the accused's command; as a result of the civil war, one in each pair
of antagonists has a game leg; in both cases the interrogator is
in turn liquidated himself. As I read on, I had the impression
of meeting the *Doppelgaenger*, the spectral doubles of Rubashov and Ivanov—a ghostly, ectoplastic regurgitation by
reality of the characters and events of my imagination.

Krivitsky had never read *Darkness at Noon*; he was dead by

the time it appeared in print. His book and mine were written at about the same time. According to his editor, Isaac Don Levine, he worked on it in 1938, and his preface is dated October 1939.

As I have repeatedly pointed out, the method by which a Mrachkovsky, a Bukharin or Rubashov was induced to confess, could only be applied to a certain type of old Bolshevik with an absolute loyalty to the Party. With other defendants, other methods of pressure were used which varied from case to case. Yet, in the controversy around the book, it was constantly alleged that I explained *all* confessions by the same method. In fact, of the three prisoners that appear in the novel, Rubashov alone confesses in self-sacrificing devotion to the Party; Harelip confesses because he is kept under torture; the illiterate peasant confesses without even understanding the charge, for he will agree to anything that Authority orders him to do. Moreover, in the passage quoted in this chapter, Gletkin himself enumerates the various methods by which others were made to confess; in yet another passage (p. 253) it is Rubashov who reflects that 'some were silenced by physical fear, some hoped to save their heads. . . .' etc., etc. Yet when the show-trials spread to the satellite countries ten years after the book was written, untiring controversialists would again point out that Cardinal Mindszenty or Mr. Vogeler owed no loyalty to the Communist Party, and thereby prove that 'the Rubashov theory of the confessions' was wrong. One might as well prove that because nails are attracted by magnets, whereas flies are attracted by fly-paper, the 'magnetic theory of attraction' must be wrong. The persistence of such, mostly quite *bona fide* misreadings, is probably due to the innate tendency of the mind to generalise and to look for a unitary explanation, a *lapis philosophicus* for puzzlingly complex phenomena. It was for precisely this reason that the defendants in each show trial were a carefully selected 'amalgam' of men of integrity, stool-pigeons and moral wrecks, who all behaved in the same manner but for entirely different reasons.

I began writing *Darkness at Noon* at the time of Munich,

and finished it in April 1940, a month before the German invasion and the subsequent fall of France. There were again, as with *The Gladiators*, several long, enforced interruptions which turned the writing of the book into an obstacle-race against time and fate, for since Munich I had been convinced that France would collapse within a few weeks under a German attack.

The first obstacle was that, half-way through the book, I again ran out of money. I needed another six months to finish it, and to secure the necessary capital I had to sacrifice two months—April and May 1939—to the writing of yet another sex book, the third and last. Then, after three months of quiet work in the South of France, came the next hurdle : on September 3 the War broke out, and on October 2 I was arrested by the French police.

At this point began the series of Kafkaesque events that I have told in *Scum of the Earth*. I spent the next four months in a concentration camp in the Pyrenees. I was released in January 1940, but continued to be harassed by the police. During the next three months I finished the novel in the hours snatched between interrogations and searches of my flat, in the constant fear that I would be arrested again and the manuscript of *Darkness at Noon* confiscated.

Yet a friendly voodoo seemed to be protecting that book. On one occasion, in March 1940, when the police searched my flat, they took away nearly all my files and manuscripts, but the typescript of *Darkness at Noon* escaped their attention. The top copy was lying on my desk, where I kept it on the theory of Edgar Allen Poe that conspicuous objects were least likely to attract suspicion; while, on an opposite theory, the carbon copy was hidden on the top of the bookshelf. In the end, I was again arrested and the original German version of the book was lost. But by that time the English translation had been completed. It was dispatched to London ten days before the German invasion of France started, and the book thus had another narrow escape.

During the next six months that it took to make my own escape to England, the book had quietly progressed to the stage of page-proofs. The page-proofs reached me in Pentonville prison in London, where I had landed on my arrival.

There was some difficulty about this, as prisoners are not supposed to receive books from outside; but as it could be proved that the book was written by the prisoner, permission was granted by the Governor. It was also in Pentonville that I heard for the first time the English title of the book. It had been suggested by Milton's 'Oh dark, dark, dark, amid the blaze of noon', and was the translator's idea. The translator, Daphne Hardy, was in fact not a translator but a young English sculptress, the 'G' in *Scum of the Earth*. She had escaped from France earlier, by a different route; our reunion took place in the visitors' room in Pentonville, where we had to talk across a wire-mesh in the presence of a uniformed guard. When the guard escorted me back to my cell, he asked me what sort of book it was we had discussed for so long. I said that it was a book I had written about a prisoner in a solitary cell. 'Then you must be a prophet,' he said, slamming the door of my solitary cell.

When *Darkness at Noon* was published, I was still in that cell.

In England, the book was discussed in Left-wing circles, but otherwise made so little stir that after the first edition of a thousand was sold out, it remained out of print for several months, and at the end of the first year had sold less than four thousand copies.

In France it was published after the end of the war, and sold over four hundred thousand copies. It is not usual for an author to mention circulation figures, but I feel that in this case an exception is justified on two grounds : firstly, because it illustrates the contrast in reading preferences between the two countries, and secondly because of certain developments which I shall presently explain.

The reason why *Le Zéro et l'Infini*[1] broke all pre-war records in French publishing history was not literary but political. After the terror of the German occupation France went through a second period of terror the history of which has not yet been written. During the chaotic weeks between the crumbling of the occupational forces' authority and the establish-

[1] The French title is an allusion to a passage in the book which says that the individual's value in the social equation is both nought and infinite.

ment of orderly government, nearly every region of France
became the scene of summary executions, arbitrary reprisals
and lawlessness. The Communists, who emerged from the Resistance movement as the best-organised force, used these
chaotic weeks, just as they had done in Spain, for a systematic
settling of accounts with their opponents under the pretext
that they had been collaborators. This rule of the *maquis*—in
the original, lawless sense of the word—abated only gradually,
and in more covert forms continued for several years; even today certain aspects of it are hushed up by tacit agreement. At
the time in question, 1946, the Communists were still the
strongest party in France; they sat in the Government, had
direct control over the trade unions, and indirectly, through
blackmail and intimidation, imposed their will to a considerable degree on the Courts, on publishing and editorial offices,
the film industry and literary cliques.

In this oppressive atmosphere, the novel on the Russian
Purges, though dealing with events that lay ten years back,
assumed a symbolic actuality, an allusive relevance which had
a deeper psychological impact than a topical book could have
achieved. It happened to be the first moral indictment of
Stalinism published in post-war France; and as it talked the
authentic language of the Party, and had a Bolshevik of the
Old Guard for its hero, it could not be easily dismissed as
'reactionary' and 'bourgeois'. Instead, the Communists at first
tried to intimidate the publishers of the book. When they did
not succeed, they bought up entire stocks of it from suburban
and provincial bookshops, and destroyed them. As a result,
the book was sold in between reprints at black-market prices
three to five times higher than the official price. When the
circulation had passed the quarter-of-a-million mark, Communist speakers were instructed to attack book and author at
their mass meetings. The pressure of intimidation may be
gathered from the fact that the French translator found it
advisable to hide behind a pseudonym, and subsequently to
withdraw even that from the cover, so that no mention of a
translator appears on later editions.

The controversy reached its peak during the fateful weeks
preceding the referendum on the future form of the French
constitution. If the Communists' formula had won, this would

have given them, as the numerically strongest party, nearly absolute control of the State. When the battle was over, one of the leading newspapers, summing up the campaign in its editorial, said that 'the most important single factor which led to the defeat of the Communists in the referendum on the Constitution, was a novel, *Le Zéro et L'Infini.*'

I have mentioned in an earlier chapter that there are two incidents in my life to which, in the frequent hours of depression and self-negation, I turn for comfort. The first is related to *Thieves in the Night*, the second is the episode that I have just told.

Communist attacks continued during the post-war years. They ranged from academic polemics to physical threats. On the academic level, Professor Merleu-Ponty, the successor to Henry Bergson's chair at the Collège de France, published a remarkable book to prove that Gletkin was right.[1] On a lower level of the echelon, the official writers of the French C.P. took a simpler, traditional line. An example of this category was M. Jean Kanapa's book *Le Traître et le Prolétaire—ou l'Enterprise Koestler and Co. Ltd.*[2] (another paraphrase of *The Yogi and the Commissar*), which revealed the well-guarded secret that I had been recruited by the British Intelligence Service in Franco's prison in Seville. The next lower level may be exemplified by a front-page article in the Party's weekly paper, *L'Action*, which revealed that the little villa in Fontaine le Port which I owned for a while, was 'the headquarters of the cold war', and that I trained there 'Fascist thugs to form a terrorist militia.'[3] This was followed up by the Party's Sunday paper *Humanité Dimanche*, which published

[1] *Humanisme et Terreur* (Paris, 1947), first published as a series of essays in Sartre's monthly, *Les Temps Modernes,* under the title *Le Yogi et le Prolétaire* (a polemical paraphrase of my *The Yogi and the Commissar*). The book defends every measure of the Soviet régime, including the Stalin-Hitler pact, as Historical Necessity, condemns Anglo-American policy as Imperialist Aggression, and regards criticism of the Soviet Union as an implicit act of war. It is an almost classic example of the controlled schizophrenia of the closed sytem, provided by the foremost academic exponent of the French Marxist-Existentialist school.

[2] Paris, 1950.

[3] *L'Action*, August 6, 1950.

a map of the area, marking the exact location of the villa by an obliging arrow. After that, our cook's relatives no longer visited her on Sunday afternoons, as they had been given to understand that the villa might blow up at any moment.

In November 1952, the last of my intimate Party comrades, Otto Katz, alias André Simon, met his fate.

Otto had spent the war years in Mexico. Then he had gone back to his native country, Czechoslovakia. After the Communist coup of 1948 he had been appointed editor of the official Party organ, *Pravo Lidu*, and later on chief of the Press Department at the Foreign Ministry. In 1952 the great purge that swept through the satellite countries, swept him away too. He was one of the nine accused in the Slansky-Clementis trial, charged with being a British spy, a saboteur and—of all things—a Zionist agent. He confessed to everything and was executed by hanging.

As I read the terrible report of Otto's confession at the trial, I received a more painful shock than on any similar previous occasion. In his last statement before the Tribunal, Otto had quoted Rubashov's last speech as textually as he could probably remember it. Otto's concluding words were :

'I . . . belong to the gallows. The only service I can still render is to serve as a warning example to all who, by origin or character, are in danger of following the same path to hell. The sterner the punishment . . .' (Voice falls too low to be intelligible).[1]

Rubashov's last speech, with its emphasis on 'rendering a last service' and 'serving as a warning example' was a paraphrase of Bukharin's confession at the Moscow trial of 1938—and Otto knew that. The phrasing by Otto of his last statement was clearly intended as a camouflaged message, to indicate that he, too, had been brought to confess to crimes as imaginary as Bukharin's and Rubashov's. Perhaps he believed that I could do for him what he had done for me when I had been in a similar, yet less hopeless predicament; perhaps he

[1] B.B.C. Monitoring Report of last statement by Otto Katz at the Slansky-Clementis trial, November 23, 1952.

hoped that his influential former friends in London, Paris and Hollywood, who had once admired and fêted the author of the *Brown Books*, the propagandist for republican Spain, would raise their voices in protest. When a man is going to be hanged, he tends to over-estimate the interest which the world takes in his windpipe. Not one voice was raised among the editors, journalists, social hostesses and film-stars who had swarmed round Otto in the romantic, pink days of the 'People's Front'. His last message was like a scribbled S.O.S. in a bottle washed ashore by the sea, and left to bob among the driftwood, unnoticed by the crowd.

XXXVIII. The End of a Friendship

IN the autumn of 1938, I became the editor of a German weekly paper in Paris, called *Die Zukunft* (The Future), and published by Willy Muenzenberg.

Willy, too, had finally broken with the Comintern by refusing to go to Moscow. The world-wide enterprise that he had built up was taken over by the Party bureaucracy, and soon fell to pieces. Willy needed an outlet for his inexhaustible store of energy; hence *Die Zukunft*.

The idea was to publish an independent, German-language weekly paper which, apart from anti-Nazi propaganda, would work for the *rapprochement* of the various groups in exile, and develop a programme for the day when the Nazi régime was no more. We had a rather good start, with original contributions from Siegmund Freud, Thomas Mann, Harold Nicolson, Duff Cooper, Norman Angell, E. M. Forster, Aldous Huxley, and others. For the planning of a long-term, post-Hitlerian policy we had assembled an editorial Brains Trust consisting of Manes Sperber (who by now had also left the Party), Paul Sering (the pen-name of Richard Loewenthal, at present on the London *Observer*), Julius Steinberg the sociologist, Willy and myself. We also had a literary supplement, edited by Ludwig Marcuse.

In spite of all this, after a few months the paper began to go stale, as sooner or later most emigré papers do, cut off as they are from their native country, and without real contact with the country of their exile. While I was editing it, I could only work at *Darkness at Noon* during the night—but the novel was growing on me like an advancing pregnancy, and, as I felt that the war was approaching, I wanted to concentrate on it while the going was good. About Christmas I resigned from the paper, but remained a member of its Brains Trust, and an occasional collaborator.

Die Zukunft continued to appear, edited by Thorman, a member of the Catholic Centre Party, until the end of 1939 or the beginning of 1940, when most of the staff were sent to internment camps, and the paper closed down. It had been a still-born idea from the beginning, but I do not regret the time spent on it, for during the first few months after the break with the Party I needed activity, and the comradeship of a like-minded team. Work on the paper brought me into even closer contact with Willy before his death, and was also the beginning of my intimate friendship with Manes Sperber, in whom, since he had left the Party, I discovered a rare mixture of lucidity, warmth, humour and penetrating analytical power behind the somewhat authoritarian façade.

We were all going through the critical period after the break, like convalescents learning to walk again after an operation. For Sperber and myself it was easier to find our feet again than for Willy, whose life had been the Party, and nothing but the Party, since his days as a young man in the shoe factory at Erfurt. Yet I never heard from him a word of complaint about the way the Party had treated him. The real test of a politician's human greatness comes after his fall from power. Deprived of their imposing desks, secretaries, acolytes, and the trappings of rank and position, most of the former Cabinet Ministers and ex-Excellencies whom I have known in the lands of exile were like old men shivering in a Turkish bath. Willy was one of the rare exceptions. His personal magic, his authority and driving power remained the same to the end.

The end came for Willy in the summer of 1940. French politicians had protected him from being interned as an enemy alien (as all German refugees were at the outbreak of the war) until a few days before the fall of Paris. He was then sent to an internment camp in Central France. When the German armies were approaching that region, the French officer in command of the camp, knowing that the inmates were political refugees, and the fate that awaited them if they were to fall into the Nazis' hands, opened the gates and wished them good luck. The internees decided that their best chance was to disperse and to make their way, singly or in small groups, towards Switzerland and the unoccupied South. Willy was last seen marching down a road towards the East in the company of two young men who had attached themselves to him in the camp. The young men were unknown in refugee circles, and supposedly members of the German Socialist Party. A few days later Willy's body was found in a forest near Grenoble, hanging from a tree by a rope round his neck. His face was battered and bruised. The position of the branch to which the rope was attached excluded the possibility of suicide. Neither German nor French troops had passed through the region. The two young men have never been heard of again.[1]

It seems surprising that a man of Willy's experience should have walked into the trap. But Trotsky, Krivitsky, Ignatz Reiss, and other victims of the G.P.U. were equally experienced men, who knew equally well that the G.P.U. was determined to get them, and sooner or later they, too, walked into a trap. The reason is simply that no man can live without a minimum of trust in his friends. Old-fashioned assassins used women as decoys. The G.P.U.'s modern dialectic of assassination is based on the psychological insight that a lonely man can resist all temptations, except one : his craving for friendship and loyalty.

It is thanks to *Die Zukunft* that I had the opportunity of making the acquaintance of Siegmund Freud, in the last year of his life. Some time during the autumn of 1938, I went to see him in London, to ask him for a contribution for a special Anglo-German issue of the paper that we were preparing.

Freud was then eighty-two. A few months before, the Nazis had annexed Austria, and Freud and his family had emigrated from his native Vienna to London. His younger son Ernst, the architect, had prepared a house for them in Hampstead. It was a pleasant Georgian house with a small, walled-in garden, surrounded by old trees. A swing couch stood on the lawn, where Freud occasionally took a nap after a sleepless night.

[1] I learned these details after my escape to England from the late Ellen Wilkinson who had been an intimate friend of Willy and Otto. In 1940, Ellen was Parliamentary Secretary to the Minister for Home Security in the Coalition Government and had detailed intelligence reports regarding Willy's death in her files.

R

There was a miniature lift that Ernst Freud had ingeniously contrived to squeeze into the narrow old staircase.

Freud's study was on the second floor. Of the furniture I remember nothing—I was so overwhelmed by the occasion that I crossed the anteroom to the study in a daze. I remember, though, that there were a great number of small oriental *objets d'art* about—Freud's famous collection, to which I gave only a sidewise glance of awe and wonder. My accursed shyness had returned, and kept me during the whole visit in a grip of perspiring paralysis, even worse than at the meeting with Thomas Mann.

Freud looked so exactly like his photograph, so exactly as I had imagined him, that it gave me a start and a feeling of unreality—as if, walking through Hyde Park, I had met the fabulous unicorn and it had said politely : 'I am the fabulous unicorn'. Freud was indeed very polite and, noticing my embarrassment, a gentleness came into his face—it was the unsmiling, grave, manly kind of gentleness. Though small and fragile, the chin and lower jaws stubbled with the white, short-trimmed beard—a beard with a crew-cut as it were—the dominating impression was not that of a sick octogenarian, but of the indestructible virility of the Hebrew patriarchs. Not even the peculiar, laboured manner of his speech could destroy it. The cancer of the mouth, which was to kill him within less than a year, forced Freud to speak with lips stretched tight and the corners of the mouth extended—rather in the manner of children imitating the speech of their toothless elders in cruel mockery. He was in intermittent pain, and easily fatigued by visitors. Anna Freud, who had led me to the study door, had asked me to take my leave in twenty minutes, but Freud made me stay another ten. He must have done it out of kindness for, unable to loosen the cramp of my timidity, I trotted out one conversational platitude after another, mostly about politics and *Die Zukunft*, subjects that could not but bore him. But perhaps the great mind-reader's curiosity about human beings, however inarticulate and gauche they were, also played a part.

My notes on the talk were confiscated with my files by the French police, and after fifteen years only three fragments of it have remained in my memory.

The first is the beginning of the conversation, which I opened with a monumental blunder. I explained that for our special issue of the paper we were trying to get contributions from all German and English Nobel Prize winners—'yourself, Herr Professor, Thomas Mann, and so on . . .'

At that Freud said, unsmiling, his mouth stretched tight :

'Well, you know, I am an old Jew now, but they never gave me the Nobel Prize.'

The second episode stands out equally sharply. I had uttered some platitude about the Nazis. Freud looked with an absent, wondering look at the trees across the window, and in a hesitating manner, said :

'Well, you know, they are *abreacting* the aggression pent up in our civilisation. Something like this was inevitable, sooner or later. I am not sure that from my standpoint I can blame them.'

He probably put it into quite different words, but there could be no misunderstanding of the meaning. He had merely given a consistent expression to the ethical neutrality inherent in the Freudian system—and in all strictly deterministic science. Not even *'tout comprendre c'est tout pardonner'*— for even forgiveness implies an ethical judgment, but simply *'Tout comprendre c'est tout comprendre'*. I did not have the temerity to contradict, to talk of the 'invisible writing', or the 'oceanic feeling' which Freud, on his own admission, had never experienced. But I wondered with admiration and compassion, how a man can face his death without it.

The third incident was an indirect answer to that question. I asked Freud whether he saw many friends and colleagues in London. He said that 'the doctors' did not allow him to see many people because 'of this thing on my lip'. He went on to say that they were treating it with X-rays and radium. Then again that wondering, absent and wistful gaze came into his eyes. He went on : 'The doctors say they can cure it. But who knows whether one can believe them?'

Freud knew that the thing on his lip was cancer. But the word was never mentioned by him either in speech or in his letters to friends, and it was never mentioned by others in his presence. The destroyer of taboos had erected a taboo of his own. He knew that there was no hope, and that 'the doctors' knew it. The man who knew more than any mortal had known about the ruses of self-deception, had chosen to enter the darkness with a transparent veil over his eyes.

Freud promised to send a short contribution, and he kept his promise. It was his first publication since he had left Austria, and a very strange one. It referred to a quotation, which Freud had once read somewhere, and of which he had forgotten the author and context. Could any reader help him to identify the book in which the quotation appeared?

We received no readers' answers. Curiously enough, I have forgotten the quotation whose source Freud had forgotten, and even the nature of its content. I believe it had something to do with anthropology or mythology. All efforts to find a copy of *Die Zukunft* in which the contribution appeared, undertaken both by the Freud Archives and myself, have so far been in vain. Perhaps a reader may help this time? Freud's article appeared nowhere else and its recovery would be of documentary interest.

I wonder whether my forgetting what Freud had forgotten had a Freudian reason, or whether it can perhaps be explained in a different way. When, during a conversation, a person is unable to remember a word or a name which he has 'on the tip of his tongue' it sometimes happens that the other person suddenly experiences the same blockage. This seems to indicate that not only emotion is infectious, but forgetting, too—a kind of negative telepathy as it were. I have often come across this phenomenon, but as far as I can remember, I have seen no mention of it in the writings of Freud or in any other analytical literature.[1]

I must now tie up some loose ends which extend into the post-war era. One is the end of Alex's story, the other

[1] Since this chapter was written, a copy of *Die Zukunft*, containing Freud's article (November 25, 1938) was found in a Paris library by Dr. K. R. Eissler, Secretary of the Siegmund Freud Archives. The subject of the article of which I could only remember that it had 'something to do with anthropology or mythology' was—anti-Semitism. I leave it (for once) to the reader to draw his own conclusions. In other respects my memory was correct: the article consists mainly of one long quotation whose source Freud had forgotten.

Németh's. The first is pleasant to tell, the second very unpleasant.

At the time when Eva was expelled from Russia and arrived in London (Spring, 1938), she only knew that Alex was in Kharkov prison, charged with spying for the Germans and fomenting an armed rising in the Ukraine. Later we learned that he had also been accused of having recruited a band of Nazi terrorists to assassinate Stalin and Marshal Voroshilov[1] on their next hunting trip to the Caucasus, and to blow up the main industrial plants in the Ukrainian capital in the event of war. There seemed to be little that could be done to save him, but I promised Eva to leave nothing untried.

As Alex was a physicist, I thought that a joint appeal, addressed directly to Stalin, by the three French winners of the Nobel Prize for Physics might make some impression. They were Frédéric and Irène Joliot-Curie, and Jean Perrin. All three sympathised with the Left, and the Joliot-Curies soon afterward joined the French C.P. I approached Frédéric Joliot, whom I knew slightly from the past days of INFA. He had never heard of Alex Weissberg, but he took my word for it that Alex was innocent, signed the letter to Stalin that I had drafted beforehand, and also obtained for me the signatures of his wife and Perrin—who too had never heard of Alex. I shall have something to say later about the significance of Joliot-Curie's generous gestures, and its political aftermath.

The joint protest of the French Nobel-laureates, supported by a simultaneous letter from Einstein to Stalin, was never acknowledged or answered, but seems nevertheless to have influenced Alex's fate. A short while after the protest had been dispatched, he was suddenly taken out of his cell, was deloused, given a shave, a haircut, a decent suit and a tie, and photographed in this jollied-up condition. After that the suit and tie were taken away again, and he was put back into the cell. The obvious explanation is that, in view of the foreign protests, the authorities wanted to be able to prove that he was alive and in good shape. And once higher quarters recognised the significance of the case, his bare life at least was safe.

Altogether, Alex was held for three years in various Ukrainian and Russian prisons. In 1940, together with about a hun-

[1] Not Kaganovich, as I have mistakenly said in *The God that Failed*.

dred other German and Austrian Communists, Socialists and anti-Nazi refugees, he was handed over by the G.P.U. to the Gestapo. This act of unfathomable baseness was one of the consequences, and at the same time the ignominious symbol, of the Stalin-Hitler pact. He survived the further ordeals of the Gestapo, played a part in the Polish underground movement, and after the war escaped to the West. In 1952 he published his remarkable book, *Conspiracy of Silence*, for which I wrote the preface.

The part played by Professor Joliot-Curie in this story was that of a courageous and warm-hearted man, prompted by a humane impulse. A year and a half later, when the war started and I was put in a concentration camp, he repeated his generous gesture by protesting against my arrest to the French government. Another five years later, when he had become the most celebrated Communist intellectual in Europe next to Pablo Picasso, he attacked *Darkness at Noon* from the public platform of a mass-meeting.

Here we have in a nutshell the tragedy of the Communist intellectual. Joliot's political conscience compelled him to attack a book which was an exposure of Soviet terror. His human conscience compelled him to defend a man who was a victim of that terror. But what faith could he have had in Soviet justice if he was satisfied with my hearsay evidence in favour of Alex, a person unknown to him, officially accused by the Soviet State of spying, sabotage, and plotting to assassinate Stalin? By taking it upon themselves to interfere with the course of Soviet justice, by taking the innocence of its victim for granted and calling the official charges against him 'absurd', the three eminent French savants revealed their true opinion of the Soviet Régime—which they nevertheless felt in duty bound to defend. They knew that Weissberg's case was not an exception, but the rule, because reports of hundreds of similar arrests on similarly grotesque charges, among their academic colleagues in the Soviet Union, were available to them. Yet hope that in spite of all this the 'Socialist Sixth' of the Earth would in the end justify their expectations, unwillingness to part with a cherished illusion, and intellectual pride which would not admit that they had been fooled, made them remain silent about the horrors of which they knew, and by their silence endorse them. The same is true of thousands of Communist or vaguely sympathising writers, painters, actors, journalists, academic teachers, including myself.

Some years later, history gave an ironic twist to this affair, and the Joliot-Perrin letter gave rise to a political scandal. It happened in 1950, during a famous French trial. Technically, it was a libel suit brought by the writer David Rousset against the Communist weekly, *Les Lettres Françaises*, which had accused him of falsifying a text in the Soviet Penal Code. Rousset's real purpose at the trial was to establish in public the facts about Soviet prisons and labour camps. He had cited as witnesses all available men and women who had been imprisoned in Russia, among them Alex Weissberg. When Alex began to testify, counsel for the Communist weekly tried to discredit him by character-smears. At this, counsel for Rousset got up and read a long testimony in Alex's favour, praising his loyalty to the Soviet régime and describing his imprisonment as arbitrary and unjust. It was the letter that I had drafted twelve years before, signed by the idol of the French Communists, Professor Frédéric Joliot-Curie, a copy of which had been preserved through all these years by Eva. The effect was that of a bombshell. Weissberg's testimony was now authenticated, as it were, by the highest intellectual authority in the Communist camp. It carried decisive weight in the trial, which ended with one of the most significant moral defeats of French Communism since the war.[1]

In the summer of 1939, Németh and Juci turned up in Paris. Németh could no longer stand the provincial atmosphere of Budapest. They had scraped together a little money to last them for two or three months, and settled down to life in exile in a small hotel room near the Rue Mouffetard, where Juci cooked their meals on the gas-ring, and washed Németh's shirts and socks in the *bidet*.

Németh was now approaching fifty, but still the same willowy, untidy, long-haired eternal student. He had successfully resisted all temptations to become a success. He had never finished a novel. He had produced a few beautifully-written

---

[1] Cf.: *Le Procès des camps de concentration sovietiques* (Paris, 1951), *Pour la Verité sur les camps concentrationnaires* (Paris, 1951), etc.

pot-boilers, among them a book on the Paris Commune of 1871. Now he was working on the Life of one Père Lieberman, the son of an Alsatian rabbi who became a Catholic convert and a celebrated missionary.

We again spent much time together. Unfortunately Sperber, who had become an equally close friend, had little in common with Németh. Sperber, the Adlerian Marxist, was brilliant, logical, didactic with a touch of the rhetorical; Németh was lazy, dreamy, and enamoured of the absurd. Between the two of them I felt like Hans Castorp in the *Magic Mountain* with his sympathies split between the discursive Settembrini and the pathos of Naphta.

When France collapsed, Németh and Juci took refuge in a small village in the South where they lived under a régime of semi-confinement under police supervision, restricted in their movements to a radius of two miles, and in the constant fear of arrest and deportation. They just managed not to starve thanks to the ingenuity of Juci, who made women's handbags and sold them to the villagers. It was typical of Németh that he had gone to France for the first time in the summer of 1914, and the second time in the summer of 1939, and had spent both wars in physical or virtual confinement.

Our last meeting, of which I did not know that it was to be the last, took place in a Paris hotel room in 1946.

It was during my first visit to Paris after the war. For six years I had not known who among my friends was still alive, who dead. For six years England had been cut off from the rest of Europe, until the occupied Continent, only twenty-odd miles away, had almost become a mythological Atlantis. During six years of sorrow and longing I had dreamt of this return; and the first few days of it I lived in a haze.

It was not only a return to the town in which the decisive years of my youth had been lived, and which I had thought I would never see again. There were other circumstances which made it so unreal. I had fled from France penniless, with false papers, spat out by a concentration camp, with a kick for a farewell. I came back at the height of the noise around *Le Zéro et l'Infini*, a best-seller and a lion. It was like a wish-fulfilment fantasy in gaudy technicolour. It was both intoxicating and bitterly disappointing, like all day-dreams come true—drunkenness and hangover telescoped into one. This may partly explain what happened at that last meeting with Németh, which destroyed a quarter-century of friendship.

The immediate reason for my coming to Paris was the rehearsals of a play produced by Jean Villar in the Théâtre de Clichy. It was a new version of *Bar du Soleil* which Németh had translated into the Hungarian, and which had almost been produced in Budapest under the joint names of 'the firm'. That manuscript, too, I had lost during the flight from France, but in 1943 I had written another play, with different characters, around the same idea, and had called it *Twilight Bar*. It was a diversion rather than a play, and without literary pretensions; I had mainly written it for my own amusement during the V-1 bombardment of London. Now it was going to be produced in Paris because my name happened to be *en vogue*. The earlier play, under our joint names, had never been produced. 'The firm' had never been *en vogue*. The past that Németh and I shared, the tie that united us, the memories that we had nursed during our separation, were of struggle, starvation and failure.

Németh and Juci arrived in Paris from the village where they had spent the war, in the middle of the rehearsals. They went back to the little hotel room with the gas-ring near the Rue Moufetard; I now occupied an apartment in one of the larger Left-bank hotels. I did not know that they were in Paris. When, after being told by the hotel porter that Monsieur K. was in conference and could not be disturbed, they finally managed to get through on the telephone, I was on my way to a rehearsal. There was a crisis on : one of the chief characters had to be re-cast a fortnight before the opening, and we could not find a suitable actor. I met Németh hurriedly in a café in the company of the producer, Villar, who would not let go of me. Villar had a car waiting outside the café—taxis were still unobtainable in Paris; after a hurried embrace with Németh, and a disjointed staccato conversation, I was whisked off to the theatre. The next two days were a mess of meeting agents and actors with Villar; I had to put Németh off twice. When, on the third day, we talked over the telephone, Németh said softly and quietly :

'Look, don't apologise. Juci and I both understand. Our

circumstances have not changed. Yours have. It is quite natural that you should be too busy to see us. I only rang because I was hoping you could spare me a few minutes on a rather urgent technical matter.'

I apologised even more profusely, knowing that the irremediable had happened. Németh's voice was, as always, free from any trace of a reproach. It was the old, matter-of-fact, taking-everything-for-granted voice which said, 'it is quite natural that you should be too busy to see us'. ('You like your boiled eggs with brilliantine? But we all do, of course'.) We arranged that they should come at once to my hotel. He arrived half an hour later, without Juci.

My sitting-room in the hotel was dark and depressing, as only a French *salon* with gilt and spindle-legged imitation period furniture can be. Németh sat on a narrow, squeaking sofa, I on a straight-backed tapestry chair. In the six years of our separation Németh had become an old man. He had always carried himself with a stoop; now he looked almost hunchbacked. The bulginess of the eyes over the bony nose had become more pronounced, beetle-like. The white dandruff on the collar of his worn, shiny black jacket was no longer an amusing eccentricity.

We sat, facing each other in the semi-obscurity; I forgot to put the electric light on until the room was almost completely dark. It was like talking across the bier of our dead friendship. I talked about England, the Blitz, the political future; it meant nothing to him. He told me about their life in the village, and the handbags that Juci had made. He had not written a line during these six years. What for? He could only write in Hungarian. Who would translate it into French? And who would publish it?

I had a formal dinner appointment that I could not cancel. After dinner I had to go to a late rehearsal. The same the next day. I was a busy little man. I began fidgeting with my appointment book.

Németh said he and Juci had read in the local paper in their village that I was in Paris. That had shaken them out of their lethargy. They had borrowed the money for the train. Otherwise they would still be there, Juci making handbags . . .

My dinner appointment was with Malraux, and there would

be several heroes of the Resistance present, men who had been parachuted into France and had survived the Gestapo. I could not be late. It did not occur to me to remember our dead friend, Maria, and her last, desperate embrace at the station in Lugano. Nor Nadeshea, standing alone on the quay in Baku.

Németh said Juci was sorry she was prevented from coming along.—And how *is* Juci?

—O thank you, very well. I hear you have married again?

—No, not yet, but we hope to get married soon. I am sure you will like her ...

And Karinthy? Dead. Rappaport? Dead. Attila? Dead. Muenzenberg? Dead. Cousin Margit? Yes, and her mother, husband and children. Never mind, we two have survived it, long live the Old Firm.

I really had to change for dinner. We talked through the open bathroom door. We came at last to that urgent technical matter. Németh explained the situation : he needed enough money for six months to live, to write a book, to find his feet again. Otherwise he and Juci had no other choice but to go back to Budapest.

I said that to go back to Budapest meant suicide. The Russian grip on the satellites would gradually tighten, everybody who had spent the war years in the West would be suspect and doomed. Németh agreed. We discussed the amount of capital he needed to pay his debts and start on the new life in Paris. It was not a small sum, nor a sum that seriously hurt me. I had no bank account in France, so we arranged that it would be delivered in cash the next day at his hotel.

The day after the money had been paid out to Németh, I rang him at their hotel, and was told by the concierge that they had paid their bill, packed their luggage, and left by the morning train for Budapest.

There is little to add, by way of comment, to this story. Németh had left no message. I never heard of him again. Through indirect sources I learnt that after his return to Budapest he was allowed to work, in a subordinate capacity, on a newspaper, and occasionally to publish a book review under his name. After the arrest of his closest friend, Paul Ignotus, his name no longer appeared in print. In July 1953 he was still free, the only one in our circle who had returned to Hungary and survived the purge. He was described to me as a destitute old man, huddled in a corner of a coffee-house, unknown and forgotten by all.

On November 13, 1953, the Hungarian newspapers carried a short notice in small print: 'Andor Németh, critic and author, died yesterday at the age of sixty-two. He had been a collaborator of *Nyugat* and other Left-wing magazines.'

When we were both young, and hopefully founded 'the firm', Dr. Rappaport, Németh's psychoanalyst, had commented: 'A literary partnership is an association of two people each of whom sees a father in the other'. In this particular partnership, Németh to me had been the Mentor, I to him the Provider. By the time we met in that Paris hotel room, one half of the silent contract could still be revived, but only one. This would be my excuse, if excuses had any meaning. Freud says somewhere that the death of the father is the most critical event in a man's life. He did not mention that this event may occur not only once, but several times.

XXXIX. The End of a Typical
Case-History

A MONTH after France declared war on Germany, on October 2, at seven-thirty in the morning, I was arrested in my Paris flat by two detectives. The next three days I spent in the company of hundreds of other suspect aliens—mostly political refugees from Germany and Spain—at Police Headquarters. During the day we were kept under guard in a large lecture-room; at night we were herded, men and women, into the coal-cellar of the Préfecture where we slept on newspapers on the coal.

On the third day the males were taken in Black Marias to the Rolland Garros Tennis Stadium in Neuilly, where we were dumped into the dressing-rooms under the stands. We spent a week there, and were then transported by train to the camp of Le Vernet, in the foothills of the Pyrenees. This place was officially designated as a Concentration Camp for Undesirable Aliens (habitual criminals and political suspects), as distinct from the normal internment camps for civilians of German nationality. It had the reputation of a penal colony, and deserved it. I stayed in Le Vernet for altogether a little under four months.

Internment in a concentration camp during a war is in itself not a pleasant experience. In my case it came too soon after imprisonment in a civil war. Only two years separate the events of *Dialogue with Death* from those of *Scum of the Earth*. The breathing space had been too short, and the experience, therefore, particularly trying. As I have described it in detail in *Scum of the Earth*, I can, to my relief, pass it over in silence.

As Hungary remained a neutral country until 1943, I did not fall into the category of enemy aliens, and my internment must have had other reasons. What these reasons were I do not exactly know to this day. I was arrested, interned, released and re-arrested without ever being interrogated or told the nature of the charge. According to one theory, the police did not know, or did not believe, that I had broken with the Communist Party; according to another, the Party had played one of its routine denunciation tricks on me; according to a third, Marshal Pétain (then French Ambassador to Spain), had given a promise to Franco's Foreign Minister to the effect that all foreigners in France who had fought with the International Brigade, or had taken a public anti-Franco attitude, would be interned for the duration of the war. At any rate, Stalin's pact with Hitler had turned all Communists and fellow-travellers in France into passive allies of the Nazis and a potential Fifth Column. In this bewildering situation, the French bureaucracy found a welcome diversion in starting a witch-hunt among the detested anti-Nazi refugees; and as usual in a witch-hunt, the first victims were the innocents.

Apart from all this, I had also been unknowingly involved in a grotesque incident about which I only learned, from French government sources, after the war. My last but one domicile in Paris had been a studio near the Porte d'Orléans, at 7 Rue Antoine Chantin. It was a furnished studio which I had taken over from my old friend, Johannes R. Becher—the Communist poet laureate and author of the 'Hymn to Stalin'—on his departure for Moscow. Becher had lived in the studio with his girl-friend—slim, pretty, red-haired Lily, who looked like a Tanagra figure and worked for the Soviet *apparat*. During my internment, a routine search was made by the police at the various domiciles that I had occupied, including the studio in the Rue Antoine Chantin. There, in the water-tank of the W.C., protected by a water-proof wrapping, they found a scroll—the blue-print of the anti-aircraft defences of Paris. Sweet Lily must have forgotten it in its hiding place when she left with Becher for Russia. I had lived for nearly a year in the studio without knowing of the document in the water tank. Had I discovered it after my break with the Party, I would have been caught in the classic conflict of conscience whether or not to hand it over to the police and thereby to denounce Lily, who had always been nice to me. Luckily, I was spared the conflict. Even more luckily, the police did not implicate me in the matter. They must have traced back the origin of the document to Lily, who was out of their reach; otherwise they would obviously have levelled a charge of espionage against me. At any rate, the story of 'the loo-tank papers', like that of the pumpkin papers, is another instance of the cloak-and-dagger atmosphere which keeps intruding, all his life, into the Party-member's world.

I was released from Le Vernet at the end of January 1940, this time, again, as a result of British pressure. But the French bureaucracy, sulky and hostile to foreigners at the best of times, was already riddled with potential collaborators who detested the anti-Nazi refugees, and six months later gleefully handed them over to the Gestapo. They were obliged to let me go, but only temporarily; they discharged me from the camp, but withheld my identity card, which meant that I ceased to have a legal existence, as it were.

During the next four months, until France capitulated, the police played cat and mouse with me. My civilian status was now that of a person under a deportation order which cannot be executed owing to wartime conditions. This entailed reporting to the police once or twice a week, and at times every day, queuing up each time for three to six hours to obtain the rubber-stamp which granted a further stay of a day or a week, according to the mood of the police-clerk at the desk. This game was called *le régime des sursis* (reprieves); it was played with thousands of political refugees in France, and led to a number of suicides among them. I kept up my morale by finishing *Darkness at Noon* and working over the English translation with Daphne.

After this short breathing space—if it can be called that—of uncertain and precarious freedom, France collapsed. The roof fell in over our heads, and the chase was on again. When the Germans were only a few miles from Paris, I was arrested once more. I managed to fool a rattled police official, bluffed my way out of the camp, and went underground. As the story of these events, and of my subsequent escape from France is described in *Scum of the Earth,* I can again confine myself to a brief outline.

For a few days I remained in hiding, first at the flat of Adrienne Monnier, then at the Paris P.E.N. Club. I then got to Limoges, where I assumed a new identity by signing up for five years with the Foreign Legion, under the assumed name of one Albert Dubert, taxi driver from Berne, Switzerland. To complete the transformation I grew a walrus moustache.

As Legionnaire Dubert I hung around for three months in various barracks in German-occupied and Vichy-France, until, in August 1940, I reached Marseilles. Uniformed and moustachioed, I must have looked fairly convincing, for I was employed as a regimental messenger between the Legion's Headquarters in the Fort St. Jean, and the German Port Supervising Commission in the Fort St. Nicholas. The messages concerned only the daily parade state and contained no military secrets, but this employment gave me a certain freedom of movement for making contacts in the town. At the end of the month I linked up with three British officers and a staff sergeant who had escaped from German captivity and had been interned by the French. By various means we all obtained false papers, which gave as our destination Casablanca, the Moroccan port not yet under German supervision.

Just before we left, I ran into an old friend, the German writer Walter Benjamin. He was making preparations for his own escape to England, by a different route; unable to obtain a French exit permit, he intended to walk into Spain across the Pyrenees, as hundreds of other refugees did. He had thirty tablets of a morphia-compound, which he intended to swallow if caught; he said they were enough to kill a horse, and gave me half of the tablets, just in case.

We travelled via Oran and Oudja. In Casablanca we established contact with a courteous and versatile representative of a hush-hush set-up which I liked to call 'the British *apparat*'. With his help the five of us, plus some fifty other escapees, embarked on a 270 ton fishing boat, which in four days somehow managed to roll and toss us past the German submarines into the neutral harbour of Lisbon. After being congratulated on our escape by the British Consulate, my four companions were flown the next day to England, whereas I was informed that I could not go, as I had no visa.

I waited in Lisbon—the 'Neutralia' of *Arrival and Departure*—for two months. The visa was never granted. With my false papers, I was again in danger of being arrested and deported, this time by the Portuguese police; and across the frontier lay Franco's Spain. Every day the refugees streaming into Lisbon brought news of the capture or suicide of our friends left behind in France. Europe was gone, and England seemed lost; in the Portuguese Press, London under the Blitz was described as 'a sea of flames'. Twice the British Consulate in Lisbon asked the Home Office to reconsider my visa, and twice it was refused.

In cell No. 40 there had been the hours by the window; in the concentration camp there had still been hope. To have, come this far, and then have the door slammed in one's face seemed to mean the end of the journey. The day after the final refusal of my visa, I learned that Walter Benjamin, having managed to cross the Pyrenees, had been arrested on the Spanish side, and threatened with being sent back to France the next morning. The next morning the Spanish gendarmes had changed their minds, but by that time Benjamin had swallowed his remaining half of the pills and was dead. I took this to be an obvious hint of the *language du destin*, and tried to follow his example. But Benjamin apparently had a better stomach, for I vomited the stuff out. It was the second time I had given in to self-pity, with the same ridiculous result : but after that, I felt much better.

I had two alternatives before me. The first was to get to a neutral country, either Palestine or the United States (where I had been offered a visa by the Emergency Rescue Committee); but I knew that to run away from Europe now would mean to condemn myself to life-long self-reproach, frustration and sterility. The alternative was to try to get to England without a visa—which in view of the Home Office's refusal, and the Fifth Column scare, would mean another certain imprisonment or internment. Nevertheless, it was the only logical choice—according to the logic of the Europe of 1940.

With the passive connivance of the British Consul General in Lisbon, Sir Henry King, and the active help of the correspondent of *The Times*, Walter Lucas, I managed to get without a permit on a Dutch KLM aeroplane bound for England. In Bristol, I handed to the Immigration Officer a written statement explaining my case—and was, as I had expected, promptly arrested. I spent one night at a Bristol police station, was taken under escort to London, spent two nights at Cannon Row police station, and six weeks in Pentonville prison. There I felt at last safe to shave off my moustache; the procedure was watched by a guard to prevent me from cutting my throat. When it was finished, I saw two sharp furrows leading from the nostrils to the corners of the lips, which six months earlier had not been there. I had always suffered from a preposterously juvenile appearance; now at last my face had caught up with my age.

If I should write a Baedeker of the prisons of Europe, I would mark Pentonville with three stars. It is the most decent gaol I have been in, though the plumbing leaves much to be desired. In Seville the installations were more modern, with water-closets and running water in each cell, and you were allowed to buy wine with your meals, but the people were shot and garrotted without much ado. In Pentonville we only had one hanging during my stay—a German spy—but on that morning the guards walked on tiptoe and there was a hush in the whole, large building. It was nice to know that you were at a place where putting a man to death was still regarded as a solemn and exceptional event. It made all the difference; it was, as a matter of fact, what this war was about.

As some of the prisoners were genuine spies and others genuine suspects, the electric light was automatically switched off in all the cells of our wing as soon as the air-raid warning went, to prevent us from making signals to the raiders. The warning usually sounded with the fading of daylight around four or five in the afternoon—for we are now in December 1940. As a consequence, we had to spend fifteen or sixteen hours of the day locked up in our dark cells, until the lights were turned on again the next morning at eight o'clock. With the black-out curtains drawn and the tight-fitting heavy cell-doors shut, it was so completely dark in the small cell that one could not even pace up and down without bumping into the wall. I had had no previous notion how dark darkness can be.

The only solution was to lie on one's bunk and to listen to the racket outside. We only had two incendiary bombs which fell through the roof on to the wire-netting across the main stair-shaft (which serves to prevent prisoners from committing suicide), but the possibility of another one falling into one of the cells, with the door locked from outside, was a worry to the administration.

The 'dark cell' is one of the most dreaded punishments among prisoners. And yet, locked up alone in a pitch-dark, second floor cell during the bombardments, I felt, for the first time since the outbreak of the war, in safety. This must sound like a deliberate paradox to minds not acquainted with the logic of the apocalypse. It becomes less paradoxical when one realises that every one of my political friends and every member of my race trapped on the occupied Continent would have felt the same, and would gladly have changed place with me. In Pentonville, I was one of the lucky few who had arrived at his destination.

I was released from Pentonville a few days before Christmas, 1940, equipped with a National Registration Card as proof that I had regained my identity, and the right to exist.

At this point ends this typical case-history of a central-European member of the educated middle classes, born in the first years of our century.

EPILOGUE: Portrait of the Author
at Thirty-five and After

'Of living English novelists I like Koestler the best.'
This was said to me recently by a friend in France,
where Darkness and Noon has, in translation, enjoyed
a sensational success. 'He is wonderfully living,' I an-
swered, 'but he is not English; he is not a novelist; and
how far is he, as a writer, even likeable?'

RAYMOND MORTIMER, 'The Art of Arthur
Koestler', *Cornhill*, November, 1946

THE day after I was released from Pentonville, I went to the Recruiting Office to enlist in the Army. I was told that it would take about two months before I was called up. I used this interval to write *Scum of the Earth*—the first book that I wrote in English. When the call-up order arrived in the middle of February, I needed just another fortnight to finish the book, and my publisher wrote to the Recruiting Office to ask whether it would be possible to obtain a deferment. The answer he received deserves to be quoted in full :

No. 3 CENTRE
LONDON RECRUITING DIVISION
DUKE'S ROAD, W.C.1.
EUSTON 5741

12th February, 1941

Jonathan Cape Esq.,
Jonathan Cape Ltd.,
30, Bedford Square,
W.C.1.

re Arthur Koestler

I am in receipt of your letter of the 11th instant contents of which have been noted.

As requested, I am therefore postponing Mr. Koestler's calling up, and would suggest that he calls at this Centre when he
is at liberty to join His Majesty's Forces.

Illegible signature

Major

A.R.O.

Having read this remarkable document, I was more than
ever convinced that England must lose the war. It took me a
month instead of a fortnight to finish *Scum of the Earth*; I
had already learnt not to hurry, and that it was bad form to
appear too eager. The process of growing roots had begun.

Up to this turning point, my life had been a phantom-chase
after the arrow in the blue, the perfect cause, the blueprint of
a streamlined Utopia. Now, with unintentional irony, I
adopted as my home a country where arrows are only used on
dart-boards, suspicious of all causes, contemptuous of systems,
bored by ideologies, sceptical about Utopias, rejecting all blue-
prints, enamoured of its leisurely muddle, incurious about the
future, devoted to its past. A country neither of Yogis nor of
Commissars, but of potterers-in-the-garden and stickers-in-
the-mud, where strikers played soccer with the police and
Socialists wore peer's crowns. I was intrigued by a civilisation whose social norms were a reversal of mine : which admired 'character' instead of 'brains', stoicism instead of temperament, nonchalance instead of diligence, the tongue-tied
stammer instead of the art of eloquence. I was even more intrigued by the English attitude to the outside world, which I
summed up in a maxim : 'Be kind to the foreigner, the poor
chap can't help it.' Most of the friendly natives on whom I
tried this nodded in modest agreement; so few saw the joke
that I began to wonder whether it was a joke after all.

In short, I was attracted by those obvious features of English life which have always fascinated the stranger. But this
was a superficial attraction. It gradually wore off, and yielded
to exasperation with the land of virtue and gloom which England became under the Labour Government of the post-war
era. So, at the end of 1947, after seven years in England, I
went tramping again. During the next four and a half years
I lived in France and the United States, and travelled in a

number of other countries. It was during this long absence from England that I became conscious of living *abroad*. In England, I felt a stranger—abroad, an Englishman. In 1952, at the age of forty-seven years, I returned to England, and bought a house in one of London's old squares, in which I shall live happily ever after, until the Great Mushroom appears in the skies.

The reasons why all the places where I have lived long before England have now become 'abroad'—which is the ultimate test of belonging to a country—are difficult for me to analyse. There is, for instance, language. Since 1940 I have been writing in English, thinking in English, and reading mostly English literature. Language serves not only to express thought, but to mould it; the adoption of a new language, particularly by a writer, means a gradual and unconscious transformation of his patterns of thinking, his style and his tastes, his attitudes and reactions. In short, he acquires not only a new medium of communication but a new cultural background. For several years, while I thought in English, I continued to talk French, German and Hungarian in my sleep. Now even this occurs only rarely; the layers are becoming integrated.

The process of changing languages is a fascinating one, and as I have gone through it twice (first from Hungarian to German, then from German to English) I hope to give one day a detailed account of the psychological problems that it involves. One curious aspect of it, from the writer's piont of view, is what one may call 'the rediscovery of the cliché'. Every cliché, even the broken heart and the eternal ocean, was once an original find; and when you begin writing and thinking in a new language, you are apt to invent all by yourself images and metaphors which you think are highly original without realising that they are hoary clichés. It is rather like the sad story of the man in a remote village in Russia, who just after the first World War invented a machine with two wheels and a saddle on which a person could ride quicker than he could walk; and who, when he rode to town on his machine and saw that the streets were full of bicycles, fell down and died of shock. Something similar happened to me when I finished the first novel that I wrote in English (*Arrival and*

Departure), with a sentence whose poetic ring made me rather proud :

'. . . at night, under the incurious stars.'

It is still there, on the last page of the book, a verbal bicycle.

Another symptom of growing roots is the homesickness that accompanies prolonged absence. I am talking of the kind of homesickness which is not focused on persons and places, but a rather diffuse nostalgia for a specific human climate. The buffetings of the past by prison guards, policemen and totalitarian bureaucrats have left their scar : an oversensitivity which reacts to slight traces of aggression or mere uncouthness in the casual contacts of the day, as a Geiger counter registers radio-activity in the air. If one is afflicted in this manner, the mood of an hour or a morning is decided by the rudeness of a taxi-driver, the temper of the charwoman, the smile of the traffic-cop, by waiters, telephone operators, the man at the petrol pump, the girl in the department store. One lives immersed in this anonymous mass, it is like a liquid medium through which one moves without being aware of it; yet its temperature and the amount of friction that it offers, constantly influence one's condition and outlook. In this respect, I have found the human climate of England particularly congenial and soothing—a kind of Davos for internally bruised veterans of the totalitarian age. Its atmosphere contains fewer germs of aggression and brutality per cubic foot in a crowded bus, pub, queue or street than in any other country in which I have lived. I felt a growing conviction that, to quote Orwell, these crowds 'with their mild knobby faces, their bad teeth and gentle manners, this nation of flower-lovers and stamp-collectors, pigeon-fanciers, amateur carpenters, coupon-snippers, darts-players and crossword-puzzle fans' lived, in its muddled ways, closer to the text of the invisible writing than any other.

In his preface to the first English translation of *Das Kapital*, Engels wrote in 1886 that Marx, 'after a life-long study of the economic history and conditions of England,' had been 'led to the conclusion that, at least in Europe, England is the only country where the inevitable social revolution might be effected entirely by peaceful and legal means'.

It is one of the few Marxian predictions that has come true. The continuity of tradition which it reflects is indeed an impressive feature, and particularly so in a declining empire. The fall of each of the great Empires of the past was an ugly and catastrophic event. For the first time in history we see an Empire gradually dissolving with dignity and grace. The rise of this Empire was not an edifying story; its decline is.

Ultimately, this may be the reason which attracted me to England. I only seem to flourish in a climate of decline, and have always felt best in the season when the trees shed their leaves.

I also like to believe that the disappearance of the Pukkah Sahib and his female equivalent at home : the *Virago Harrodsiensis,* will make the English more European. It even seems to me, at times, that they are the last Europeans, without being aware of it.

'If I find Mr. Koestler's writing unlikeable, it is because he accepts as normal what I believe and hope is abnormal,' wrote Mr. Raymond Mortimer in an essay from which I quote again, because the former literary editor of *The New Statesman and Nation* seems to me fairly representative of the general attitude of men of letters in his country and generation. I can see their point on the question of likeableness only too well, but on the question of what is normal I disagree with them. For the life that I have described was indeed, up to 1940, the typical case-history of a Central-European member of the intelligentsia in the totalitarian age. It was entirely normal for a writer, an artist, politician or teacher with a minimum of integrity to have several narrow escapes from Hitler and/or Stalin, to be chased and exiled, and to get acquainted with prisons and concentration camps. It was by no means abnormal for them, in the early 'thirites, to regard Fascism as the main threat, and to be attracted, in varying degrees, by the great social experiment in Russia. Even today, about one quarter of the electorate in France and Spain, and a much higher percentage among the intellectuals, regard it as 'normal' to vote for the Communist Party. Even today the displaced persons, the scum of the earth of the post-war era, number several millions. Finally, it was quite normal for six million European Jews to end their lives in a gas chamber.

The awareness that the first thirty-five years of my life were a typical sample of our time, and the chronicler's urge to preserve the sample, were my main reasons for writing these memoirs. Yet the majority of well-meaning citizens of the country in which I live, believe and hope that prisons and firing squads and gas chambers and Siberian slave camps just 'do not happen' to ordinary people unless they are deliberately looking for trouble. This protective filter of the mind which, when reality become too shocking, only allows a thin trickle of it to pass, has its useful function in keeping us all sane; yet at times it can become rather exasperating. In 1943, when the facts about gas chambers had already become general knowledge, the literary monthly *Horizon* published a chapter from *Arrival and Departure* which described an episode in the mass-killings. I received a number of letters, some of them accusing me of atrocity-mongering to satisfy my morbid imagination; others naïvely asking whether or not the episode had some factual basis. I had just received the news that members of my family were among the victims, and this may explain the following outburst:

A collective Answer to some Inquiries.[1]
Dear Sir,

In your letter you asked me the idiotic question whether the events described in The Mixed Transport *were 'based on fact' or 'artistic fiction'.*

Had I published a chapter on Proust and mentioned his homosexuality, you would never have dared to ask a similar question, because you consider it your duty 'to know' although the evidence of this particular knowledge is less easily accessible than that of the massacre of three million humans. You would blush if you were found out not to have heard the name of any second-rate contemporary writer, painter or composer; you would blush if found out having ascribed a play by Sophocles to Euripides; but you don't blush and you have the

[1] *Horizon*, December 1943.

brazenness to ask whether it is true that you are the contemporary of the greatest massacre in recorded history.

If you tell me that you don't read newspapers, White Books, documentary pamphlets obtainable at W. H. Smith bookstalls —why on earth do you read Horizon and call yourself a member of the intelligentsia? I can't even say that I am sorry to be rude. There is no excuse for you—for it is your duty to know and to be haunted by your knowledge. As long as you don't feel, against reason and independently of reason, ashamed to be alive while others are put to death; not guilty, sick, humiliated because you were spared, you will remain what you are, an accomplice by omission.

Yours truly,

A. K.

I am quoting this grossly unfair letter, written under emotional strain, because it shows that the process of acclimatisation was not quite as smooth and idyllic as it might appear from the preceding pages; and that has remained true to this day. The smug contentment that I feel each time I arrive at the Passport Control at Dover, joining the queue which says 'For British Subjects' and casting a cold eye at the queue 'For Foreigners' (the poor chaps can't help it), alternates with moods of impatience and fits of exasperation. But a relationship without ambivalence would be lacking in spice.

The irony of this relationship is reflected in the sales figures of my books, which are proportionately lower for England than for any other country including Iceland. However, I have gradually become reconciled to the fact that in England I am only read by highbrows, and even by them only as a penance. For I realise that the reasons why the English find my books unlikeable are to be found in precisely that lotus-eating disposition which attracts me to them. Their supreme gift of looking at reality through a soothing filter, their contempt for systems and ideologies, is reflected in their dislike of the *roman a thèse*, the political and ideological novel, of anything didactic and discursive in art, of any form of literary sermonising. In addition to this native trend, English literary criticism has, since the collapse of the 'socially conscious' literature of the 'thirties, developed what seems to me an ultra-Flaubertian tendency—'Flaubertian' in a sense in which the author of *Bouvard et Pécuchet* never was one. It was largely because of this trend that Orwell, too, remained a lifelong outsider in his country, though he came from solid British stock, and not from Budapest; and that even Wells died in the literary doghouse.

On the whole, I find life in the doghouse quite cosy, and at any rate a good cure for one's vanity—which, when one thinks one has purged and cauterised it finally out of one's system, pops up again like intermittent fever. Or, to change the metaphor : better a few sour grapes over one's head than the indigestion of surfeit.

There is a certain arbitrariness in every statement referring to the age of individuals and nations. A cross-section through a nation at any given date will reveal that some parts of the population live twenty, others two hundred years, behind their time, while some small minorities seem to live ahead of it.

Individuals are even less homogeneous. There are wilted heads on young bodies, and girlish faces framed by grey hair. As for the mind, it has no fixed age at all; it contains layers or circuits that got stuck in infancy, and others that have gone prematurely senile, and still others that function on the paleolithic level. The brain is a clockmaker's workshop where all the clockfaces mark different times. These are supposed to be somehow synchronised in those mythical beings that psychiatrists call 'integrated personalities'. Unfortunately, the wider the range of contrasts within a person the more difficult it becomes to bring them into harmony, and Goethe's 'perpetual adolescence of the artist' may well be prolonged into the age of dotage. The completely integrated person is the complete bore.

The above is intended as an apology for that web of contradictions that blurs the features of my youth not only in the reader's, but also in my own eyes. It seems difficult to make sense of a brazen Comintern agent who gains access to the enemy's headquarters in a civil war, but turns into a stammering schoolboy in the presence of Herr Docktor Mann and Herr Professor Freud. It seems difficult to 'integrate' the contemplative figure of the hours by the window with the bustling, gregarious extrovert; or to reconcile guilt, anxiety and an obsession with prison and torture, with Orwell's damning (yet correct) verdict : 'The chink in K.'s armour is his hedonism.' The contradictions between sensitivity and callousness, integrity and shadiness, egomania and self-sacrifice which appear in every chapter would never add up to a credible character in a novel; but as this is not a novel, he must stand as he was. The seemingly paradoxical can only be resolved by holding the figure against the background of his time, by taking into account both the historian's and the psychologist's approach. It was my aim throughout this autobiography not to withhold from the reader any clue, however embarrassing, that is relevant to the solution. This basic rule of the mystery-story should, I believe, apply equally to the writing of memoirs, if the latter are to satisfy not only the chronicler's urge, but also that second impulse that I have called the *'ecce homo* motive'.

Here this case history, which has now grown to four volumes, comes to an end. A fitting epitaph for it was sent to me a few months ago. It is a poster, three feet by two, put out by the Social Democratic Party of Germany, reproduced on the opposite page. The translation of the text reads :

1933 . . .
In those days the pyres were blazing in Germany's towns. By the order of Goebbels millions of books were burned in the flames.

The design below this text shows Goebbels hurling a book into the fire while Hitler looks on; the book shows the name Köstler on its cover.

1952 . . .
In these days new pyres were blazing in the German towns of the Soviet zone. Again 9 million books perished in the flames.

The design shows Pieck throwing another book, again marked 'Köstler', into the fire, while Stalin looks on.

Though one may object that in 1933 I had only published one book of which no large quantities were available for burning,

I found the fact that these posters were being displayed in the towns of Germany nevertheless gratifying. A copy of it now hangs outside my study, framed like a professional diploma certifying that its owner has passed his examinations and is entitled to exercise his craft. For, to be burned twice in one's lifetime, is, after all, a rare distinction.

London, June 1952—October 1953.

VINTAGE CLASSICS

Vintage launched in the United Kingdom in 1990, and was originally the paperback home for the Random House Group's literary authors. Now, Vintage is comprised of some of London's oldest and most prestigious literary houses, including Chatto & Windus (1855), Hogarth (1917), Jonathan Cape (1921) and Secker & Warburg (1935), alongside the newer or relaunched hardback and paperback imprints: The Bodley Head, Harvill Secker, Yellow Jersey, Square Peg, Vintage Paperbacks and Vintage Classics.

From Angela Carter, Graham Greene and Aldous Huxley to Toni Morrison, Haruki Murakami and Virginia Woolf, Vintage Classics is renowned for publishing some of the greatest writers and thinkers from around the world and across the ages – all complemented by our beautiful, stylish approach to design. Vintage Classics' authors have won many of the world's most revered literary prizes, including the Nobel, the Man Booker, the Prix Goncourt and the Pulitzer, and through their writing they continue to capture imaginations, inspire new perspectives and incite curiosity.

In 2007 Vintage Classics introduced its distinctive red spine design, and in 2012 Vintage Children's Classics was launched to include the much-loved authors of our childhood. Random House joined forces with the Penguin Group in 2013 to become Penguin Random House, making it the largest trade publisher in the United Kingdom.

@vintagebooks

penguin.co.uk/vintage-classics